The Psychology of Problem Solving

Problems are a central part of human life. *The Psychology of Problem Solving* organizes in one volume much of what psychologists know about problem solving and the factors that contribute to its success or failure. There are chapters by leading experts in this field, including Miriam Bassok, Randall Engle, Anders Ericsson, Arthur Graesser, Norbert Schwarz, Keith Stanovich, and Barry Zimmerman.

The Psychology of Problem Solving is divided into four parts. Following an introduction that reviews the nature of problems and the history and methods of the field, Part II focuses on individual differences in, and the influence of, the abilities and skills that humans bring to problem situations. Part III examines motivational and emotional states and cognitive strategies that influence problem-solving performance, while Part IV summarizes and integrates the various views of problem solving proposed in the preceding chapters.

Janet E. Davidson is Associate Professor of Psychology at Lewis & Clark College. She conducts research on several aspects of problem solving, including the roles that insight and metacognitive skills play in problem solving.

Robert J. Sternberg is IBM Professor of Psychology and Education at Yale University and Director of the Yale Center for the Psychology of Abilities, Competencies and Expertise (PACE Center). Professor Sternberg is Editor of *Contemporary Psychology* and past Editor of *Psychological Bulletin*.

Together, Professors Davidson and Sternberg have edited two previous books, *Conceptions of Giftedness* (Cambridge, 1986) and *The Nature of Insight* (1995).

The Psychology of Problem Solving

Edited by

JANET E. DAVIDSON
Lewis & Clark College

ROBERT J. STERNBERG
Yale University

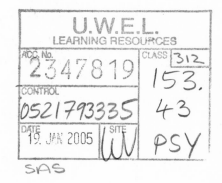
 **CAMBRIDGE**
UNIVERSITY PRESS

PUBLISHED BY THE PRESS SYNDICATE OF THE UNIVERSITY OF CAMBRIDGE
The Pitt Building, Trumpington Street, Cambridge, United Kingdom

CAMBRIDGE UNIVERSITY PRESS
The Edinburgh Building, Cambridge CB2 2RU, UK
40 West 20th Street, New York, NY 10011-4211, USA
477 Williamstown Road, Port Melbourne, VIC 3207, Australia
Ruiz de Alarcón 13, 28014 Madrid, Spain
Dock House, The Waterfront, Cape Town 8001, South Africa

http://www.cambridge.org

First published 2003

Printed in the United States of America

Typeface Palatino 10/12 pt.   *System* LATEX 2_ε [TB]

A catalog record for this book is available from the British Library.

Library of Congress Cataloging in Publication Data

The psychology of problem solving / edited by Janet E. Davidson, Robert J. Sternberg.
    p.   cm.
Includes bibliographical references and index.
ISBN 0-521-79333-5 – ISBN 0-521-79741-1 (pb.)
1. Problem solving.   I. Davidson, Janet E.   II. Sternberg, Robert J.
BF449 .P78   2003
153.4'3–dc21   2002041238

ISBN 0 521 79333 5 hardback
ISBN 0 521 79741 1 paperback

Contents

v

Contributors

Miriam Bassok
University of Washington

Magda Campillo
Graduate School and University Center,
City University of New York

Janet E. Davidson
Lewis & Clark College

Randall W. Engle
Georgia Institute of Technology

K. Anders Ericsson
Florida State University

Peter A. Frensch
Humboldt-University at Berlin

Arthur C. Graesser
The University of Memphis

David Z. Hambrick
Michigan State University

Kenneth Kotovsky
Carnegie Mellon University

Todd I. Lubart
Université René Descartes, Paris

Christophe Mouchiroud
Université René Descartes, Paris

Adam J. Naples
Yale University

Jean E. Pretz
Yale University

Norbert Schwarz
University of Michigan

Ian Skurnik
University of Michigan

Keith E. Stanovich
University of Toronto

Robert J. Sternberg
Yale University

Dorit Wenke
Humboldt-University at Berlin

Shannon Whitten
The University of Memphis

Barry J. Zimmerman
Graduate School and University Center,
City University of New York

Preface

Almost everything in life is a problem. Even when we go on vacations to escape our problems, we quickly discover that vacations merely bring problems that differ in kind or magnitude from the ones of daily living. In addition, we often find that the solution to one problem becomes the basis of the next one. For example, closing on a house solves the problem of buying a house, but usually means the initiation of a whole new set of problems pertaining to home ownership.

Because problems are a central part of human life, it is important to understand the nature of problem solving and the sources that can make it difficult. When people have problems, how do they identify, define, and solve them? When and why do they succeed at problem solving and when and why do they fail? How can problem-solving performance be improved?

Our goal for this book is to organize in one volume what psychologists know about problem solving and the factors that contribute to its success or failure. To accomplish this goal, we gave each of our contributors the following problem: "Use your area of expertise to determine what makes problem solving difficult." By examining why problem solving is often difficult for people, we hope to discover how to make it easier and more productive. However, the book's focus is not a discouraging one that emphasizes only failures in problem solving. Instead, it provides a balanced view of why problems are and are not solved successfully. Therefore, the book is organized by factors that affect problem-solving performance, such as intellectual abilities, working memory, motivation, and transfer of training, rather than by area of endeavor, such as mathematics, social science, natural science, and history. Each chapter focuses on one or more factors that are common to the solution of a wide range of problems. However, the extent to which these factors affect problem-solving performance can vary from one type of problem to another.

The book is divided into four parts. Part I comprises the introduction to the book and to the field of problem solving. In chapter 1, Jean Pretz,

Adam Naples, and Robert Sternberg describe the steps and mental processes that individuals use when successfully solving a wide range of problems. These authors then discuss different types of problems and how these types influence our recognition, definition, and mental representation of problem situations. Anders Ericsson, in chapter 2, reviews the historical context and methodology for research on problem solving. In addition, he presents contemporary research in a variety of domains that demonstrates how and why deliberate practice affects problem-solving performance.

Part II focuses on individual differences in, and the influences of, the abilities and skills that humans bring to problem situations. In chapter 3, Dorit Wenke and Peter Frensch discuss whether intellectual ability influences individuals' ability to solve complex problems. Chapter 4, by Todd Lubart and Christophe Mouchiroud, reviews when and why creative problem solving is difficult for many individuals. In chapter 5, Janet Davidson describes the difficulties surrounding insightful problem solving and discusses four approaches that explain individual differences in its occurrence. David Hambrick and Randall Engle propose, in chapter 6, that working memory and differences in its capacity play an important role in problem solving, especially when irrelevant information needs to be suppressed or tasks are complex. The final chapter in this part, written by Shannon Whitten and Arthur Graesser, describes the roles that text comprehension and knowledge base play in most problem-solving situations. This chapter also reviews models that explain how text is represented mentally after it is comprehended.

Part III covers motivational and emotional states and cognitive strategies that influence problem-solving performance. In chapter 8, Barry Zimmerman and Magda Campillo review how and why motivation and personal resourcefulness influence problem-solving performance in both formal and informal contexts. In addition, these authors present a cyclical model of problem solving that identifies self-regulatory processes and sources of motivation that are central to successful problem solving in a wide range of situations. Norbert Schwarz and Ian Skurnik, in chapter 9, describe how our moods and emotions inhibit or facilitate thinking and problem solving. In chapter 10, Keith Stanovich presents a collection of related processing styles or computational biases that predispose individuals, for evolutionary reasons, to make particular judgments and pursue certain problem-solving paths. Miriam Bassok, in chapter 11, discusses the conditions that allow or prohibit individuals from transferring well-learned problem-solving procedures to new problem situations.

It should be noted that the division of chapters into parts II and III is not meant to imply that individuals are the sole source of problem-solving success or failure. The role of the problem is discussed throughout the book. Some problems require certain abilities, skills, states, and strategies that other problems do not require.

The final section, part IV, is a chapter written by Kenneth Kotovsky. This chapter summarizes and integrates the various contributions to the book. It also challenges us to approach the field of problem solving in new ways.

Many people helped make this book possible. We thank all of the authors for working with us and producing excellent chapters. Their chapters will help us solve the problem of why problem solving can be difficult. Philip Laughlin, our wonderful editor at Cambridge University Press, expertly solved the problems that arose in all phases of the book's development. Our colleagues at Lewis & Clark College and Yale University provided the intellectual stimulation that inspired us to pursue this book. We also thank each other. Over the years, we have learned how to work together to solve the problems that naturally occur during cross-continental collaborations.

Preparation of this book was supported, in part, by Grant REC-9979843 from the National Science Foundation and by a government grant under the Javits Act Program (Grant No. R206R000001) as administered by the Office of Educational Research and Improvement, U.S. Department of Education. The views and findings presented in this volume do not necessarily represent the policies or the positions of the National Science Foundation or the U.S. Department of Education.

J.E.D.
R.J.S

PART I

INTRODUCTION

1

Recognizing, Defining, and Representing Problems

Jean E. Pretz, Adam J. Naples, and
Robert J. Sternberg

What are the problems that you are currently trying to solve in your life?
Most of us have problems that have been posed to us (e.g., assignments
from our supervisors). But we also recognize problems on our own (e.g.,
you might have noticed the need for additional parking space in the city
where you work). After identifying the existence of a problem, we must
define its scope and goals. The problem of parking space is often seen as a
need for more parking lots or parking garages. However, in order to solve
this problem creatively, it may be useful to turn it around and redefine it as
a problem of too many vehicles requiring a space in which to sit during the
workday. In that case, you may be prompted to redefine the problem: You
decide to organize a carpool among people who use downtown parking
lots and institute a daytime local taxi service using these privately owned
vehicles. Thus, you solve the problem not as you originally posed it but as
you later reconceived it.

Problem solving does not usually begin with a clear statement of the
problem; rather, most problems must be identified in the environment;
then they must be defined and represented mentally. The focus of this
chapter is on these early stages of problem solving: problem recognition,
problem definition, and problem representation.

THE PROBLEM-SOLVING CYCLE

Psychologists have described the problem-solving process in terms of a
cycle (Bransford & Stein, 1993; Hayes, 1989; Sternberg, 1986). The cycle
consists of the following stages in which the problem solver must:

1. Recognize or identify the problem.
2. Define and represent the problem mentally.
3. Develop a solution strategy.
4. Organize his or her knowledge about the problem.

5. Allocate mental and physical resources for solving the problem.
6. Monitor his or her progress toward the goal.
7. Evaluate the solution for accuracy.

The cycle is descriptive, and does not imply that all problem solving proceeds sequentially through all stages in this order. Rather, successful problem solvers are those who are flexible. The steps are referred to as forming a cycle because, once they are completed, they usually give rise to a new problem, and then the steps need to be repeated. For example, if you solve the parking-space problem by carpooling, then you may find that you are facing the problem of a work schedule that diverges from that of the person or people with whom you carpool. In other words, the solution to one problem gave rise to another problem, which then again needs to be solved through the problem-solving cycle.

CLASSES OF PROBLEMS

There are two classes of problems: those that are considered well defined and others that are considered ill defined. Well-defined problems are those problems whose goals, path to solution, and obstacles to solution are clear based on the information given. For example, the problem of how to calculate the price of a sale item is well defined. You see the original price on the tag, calculate the discount percentage, and subtract this amount from the original price. The solution is a straightforward calculation. In contrast, ill-defined problems are characterized by their lack of a clear path to solution. Such problems often lack a clear problem statement as well, making the task of problem definition and problem representation quite challenging. For example, the problem of how to find a life partner is an ill-defined problem. How do you define "life partner"? What traits should that individual have? Where do you look to find such a person? Only after considerable work has been done to formulate the problem can an ill-defined problem become tractable. Even at this stage, however, the path to solution may remain fuzzy. Multiple revisions of the problem representation may be necessary in order to find a path to a solution. In contrast to well-defined problems, ill-defined problems can lead to more than one "correct" solution.

The solution process for well-defined problems has been studied extensively, often using algorithms to describe how each step of a problem is solved (e.g., Newell & Simon, 1972). A well-defined problem can be broken down into a series of smaller problems. The problem may then be solved using a set of recursive operations or algorithms. In contrast, algorithms cannot be used to solve ill-defined problems precisely because the problem cannot be easily defined as a set of smaller components. Before a path to solution is found, ill-defined problems often require a radical change in representation. For example, consider the following problem:

> You have a jug full of lemonade and a jug full of iced tea. You simultaneously empty both jugs into one large vat, yet the lemonade remains separate from the iced tea. How could this happen?

At first, this puzzle is difficult. You imagine two pitchers of refreshing drinks being poured into a common vessel and wonder how they could not mix. (It is safe to assume that the lemonade and iced tea have similar densities). However, if you change your mental representation of the lemonade and iced tea, you see that *frozen* drinks could be easily poured into the same vat without mixing. Though the problem itself does not specify the state of the drinks, most people assume that they are liquid, as is usually the case. But this constraint is simply an assumption. Of course, this puzzle is a fairly trivial one. But in life, we often make unwarranted assumptions in our everyday problem solving. Such assumptions can interfere with our ability to discover a novel solution to an ordinary problem.

PROBLEM RECOGNITION, DEFINITION, AND REPRESENTATION

Problem recognition, definition, and representation are metalevel executive processes, called metacomponents in Sternberg's (1985) triarchic theory of human intelligence. This theory proposes that metacomponents guide problem solving by planning, monitoring, and evaluating the problem-solving process. The metacomponents include such processes as (1) recognizing the existence of a problem, (2) defining the nature of the problem, (3) allocating mental and physical resources to solving the problem, (4) deciding how to represent information about the problem, (5) generating the set of steps needed to solve the problem, (6) combining these steps into a workable strategy for problem solution, (7) monitoring the problem-solving process while it is ongoing, and (8) evaluating the solution to the problem after problem solving is completed. In this theoretical context, the processes of problem recognition, definition, and representation correspond to the first, second, and fourth metacomponents, which are used in the planning phase of problem solving.

Problem recognition, also referred to as problem finding, is one of the earliest stages of problem solving. Getzels (1982) classified problems based on how they were "found." According to Getzels, there are three kinds of problems: those that are presented, those that are discovered, and those that are created. A presented problem is one that is given to the solver directly. In this case, there is no need to recognize or find the problem; it is stated clearly and awaits solution. A discovered problem, however, is one that must be recognized. Such a problem already exists, but it has not been clearly stated to the problem solver. In this case, the problem solver must put together the pieces of the puzzle that currently exist and seek out a gap in current understanding in order to "discover" what the problem is. In contrast to presented and discovered problems, the third class of problems comprises those that are created. Created problems are those in which the problem solver invents a problem that does not already exist in the field. For this reason, one can argue that a created problem will, in some sense, always produce a creative solution, simply because its problem statement deviated from the usual way of thinking about the problem. Getzels and Csikszentmihalyi (1976) found that artists who spent more time in the problem-finding stage while creating an artwork were judged to have more creative products than did artists who spent less time in problem finding. In fact, the artists who spent more time also remained highly creative seven years later. For the purposes of this chapter, problem recognition refers to both discovered and created problems.

Problem definition is the aspect of problem solving in which the scope and goals of the problem are clearly stated. For example, a presented problem may be easy to define if the problem statement has been prepared for the solver. However, some presented problems are not clearly stated, requiring the problem solver to clarify the precise definition of the problem. Discovered problems usually require definition because the problem solver has identified the problem in his or her field. Defining a created problem is likely to be a challenge, given that the problem solver has gone beyond the current field in inventing the need for a solution in the first place.

Problem representation refers to the manner in which the information known about a problem is mentally organized. Mental representations are composed of four parts: a description of the initial state of the problem, a description of the goal state, a set of allowable operators, and a set of constraints. By holding this information in memory in the form of a mental representation, the problem solver is able to remember more of the problem by chunking the information, in order to organize the conditions and rules of a problem to determine which strategies are useful, and to assess progress toward the goal state (Ellis & Siegler, 1994; Kotovsky, Hayes, & Simon, 1985; Newell & Simon, 1972). A problem may be represented in a variety of ways, for example, verbally or visually. Even a presented problem may require the generation of a new representation in order to be solved. For example, given the problem of finding your way to a new location, you may find it much easier to follow a map than to read a set of directions. If you have trouble following the map, then it may be worthwhile to write out a description of the route in words, re-representing the information in a way that makes it easier to get to your destination.

It is important to note that these three aspects of problem solving are not discrete, sequential stages in the solution process, but rather are interactive and often difficult to tease apart in a real problem-solving situation. When a problem is represented in a new way, the problem solver may decide to redefine the goal accordingly. Similarly, a redefinition may lead to a new representation.

It is useful to consider the roles of problem recognition, definition, and representation in the solution of well-defined versus ill-defined problems. Recall that a well-defined problem is one whose path to solution is straight-forward, whereas an ill-defined problem is one that does not lend itself to a readily apparent solution strategy. Consider the following well-defined problem, referred to as the Tower of Hanoi problem:

> There are three discs of unequal sizes, positioned on the leftmost of three pegs, such that the largest disc is at the bottom, the middle-sized disc is in the middle, and the smallest disc is on the top. Your task is to transfer all three discs to the rightmost peg, using the middle peg as a stationing area, as needed. You may move only one disc at a time, and you may never move a larger disc on top of a smaller disc. (Sternberg, 1999)

The problem here is easy to recognize: One needs to move the discs onto the rightmost peg. The problem is also defined clearly; the relative sizes of the discs as well as their locations are easy to distinguish. Also, the solution path is straightforward based on this representation. Working backward, one realizes that the largest disc must be placed onto the rightmost peg, and in order to do so, the other two discs must be removed. So that the medium-sized disc does not end up on the rightmost peg, the smallest disc must first be moved to the far right. Then the medium disc is placed on the middle peg; the small disc is placed on top of the medium disc. The large disc is then free to be placed on the rightmost peg. Finally, the small disc is moved to the left so that the medium disc is free to move to the rightmost peg. The last step is then to move the small disc atop the other two and the problem is solved. Note that this well-defined problem can be expanded to include many pegs and many discs of varying sizes, but its solution will always proceed according to the algorithm described in this, the simplest case.

For the most part, well-defined problems are relatively easy to recognize, define, and represent. However, a well-defined problem may entail some degree of "problem finding," in the sense that a problem exists but must first be discovered. For example, a scientist may struggle to identify a gap in the existing literature on a problem, but the actual process of filling that gap may come easily once the problem itself has been identified. The solution to the discovered problem may follow a path similar to that of other problems in the field (e.g., experimental methods). For example, much early psychological research was conducted using male participants. When a researcher questioned the validity of the results for females, a new problem had been discovered. Given this new problem, the path to solution was well defined: Simply use the same experimental method but include female participants in the study. In this sense, this well-defined problem was somewhat difficult to recognize, yet once identified, it was easily defined and represented in familiar terms.

The representation of well-defined problems is not necessarily easy, however. Consider another problem:

> Three five-handed extraterrestrial monsters were holding three crystal globes. Because of the quantum-mechanical peculiarities of their neighborhood, both monsters and globes come in exactly three sizes, with no others permitted: small, medium, and large. The small monster was holding the large globe; the medium-sized monster was holding the small globe; and the large monster was holding the medium-sized globe. Since this situation offended their keenly developed sense of symmetry, they proceeded to transfer globes from one monster to another so that each monster would have a globe proportionate to its own size. Monster etiquette complicated the solution of the problem since it requires that: 1. only one globe may be transferred at a time; 2. if a monster is holding two globes, only the larger of the two may be transferred; and, 3. a globe may not be transferred to a monster who is holding a larger globe. By what sequence of transfers could the monsters have solved this problem? (See Kotovsky et al., 1985)

Most people find this problem to be more difficult than the Tower of Hanoi problem (Newell & Simon, 1972). However, it is actually directly isomorphic to (i.e., its structure is exactly the same as that of) the Tower of Hanoi problem. In this case, it is the difficulty of representing the problem correctly that increases the level of difficulty of the problem as a whole. After you are told of the isomorphism between the two problems, the solution is simply a matter of mapping relationships from one problem to the other. In summary, problem definition is usually easy for the class of well-defined problems; however, accurate problem recognition and representation are not necessarily straightforward, even when the scope and goals of the problem are clear.

In the case of ill-defined problems, however, it is often the case that all aspects of problem formulation are relatively challenging. Perhaps the easiest stage in attempting to solve an ill-defined problem is that of problem recognition. It is often relatively simple to identify a fuzzy problem. For example, it is easy to identify the problem of developing a test of creativity. It is hard, however, to define the exact contents of such a measure.

The real difficulty in solving an ill-defined problem is in clarifying the nature of the problem: how broad it is, what the goal is, and so on. Although well-defined problems have a clear path to solution, the solution strategy for an ill-defined problem must be determined by the problem solver. To develop a problem-solving strategy, it is first necessary to specify the goals of the task. For example, if we take on the task of designing a creativity test, we must decide whether the goal is (a) to estimate the creativity of under-graduate psychology majors or (b) to measure creative potential among people of all ages and educational and cultural backgrounds. Before the path to solution can be constructed, the goal must be clear.

Representing information about the problem is also difficult in the formulation of an ill-defined problem. Consider again the problem of parking mentioned at the beginning of the chapter. The representation of the problem affects the solution. If we think of the parking problem in terms of parking spaces, we are likely to seek additional spaces when there are too many cars to park. However, if we think of parking in terms of too many idle vehicles, we are more likely to consider new ways of making use of the cars that have remained idle during the workday (e.g., driving other people who need transportation around the city). This latter perspective will guide us to seek solutions that maximize efficiency rather than maximizing the amount of concrete and asphalt in the downtown area. To solve a problem, it often is necessary or, at least, desirable to try out several representations of the problem in order to hit upon one that leads to an acceptable solution.

Problem-solving research has not revealed a great deal about the processes involved in problem recognition, problem definition, and problem representation. Indeed, the emphasis in research has been on the latter rather than the earlier phases of problem solving. Yet these earlier phases are critical to accurate and efficient problem solving, especially in the solution of ill-defined problems. The study of ill-defined problems generally has been less fruitful than the study of well-defined problems. Well-defined problems are well described by current theories of problem solving; however, ill-defined problems are ill understood by psychologists. Yet arguably most of the problems in the real world are not well defined. Most are fuzzy problems, often difficult to delineate and sometimes even harder to represent in a way that makes them solvable. Our current educational system better prepares children to answer questions that are well defined and presented to them in the classroom than it does to formulate the nature of problems in the first place. Often the skills involved in solving well-defined problems are not the same as those involved in recognizing a nonobvious problem or creating a problem. The skills needed clearly to state a problem and to represent information about it in a way that permits solution are also often not emphasized in current classrooms. In this chapter we consider what factors influence the metacognitive processes involved in recognizing, defining, and representing problems.

Research on problem solving has identified several variables that influence problem-solving performance. Among these are knowledge, cognitive processes and strategies, individual differences in ability and dispositions, as well as external factors such as social context. Those variables known to influence general problem solving will be examined with respect to the three particular aspects of problem solving that are the focus of this chapter: problem recognition, problem definition, and problem representation.

KNOWLEDGE

Everyone approaches a problem situation with a unique knowledge base. That knowledge base is essentially a set of expectations about the way the world works. As you began to read this chapter, your experience with reading chapters in similar books led you to expect a certain structure and content. Similarly, when you identify, define, and represent a problem, it is in terms of what you already know. For example, consider how the parking problem mentioned in the beginning of the chapter would be approached differently by individuals with different knowledge bases. An urban planner is more likely to identify or notice that problem as one of primary importance than is a person who does not live in an urban area. The urban planner is also more likely to consider different variables in defining the problem than someone from a small town. For example, the urban planner defines the problem in terms of how it may affect the city's income (e.g., parking meters or garages) and use the city's resources (e.g., administrative factors associated with employees and regulation of parking). In contrast, the small town resident may define the problem in terms of the esthetics of housing many vehicles (e.g., parking garages are often not welcome sights in small towns) because the solution of this problem is less likely to generate funds for the town than it would in an urban setting. According to the definition of the problem, the problem would be represented differently depending on the knowledge of the problem solver, be it an urban planner or small town parking supervisor. Problem-solving research has accumulated a tremendous amount of information regarding the relationship between knowledge and problem definition and representation and, to a lesser extent, regarding problem recognition.

It is important to keep in mind that knowledge may help or hinder problem solving. For example, knowledge plays an important role in the solution of analogies. In such problems, your task is to map the relationship between two items onto two other items. For example, *apple* is to *apple tree* as *pear* is to *pear tree*. The relationship here should be clear: You are pairing fruits with their respective trees of origin. Consider the following analogy problem.

Nefarious is to Dromedary as Eggs are to:
A: Chapel
B: Yellow
C: Bees
D: Friend   (Concept Mastery Test; Terman, 1950)

The correct answer to this problem is bees. The mapping rule here is that the number of letters in each part of the analogy must match. The typical approach to analogy problems is to look for a semantic connection between the constituents rather than a surface similarity such as the number of letters. In this example, knowledge is actually an impediment to problem-solving success.

Everyday Knowledge and Problem Definition and Problem Representation

Research has demonstrated the effects of knowledge in general on problem solving, as well as its effect on domain-specific expertise. Most of this research has focused on problem representation and can also be applied to our understanding of problem definition. One source of evidence of the effect of knowledge on problem definition and representation stems from early research on the solution of well-defined problems.

Early problem-solving research sought to describe the problem-solving process as a set of steps in higher order, isomorphic problem spaces (e.g., Newell & Simon, 1972). Such research on problem solving and the concept of "problem space" grew from Newell and Simon's (1972) work on the General Problem Solver, or GPS, a model of human problem-solving processes. This model defined a problem as composed of a problem space, a starting state, a goal state, rules of transition, and heuristics. The problem space refers to all the possible states a problem could be in, such as during a bridge or checkers game. The starting state refers to the initial state of the problem. The goal state is the state to be reached by the system. Rules of transition refer to those functions that move the system from one state to another. Finally, heuristics are defined as rules that determine which moves are to be made in the problem space, as opposed to a random walk. Essentially, the GPS employs means-end analysis, a process that compares the starting state of a problem with the goal state and attempts to minimize the differences between the two. These components are well suited for solving well-defined problems where the space and transitions between states are unambiguous. However, the model offers no solution whatsoever for dealing with ill-defined problems. Nevertheless, the idea of a problem space has become a widely used and effective way of formalizing well-defined problems.

Recall the Tower of Hanoi and Monsters and Globes problems mentioned previously. According to the GPS, isomorphic problems should theoretically be solved similarly regardless of the way the information in the problem is represented. However, this model has been called into question by further studies of problem-solving performance on problems identified to be isomorphic to the Tower of Hanoi problem. Although these problems share with the Tower of Hanoi problem an identical problem space and solution structure, it is clear that the constituents chosen to represent the surface structure of each problem do have an effect (sometimes negative) on the mental representation of the problem space. One source of such evidence comes from a study that used isomorphs of the Tower of Hanoi problem involving acrobats of differing sizes (Kotovsky et al., 1985). Consider one such isomorph:

> Three circus acrobats developed an amazing routine in which they jumped to and from each other's shoulders to form human towers. The routine was quite spectacular because it was performed atop three very tall flagpoles. It was made even more impressive because the acrobats were very different in size: The large acrobat weighed 700 pounds; the medium acrobat 200 pounds; and the small acrobat, a mere 40 pounds. These differences forced them to follow these safety rules.
>
> 1. Only one acrobat may jump at a time.
> 2. Whenever two acrobats are standing on the same flagpole one must be standing on the shoulders of the other.
> 3. An acrobat may not jump if someone is standing on his shoulders.
> 4. A bigger acrobat may not stand on the shoulders of a smaller acrobat.*
>
> At the beginning of their act, the medium acrobat was on the left, the large acrobat in the middle, and the small acrobat was on the right. At the end of the act they were arranged small, medium, and large from left to right. How did they manage to do this while obeying the safety rules?
>
> *For the Reverse Acrobat problem this rule was reversed so that the smaller acrobat could not stand on the larger one; thus, the large ones had freedom of movement in that version. (Kotovsky et al., 1985, p. 262)

In the reversal of the situation where the large acrobats were standing on the smaller acrobats, participants took significantly more time to solve the problems. When an individual's expectations about a problem are violated (i.e., smaller acrobats should stand on top of larger acrobats), it requires more time successfully to build and navigate a solution to the problem. Alternatively, performance was facilitated when the information presented was in synchrony with the individual's knowledge, or in a form that did not lead to inadequate representations. Clement and Richard (1997) again used the Tower of Hanoi framework to examine problem solving, coming to the conclusion that the most difficult versions of the problem were those that required an individual to abandon their initial point of view in favor of a new, more appropriate one.

These findings pose a challenge to the idea that an individual's representation of a problem is based solely on structure, as implied by the GPS model. Even when the structure of two problem spaces is identical, the solution of those problems will depend on dissimilarities in surface elements and modalities of thought (Kotovsky et al., 1985; Simon & Newell, 1971). Simply put, these results show that one does not enter a problem as a blank slate. Prior knowledge provides a tool to structure the information in the problem, allowing the individual to apply a familiar scaffold to the information, regardless of how helpful or harmful it might be. Prior knowledge mediates an individual's ability to represent the problem in the most efficient fashion.

There is also evidence to suggest a developmental trend in the ability to use knowledge, a skill that affects problem definition. Siegler (1978) found that older children outperform younger children on a balance-scale task because of their attention to all the relevant information about the problem. Older children realize that it is necessary to encode information about multiple dimensions of the task, but younger children do not without prompts to do so. Thus, to the extent that problem definition relies on the knowledge that multiple sources of information need to be attended to and encoded, the skill of defining problems will also increase with age.

Expert Knowledge and Problem Definition and Problem Representation

Prior knowledge has been discussed in terms of everyday knowledge about the world; however, research in cognitive psychology has found a qualitative distinction between the knowledge of individuals who have more or less experience with a particular domain. Specifically, studies show that individuals who have accumulated considerable knowledge in a domain represent information about problems differently from the ways these problems are represented by individuals without extensive knowledge bases (see Chi, Glaser, & Farr, 1988). Often experts have more efficient representations of their domain than do novices. These representations have stripped away irrelevant details and get at the deeper structure of the problem, in part by chunking information. These differences in knowledge structure affect the way an expert identifies, defines, and represents problems. For example, experts and novices typically differ in how they define problems, as illustrated in the following example.

Two groups of students were given physics problems and asked to sort them into several groups, based on their similarity (Chi, Feltovich, & Glaser, 1981). The students were either graduate students in physics (experts) or undergraduates with some physics knowledge (novices). Level of expertise determined how the students defined the problems. The novice students organized their problems based on the surface features of the problem, such as whether the problem contained a spinning object, a falling object, or some other similar surface feature. The graduate students, in contrast, organized problems based on deeper, structural similarities, such as what principles of physics were required to solve the problems. This sort of deep-level process is exactly what is needed to sift through most of the unimportant information contained in the texts of many well-defined problems. It also is most likely what impairs people when they are confronted with problems that present the information in a fashion that causes them to frame the problems in an inappropriate manner.

The expert-novice differences in problem representation are well illustrated by the famous studies of chess expertise. Chase and Simon (1973) studied the reconstructive memory of individuals for arrangements of chess pieces on boards. The chess experts performed better than the novices in reconstructing the board when the pieces were placed as they would be in the middle of a chess game. However, when the pieces were arranged randomly, the experts performed no better than the novices, suggesting that the violation of these deep-level rules about the structures of chess lessened the usefulness of the expert knowledge. Experts' mental representations of chess pieces on a chessboard are more sophisticated than those of novices in that they contain more chunked information. When chess pieces are arranged on the board randomly, expert mental representations based on familiar board configurations are of no help. Randomly placed pieces cannot be chunked together according to patterns that naturally occur in chess play, rendering expert players as naive as novices when it comes to remembering random arrangements of pieces.

Empirical studies of problem solving have demonstrated a distinction between expert and novice problem representation in terms of the time spent on various stages of the problem-solving process (Lesgold, 1988). Specifically, Lesgold found that experts spent more time determining an appropriate representation of the problem than did novices. Novices were found to represent the problem relatively quickly and spend their time working on a solution. In contrast, experts spent more time comparing their current knowledge to the information they needed to discover in order to best represent the problem. After the problem was set up in the expert problem solver's mind, the process of solving it proceeded quickly relative to the novices. Thus, the effect of expertise provides the problem solver with skills that aid problem solving from the very early stages. Because novices may not notice the flaws in their representations of the problem, they will often be forced to start over, forfeiting a lot of hard work on a poorly represented problem. An expert's well-organized knowledge base is better equipped to assess the appropriateness of a problem representation even before further work is done on the problem.

While expertise is often hailed as a key to problem-solving success, it seems that the development of a highly specialized body of knowledge can lead to an impairment in the ability of experts to incorporate new rules into their thinking or to modify older ones. For example, Frensch and Sternberg (1989) have studied expert and novice bridge players. In games of bridge, the expert players performed much better than the novice players when a surface rule was changed. However, when a deeper rule was changed (for example, the rules that specified who played the lead card on the next trick), the experts' performance deteriorated more, in the short run, than did that of the novices. Frensch and Sternberg concluded that experts' entrenched strategies interfered with, rather than facilitated, their performance. The preceding examples highlight the fact that even though experts often both define and represent problems differently than do novices, the experts can suffer when the fundamentals of their representations are altered, resulting in significantly different performance profiles.

Problem Recognition

Problem recognition occurs with respect to the knowledge a person has about a domain. The fact that an expert's knowledge about a domain is organized differently from that of a novice will affect the nature of the problems that are recognized in a domain. Studies of creativity have found that it requires a considerable amount of expertise in a domain before an individual begins to recognize and create valuable new problems (Csikszentmihalyi, 1996; Simonton, 1999). Only after a person knows a field well can that person recognize gaps in the field's body of knowledge; novices are more susceptible to recognizing problems that have already been addressed by the field in the past. Not only do experts need to be thoroughly familiar with their domain; Csikszentmihalyi and Sawyer (1995) found that problem recognition often also involves the synthesis of knowledge from more than one domain. It is unfortunate that so few researchers have directly examined the effect of knowledge on problem recognition.

Both everyday knowledge and expert knowledge of a particular domain play an important role in the recognition of a problem, as well as the nature of a problem's definition and representation. However, more research has focused on the latter than the former aspects of problem solving. The next section considers the *process* of using knowledge in the course of problem solving.

COGNITIVE PROCESSES AND STRATEGIES

How do cognitive processes and strategies play a role in problem recognition, definition, and representation? Mumford, Reiter-Palmon, and

Redmond (1994) have developed one of the few models that attempts to describe the cognitive processes involved in the early stages of problem solving. Their model of problem construction proposes a set of processes that are implemented in finding, defining, and representing problems. First, problem solvers must be aware of cues, patterns, and anomalies in the environment (attention and perception). Second, analogous problem representations must be accessed from memory (activation of representations). Third, these representations must be evaluated (screening strategy selection). Fourth, the goals and constraints of the problem must be defined (element selection strategy). Fifth, these elements of the problem must be represented mentally (element reorganization).

Consider again the example of finding a life partner in the context of this model. First, the problem is recognized through attention to cues in the environment, such as noting who you are, what your needs are, and what type of person might possess the qualities you are seeking. Second, as you think of where to find such an individual, you consider analogous problems, such as how you went about selecting a suitable career or how you found friends when you moved to a new area. Third, you screen these possible analogous representations for importance. Whereas the strategy of choosing friends may have been governed by proximity and common interests, you may find that the strategy of choosing a career is more appropriate to finding a life partner if your career is one that you are passionate about, that takes into account your values and interests, and that is something that you are committed to for the long term (as opposed to a superficial friendship, which may last only as long as you remain in the same city or neighborhood). Fourth, you examine the goals and constraints of the problems. For example, it may be more important to consider the compatibility of lifestyles (e.g., career, values) with a life partner than it is with a friend. That is, you may maintain friendships with individuals whose political or religious ideals are very different from your own, but you would be less likely to choose to initiate a romantic relationship with someone with incompatible values. Fifth and finally, all of the considerations you have identified as relevant to finding a life partner are represented in a way that makes it possible to conceptualize who that person might be.

Processes in Problem Recognition

Another model of problem solving has focused more specifically on problem recognition. Brophy (1998) described a series of processes that artists and scientists report engaging in prior to defining a problem. These presymbolic processes set out the goals and obstacles in a problem situation. Brophy described these processes as "unconscious, intuitive thought that combines perceptual pattern recognition, abstract analogy creation, and search for useful ways to organize experience in problem domains" (p. 126). This idea is echoed more explicitly by Goldstone and Barsalou (1998), who suggested that while the early phases of our concepts may be couched in perceptual imagery, later abstractions arise as a function of the transformation of these nascent perceptual objects. While it is not clear just how reliable introspective self-reports are (Nisbett & Wilson, 1977), the support for these perceptually based concepts (Barsalou, 1999; Goldstone & Barsalou, 1998) lends credence to the idea that early stages of problem formation employ these presymbolic processes.

Although there is not a large body of research on these presymbolic processes or the process of problem recognition, we suggest one possible hypothesis in regard to the phenomenon of problem finding. This hypothesis is that problem recognition in a given domain depends on a sensitivity to gaps in domain knowledge that cannot be filled in by interpolating information from the existing knowledge space. Put more simply, when a person knows a certain amount of information about a domain, there will be holes in his or her knowledge, and if the person is unable satisfactorily to fill these gaps, the person will seek to fill these gaps. This hypothesis complements the Mumford et al. (1994) model in that it requires the problem solver to have a reasonable internal representation of the knowledge space and to be attentive to gaps in that knowledge.

Problem recognition as sensitivity to gaps is also consonant with Boden's (1999) model, which describes creative problem solving as the exploration and possible transformation of a psychological (or computational) knowledge space. Boden proposes that creativity is embodied in an agent exploring its knowledge space in a domain, and that creative products are created by tweaking and transforming these spaces in accordance with computational approaches to information processing. As an individual explores his or her knowledge, he or she is likely to recognize gaps or see patterns in the knowledge base, leading to the recognition of new problems. This research supports the hypothesis that problem recognition is heavily reliant on the type of information encountered and explored by the individual.

Processes in Problem Definition and Representation

Research on specific processes involved in problem solving has described problem solving in terms of algorithms, analogical transfer, convergent and divergent thinking, as well as incubation and insight. Before examining each in relation to the early stages of problem solving, let us define the constructs. As mentioned previously, algorithms are sets of operations often applied recursively to solve a problem. Analogical transfer is a process by which a problem is solved by mapping its components onto a similar problem whose solution path is already known. Convergent thinking refers to the process of narrowing down a set of ideas in order to converge on the most appropriate one. Divergent thinking is the process of generating multiple ideas in order to create a set of possibilities from which to choose. Incubation is a stage of problem solving in which the problem is set aside and not worked on consciously, but which may lead to a solution, often manifested in a sudden moment of insight. Though these processes have been studied with regard to the whole problem-solving process, we are interested in the operation of these processes in problem definition and representation.

After the problem has been recognized, the process of defining and representing the problem may proceed with processes such as analogical thinking. To form an appropriate representation, a problem solver must often try out several different perspectives on a problem before finding one that gives insight to a solution path. One way in which a variety of representations can be found is through analogical thinking. When an analogous problem can be identified, then the solution of the present problem is partly a matter of mapping one element onto another (Reed, 1987). For example, mapping involves comparing the problems for similarity in structure and identifying their parallel elements. The solution of one problem then can guide the process of solving a novel one through this analogical mapping process.

When an appropriate analogy is found, the problem solver may experience a leap in understanding – an insight. Some researchers consider insight to reflect a sudden restructuring process that yields an immediate understanding of the path to solution (Metcalfe & Wiebe, 1987). Other researchers disagree with this view, claiming that insight is incremental and does not reflect any sudden changes in representation (Weisberg & Alba, 1981). However, the current point is that re-representation of a problem can lead to a new and different solution path. Consider this example of a problem, which often yields an insight upon solution:

> A man who lived in a small town in the U.S. married 20 different women of the same town. All are still living and he has never divorced one of them. Yet he has broken no law. Can you explain?

You may find this problem difficult to solve until you remember that the verb "to marry" can also mean "to perform a marriage." Until an appropriate representation of the problem is found, the solution to the problem remains elusive.

Many psychologists have attempted to explain the processes underlying insight. Gestalt psychologists (Wertheimer, 1945) as well as contemporary psychologists (Metcalfe & Wiebe, 1987) have described insight as a sudden understanding that results when the problem solver realizes how all parts of the problem fit together to form a coherent whole, or *Gestalt*.

Other psychologists have criticized this view, claiming that the processes involved in having an insight are nothing special, and are in fact no different from the processes implicated in solving a problem that does not involve insight (Weisberg & Alba, 1981).

Still other psychologists (Davidson, 1995; Sternberg, 1985) have proposed a three-process theory, according to which insights arise out of processes called selective encoding, selective combination, and selective comparison. Selective encoding refers to the process of attending to and encoding information that is relevant for the solution of a particular problem. Selective combination is the process of recombining elements of the problem in a way that changes the representation of the problem. Selective comparison is the processing in which elements of the current problem are recognized as related to problems that have been encountered in the past. Any one of these three processes can lead to a change in problem definition or representation, possibly resulting in an insight.

What leads to an insightful moment of re-representation? Some researchers have claimed that a period of time spent away from the problem may help in the incubation of ideas and thus lead to an insight. Wallas's (1926) model suggests that after the period of (1) preparation, in which relevant information is gathered about the problem, a period of (2) incubation follows, and after this, time is spent away from the problem, and then a moment of (3) illumination occurs. The solution is then subject to (4) verification. Various researchers have tried to test this model. Two tests are described below.

Smith's (1995; Smith & Blankenship, 1989) research on incubation suggests that a period of time spent away from the problem can allow the problem solver to let go of unfruitful approaches and to allow an appropriate representation to come to mind, thus culminating in a moment of insight. Smith explains that initial, failed attempts to solve a problem interfere with the solver's ability to access the correct solution. Only after the solver takes a break from the problem can the initial misleading solution paths be forgotten so that new, accurate solution paths may be found. Other theories of incubation propose that the incubation period allows for the assimilation of new information, which then is incorporated into the solution of the problem (Seifert, Meyer, Davidson, Patalano, & Yaniv, 1995). According to this theory, incubation not only allows the problem solver to let go of misleading information, but also provides an opportunity to notice new information that helps form a viable mental representation of the problem. Neither of these theories requires special cognitive processes in order to explain the evolution of an insight.

The metacognitive task of how to represent information given in a problem is subject to the effects of fixation and negative transfer (Gick & Holyoak, 1980, 1983). Fixation occurs when an individual gets stuck in a particular way of looking at a problem. When a person is attempting to solve the problem mentioned above about a man with multiple marriages, that person may become fixated on the fact that one person cannot marry several times without being married to more than one person. Only when a person lets go of the misleading (though more common) definition of the word "marry" can the person break this fixation.

Fixation is a common result of the ordinary processes of problem solving. When faced with any type of problem, an individual brings to the task his or her experience with similar problems, such as the knowledge about the domain and the individual's expectations or intuitions about how to approach the problem. Often schemas provide useful short-cuts in the solution of well-defined problems. For example, most people have schemas for solving word problems in math, based on their previous experience with such problems (Newell & Simon, 1972). Usually, we examine the question and use the given numeric values to set up a familiar formula for solution. However, when a problem's definition and its goals are ill structured, our expectations about how the problem should be approached may be more detrimental than helpful. In fact, the key difficulty in many insight problems is that they are based on the premise that the problem solver will build on an incorrect or misleading expectation that must be overcome in order to solve the problem.

For example, consider the following problem:

> If you have black socks and brown socks in your drawer, mixed in a ratio of 4 to 5, how many socks will you have to take out to make sure that you have a pair of the same color?

When people see a problem involving numbers, they usually assume, correctly, that there are some calculations to be done. Therefore, they concentrate on the numerical information, in this case the ratio information, in pursuing a solution (Davidson, 1995). However, this assumption is an example of negative transfer, a misleading expectation. If the problem is represented without this numerical information, we notice that it can be solved in a straightforward manner without considering the ratio information at all: Pull out two socks and they may match. If not, the third sock will definitely match one of the other two, given that there are only two colors of socks in the drawer.

Based on the limited amount of research that has been done on the information-processing components of problem recognition, definition, and representation, it appears that these aspects of problem solving may not require special kinds of thinking. However, attention and openness are likely to be crucial to the discovery and creation of problems and to the selection of a problem representation. The metacognitive processes involved in these early stages of problem formulation are both divergent and convergent and appear to rely on analogical thinking as well as incubation and insight.

INDIVIDUAL DIFFERENCES: ABILITIES AND DISPOSITIONS

Traditionally, problem solving research has not focused on the role of individual differences beyond a consideration of general cognitive ability. However, psychologists who have examined the early stages of problem solving have found that there are important sources of individual variation that affect the processes of problem recognition, definition, and representation.

Individual differences have been found to play a role in the early stages of well-defined problem solving (MacLeod, Hunt, & Mathews, 1978; Sternberg & Weil, 1980). For example, MacLeod et al. (1978) found that individual differences in ability influence problem representation. In their study, participants were presented with simple declarative sentences such as "Plus is above star." Their results showed that most participants represented the sentence linguistically. In contrast, participants who had high spatial abilities were more likely to represent the content of the sentence pictorially. The authors concluded that the processes in sentence comprehension are not universally generalizable, but rather depend on the abilities of the individual. Similarly, mental representations of problems are also affected by individual differences in ability.

Getzels and Csikszentmihalyi (1976) found that individuals who were successfully creative exhibited a concern for problem finding throughout the creative process. This "concern" can be characterized as a disposition or a mental set that attends to the nature of the problem definition and representation throughout the process of solving the problem at hand. Their study found that the most products were produced by individuals who reevaluated the way they had initially defined and represented the problem during all stages of the problem-solving process.

One source of information about the abilities and dispositions that may be influential factors in the processes of problem recognition, definition, and representation in ill-defined problem solving is the literature on creativity. As discussed earlier, the processes of recognizing a problem, redefining problems, and representing them in various ways are essentially creative processes. The creativity literature has identified several individual-difference variables that appear to influence creative problem solving, including divergent thinking, openness, tolerance of ambiguity, and intrinsic motivation.

Do some people have the ability to think more divergently or flexibly than others? Individual differences in intelligence and personality have been linked to differences in creative performance in various studies (see Sternberg & Lubart, 1995). Psychologists have often pointed out the importance of divergent-thinking abilities in creative problem solving. One way divergent thinking has been measured is using the Torrance Tests of Creative Thinking (Torrance & Ball, 1984), which include several measures of an individual's ability to think divergently and flexibly. For example, the Alternate Uses Task asks participants to name as many uses as they can for an everyday object, such as a paper clip or an eraser. Responses of great diversity and number allegedly indicate greater divergent thinking ability and cognitive flexibility. Scores on the Torrance Tests have been associated with greater creative performance. This association between divergent thinking and creativity may be due to the ability to think of many and diverse ways of defining and representing a problem. Thinking divergently and flexibly may not help in the latter stages of problem solving, when a solution must be evaluated for accuracy; evaluation relies on analytical and convergent thinking abilities. However, divergent thinking ability is more likely to be critical in the early stages of solving, when the problem remains open-ended and various definitions and representations of the problem must be considered.

As mentioned earlier, one of the critical processes associated with problem finding is attention to and perception of the environment in which a problem is discovered (Mumford et al., 1994). Research on creativity has demonstrated that highly creative individuals are those who have a broad range of attention relative to less creative people. When experiencing the world, creative people tend to filter out fewer distracters in the environment (Eysenck, 1997). Because creative individuals take in information that other people would consider irrelevant, a highly creative person's chances of detecting subtle patterns and hidden anomalies are greater than the chances of a less creative person doing so.

Besides abilities, are there dispositional traits, such as personality attributes or cognitive style, that predispose people to being able to identify problems and realize creative ways to define and represent them? Many psychologists have argued that dispositions are a key factor in problem finding (e.g., Ennis, 1987; Jay & Perkins, 1997). Jay and Perkins (1997) have claimed: "Abilities, knowledge, and strategies enable a person to problem find, and contexts provide the stimulus, but it is dispositions that actually promote the initiation of problem finding" (p. 286). Jay (1996) found that problem-finding behavior was enhanced when it was encouraged and guided. Given the fact that real-world problem-solving situations often do not include such guidance and prompts, it appears that the disposition *spontaneously* to engage in problem-finding behavior is very important. Perhaps individuals who are prompted to take a lot of time during the identification, definition, and representation phases of problem solving will eventually internalize these strategies and spontaneously engage in problem-finding behavior, even in the absence of prompts and encouragement to do so.

Are there personality traits associated with creative problem solving? Quite a bit of research has sought to find a link between personality and creativity. In a meta-analysis of the relationship between personality traits and creativity, Feist (1998) found that creative individuals tended to be "autonomous, introverted, open to new experiences, norm-doubting, self-confident, self-accepting, driven, ambitious, dominant, hostile, and impulsive" (p. 299). Other traits associated with creativity include tolerance of ambiguity (MacKinnon, 1978; Sternberg & Lubart, 1995) and intuitiveness (Bastick, 1982).

Eysenck (1997) has discussed the creative individual in terms of ego strength and psychopathology. Ego strength is a term used by Barron (1969) and others to refer to a strong, self-determined, dominant, self-reliant, and independent person. Eysenck has found a link between creativity and subclinical levels of psychoticism as measured by the Eysenck Personality Questionnaire (Eysenck & Eysenck, 1975). Eysenck conceived of psychoticism as a continuum ranging from conventional, socialized, and altruistic traits to aggressive, impulsive, and psychotic traits. Creative individuals were found to be slightly more psychotic than average with respect to this continuum. This observation has been supported by various reports of heightened levels of actual psychopathology among creative populations (e.g., Kaufman, 2001).

Most research that has attempted to identify the personality characteristics associated with creativity has found a great deal of variability among creative individuals, suggesting that the ability to create problems and solve them in a way that is considered useful and original may vary greatly from domain to domain. For example, the traits that are associated with being a creative visual artist may be very dissimilar from the traits associated with being a creative business manager. For a creative visual artist to transform his or her creative idea into a reality, he or she often must spend long hours in the studio. But a creative business manager will probably need to interact intensely with many different types of people in order to carry out her creative vision for her organization.

Another important factor that has been identified as critical to the creative process (e.g., Amabile, 1996), as well as to the early stages of problem solving, is motivation. It is logical that you will not recognize problems that you are not motivated to find. For example, recall the problem of lack of parking mentioned at the beginning of this chapter. If you walk or take public transportation to work every day, you may not even notice, let alone be concerned with, the problems facing automobile commuters. If you lack intrinsic motivation, you are less likely to pursue a difficult problem such as this one. Extrinsic motivation can also encourage creative problem solving if it provides more information or somehow makes it easier to solve the problem; however, extrinsic motivation that simply offers a reward but does not aid the problem-solving process (such as being paid to work on the downtown parking problem despite your lack of interest in the issue) will not lead to more creative solutions (Collins & Amabile, 1999). Amabile (1996) has also noted the importance of curiosity and a playful attitude in the facilitation of creative problem solving. People who enjoy experimenting with unusual ideas are more likely to recognize novel ways of defining and representing problems, in the same way that curious people are more likely to discover or create problems that escape the awareness of others.

These abilities and dispositions have been associated with creativity. However, the relationship of these with problem recognition, definition, and representation remains to be investigated carefully. Individual difference variables that are associated with creativity may prove to be a fruitful starting point for further research on the factors that influence the early stages of problem solving.

SOCIAL CONTEXT

Any discussion of problem-solving abilities must survey the environment in which an individual encounters a problem. Peers, culture, and even language structure play a role in the recognition, definition, and representation of a problem.

Social forces can influence substantially an individual's efforts in creatively defining, recognizing, or representing a problem (e.g., Sternberg, Kaufman, & Pretz, 2001; Sternberg, Kaufman, & Pretz, 2002). When an individual recognizes a problem in his or her field, this recognition may be viewed as "rocking the boat." The existence of a new problem may suggest an overlooked or ignored shortcoming in a field or situation. The social context affects problem recognition and definition through the field's adherence to current paradigms. For example, problems studied in the field of social cognition previously employed social-psychological methodology to examine the effect of beliefs about social groups on behavior. However, recent attraction to the use of functional magnetic resonance imaging techniques in research by neuroscientists and cognitive psychologists has become a tool of interest to some social psychologists who are interested in social cognition (e.g., Cunningham, Johnson, Gatenby, Gore, & Banaji, 2001). The availability of such resources, the field's acceptance of the validity of the methodology, as well as the neuroscience community's acceptance of social psychologists will affect the way that social psychologists discover and define problems in their field, especially among researchers interested in embarking on the new subdomain of "social cognitive neuroscience" (Ochsner & Lieberman, 2001).

Problem definition is affected by social context in any domain. Individuals can become unable to redefine problems or evaluate progress on current problems due to the attitudes of the group. For example, in an office environment, individuals may be familiar with a particular computer application for word processing. However, the program eventually may become outdated or unsupported. Initially, the group may simply go through the process of converting files or rewriting documents, rather than abandoning the program for one that is more appropriate. Here the problem has become not word processing, but rather the word processing program itself. The problem is not particularly difficult to spot, but the ways of the group may be so entrenched that changing programs becomes an unacceptable option. In other words, the attitudes of a group can be pervasive in the decision process of the individual.

The influence of the social context on problem recognition can be illustrated by an example from the field of psychology. In the late 1950s, Rosenblatt (1958) developed neural networks using elements that were designed to model human cognition, which he called perceptrons. Following this early work, other researchers in the field pointed out limitations of Rosenblatt's networks (Minsky & Papert, 1969). Minsky and Papert claimed that these early networks were unable to solve classification problems whose solutions were nonlinear (Beale & Jackson, 1990). Based on the argument that most interesting problems attempted by humans often require a nonlinear solution, this weakness was regarded as a fatal flaw in Rosenblatt's network design. As a result of the field's influence, there was little research in the field of neural networks for almost three decades; networks had been deemed inappropriate for modeling cognition. It was not until much later that the field gave neural networks another chance (Rumelhart, McClelland, & University of California San Diego, 1986). Rumelhart and McClelland's new vision of neural networks illustrated that such models did have the power to model more complex human cognition, and resulted in a rush of research interest in this area. Despite the fact that there was not a tremendous amount of evidence against the viability of neural networks at the time of Minsky and Papert's critique, the social context of the field hindered the progress of research in this vein for quite some time.

The social context has a strong, sometimes unnoticed, effect on problem solving, beginning with the very early stages. Immediate clues from the environment can affect the type of definition or representation used to solve a problem (Gick & Holyoak, 1980, 1983). Even the traditions and attitudes of a group will affect the types of problems recognized by its members, the terms in which they define those problems, and the ways they represent the problems as they prepare to solve them. Often, the most difficult part of problem formulation requires an individual to call into question these norms and expectations in order to most appropriately examine the phenomenon of interest.

SUMMARY AND CONCLUSIONS

What We Know

The earliest stages of problem solving involve recognizing that a problem exists, defining the scope and goals of the problem, and representing information about that problem in a way that helps establish a viable path to solution. For the most part, research on problem solving has focused on explaining the solution of well-defined problems that are already recognized and presented directly to the problem solver.

When we approach a new situation, our knowledge based on prior experiences will influence our ability to define and represent a problem correctly. In fact, we may fail to notice the existence of a problem if it runs counter to our strongly held expectations. To the extent that an individual has misleading expectations or schemas about a problem, due either to crystallized expertise or to the effects of misleading context, that person may have difficulty thinking flexibly about how to approach the dilemma. Recall the lemonade and iced tea example. Our assumption that lemonade and iced tea are beverages in liquid form impedes our ability to think of them in any other form.

The processes involved in problem recognition, definition, and representation are quite varied. To notice a problem, a person must attend broadly to all pieces of relevant information in a situation. Additional knowledge from past experience with similar problems must also be accessed. However, the likelihood that an individual will spontaneously notice analogies between problems in disparate domains is rather small (Gick & Holyoak, 1980). Individual differences in cognitive abilities and personality may explain why some people are better at solving ill-defined problems than are others.

The ability to think divergently and flexibly is valuable in the process of problem formulation, as is an open and intrinsically motivated disposition. Perhaps the most critical variable in determining whether a person discovers or creates a novel problem is that individual's motivation to find it and work on developing an appropriate definition and representation of the issue. This disposition characterized by openness and curiosity may be regarded as a trait version of a mental set, a constant metacognitive attentiveness to the environment and the process of problem solving. Individuals with this disposition are always thinking of different ways to regard the information in their environment and the information they possess in long-term memory. When they are working on a problem, they naturally attempt to redefine and re-represent the problem, thus increasing their chances of finding a definition and representation that will yield a creative solution.

Finally, the social context may also facilitate the likelihood of noticing problems and thinking divergently about their solutions. If an environment does not encourage potentially creative individuals to seek and explore, they will not discover gaps in their understanding, and they will not learn to play with ideas nor practice taking different perspectives on problems with which they are confronted.

What We Need to Know

In contrast to the later stages of problem solving, the stage of problem formulation appears to rely more heavily on disposition and social context. Unfortunately, relatively little empirical research has addressed these topics. We need to understand what makes a person more likely to engage him- or herself in seeking out ill-defined problems and experimenting with various ways to represent them. We need to know how people who are constrained by misleading expectations and schemas break out of their mental sets in order to gain new perspectives on problems. Can we teach children to think with this kind of mindful curiosity? We hope that teachers will allow children to practice suspending their judgment when necessary, to be playful in their search for a variety of solutions to problems.

If our ultimate goal is to help people become better able to solve problems that confront them in their personal and professional lives and in the concerns of the world, we must be prepared to examine the fuzzy issues surrounding problem recognition, definition, and representation. Because most of life's problems are not cleanly packaged with one correct path to solution, it is important that we take on the ill-defined challenge of studying these early phases of problem solving in an effort to understand how problem solving can be enhanced in these initial stages. Rather than educate others to become followers, it is in our best interest to encourage problem solvers to become active problem finders, to stay curious so that they discover and create novel problems, and to think flexibly in the process of solving those problems.

REFERENCES

Amabile, T. M. (1996). *Creativity in context: Update to "The social psychology of creativity."* Boulder, CO: Westview Press.
Barron, F. (1969). *Creative person and creative process.* New York: Holt, Rinehart & Winston.
Barsalou, L. W. (1999). Perceptual symbol systems. *Behavioral & Brain Sciences, 22,* 577–660.
Bastick, T. (1982). *Intuition: How we think and act.* New York: Wiley.
Beale, R. J., & Jackson, T. (1990). *Neural computing: An introduction.* Bristol: Institute of Physics Publishing.
Boden, M. (1999). Computer models of creativity. In R. J. Sternberg (Ed.), *Handbook of Creativity* (pp. 351–372). New York: Cambridge University Press.
Bransford, J. D., & Stein, B. S. (1993). *The ideal problem solver: A guide for improving thinking, learning, and creativity* (2nd ed.). New York: W. H. Freeman.
Brophy, D. R. (1998). Understanding, measuring and enhancing individual creative problem solving efforts. *Creativity Research Journal, 11,* 123–150.
Chase, W. G., & Simon, H. A. (1973). Perception in chess. *Cognitive Psychology, 4,* 55–81.

Chi, M., Feltovich, P. J., & Glaser, R. (1981). Categorization and representation of physics problems by experts and novices. *Cognitive Science, 5,* 121–152.

Chi, M. T. H., Glaser, R., & Farr, M. J. (Eds.). (1988). *The nature of expertise.* Hillsdale, NJ: Erlbaum.

Clement, E. & Richard, J. (1997). Knowledge of domain effects in problem representation: The case of Tower of Hanoi isomorphs. *Thinking and Reasoning, 3,* 133–157.

Collins, M. A., & Amabile, T. M. (1999). Motivation and creativity. In R. J. Sternberg (Ed.), *Handbook of creativity* (pp. 297–312). New York: Cambridge University Press.

Csikszentmihalyi, M. (1996). *Creativity.* New York: Harper Collins.

Csikszentmihalyi, M., & Sawyer, K. (1995). Creative insight: The social dimension of a solitary moment. In R. J. Sternberg & J. E. Davidson (Eds.), *The nature of insight* (pp. 329–363). Cambridge, MA: MIT Press.

Cunningham, W. A., Johnson, M. K., Gatenby, J. C., Gore, J. C., & Banaji, M. R. (2001, April). *An fMRI study on the conscious and unconscious evaluations of social groups.* Paper presented at the UCLA Conference on Social Cognitive Neuroscience, Los Angeles, CA.

Davidson, J. E. (1995). The suddenness of insight. In R. J. Sternberg & J. E. Davidson (Eds.), *The nature of insight* (pp. 125–155). Cambridge, MA: MIT Press.

Ellis, S., & Siegler, R. S. (1994). Development of problem solving. In R. J. Sternberg (Ed.), *Thinking and problem solving. Handbook of perception and cognition* (2nd ed.) (pp. 333–367). San Diego, CA: Academic Press.

Ennis, R. H. (1987). A taxonomy of critical thinking dispositions and abilities. In J. B. Baron & R. J. Sternberg (Eds.), *Teaching thinking skills: Theory and practice.* Series of books in psychology (pp. 9–26). New York: Freeman.

Eysenck, H. J. (1997). Creativity and personality. In M. A. Runco (Ed.), *The creativity research handbook* (pp. 41–66). Cresskill, NJ: Hampton.

Eysenck, H. J. & Eysenck, S. B. G. (1975). *Manual of the Eysenck personality questionnaire.* London: Hodder & Stoughton.

Feist, G. J. (1998). A meta-analysis of personality in scientific and artistic creativity. *Personality and Social Psychology Review, 2,* 290–309.

Frensch, P. A., & Sternberg, R. J. (1989). Expertise and intelligent thinking: When is it worse to know better? In R. J. Sternberg (Ed.), *Advances in the psychology of human intelligence* (Vol. 5, pp. 157–188). Hillsdale, NJ: Erlbaum.

Getzels, J. W. (1982). The problem of the problem. In R. Hogarth (Ed.), *New directions for methodology of social and behavioral science: Question framing and response consistency* (No. 11). San Francisco: Jossey-Bass.

Getzels, J. W., & Csikszentmihalyi, M. (1976). *The creative vision: A longitudinal study of problem finding in art.* New York: Wiley.

Gick, M. L., & Holyoak, K. J. (1980). Analogical problem solving. *Cognitive Psychology, 12,* 306–355.

Gick, M. L., & Holyoak, K. J. (1983). Schema induction and analogical transfer. *Cognitive Psychology, 15,* 1–38.

Goldstone, R. L., & Barsalou, L. (1998). Reuniting perception and conception. In S. A. Sloman and L. J. Rips (Eds.), *Similarity and symbols in human thinking* (pp. 145–176). Cambridge, MA: MIT Press.

Hayes, J. R. (1989). *The complete problem solver* (2nd ed.). Hillsdale, NJ: Erlbaum.

Jay, E. S. (1996). *The nature of problem finding in students' scientific inquiry*. Unpublished doctoral dissertation, Harvard University, Graduate School of Education, Cambridge, MA.

Jay, E. S., & Perkins, D. N. (1997). Problem finding: The search for mechanism. In M. A. Runco (Ed.), *The creativity research handbook* (pp. 257–293). Cresskill, NJ: Hampton.

Kaufman, J. C. (2001). The Sylvia Plath effect: Mental illness in eminent creative writers. *Journal of Creative Behavior, 35*(1), 37–50.

Kotovsky, K., Hayes, J. R., & Simon, H. A. (1985). Why are some problems hard? Evidence from the Tower of Hanoi. *Cognitive Psychology, 17*, 248–294.

Lesgold, A. M. (1988). Problem solving. In R. J. Sternberg & E. E. Smith (Eds.), *The psychology of human thought* (pp. 188–213). New York: Cambridge University Press.

MacKinnon, D. W. (1978). *In search of human effectiveness: Identifying and developing creativity*. Buffalo, NY: Creative Education Foundation.

MacLeod, C. M., Hunt, E. B., & Mathews, N. N. (1978). Individual differences in the verification of sentence-picture relationships. *Journal of Verbal Learning and Verbal Behavior, 17*, 493–507.

Metcalfe, J. A., & Wiebe, D. (1987). Intuition in insight and noninsight problem solving. *Memory & Cognition, 15*, 238–246.

Minsky, M., & Papert, S. (1969). *Perceptrons: An introduction to computational geometry*. Cambridge, MA: MIT Press.

Mumford, M. D., Reiter-Palmon, R., & Redmond, M. R. (1994). Problem construction and cognition: Applying problem representations in ill-defined domains. In M. A. Runco (Ed.), *Problem finding, problem solving, and creativity* (pp. 1–39). Norwood, NJ: Ablex.

Newell, A., & Simon, H. (1972). *Human problem solving*. Englewood Cliffs, NJ: Prentice-Hall.

Nisbett, R. E., & Wilson, T. D. (1977). Telling more than we can know: Verbal reports on mental processes. *Psychological Review, 84*, 231–259.

Ochsner, K. N., & Lieberman, M. D. (2001). The emergence of social cognitive neuroscience. *American Psychologist, 56*, 717–734.

Reed, S. K. (1987). A structure-mapping model for word problems. *Journal of Experimental Psychology: Learning, Memory, & Cognition, 13*, 125–139.

Rosenblatt, F. (1958). The perceptron: A probabilistic model for information storage and organization in the brain. *Psychological Review, 65*, 386–408.

Rumelhart, D. E., McClelland, J. L., & University of California San Diego, PDP Research Group. (1986). *Parallel distributed processing: Explorations in the microstructure of cognition*. Cambridge, MA: MIT Press.

Seifert, C. M., Meyer, D. E., Davidson, N., Patalano, A. L., & Yaniv, I. (1995). Demystification of cognitive insight: Opportunistic assimilation and the prepared-mind perspective. In R. J. Sternberg & J. E. Davidson (Eds.), *The nature of insight* (pp. 125–155). Cambridge, MA: MIT Press.

Siegler, R. S. (1978). The origins of scientific reasoning. In R. S. Siegler (Ed.), *Children's thinking: What develops?* (pp. 109–49). Hillsdale, NJ: Erlbaum.

Simon, H. A., & Newell, A. (1971). Human problem solving: The state of the theory in 1970. *American Psychologist, 26*, 145–159.

Simonton, D. (1999). Creativity from a historiometric perspective. In R. J. Sternberg (Ed.), *Handbook of creativity* (pp. 116–136). New York: Cambridge University Press.

Smith, S. M. (1995). Fixation, incubation, and insight in memory and creative thinking. In S. M. Smith, T. B. Ward, & R. A. Finke (Eds.), *The creative cognition approach* (pp. 135–156). Cambridge, MA: MIT Press.

Smith, S. M., & Blankenship, S. E. (1989). Incubation effects. *Bulletin of the Psychonomic Society, 27,* 311–314.

Sternberg, R. J. (1985). *Beyond IQ: A triarchic theory of human intelligence.* New York: Cambridge University Press.

Sternberg, R. J. (1986). *Intelligence applied? Understanding and increasing your intellectual skills.* San Diego, CA: Harcourt Brace Jovanovich.

Sternberg, R. J. (1999). *Cognitive psychology* (2nd ed.). New York: Harcourt Brace.

Sternberg, R. J., & Davidson, J. E. (Eds.) (1995). *The nature of insight.* Cambridge, MA: MIT Press.

Sternberg, R. J., & Weil, E. M. (1980). An aptitude-strategy interaction in linear syllogistic reasoning. *Journal of Educational Psychology, 72,* 226–234.

Sternberg, R. J., Kaufman, J. C., & Pretz, J. E. (2001). The propulsion model of creative contributions applied to the arts and letters. *Journal of Creative Behavior, 35,* 75–101.

Sternberg, R. J., Kaufman, J. C., & Pretz, J. E. (2002). *The creativity conundrum: A propulsion model of kinds of creative contributions.* Philadelphia: Psychology Press.

Sternberg, R. J., & Lubart, T. I. (1995). *Defying the crowd: Cultivating creativity in a culture of conformity.* New York: Free Press.

Terman, L. M. (1950). *Concept Mastery Test.* New York: Psychological Corporation.

Torrance, E. P., & Ball, O. E. (1984). *Torrance Tests of Creative Thinking: Revised manual.* Bensenville, IL: Scholastic Test Service.

Wallas, G. (1926). *The art of thought.* New York: Harcourt, Brace.

Weisberg, R. W., & Alba, J. W. (1981). An examination of the alleged role of "fixation" in the solution of several "insight" problems. *Journal of Experimental Psychology: General, 110,* 169–192.

Wertheimer, M. (1945). *Productive thinking.* Westport, CT: Greenwood Press.

AUTHOR NOTE

Preparation of this book chapter was supported by Grant REC-9979843 from the National Science Foundation and by a government grant under the Javits Act Program (Grant No. R206R000001) as administered by the Office of Educational Research and Improvement, U.S. Department of Education. Grantees undertaking such projects are encouraged to express freely their professional judgment. This article, therefore, does not necessarily represent the positions or the policies of the U.S. government, and no official endorsement should be inferred.

Requests for reprints should be sent to Robert J. Sternberg, Yale University, The Yale Center for the Psychology of Abilities, Competencies, and Expertise, P.O. Box 208358, New Haven, CT 06520–8358.

2

The Acquisition of Expert Performance as Problem Solving

Construction and Modification of Mediating Mechanisms Through Deliberate Practice

K. Anders Ericsson

How do experts reach their high level of performance? Recent reviews (Ericsson, 1996, 1998b, 2001; Ericsson & Lehmann, 1996) dispel the common belief that "talented" expert performers attain very high levels of performance virtually automatically through cumulative domain-related experience. Instead, empirical evidence strongly implies that even the most "talented" individuals in a domain must spend over ten years actively engaging in particular practice activities (deliberate practice) that lead to gradual improvements in skill and adaptations that increase performance.

In this chapter I argue that the acquisition of expert performance can be described as a sequence of mastered challenges with increasing levels of difficulty, such as playing pieces of music, performing challenging gymnastic routines, and solving complex mathematical problems. Different levels of mastery present the learner with different kinds of problems that must be solved for the skill to develop further. And each individual's path toward skilled performance is distinct; it depends on when technical challenges were encountered and the specific methods used to help the individuals continue their development.

When beginners are first introduced to a domain of expertise they can successfully perform only the most simple tasks and activities. With the aid of instruction and training many individuals are able to master increasingly difficult tasks, thus gradually improving and slowly approaching the level of expert performers. The incremental nature of gaining mastery means that tasks that were initially impossible to perform can be executed effortlessly as increased skill is attained.

When an individual attempts to perform a task that is too difficult, his or her available repertoire of methods and skills is insufficient to perform the task successfully. In this chapter I argue that when motivated individuals strive to overcome obstacles and master prerequisite aspects of a given task, they must engage in problem solving. Studies of how individuals eventually master various types of problems should provide unique insights into how their cognitive mechanisms, representations, and knowledge change to solve those problems. Mastery of very difficult problems, such as an unfamiliar technique or developing a better scientific theory, might require days, weeks, months, or even years, rather than minutes or hours available in most studies of problem solving in psychological laboratory.

Some people will probably object that the label *problem solving* is inappropriate when applied to the process of mastering tasks in a domain of expertise. They will propose that these phenomena should be classified as skill acquisition or complex learning. To be sure, when most textbooks in psychology discuss problem solving, they rarely refer to highly skilled performance, focusing instead on studies of classic problems, such as the Tower of Hanoi (Gagne & Smith, 1962; Simon, 1975), the tumor radiation problem (Duncker, 1945), and the pendulum problem (Maier, 1931). The large differences in tasks seem to support the argument that the two types of phenomena have always been viewed as distinct. However, a historical survey suggests that at one time a much closer relationship was assumed to exist between problem solving with puzzles and expert performance.

In the foreword to his classic paper, Duncker (1945, p. v), one of the foremost pioneers in the study of problem solving, claimed that he was tempted "to study productive thinking where it is most conspicuous in great achievements" and that "important information about the genesis of productive thought could be found in biographical material." However, he concluded that "although a thunderstorm is the most striking example of electrical discharge, its laws are better investigated in little sparks within the laboratory. To study in simple, convenient forms what is complicated and difficult to access is the method of experimental science; to lose in this simplification just the essential aspects, is its notorious danger. Experimental psychology, more than all other sciences, is continually faced with this danger."

Drawing on the analogy with the study of lightning, Duncker (1945, p. v) intentionally restricted his study of problem solving to "practical and mathematical problems," "because such material is more accessible, more suitable for experimentation." Duncker assumed that the process of solving mathematical problems in the laboratory induced the same phenomenon of problem solving as the one observed in generation of great achievements and expert performance; the differences were primarily a matter of degree.

The hypothesis that it is possible to use the laboratory to capture pure manifestations of mental functions observed in everyday life, such as problem solving and memory, in simpler form, is one of the cornerstones of modern experimental psychology. Let us first use the example of lightning to show convincing evidence for the parallels between laboratory and everyday phenomena, and then examine the evidence for parallels between problem solving in the laboratory and great achievements.

How did 18th-century scientists establish that sparks of static electricity encountered in everyday life were miniature versions of the lightning observed during thunderstorms? Since the earliest times people have recognized the strange effects of static electricity that cause invisible effects and sparks of discharge. In the 17th and early 18th century, scientists designed and refined machines to produce and store very high levels of static electricity and discharge bright sparks. Several scientists, among them Benjamin Franklin (Clark, 1983), proposed that lightning was a more intense version of the same phenomenon. Franklin listed many similarities, 'They both gave out light of the same color and had crooked direction and swift motion ... both were conducted by metals, made noise, 'subsisting' in water and ice, and could tear apart materials that they went through. In addition, both could kill animals, melt metals, set fire to inflammable substances and produce sulfurous smell" (Clark, 1983, p. 80). Franklin then demonstrated that he could tap the static electricity in a thunderstorm by sending up a kite and conducting the static electricity down the wet string from the cloud. He was able to use the naturally occurring phenomenon of the storm to reproduce characteristics of static electrical discharge induced under laboratory conditions.

Do we know enough about the characteristics of productive thinking used to solve practical and mathematical problems and the processes mediating great achievements to draw the conclusion that productive thinking captured in the laboratory will automatically apply to great achievements? The answer must be "No." The progress on understanding puzzle problem solving during the 20th century was remarkable, and was largely attributable to Duncker's (1945) research. However, as I show in the next section, the concept of problem solving does not correspond to a single well-defined phenomenon. It has changed considerably during the last century in tight connection with the changes in the dominant theoretical framework of general psychology. In fact, as more knowledge has been accumulated about various forms of thinking, such as decision making, comprehension, reasoning, planning, and creative thinking, the harder it has become to distinguish problem solving as a separate phenomenon with its unique processes and mechanisms.

The research efforts to identify the structure of thinking led to great advances in the design of experiments and the methodology for tracing complex cognitive processes in the laboratory with recordings of eye movements and concurrent verbalization. These developments revealed that performance on simple laboratory tasks is often mediated by complex knowledge and semantic memory, and they provided tools for studying complex performance.

Ericsson and Smith (1991) showed that the same methodology can be adapted to study expert performance and its mediating cognitive processes as well as the learning processes that led to this superior level of performance. For example, if we are interested in how world-class chess players are able to play better than other less accomplished players, we should study the cognitive processes involved in playing at the world-class level. If we are interested in how scientists are able to produce consistently superior pieces of research and how musicians are able to produce rich musical experiences for their audiences, we should study the processes involved in producing these achievements. Once we are able to reproduce expert performance with representative tasks in the laboratory (de Groot, 1946/1978; Ericsson & Smith, 1991), it is possible to submit the mediating processes to analysis and experimental variation.

Consider how Benjamin Franklin waited for a thunderstorm to send up his kite to siphon off static electricity from the clouds. In much the same way, it is possible to reproduce the necessary representative conditions for expert performance and then merely request that willing expert performers exhibit their superior performance under those conditions. When the everyday phenomenon of expertise can be reproduced in the laboratory, then the difficult problem of establishing the equivalence between phenomenon in everyday life and the laboratory can be avoided.

OUTLINE OF THE CHAPTER

Until the 19th century, most scientists and philosophers believed that it would be impossible to use scientific methods in the rigorous study of thinking and problem solving. I therefore briefly discuss how the study of problem solving evolved within the scientific discipline of psychology and how it led to studies of problem solving primarily using puzzles and traditional laboratory tasks. Then I focus on the methodological advances in studying thinking and how they allowed scientists to describe the structure of problem solving with puzzles. In the main body of the chapter I discuss how the same methods can be used to study problem solving and thinking within the context of representative tasks that capture expert performance and its acquisition. I conclude with a brief discussion of our emerging knowledge of problem solving in highly skilled performance and its relation to problem solving with traditional puzzles and discuss some future directions of problem solving research.

Approaches to the Study of Problem Solving and Thinking: Historical Background

Conceptions of the structure of the human mind have gone through dramatic changes during the history of our civilization. Humans have always reflected on experiences and feelings. With Aristotle and other Greek philosophers, the search for the structure of consciousness and its basic elements became more systematic, based on observation and analysis of one's own thinking. One of the central problems of these introspective efforts was the private nature of consciousness; one person's conscious awareness could not be directly experienced by others. Only a few centuries ago prominent philosophers such as Immanuel Kant denied the possibility of even studying complex mental phenomena and subjective experience with scientific methods.

When the first psychological laboratory was established in Germany toward the end of the 19th century, Wilhelm Wundt, the founding father of experimental psychology, deliberately focused his research on the most basic phenomenon, namely, sensory perception. Other pioneering researchers in psychology, such as Hermann Ebbinghaus, also designed techniques to measure basic forms of memory processes in which thinking and meaningful associations were minimized, such as Ebbinghaus's famous nonsense syllables. Ebbinghaus showed that it was possible to design experimental situations in which the results of complex mental capacities, such as memory, could be directly observed and measured. His empirical studies focused on general processes and capacities so basic that they were not mediated by thinking and therefore could not be analyzed by introspective methods. These empirical paradigms allowed measurement with quantitative methods and the mathematical expression of general laws that were consistent with other natural sciences.

The scientific approach of identifying general laws and simple basic mechanisms to account for the complex natural phenomena had been very successful in the natural sciences. The application of this analytical approach to psychological phenomena is nicely summarized in Morgan's canon: "In no case may we interpret an action as the outcome of the exercise of a higher faculty, if it can be interpreted as the outcome of the exercise of one which stands lower in the psychological scale" (Morgan, 1894, p. 53).

This general commitment to reductionism has had major impact on the study of higher level cognitive processes, such as problem solving. First, it led to prioritization of research that would extend our knowledge about the basic processes of sensation, perception, memory, and action. Second, the study of thinking and other complex mental phenomena was primarily motivated by the question of whether these complex phenomena could be accounted for within the current theoretical framework, and thus reduced to explanations based on the existing set of basic processes and capacities. As new knowledge emerged and new theoretical frameworks were developed, the boundary between phenomena that could and could not be accounted for within the dominant theoretical framework kept changing. These theoretical transitions had far greater effect on the study of complex phenomena such as problem solving than they did on phenomena that could be explained by less complex mechanisms.

The central challenge when studying thinking and problem solving in everyday life is their covert nature and complexity. Scientists must either find methods that allow them to monitor the complexity of thought in a task or find unfamiliar tasks in which participants' relevant knowledge is minimized. I sketch some important methodological developments that were significant stepping stones in the modern study of thinking and problem solving. I also briefly point out how the dominant theoretical frameworks in psychology changed during the 20th century, how new frameworks conceived of problem solving differently and favored different empirical tasks for its study.

Initial Attempts to Study Thinking

The pioneering researchers in the 19th century, such as Wilhelm Wundt, were explicit about the limitations of their methods and rejected the possibility of extending them to the study of complex experience and thinking in everyday life. Their studies were restricted to simple sensations, such as pure tones and points of light. The primary focus of the research was establishing how variations in the physical aspects of a stimulus are registered by neural receptors and processed by the nervous system. It is important to remember that the very existence of many of these receptors was controversial at the start of this research. Wundt also studied the speed of neural transmission of information and recorded the time to react and make other judgments about simple stimuli (cf. Donders, 1868/1969).

It is not typically recognized that Wundt deliberately limited his research to simple sensory stimuli to map out their encoding by receptors and the nervous system. Wundt argued that complex experience of the type analyzed by contemporary philosophers was qualitatively different from sensory stimulation. According to Wundt, an individual's experience in everyday life is a complex mixture of sensory information that is merged with the vast amount of accumulated prior experience. Wundt believed that his analytic methods could not be used to uncover the fluid and complex structure of experience and thinking.

Around the beginning of the 20th century, many psychologists became increasingly interested in going beyond simple sensory stimuli and studying complex thought. They tried to develop Wundt's rigorous introspective methods and the old philosophical method of self-observation into a scientifically acceptable method for describing the detailed elements of complex thought. The most famous developments occurred at the University of Würzburg where highly trained observers (often professors of psychology) were asked to perform various tasks involving reasoning and decision making and afterward give introspective analyses of their thoughts. To induce original thinking the investigators designed tasks that observers were unlikely to have encountered previously. Some of the tasks involved answering questions, such as "Do you understand the meaning of the following saying 'We depreciate everything that can be explained'?" (Bühler in Rapaport, 1951, p. 41)

These introspective analyses revealed many different types of thoughts and mental elements, even thoughts without associated sensory images – imageless thoughts. Karl Bühler argued in a series of papers that because Wundt's theory could not account for the existence of imageless thought, it must be incorrect. Wundt countered that it was impossible to simultaneously perform the assigned task and observe neural activity in the brain. Wundt emerged victorious from his famous exchange with Bühler, and some of Karl Bühler's original observers even conceded that their reports of imageless thought must have been flawed.

It is important to note that Wundt forcefully argued all along that concurrent *introspective analysis* of thinking is not possible because it would disturb the flow of thinking and produce potentially biasing inference. Subsequently, all of the main psychological theories for studying thinking, such as behaviorism, gestalt psychology, and information processing, developed verbal reports methodologies to externalize thinking that would not disturb the associated thought processes and bias the verbalized information.

Behaviorism and Studies of Thinking

When John B. Watson (1913) introduced behaviorism in his seminal paper he criticized the introspective analysis of experience and proposed an alternative approach based on observable behavior and performance. A careful reading of this paper shows that there was considerable agreement between Wundt and Watson. Both rejected introspective analysis of complex mental phenomena such as thinking, although their theoretical rationales differed. Furthermore, Watson accepted the research contributions on sensory perception and psychophysics by Wundt and his colleagues because these findings were supported by observable performance in the form of accurate perceptual judgments of presented stimuli.

A fundamental assumption of behaviorism is that behavior can be described by sequences of responses elicited by selected aspects of environmental stimuli. This assumption closely matches the consensus view of thinking as a sequence of thoughts (Ericsson & Crutcher, 1991), illustrated in Figure 2.1. Watson (1924) proposed that thinking could be described as covert, internalized behavior, especially in the form of inner subvocal speech. If one wished to study thinking, he or she should instruct subjects to "think aloud." Watson (1920) was the first investigator to publish a case study of thinking aloud. These think-aloud verbalizations provided a direct externalization of the subject's inner speech. They provided an unbiased trace of thinking that could be readily elicited by untrained adults, thus alleviating the problems of the extensive training and retrospective analysis associated with introspection.

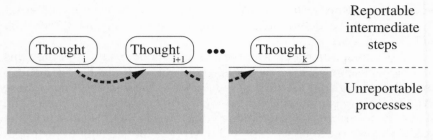

FIGURE 2.1. Thinking illustrated as a sequence of thoughts where each thought emerges in attention as the end result of covert retrieval processes.

The primary focus of behaviorism was on the learning and acquisition of stimulus-response (S-R) connections rather than the access and use of previously stored S-R connections to guide thinking and problem solving. Within this theoretical framework, the difficulty of completing a task and finding the correct answer was directly related to the number and relative strength of competing responses. Extensive research was conducted on anagram tasks in which a subject is asked to identify an English word, such as CRIME, from a scrambled sequence of letters, such as RECMI. By analyzing the letter combinations within the target word and the presented anagram, researchers were able to predict subjects' difficulty in generating and retrieving the solution word.

Researchers were able to demonstrate that inconsistent prior experience, such as functional fixedness and set, could increase solution difficulty across a wide range of tasks. Subsequent theoretical frameworks including gestalt and information-processing psychology identified types of tasks that could not be easily explained in terms of acquired S-R connections.

Gestalt Psychology and Human Information-Processing Psychology

It is very difficult to refute the behaviorist assertion that relevant prior experience and previously acquired S-R relations could explain the generation of solutions to encountered problems in everyday life. It is practically impossible to describe the experience and skills that adults could have acquired during their extended development; hence, one cannot rule out the possibility of mediation by relevant S-R connections. In some truly pioneering work, Karl Duncker (1926) decided to test problems on which individuals were virtually assured to be inexperienced, and thus could not have acquired S-R connections. He selected problems to be as simple as possible and yet offer compelling refutation of the sufficiency of acquired S-R connections. Duncker (1945) monitored his subjects' thought processes during problem solving by asking them to think aloud. Their verbal protocols revealed that subjects developed solutions by reasoning where a mental presentation of the presented problem mediated the generation and evaluation of possible solution characteristics.

A significant advance in our understanding of problem solving was attained when Newell and Simon (1972) proposed the information-processing theory of human problem solving. Puzzles such as the Tower of Hanoi and Missionaries and Cannibals are particularly suitable to accounts based on information processes. These problems are easy to understand and represent some of the simplest structures that can induce problem solving in adults. The problem descriptions contain all the essential information necessary to solve the puzzles.

Newell and Simon (1972) proposed a formal description of the tasks and showed that it was possible to use task analysis to identify participants' possible solution paths, based on their prior knowledge and limits in information-processing capacity. The task analysis for many puzzles is relatively easy because participants' relevant knowledge is limited and the task instructions refer primarily to rules for making local moves between different situations or states. Within this type of description a solution corresponds to a path that connects the starting state to the goal state by a sequence of states. When all the possible states and their connecting transitions in the state space are illustrated in the form of a map, then it is easy to depict the possible alternative paths and solutions uncovered in the task analysis.

This map of the state space allows investigators to study generation of the solution and how individuals approach the goal state by successive moves that lead to transitions to new states. Given that there is often a close mapping between the external configuration of the problem and the theoretical analysis of states, it is possible to view an individual's solution path as a series of discrete transitions in a maze, as is illustrated in Figure 2.2.

The formal description of the problem and the associated state space allowed Newell and Simon (1972) to propose formal models of problem solving in the form of computer models *within* the constraints of human information-processing capacities. Newell and Simon (1972) designed the mechanisms so their computer models generated solutions that matched closely with thoughts verbalized by individuals solving the same problems. Hence, the main characteristics of the sequences of generated thoughts could be regenerated and thus accounted for by the proposed information-processing models (Ericsson & Simon, 1984, 1993).

Information-processing analysis is particularly powerful when the task structure is well defined and the associated rules are included in the task instructions. Given that most tasks studied in the laboratory have been developed to be clear and well defined, it was possible to extend this type of analysis to a wide range of tasks other than problem solving. Information-processing analyses were developed for tasks studying memory,

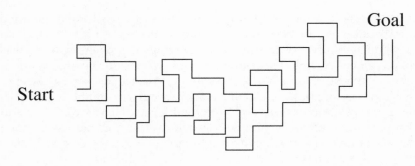

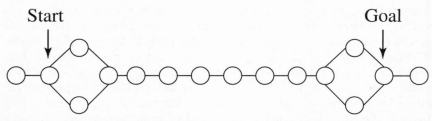

FIGURE 2.2. Two types of highly structured task environments. *Top*: A maze used in learning experiments with animals and humans. *Bottom*: A graphical depiction of all possible states with the associated legal moves and transitions in the problem space for the missionaries and cannibals problem.

comprehension, concept formation, decision making, and reasoning (see Greeno & Simon, 1988, for a review). Cognitive processes in these different tasks didn't differ from each other in any qualitative manner, and all tasks involved sequences of thoughts. The differences could be fully explained in terms of the different tasks used to induce the different forms of thinking, where the goals and relevant knowledge differ from task to task.

Information-processing psychology and gestalt psychology were able to analyze the processes mediating solutions to traditional problems and puzzles and show that the elements of problem solving corresponded to preexisting processes, representations, knowledge, and experience. Information-processing models demonstrated how general processes and representations could generate solutions similar to those of human participants. Both of these approaches were able to account for productive problem solving and solutions to new puzzles within the same framework used to explain other types of cognitive phenomena, such as perception, memory, concept formation, and reasoning. The study of problem solving led to successful theoretical accounts without the need for unique problem-solving capacities. In fact, problem solving could no longer be distinguished as a well-defined empirical phenomenon. However, it turned out to be far more difficult to explain the sources of stable individual differences in speed and accuracy of performance within the theoretical framework of information processing (Hunt, 1978; Sternberg, 1977).

Some Conclusions From Traditional Laboratory Studies of Problem Solving

In the last couple of centuries, the dominant theoretical framework for describing thinking and problem solving has changed so much that true accumulation of theoretical knowledge has been difficult. The changes have frequently been revolutionary, such as the transition from structuralism to behaviorism, and from behaviorism to cognitive theories. Around the beginning of the 20th century, the introspective method for studying the sensory aspects of consciousness was viewed to be a defining aspect of psychology. Within decades it was discarded as a valid method for analyzing the structure of thought. The behaviorists' rejection of mediating unobservable representations in favor of what could be directly observed was followed by alternative proposals by gestalt psychology, and later the information-processing theories that described how cognitive processes mediate thinking.

Theoretical differences were also clearly revealed by the types of tasks selected to elicit problem solving. All theoretical frameworks focused on the simplest tasks that would be sufficient to induce problem solving. For behaviorists, the task of rearranging anagrams to form words was simple; the primary challenge concerned retrieving words from the lexicon, especially infrequent words with weak associations to the presented letters. The gestalt and information-processing theorists searched for unfamiliar tasks that forced participants to generate thoughts and actions using general processes and representations, based on very limited direct experience. In spite of these major differences in theoretical perspectives and task selection, there appears to have been remarkably general agreement on the structure of thinking and the methodology for studying thinking.

All theoretical frameworks for describing thinking, including problem solving, have proposed that thinking can be accounted for by a sequence of thoughts, as illustrated in Figure 2.1. Thinking processes that are normally covert can be made overt by instructing subjects to vocalize their inner speech and to verbalize mediating thoughts. The behaviorist John B. Watson pioneered the procedure of instructing participants to "think aloud" as they solved problems.

The techniques used for collecting valid verbal protocols instruct participants to remain focused on the primary task and to verbalize thoughts mediating the primary performance. When participants are given this type of instruction, no reliable differences in performance have been found between silent participants and participants who are thinking aloud (Ericsson & Simon, 1993). However, when participants are asked to do more than merely verbalize their thoughts, then giving verbal reports has been found to influence thinking and performance on the experimental task. Even the introspectionists agreed that attempts to concurrently analyze the structure of one's thoughts while verbalizing them influenced the sequence of thought processes and led to associated changes in task performance (Lindworsky, 1931). Similarly, when participants are instructed to explain how they generate their answers or give detailed descriptions of their thoughts, then their thinking processes also change. In most cases participants do not spontaneously generate explanations for their solutions, and therefore they have to generate thoughts associated with the explanations just to be able to verbalize them. Generating the requested explanations or other detailed descriptions changes the sequence of thoughts, which in turn influences performance (Ericsson & Simon, 1993).

Figure 2.3 illustrates a variety of other dependent measures that, along with concurrent and retrospective verbal reports, provide convergent evidence of performance (Ericsson & Oliver, 1988; Ericsson & Simon, 1993). For example, when individuals report mediated thoughts when generating an answer, reaction times (RTs) are usually longer than when the answer is accessed directly, and the number of intermediate thoughts reported is correlated with longer RTs.

Similarly, when individuals verbalize perceptual details of stimuli in a visual task, there is generally a close temporal relation between the direction of their gaze recorded in eye fixations and their subsequent verbalization. Researchers have also related verbal reports to electrophysiological recordings, such as EEG, and more recently to patterns of blood flow determined by brain images, such as functional magnetic resonance imaging. In sum, the methodology for recording and analyzing detailed cognitive processes has developed dramatically during the 20th century, and these improvements are likely to continue as technology advances. With current methodology for recording verbal reports, eye movements, and electrical activity and blood flow in the brain, it is now possible to collect a rich set of indicators of an individual's cognitive processes during a single trial.

It has been possible to record and analyze correlates of the detailed structure of thinking for some time. However, the vast majority of scientists have not been interested in the detailed characteristics of thinking of individual participants. Their main focus has been on identifying capacities and processes that generalize across trials, task domains, and participants.

The Search for Generalizable Capacities and Processes

When the pioneers of psychology, such as Wundt and Ebbinghaus, founded our discipline the primary goal was to develop empirical and experimental

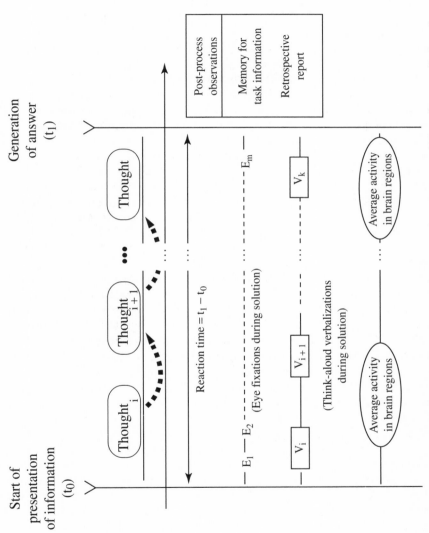

FIGURE 2.3. Different types of observations relevant to the sequence of thoughts mediating the successful production of the correct answer for a task.

methods to study psychological phenomena in the laboratory. Following the general approach of natural science, researchers were interested in studying psychological phenomena in their most basic and general form. Wundt and Ebbinghaus acknowledged the complex structure of experience and had no objective methods to study that level of complexity except for the reactive and subsequently discarded method of introspective analysis of complex thoughts.

These pioneering psychologists followed the approach of the natural sciences in which laboratory tasks were designed to reduce the role of the complex factors influencing performance in everyday life. For example, if one is interested in a general law such as gravity, it is better to study free fall under conditions of vacuum, without the complications of air resistance and displacement, rather than study the free movements of common objects, such as feathers, balloons, or coins.

It is interesting to examine how Ebbinghaus and his colleagues followed these principles when designing their memory experiments. Participants were encouraged to merely pay attention to the presented information without actively encoding the information and without generating associations to prior knowledge and experience. By designing nonsense syllables that were not inherently meaningful, such as PIQ and TEB, and increasing the rate of item presentation, researchers attempted to minimize the possibility that participants could draw on prior experience and related knowledge. They hoped to study the "direct" memory effects of multiple exposures to stimuli. Similarly, researchers interested in perceptual phenomena studied combinations of perceptual elements and generally developed simple tasks involving detection and recognition in which performance primarily reflected perception. Keeping the perceptual stimuli and tasks simple minimized attentional demand and its effects on memory. Problem-solving researchers have often studied tasks in which most task-relevant information was limited and available to the participants, thus reducing the effects of memory. Most problems and puzzles selected for problem-solving research minimized the role of prior experience and often provided the information needed to solve them.

If we consider a dimension measuring the number of factors that define the context and situation of behavior, then typical laboratory tasks would fall at one extreme and expert performance at the other, as illustrated in Figure 2.4. The laboratory tasks should, according to the traditional view, capture the general and basic aspects of mental processes and capacities and provide investigators with ideal conditions for studying and describing these basic capacities. These general capacities are assumed to mediate and constrain performance in all everyday cognitive activities. Although individuals acquire knowledge and skills that help them master the behavior required in everyday life, the basic underlying processes and capacities are assumed to remain invariant for adult participants.

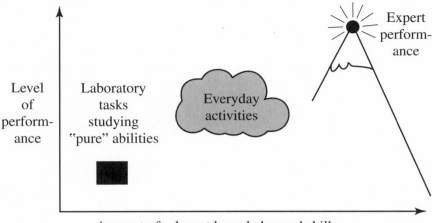

FIGURE 2.4. Three laboratory-based approaches to the study of working memory for skilled everyday activities.

The crucial assumption that basic mental functions studied with traditional laboratory tasks are the same as those that underlie and constrain performance in everyday life has not been directly tested empirically in psychology. A direct test of this assumption in psychology would entail capturing everyday performance, then examining its mediating mechanisms to show their relationship with basic functions studied in the laboratory. In the second half of this chapter I discuss approaches to capturing performance in everyday life and examine these phenomena with the full range of scientific methods, such as experimental variation and procedures for tracing the cognitive processes. Before describing these studies of reproducible performance in everyday life, such as expert performance, I briefly review some concerns raised about the generalizability of processes and capacities assumed to mediate standard laboratory tasks.

Do Basic, Invariant Processes and Capacities Mediate Performance on Laboratory Tasks?

The assumption that performance of "simple" tasks reflects elementary basic processes and capacities has a long, contested history. As far back as the 19th century, Ebbinghaus's original proposal for the mediation of basic associative processes in his memory tasks was almost immediately contested (Müller & Pilzecker, 1900; Müller & Schumann, 1894). Müller and his collaborators reported analyses of errors that indicated the mediation of more complex mechanisms. Another general source of evidence questioning the mediation of basic processes on simple tasks was discussed by Binet (Varon, 1935). Binet reached the conclusion that elementary tasks of perception, judgment, and memory were unsuitable for measuring mental abilities such as IQ, because participants' performance improved greatly with practice. He found much higher reliability and stability for tests of knowledge, comprehension, and skills, so his IQ test was based on those types of test items. More recent reviews (Gibson, 1969) have shown that practice effects are found with tests of basic perceptual and perceptual-motor performance for virtually every task, and that the improvements are large. When performance on tasks can be greatly improved with further practice, it is unlikely that the task performance closely reflects basic and invariant processes and capacities.

How can we reconcile large performance improvements on simple tasks that are presumed to be mediated by basic unmodifiable capacities? Just because a scientist designs a very simple task, one cannot take for granted that all participants perform the task by a simple sequence of operations in the manner hypothesized by the scientist. In fact, hardly any theories of cognitive phenomena provide a complete account of how individuals perform laboratory tasks: how they comprehend task instructions, familiarize themselves with the experimental situation, and generate a strategy or method for completing the tasks. Most laboratory tasks are designed to be unfamiliar, so participants must draw on their general knowledge and skills to comprehend the tasks and generate strategies for performing them. Though the tasks may be novel, most of the stimuli used are familiar and often involve digits, letters, words, and pictures of familiar objects. Subjects' encodings of these stimuli therefore reflect the acquired systems of symbols as well as associated representations, skills, and knowledge involving these encodings.

When individuals confront unfamiliar tasks – even seemingly simple tasks with familiar stimuli – there is no assurance that they will rely on the same sequence of mediating complex processes such as the one that is illustrated in Figure 2.3. In fact, evidence from concurrent and retrospective reports, analyses of patterns of RTs, errors, and eye fixations show that participants actively search for the best strategy to perform tasks as accurately and rapidly as possible (see Ericsson & Oliver, 1988, for a review). Once they have settled on a consistent strategy, their performance often requires intermediate thoughts and processing steps (Ericsson & Simon, 1993). In sum, the structure of performance on most laboratory tasks is complex and variable across subjects.

The performance is not necessarily stable on memory tasks assumed to measure basic memory capacity, since this performance can be greatly improved by acquired skills. Chase and Ericsson (1981, 1982) showed that memory performance on a test for immediate recall of presented sequences of digits was qualitatively changed as a function of practice.

After extended practice, their participants' memory performance had improved from seven digits to over eighty digits – an improvement of over 1000%, corresponding to an effect size of over 50 standard deviations. Such dramatic improvements in memory performance have since been replicated by many different researchers (Ericsson, 1988; Kliegl, Smith, Heckhausen, & Baltes, 1987; Wenger & Payne, 1995). These studies show that performance on memory tasks for briefly presented information increases when the individuals engage in *more rather than less* cognitive activity involving the generation of complex encodings based on semantic memory for related information (Chase & Ericsson, 1982).

When participants work with laboratory tasks designed to elicit concept formation (Bourne, Goldstein & Link, 1964; Coltheart, 1971), problem solving (Atwood, Masson, & Polson, 1980; Karat, 1982; Newell & Simon, 1972), and decision making (Payne, 1976; Svenson, 1979), they develop strategies to minimize the number of goals and hypotheses that have to be maintained in short-term memory. Their performance would appear to be tightly constrained by the limited capacity of their working memory when they first encounter these tasks. Yet how can one reconcile the constraints of working memory in laboratory tasks with their apparent absence in skilled activities? One possibility is that individuals are not rigidly constrained by the limited capacity of short-term memory, but are able to expand their memory capacity for a particular type of information within a given task activity by acquiring appropriate skills (Ericsson & Kintsch, 1995; Ericsson, Patel, & Kintsch, 2000).

When participants confront unfamiliar tasks, their specific acquired memory skills cannot be applied and they are forced to rely on very general skills for maintaining information, such as rehearsal (Ericsson & Delaney, 1999). Many common procedures in the design of laboratory studies are likely to interfere with accurate memory of the current task. Typically, experimenters attempt to control for incidental stimulus characteristics by counterbalancing and factorial designs, presenting a large number of similar tasks within the same session, which may lead to considerable proactive inference and the need to maintain information by rehearsal. When investigators design tasks that minimize the relevance of prior knowledge and eliminate redundant stimuli, their findings have limited relevance to behavior in everyday life.

In sum, when encountering laboratory tasks participants have to understand the tasks and design suitable strategies to perform them. They often develop complex methods and strategies to perform seemingly simple tasks, and strategies differ across subjects. These findings raise further concerns about the assumption that basic capacities mediate performance on laboratory tasks as well as behavior in everyday life. To empirically assess that assumption one needs to describe and analyze the processes and capacities mediating performance in everyday life.

Capturing Processes With Representative Tasks From Everyday Life: Another Approach

The issue of how to study psychological phenomena in everyday life has been discussed extensively by many influential psychologists (Barker, 1978; Bronfenbrenner, 1979; Brunswik, 1943; Gibson, 1979; Neisser, 1976). Rather than discussing their important contributions, I point to a new and different approach focusing on a very constrained phenomenon in everyday life, namely, the superior performance of experts.

Most behavior in everyday life cannot be viewed as performance, where individuals make efforts to attain the highest level of achievement. If individuals are not trying to produce their maximal performance, it is unlikely that the observed behavior will reflect underlying limits of information processing and basic capacity. In direct contrast to the complete focus on the subjects' best task performance in laboratory studies, individuals in everyday life value relaxation and spontaneous interactions. When people watch television they do not intentionally attempt to memorize the presented information to be prepared for a subsequent memory test. Instead, the resulting memory is an indirect consequence of their comprehension of the television program. When they type a message they do not try to complete the message at maximal speed. Instead, they take their time and pace themselves. When people drive home they typically do not try to get home in the shortest possible time. Most people are more focused on relaxing and getting home safely with a minimal amount of effort.

There are relatively few instances of everyday behavior that can be viewed as efforts to attain maximal performance. However, there are types of behavior in everyday life where some individuals are motivated to attain high levels of performance, such as their work performance and achievements in recreational activities. Within these types of activities individuals reach a stable level of performance when they are able to perform at a consistent level in similar situations. Within these domains there are large individual differences in achievement. Some individuals, often referred to as experts, can easily accomplish tasks that are outside the range that most other individuals have been able to master. If it is possible to measure these individual differences in stable performance, then it should be possible to reproduce the performance and the associated individual differences under standardized conditions in the laboratory. By experimental examination of the performance, it should be possible to identify the processes and capacities that mediate and constrain the superior performance.

THE SCIENTIFIC STUDY OF EXPERT PERFORMANCE

Most types of human activity are evaluated. When individuals perform in front of an audience during athletic competitions or music and dance performances, their achievement is nearly always evaluated and compared with related achievements by others. Similarly, most types of work have to be evaluated to set appropriate compensation. Professionals in specific domains often form organizations that identify individuals with exceptional achievements. It is generally assumed that as individuals become increasingly experienced and knowledgeable, they become experts and can perform at a higher level, as pioneering expertise researchers (Chase & Simon, 1973; Glaser & Chi, 1988) have proposed.

In many but not all domains of expertise, individuals have been concerned about assessing the level of reproducible performance under fair and controlled circumstances. Most sport competitions are highly standardized and even approach the level of rigorous control over conditions attained in laboratory studies. In a similar manner, musicians, dancers, and chess players perform under controlled conditions during competitions and tournaments. Individuals who display superior performance from competition to competition meet the standards of reproducible superior performance.

In most professional domains, such as medicine, accounting, and psychology, formal evaluation is ended when the individual has completed his or her education and is licensed as a regular professional. Do individuals continue to improve with further experience in their domains? As a first step to address that question, Ericsson and Smith (1991) discussed how various types of professional expertise could be measured by performance under comparable conditions. Recent reviews find that only experts in certain domains have been shown to perform at a level consistently superior to less experienced individuals (Ericsson & Lehmann, 1996). For example, highly experienced psychotherapists are not more successful in treatment of patients than novice therapists (Dawes, 1994), and stock-market experts and bankers are not able to forecast stock prices reliably better than university teachers and students (Stael von Holstein, 1972). If we are interested in understanding the structure and acquisition of excellence in the representative activities that define expertise in a given domain, we need to restrict ourselves to domains in which experts can be shown to exhibit objectively superior performance.

When expert performers can reliably reproduce their superior performance in public, it is likely that they could do the same during training, and even under laboratory conditions, a finding confirmed by recent research (Ericsson & Lehmann, 1996). Unfortunately, the conditions of naturally occurring expert performance are quite complex and frequently differ markedly across domains. For example, musicians are allowed to select their own pieces of music for their performance. The sequences of moves that chess players select are virtually never the same across games, and thus the chess positions encountered will differ. Medical doctors are very unlikely to encounter patients with the same configuration of symptoms, even when they are suffering from the same disease.

The large variability in difficulty and complexity of situations that experts encounter makes it difficult to compare the success of their performance. For example, the most accomplished doctors are frequently given the most challenging medical cases that other doctors have been unable to diagnose and treat successfully. A low success rate with the most difficult cases might well correspond to a higher level of performance than a high success rate for the most routine and easy cases. Unless all performers are given tasks of comparable difficulty, accurate measurement of their relative performance will be difficult or even impossible.

Capturing Expert Performance Under Standardized Controlled Conditions

Is it possible to identify situations in which the observed performance closely reflects the individuals' level of expertise? Is it possible to present all performers with the same set of tasks so they will all confront situations of the identical difficulty level and encounter the same specific challenges? Ericsson and Smith (1991) proposed that naturally occurring performance should first be analyzed to identify critical activities that capture the defining characteristics of expertise in a domain, such as winning chess games for chess players. Next, representative situations should be identified that elicit the experts' superior performance in a way that allows it to be recorded and measured. Once performance in the representative situations can be specified, it should be possible to recreate essential elements of it under controlled laboratory conditions and test experts' responses. By instructing individuals to react to a collection of representative situations, the superior performance of experts can often be reproduced in the laboratory and investigators can identify the mediating mechanisms responsible for the experts' superiority.

The first scientist to develop this methodology in studying expertise was Adrian de Groot (1946/1978). He found that chess playing could be described as a sequence of moves and that the current chess position contained the necessary information for selecting the best next move. De Groot (1946/1978) identified chess positions from unfamiliar games between chess masters, and these could be used as stimuli. All chess players could now be presented with the same chess positions and perform the same task of selecting the next best move, as illustrated in Figure 2.5. Any chess player who consistently selects better chess moves would by definition be a superior chess player.

De Groot (1946/1978) found that better class players consistently selected superior moves, and the chess moves they selected were sometimes not even considered by the less accomplished players. Subsequent research has shown that the move-selection task provides the best laboratory test for predicting actual chess skill as measured by performance

Domain	Presented Information	Task

Chess

Select the best chess move for this position

Typing

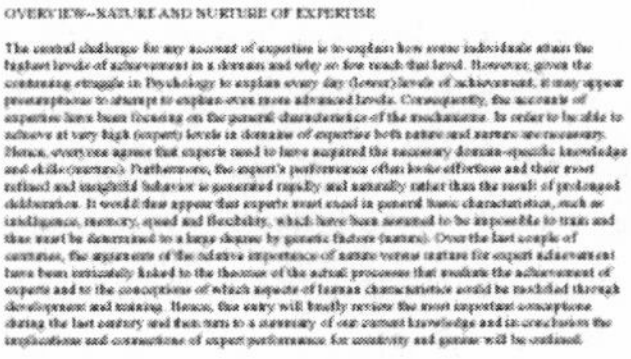

Type as much of the presented text as possible within one minute

Music

Play the same piece of music twice in same manner

FIGURE 2.5. Three examples of laboratory tasks that capture the consistently superior performance of domain experts in chess, typing, and music. (From K. A. Ericsson & Andreas C. Lehmann, "Expertise," in *Encyclopedia of Creativity* (1999). Copyright by Academic Press.)

in chess tournaments (Charness, 1981; Pfau & Murphy, 1988). The task of finding the best move for representative chess positions certainly meets the criteria for a domain-relevant lab task. In the next section we review research examining the process expert chess players use to generate superior moves.

Unless we consider the fact that expert chess players were once unable to generate and select superior moves, it would be easy to attribute their superior chess skill to innate abilities and mysterious capacities. Similar qualitative differences between experts and novices can be found in many domains, including medicine. Medical experts are better able to diagnose diseases of medical patients, especially when the diseases are rare or complicated by other simultaneous medical conditions (Norman, Trott, Brooks, & Smith, 1994; Patel & Groen, 1991).

The second panel of Figure 2.5 illustrates measurement of expert performance in typing. It is an activity in which anyone can select the appropriate keys. It is the speed of accurately typing that distinguishes experts. In a typical test of typing speed, all participants are asked to type a presented text as fast as possible. The texts have been selected from a large body of representative, unfamiliar texts. By asking the participants to type different texts on different occasions, we are able to reproduce the expert typists' superior performance and analyze its mediating mechanisms. There are many other domains of expertise, especially sports, where virtually every adult can perform the activity and individual skill differences are evident in speed, strength, or endurance.

The third panel of Figure 2.5 illustrates yet another characteristic evident in many types of expert performance: the ability to control one's performance and to reproduce the detailed aspects of a performance repeatedly. When studying music expertise, we confront the problem that expert musicians typically perform pieces of music that are too difficult for less accomplished musicians to master. However, it is possible to instruct all musicians to play easier pieces, then ask each of them to reproduce their performance for each piece as accurately as possible. Expert musicians were able to repeat their original performance with much less variability than less skilled musicians, thus exhibiting greater control over their performance. More generally, the ability to reproduce one's behavior multiple times with minimal variation is the hallmark of many types of expertise. For example, more skilled golfers are able to putt the golf ball so it stops closer to the hole and can shoot multiple drives to the same target with less variability than less skilled players. The performance of dart players, rifle shooters, and archers is directly measured by the ability to reproduce the same identical performance with minimum deviation from the bull's eye.

As long as experts are given representative tasks that capture essential aspects of their expertise, they can rely on existing skills and will exhibit the same stable performance as they do in everyday life. It is unlikely that repeated testing on randomly sampled situations would allow the experts to improve their performance. Most experts have attained their highest levels of performance over several decades, so it would be highly unlikely that several hours of additional experience and testing could lead to marked improvements of their performance. The stability of experts' performance during testing with representative tasks is a major methodological advantage of the expert performance approach over the traditional approaches to laboratory testing discussed earlier in this chapter. When the tasks are unfamiliar, participants have to search for efficient methods, which results in considerable learning and few stable characteristics mediating performance.

CAPTURED EXPERT PERFORMANCE AND PROBLEM SOLVING

In most domains of expertise, investigators have identified representative tasks that capture essential aspects of experts' superior performance. When we present individuals with the same series of tasks, we expect to measure

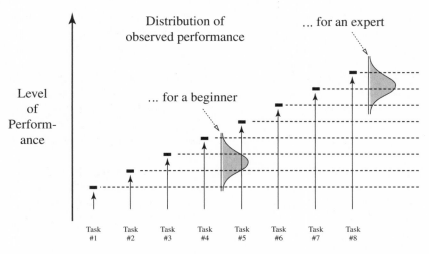

Distribution of observed performance

... for an expert

Level of Perform- ance

... for a beginner

Task #1 Task #2 Task #3 Task #4 Task #5 Task #6 Task #7 Task #8

Tasks ordered according to their level of difficulty

FIGURE 2.6. An illustration of the distribution of performance for a beginner and an expert as measured by success in mastering representative tasks from the domain of expertise that differ in difficulty. The representative tasks have been arranged according to their difficulty levels, which are marked by horizontal lines in the figure.

stable individual differences that correspond to different levels of expertise. The tasks are of graduated difficulty, so it is often possible to generate an approximate rank order of difficulty, where the associated performance is related to the attained skill level, as illustrated in Figure 2.6.

As a first approximation when testing, one can identify unchallenging tasks that are well below an expert's skill level. It is also possible to identify other tasks well above the current skill level that would be difficult, perhaps even impossible, to perform at an acceptable level at the required speed set for the test. Performance on problems of the same difficulty varies from test to test. An individual's performance is therefore better described as a distribution, in which performance is sometimes substantially above the current mean and sometimes well below. Sampling tasks from large collections containing many different difficulty levels makes it possible to challenge most performers in a domain and evaluate their performance under a variety of conditions.

The domain of expertise offers an excellent opportunity for researchers of problem solving to repeatedly study how individuals at a given skill level are able to reach an initially unobtainable performance. Even more appealing is the opportunity to examine the mechanisms that allow more skilled performers to generate the required performance with minimal processing. By comparing the performance of experts and novices on the same task, it is possible to assess the mediating mechanisms responsible for the difference in performance and then to analyze these mechanisms by process-tracing methods and experimental manipulation of the presented tasks.

In the next section I consider studies that assess mechanisms that mediate problem-solving ability in a domain. After that I focus on the important fact that every individual's performance, including that of world-class performers, started out at a very low level, typically when the individual was a child. Most every youngster knows that it is possible to improve consistency through practice, but that fairly soon the improvements become smaller until eventually most people reach some kind of plateau where further improvement of performance is impossible. The thrust of this section is that individuals who are able to keep improving after that stage is reached are engaged in a type of problem solving referred to as deliberate practice (Ericsson, Krampe & Tesch-Römer, 1993).

Analysis of Superior Representative Performance With Experiments and Process Tracing

The complexity of mechanisms mediating expert performance might seem overwhelming, especially for scientists committed to building complete computer models that would fully reproduce all aspects of the experts' performance (see Ericsson & Kintsch, 2000, for further discussion). However, it appears possible to describe and analyze even complex cognitive processes by identifying subsystems and methods for controlling performance. When scientists observe experts and less skilled individuals repeatedly performing representative tasks, they often apply process-tracing techniques (see Fig. 2.3 and the associated discussion) to gain information about the cognitive processes that mediate performance. Hypotheses about mechanisms mediating superior performance can then be evaluated by a task analysis of the possible methods for completing the task, as well as carefully designed experiments. In the following three subsections I briefly summarize how this interaction among process tracing, task analysis, and experimental tests has improved our understanding of the mechanisms mediating expert performance in chess, typing, and music.

Analyzing Expert Performance in Chess
In his pioneering research on chess expertise, De Groot (1946/1978) instructed highly skilled chess players to think aloud as they selected the best next move for chess positions extracted from unfamiliar games between chess masters. The verbal protocols of both world-class and skilled club-level players showed that the players first familiarized themselves with the position and verbally reported salient and distinctive aspects of the position along with potential lines of attack or defense. The players

then explored the consequences of longer move exchanges by planning alternatives and evaluating the resulting positions. During these searches the players would identify moves with the best prospects in order to select the single best move.

The chess players' protocols allowed De Groot (1946/1978) to identify when and how the best players generated their superior moves. De Groot found that the less skilled players didn't even discover the lines of play with the best moves during their analysis – at least not for the chess position that he studied. The world-class players mentioned many strong first moves even during their initial familiarization with the chess position. For example, they would notice weaknesses in the opponent's defense that suggested various lines of attack, then examine and systematically compare the consequences of various sequences of moves. During this detailed phase of analysis, these players would often discover new moves that were superior to all the previously generated ones.

We need to consider two different mechanisms when developing a complete explanation of the world-class players' superiority in finding moves. First, the best players were able to rapidly perceive the structure of the presented chess position, thus allowing them to identify weaknesses and associated lines of attack that the less accomplished players never reported noticing in their verbal protocols. The highly skilled players' ability to rapidly perceive superior moves has been validated by experiments in which players of different skill levels were forced to select a move within a very short time, such as 5–10 seconds (Calderwood, Klein, & Crandall, 1988; Gobet & Simon, 1996b). Furthermore, experiments have shown that highly skilled players are able to rapidly perceive meaningful relations between most chess pieces within presented positions. After a brief exposure of a chess position, often in the 5-second range, the world-class chess players have virtually perfect recall of the location of pieces, and the ability to reproduce positions from regular chess games increases as a function of chess skill (Charness, 1991; Gobet & Simon, 1996a).

The brief perception of an unfamiliar chess position is rapidly encoded in long-term memory, and disruptions of short-term storage between the presentation and the recall of the position have modest effects on the amount recalled (Ericsson & Kintsch, 1995). Highly skilled chess players can accurately reproduce a series of unrelated chess positions even when they are presented in rapid succession (Gobet & Simon, 1996c). For a recent discussion of the relation between the superior memory for presented chess positions and the memory demands integral to selecting chess moves, see Ericsson et al. (2000).

The second mechanism that underlies the superior performance of highly skilled players is the ability to select among the best potential moves by evaluating their consequences. During this planning and evaluation process, the experts often discovered new moves that were better than those perceived during the familiarization phase. The superior ability of highly skilled players to plan out consequences of move sequences is well documented. In fact, chess masters are able to play blindfold, without a visible board showing the current position, at a relatively high level (Karpov, 1995; Koltanowski, 1985). Experiments show that chess masters are able to follow chess games in their heads when the experimenter reads a sequence of moves from a chess games (Saarilouma, 1991). The chess masters can mentally generate the current chess position with high accuracy and are able to retrieve any aspect of the position when probed by the experimenter (see Ericsson & Oliver's studies described in Ericsson & Staszewski, 1989). Highly skilled players can even play several simultaneous games mentally, thus maintaining multiple chess positions in memory (Saarilouma, 1991).

Expert chess players' ability to generate better moves cannot be completely explained by their more extensive knowledge of chess patterns, the large body of associations between patterns, and appropriate moves that they have stored in memory during chess playing. As their skill increases, they become increasingly able to encode and manipulate internal representations of chess positions to plan the consequences of chess moves, discover potential threats, and even develop new lines of attack (Ericsson & Kintsch, 1995).

These mental representations supporting move selection and the associated memory skills are highly specialized and do not generalize well to patterns other than regular chess positions. For example, chess experts' memory advantage is dramatically reduced for randomly arranged chess positions or random chess games when the presentation time is brief (Chase & Simon, 1973; Gobet & Simon, 1996a). Furthermore, the skilled chess players' superior selection of chess moves does not generalize to all chess positions. Some players construct puzzling chess positions in which it is possible to force a checkmate in three moves, for example. These chess puzzles have been carefully designed to violate the structure of regular chess positions, which renders the solution difficult and counterintuitive. Even the best chess players are less able to find solutions for these chess puzzles compared with weaker chess players who have extensive experience of such chess puzzles (Gruber & Strube, 1989). Hence, superior ability to select moves for regular chess positions does not generalize fully to chess puzzles solutions that require moves rarely used in regular games. On the other hand, Frensch and Sternberg (1989) found that expert players in bridge were more able than nonexperts to generate the correct responses in a modified task of bridge, even when the deep rules of the bridge game were altered. The rule changes in the surface and deep structure of bridge seemed primarily to increase the amount of time taken by the experts to select the appropriate play. In a similar manner, Saariluoma (1989) found that expert chess players display vastly superior memory to novices even for randomly rearranged chess positions when the experts can study the configurations for more than a brief presentation time (see Ericsson et al., 2000, for a review). Hence, the mental representations of experts appear to be qualitatively different from those of less skilled individuals (Ericsson, 1996, 1998b, 2001).

Experts' ability to generate products of consistently superior quality, such as superior chess moves, accurate medical diagnoses, and solutions to domain-specific problems, requires the mediation of complex cognitive mechanisms. These mechanisms allow experts to perceive the structure of representative situations and assess relevant relations underlying actions. The same mechanisms allow experts to plan and evaluate various options in order to assure the generation of high-quality responses.

The difference in performance between experts and less skilled individuals is not a simple difference in accumulated knowledge about past experience. Expert-novice differences appear to reflect differential ability to react to representative tasks and situations that have never been previously encountered. Less skilled performers may not even be able to generate the appropriate action when confronted with a difficult task, at least not in the time that is usually available. Highly skilled performers are likely to perceive a solution to the same task as one of several possible actions, then identify the best choice after rapid evaluation and planning.

Expert Performance Characterized by Superior Speed

Typing is a skill that most adults in industrialized countries acquire to some degree. The challenge in typing is not how to generate the appropriate series of keystrokes, because even beginners can do so at very slow speeds. The real measure of expert typists is their ability to be able to type very fast and accurately for an extended period of time.

Careful observation of superior typing performance shows that expert typists don't look at the text that is typed, but instead look ahead to prepare for what comes next. High-speed filming shows that expert typists move their fingers toward the corresponding keys well ahead of time whenever possible (Norman & Rumelhart, 1983). The strongest correlate of individuals' typing speed is how far ahead in the text they look while typing. The importance of looking ahead in the text for expert typists has been studied experimentally by manipulating how far the typists are able to see while typing. When preview of the text is eliminated or dramatically reduced, the experts' speed advantage is almost eliminated, or greatly reduced, which validates the importance of expert typists' ability to capitalize on advance preparation of key press sequences (Salthouse, 1984; Shaffer, 1973). On the other hand, expert typing is surprisingly independent of meaningfulness of the material, and expert typists can type almost as fast when the text consists of randomly arranged words or even when the text is written in some foreign languages. The critical aspect determining generalizability is whether the frequencies of pairs and triplets of letter combinations in the typed material matches those in the native language of the expert typist (Logan, 1983).

A similar mechanism that enables look-ahead and advance preparation mediates other skills where rapid execution is essential. For example, musicians' ability to play a music piece without prior preparation is correlated with how far they look in advance of the music actually played (Sloboda, 1984). Everyday skills such as reading are mediated by similar mechanisms. When individuals are asked to read an unfamiliar text aloud as rapidly as possible, individuals' speed of reading is closely related to the eye-voice span, namely, the distance in the text between the words spoken and the words that the eyes gaze at (Levin & Addis, 1979).

More generally, many different domains of expertise in sports provide similar evidence for the critical role of preparation and anticipation in rapid responses (see Abernethy, 1991; and Ericsson & Lehmann, 1996, for recent overviews). It is well established that it takes humans at least 200 ms (one fifth of second) to produce an action in a test of simple reaction time. Consequently, any sport involving hitting a moving target, such as a tennis ball, requires that motor action has to be programmed and initiated well in advance of the contact between ball and the racquet. Research in many different sports shows that as skill increases, individuals are better able to anticipate the future trajectory of the ball based on perceptual cues in the situation. In fact, based on the mechanical constraints of physically hitting a ball with a racquet, it is possible to anticipate the eventual trajectory of the ball before the racquet ever comes in contact with it. Expert tennis players can better predict the trajectory of a future tennis serve than less skilled players, even when the latter are shown pictures or film sequences of a tennis serve before the serving tennis player has made contact with the ball. Superior predictive ability is also found among ice hockey goalies who gauge the trajectory of future shots and baseball hitters who estimate the trajectory of pitched balls (Abernethy, 1991).

In sum, skilled rapid motor production is not simple, nor is it completely automatic. Expert performers acquire complex representations and skills to anticipate future actions. Their speed advantage appears to be a result of acquired mechanisms that enable skilled preparatory processing rather than any basic superiority in speed. There is ample evidence showing that large differences between experts and novices in the speed of execution are restricted to responses to representative tasks from the domain of expertise. No reliable and comparable differences in speed are found when the same individuals are tested for general speed and simple reaction time (Abernethy, 1987; Starkes & Deakin, 1984). These findings suggest that individuals should be able to improve the speed of their reactions by improving their representations so they can anticipate and prepare their actions in advance.

The Acquisition of Expert Performance Requiring Increased Control

In the earlier discussion it was noted that expert musicians differ from less accomplished ones in their superior ability to reproduce the same interpretation of a piece of music many times, even on different occasions. The mark of expert performance in music and many other domains is the ability to control one's performance and its results. This manifests not only in consistency, but also in the ability to shape the experience of an audience. The primary goal of expert musicians is to provide the audience with an enjoyable music experience. Hence, expert musicians strive to provide a unique music experience characterized by their particular interpretation and style. If highly skilled musicians insist on playing the same piece differently, how can we assess individual differences in the level of expert performance?

Expert music performance requires several different representations, such as those illustrated in Figure 2.7. Musicians must have acquired representations of the music itself that allow them to form performance goals that can be modified to induce new musical experiences, favor the acoustics of a concert hall, or accommodate the wishes of an orchestra conductor. They also need to have different representations that guide the production of sound from their instruments. Finally, they need to have representations that allow them to monitor the music being produced by their performance.

Drawing on these three kinds of representations, an expert musician can produce interpretations that approach an imaged experience of how the music should sound. However, reaching a performance level suitable

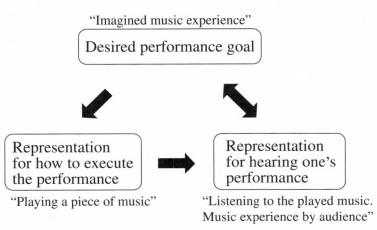

FIGURE 2.7. Three types of internal representations that mediate expert music performance and its continued improvement during practice. (From K. A. Ericsson, "The scientific study of expert levels of performance: General implications for optimal learning and creativity," *High Ability Studies, 9*, p. 92. Copyright 1998 by European Council for High Ability).

for public performance requires an extended period of study and practice in which musicians mold their performance by gradually reducing deviations between the produced sound and the desired experience. The resulting music performance should not be seen as a fixed and automated sequence of motor actions. It should be viewed as a flexible, controllable outcome based on these representations. For example, it is well known that expert musicians can hide unexpected local mistakes by changing the sound of their continued performance or improvising to cover the lapses. They can later correct the errors by adjustments and improvements during subsequent practice. Finally, expert musicians can use these representations when listening to other musicians' performances, such as those by music students, to diagnose errors and make recommendations about further improvements.

Laboratory studies of expert musicians have been able to provide empirical evidence for the mental representations illustrated in Figure 2.7. When expert musicians perform unfamiliar music, a technique called sight reading, they demonstrate their ability to mentally plan how their fingers will strike the keys to retain control and minimize interference between fingers (Drake & Palmer, 2000; Lehmann & Ericsson, 1993, 1996; Sloboda, Clarke, Parncutt, & Raekallio, 1998). Evidence for the mental representation of pieces of music comes from studies showing that expert pianists retain control over their motor performance even after a piece of music has been memorized. In laboratory studies, expert pianists have been able to perform music without additional practice under changed conditions, such as a different key or a slower tempo (Lehmann & Ericsson, 1995, 1997). Empirical evidence has also been collected for the representation that allows the experts to monitor and compare their concurrent performance with their desired goal, such as the intended musical sound or the intended sequence of a pianist's finger movements. In some recent studies, Woody, Lehmann, and Ericsson (1998) documented expert musicians' ability to reproduce several different versions of prerecorded interpretations of pieces of music.

Summary
The differences between expert and novice performance cannot be explained by innate differences in basic speed and capacity. They are attributable primarily to complex, highly specialized mechanisms that allow experts to perform at superior levels in representative domain-specific tasks. In fact, the only basic innate difference that has been conclusively shown to differentiate expert and novices is physical size and height in sports (Ericsson, 1996). For instance, the best basketball players tend to be taller than average and the best gymnasts tend to be shorter than average.

The complex mechanisms and representations mediating expert performance are directly applicable to our understanding of problem solving. The difference between the performance of experts and novices on representative domain-specific tasks is attributable to the quality of complex mediating mechanisms, such as planning, anticipation, and reasoning. Hence, to improve problem-solving ability in a given domain, it is necessary to develop and refine domain-specific mechanisms and representations. In the next section I discuss how individuals use problem-solving techniques to improve the mediating mechanisms that underlie skill.

Acquiring Expert Levels of Performance: The Role of Experience and Problem Solving

Skill acquisition is usually considered to be dependent on instruction and extended experience, not on problem solving. Once individuals understand what they need to do in a domain, they primarily need a lot of experience to increase their performance to a level that is limited by their innate abilities and capacities. According to this dominant view, skill acquisition is simple and an almost inevitable consequence of extended experience in a domain. It is assumed that learners rapidly master all the rules and knowledge necessary to become skilled in a domain. Consequently, as long as they remain actively engaged in the domain their performance will improve with experience until they reach the highest level of achievement that their innate capacities and abilities allow.

It is difficult to reconcile this view with the empirical evidence reviewed in the section above that shows superior expert performance to be mediated by complex representations and mechanisms. However, the assumption that skilled performance is primarily acquired faces at least two major related challenges. First, if the development of expert performance involves the acquisitions of skills and representations, then why do individuals who remain active in the domains differ so greatly in their attained performance? Perhaps the acquisition of the complex representations and mechanisms is not a direct consequence of experience, which leads to the second challenge. Which learning activities lead to the acquisition of these complex mechanisms and representations? I first describe the dominant view based on experience and show how it provides for an account of many characteristics associated with acquisition of some skills, such as many everyday skills. Next I argue that there are qualitative differences in processes mediating typical skill acquisition in the laboratory and in everyday life, and the processes based on problem solving that mediate expert levels of performance.

Skill Acquisition in Everyday Life and in the Laboratory
Most everyday skills are relatively easy to acquire, at least to an acceptable level. Adults often learn to drive a car, type, play chess, ski, and play golf within weeks or months. It is usually possible to explain what an individual needs to know about a given skill, such as rules and procedures, within a

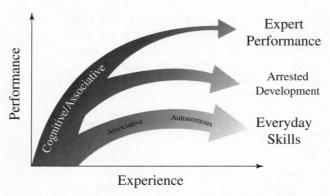

FIGURE 2.8. An illustration of the qualitative difference between the course of improvement of expert performance and of everyday activities. The goal for everyday activities is to reach as rapidly as possible a satisfactory level that is stable and "autonomous." After individuals pass through the "cognitive" and "associative" phases, they can generated their performance virtually automatically with a minimal amount of effort (see the gray/white plateau at the bottom of the graph). In contrast, expert performers counteract automaticity by developing increasingly complex mental representations to attain higher levels of control of their performance and will therefore remain within the "cognitive" and "associative" phases. Some experts will at some point in their careers give up their commitment to seeking excellence and thus terminate regular engagement in deliberate practice to further improve performance, which results in premature automation of their performance. (Adapted from K. A. Ericsson, "The scientific study of expert levels of performance: General implications for optimal learning and creativity," *High Ability Studies, 9*, p. 90. Copyright 1998 by European Council for High Ability).

few hours. Traditional theories of skill acquisition (Anderson, 1982, 1987; Fitts & Posner, 1967) distinguish an initial "cognitive" phase (see Fig. 2.8) when individuals learn the underlying structure of the activity and what aspects they must attend to. During this early phase of learning, they get clear feedback about their lack of mastery when outcomes of actions don't match desired expectations. Novices gradually learn to avoid gross errors. And eventually, during the second "associative" phase, they can attain a functional level of performance. During the third and final "autonomous" phase, learners typically perform the activity without having to think about it. After a limited period of training and experience, frequently less than 50 hours for most recreational activities, an acceptable standard of performance can be generated without much need for effortful attention. At this point, execution of the everyday activity has attained many characteristics of automated performance (Anderson, 1982, 1987; Fitts & Posner, 1967; Shiffrin & Schneider, 1977), and requires only minimal effort.

Most laboratory studies of skill acquisition within the information-processing framework have presented well-designed tasks in which participants easily learn how to represent the task and generate the correct response. The focus of these studies is thus primarily on the second and third stages where the speed of correct responses is increased as a function of further experience.

Skill acquisition in everyday life and in the laboratory reveals a rather similar pattern in which individuals' performance fairly rapidly approaches asymptote, and further improvements appear to be negligible. One of the primary reasons for this general pattern of improvement is that individuals very rapidly commit to an understanding and a representation of the structure of the activity. They then move on to the next two stages, in which the methods of performance are made more efficient and eventually become fixated, as individuals lose conscious control over intentionally modifying and changing them.

Everyday activities have evolved to the point where they are readily understood, at least on a superficial level. Leisure activities such as games and sports would not gain popularity unless individuals could easily master them at some acceptable level. Similarly, most tasks developed in the laboratory have been explicitly designed to be easily understood and to be rapidly mastered in the same manner by all participants. In these two types of environments the evolution and adaptation of these activities have led individuals to easily find a functional representation of the relevant activities. This first phase of skill acquisition is therefore relatively short and uniform for most individuals. During the next two stages, usually lasting weeks or months, individuals' performance approaches a stable level as a function of additional activity. Given that individuals do not intentionally do anything to change their behavior, the factors controlling these phases are believed to be outside the individuals' control. For skill acquisition in the laboratory and in most everyday activities, the structure of the attained skill is simple, based on recognized patterns and configurations that trigger autonomous actions.

The Acquisition of Expert Performance

This popular conception of how everyday skills are acquired cannot explain the acquisition of expert performance and its complex mediating mechanisms described in the preceding section. In contrast to the rapid automatization of everyday skills and the emergence of a stable asymptote for performance, expert performance has been shown to improve as a function of increased experience and deliberate practice, as illustrated in Figure 2.8. One of the most crucial challenges for aspiring expert performers is to avoid the arrested development associated with generalized automaticity of performance and to acquire cognitive skills to support continued learning and improvement.

Expert performers counteract the arrested development associated with generalized automaticity of skill by deliberately acquiring and refining cognitive mechanisms to support continued learning and improvement. These mechanisms increase experts' control and ability to monitor performance. Improving performance to the level of expertise requires deliberate practice – essentially a form of problem solving, where individuals engage in tasks with goals that exceed the current level of performance. The experts and their teachers and coaches have to continue to design training situations where the goal is to attain a level beyond their current performance in order to keep improving. I first show how the concept of deliberate practice is consistent with the known requirements for extended experience to attain expert levels of performance before I turn to a discussion of the detailed structure of deliberate practice.

Necessary Conditions for the Acquisition of Expert-Level Performance: Experience and Deliberate Practice

The theoretical framework of deliberate practice shows how extended engagement in domain-related activities, especially deliberate practice, is a necessary prerequisite for acquiring mechanisms to meet the task demands of that domain. More important, this framework also explains why some types of experience don't improve an already attained level of performance. Merely engaging in the same types of activities will only maintain a stable level of performance for many recreational athletes, such as tennis players and golfers, and they will remain at roughly the same level of achievement for decades of continued activity and experience.

There are several types of evidence that extended domain-specific experience is necessary (see reviews by Ericsson, 1996; Ericsson & Lehmann, 1996). First, when individuals' performance is measured repeatedly under the same standardized conditions over years and decades, their performance is found to improve gradually. There is no evidence for abrupt changes in the reproducible performance from one time to the next. Even the performance of child prodigies in music and chess, whose performance is vastly superior to that of their peers, shows gradual, steady improvement over time when measured by adult standards.

If the level of performance of young performers were limited primarily by the functional capacity of their developing bodies and brains, one would expect performance to peak around the age of physical maturation – the late teens in industrialized countries. However, experts' best performances often occur many years or even decades later. The age at which expert performers typically reach their highest level of performance in many vigorous sports is the mid- to late 20s; for fine-motor athletic activities, the arts, and science, it is a decade later, in the 30s and 40s (Lehman, 1953; Schulz & Curnow, 1988, Simonton, 1997).

Finally, some of the most compelling evidence for the role of certain kinds of extended experience in developing expertise is that even the most "talented" need around ten years of intense involvement before they reach an international level, and for most individuals it takes considerably longer. Simon and Chase (1973) originally proposed the ten-year rule, showing that no modern chess master had reached the international level in less than approximately ten years of playing. Subsequent reviews show that the ten-year rule extends to music composition, as well as to sports, science, and the arts (Ericsson et al., 1993). In sum, the fact that prolonged engagement in specific, domain-related activities is necessary to acquiring expertise is well established. Most important, given that very few individuals sustain commitment for more than a few months, much less years, most of us will never know the upper limit of our performance.

Bloom and his colleagues' (Bloom, 1985) retrospective interviews of international-level performers in many domains show that the development of these experts differs from that of amateurs in fundamental ways. However, the future experts are often introduced to their domain in a playful manner at an early age without any objective evidence that their ultimate performance will be outstanding. When they enjoy the activity and show promise compared with their peers in the local school or neighborhood, they are typically encouraged to seek out a teacher and a coach and begin regular practice. From this point on the future experts will – with their parents' help – devote an increasing proportion of their lives to reaching their highest levels of performance through work with teachers and coaches, traveling to training facilities, practicing, and participating in competitions. Bloom (1985) has argued that access to the best training resources is a necessary constraint for reaching the highest levels.

The best single source of evidence for the value of current training methods comes from historical comparisons (Ericsson et al., 1993; Lehmann & Ericsson, 1998). The most dramatic improvements in the level of performance over historical time are found in sports. In some events, such as the marathon and swimming events, many serious amateurs of today could easily beat the gold medal winners of the early Olympic games. For example, after the IVth Olympic Games in 1908, officials almost prohibited the double somersault in dives because they believed that these dives were dangerous and no human would ever be able to control them. Similarly, some music compositions deemed nearly impossible to play in the 19th century have become part of the standard repertoire today. Exceptional levels of performance are originally attained only by a single eminent performer. However, after some time other individuals are able to discover training methods so they can attain that same level of performance. Eventually, this training becomes part of regular instruction and all elite performers in the domain are expected to attain the new higher standard.

Only a small number of individuals reach the absolutely highest level of achievement in a domain, even among those given access to the best training environments. Just participating in such environments is clearly not sufficient, and individuals differ in how they generate opportunities for learning and actively attain improvement even within an optimal learning environment. Can individual differences in amount and quality of practice explain differences in the level of achievement among expert performers?

To address that question, my colleagues and I (Ericsson et al., 1993) searched for a domain in which the techniques for training outstanding performers have been refined over a long period of time. We selected music, because historically the training of expert musicians often begins at a relatively young age, often around 5 to 7 years, and has for centuries been conducted by professional teachers who developed systematic training methods. Based on interviews with expert violinists at the music academy in Berlin, we identified measurable activities that violinists had engaged in during their development. We were particularly interested in activities that had been specifically designed to improve performance – the components of deliberate practice.

One excellent example of deliberate practice is solitary practice, which successful students use to increase their mastery of new music pieces and techniques. Music teachers typically evaluate students' current performance at weekly lessons to assess improvement, diagnose weaknesses, and help the student overcome problems by assigning focused practice techniques. We were able to compare several groups of musicians representing different levels of achievement based on their daily diaries and retrospective estimates of time use. Even among these expert groups, the most accomplished musicians had spent more time in activities classified as deliberate practice during their development, and skill differences were reliably observable even before their admittance to the academy at around age 18. By the age of 20, the best musicians had spent over 10,000 hours practicing, which is 2,500 and 5,000 hours more than two less accomplished groups, respectively, and 8,000 hours more than amateur pianists of the same age (Krampe & Ericsson, 1996).

Several other studies and reviews have also found a consistent relationship between performance level and the quality and amount of deliberate practice in a wide range of domains, such as chess (Charness, Krampe & Mayr, 1996), sports (Helsen, Starkes, & Hodges, 1998; Hodges & Starkes, 1996; Starkes, Deakin, Allard, Hodges, & Hayes, 1996), and music (Krampe & Ericsson, 1996; Lehmann & Ericsson, 1996; Sloboda, 1996). The concept of deliberate practice also accounts for many earlier findings in other domains (Ericsson & Lehmann, 1996), as well as for the results from the rare longitudinal studies of experts (Schneider, 1993).

The relation between the quality and amount of practice and performance is only correlational (Sternberg, 1996), and hence it is difficult to prove that deliberate practice causes improvements in performance. A closer analysis of deliberate practice shows that it involves designing a training activity to improve specific aspects of performance. To improve, individuals must try to exceed their current level of performance, and thus they have to experience many discouraging failures until they finally succeed and reach the new higher levels. Hence, deliberate practice activities are necessary for performers to attain each of the local improvements, thus offering evidence for the causal effects of this type of practice.

Elite performers must frequently engage in problem solving and challenging learning to make the necessary modifications to reach their new and higher levels of performance. Consistent with the characteristics of problem solving, elite performers report a very high level of focus and concentration during deliberate practice. In fact, master teachers and expert performers claim that full concentration is a necessary prerequisite for deliberate practice (Ericsson, 2001). When concentration wavers, practice must stop. Ericsson et al. (1993) found support for this claim in the violinists' diaries; their practice sessions were limited to around an hour at a time. Ericsson et al. also found a general limit on how much daily practice individuals are able to sustain without exhaustion, and that seemed to generalize across many different domains of expertise. The maximal level of deliberate practice was found to be 4–5 hours when sustained daily for months and years.

In sum, to attain the highest level of performance, all individuals, even the most "talented," devote years, typically over a decade, to engaging in thousands of hours of practice, typically over 10,000. This massive amount of concentration and deliberate practice focused toward mastery in a domain is an achievement in itself – and one that very few individuals can claim. During this extended period of deliberate practice, complex adaptations and acquired mechanisms gradually emerge, and their development is the primary cause of improved performance. In the next section I describe how deliberate practice causes these changes in acquired mechanisms and representations.

The Acquisition of Mechanisms Mediating Expert Performance Through Deliberate Practice

In everyday life the acquisition of skills in one domain is relatively hard to distinguish from development of other related skills, especially for low levels of achievement in childhood. For example, when children first get a chance to play tennis, they have engaged in many related activities, such as hitting, catching, and kicking balls. Hence, skill acquisition, even from the first active encounter, always involves changing, transforming, and modifying existing behavior and skills, and thus can never be adequately represented as building completely new structures unrelated to previously acquired knowledge and skills.

When individuals increase their level of skill, improvements involve changes to different knowledge structures and complex acquired mechanisms. These changes in the structures and mechanisms associated with further improvements differ among individuals and require idiosyncratic modification and adjustment according to each individual's acquired mechanisms and representations. This view of skill acquisition as a series of deliberate adjustments requires that performers actively construct their skills. Continued learning will reflect successful problem solving. I first use typing as an example of the acquisition and modification of mediating mechanisms, then extend the discussion to chess and music.

Most everyday skills, such as typing, must be simple to understand and master, at least at an acceptable level. When individuals type information into an automatic teller machine or enter a password to open a lock, they simply push a sequence of keys. They first find the key on the keypad and then push it with the index finger on their dominant hand until all the keys are pressed. Children and adults tend to use this hunt-and-peck method when they encounter an unfamiliar keypad. Similarly, when people encounter a typewriter or computer keyboard for the first time they tend to spontaneously adopt this "natural" method. When an individual gains familiarity with the locations of the keys after extended experience, his or her performance generally speeds up and becomes increasingly autonomous, and perhaps even automatic. As long as the hunt-and-peck method is maintained, there is no need for problem solving.

If individuals need to type faster than the hunt-and-peck method allows, they must search for an alternative method. They may generate a new method using index fingers of both hands. If the individual has already become proficient with the one-finger method, it is likely that the two-finger method will initially be less efficient. When an additional finger is introduced into the typing process, the new finger-to-key assignments must override the old ones by means of attentional control. It is easy to understand how some individuals would decide against investing the attention necessary for learning a new method and settle for the familiar, if slower, method, as is illustrated in the premature automation of a skill in Figure 2.8. Alternatively, they might improve their skills by adopting increasingly efficient techniques until they have acquired something equivalent to the standard touch-typing method.

When the typing skill involves all the digits on both hands and the finger-to-key assignments have been learned, it might seem that typing speed would rapidly reach asymptote because the skill is now based on the most efficient method. However, it is well known that even highly skilled typists can substantially improve their typing speed if they are highly motivated. Typing speed is variable and corresponds to a distribution of observed speeds. By exerting full concentration, individuals can increase their typical typing speed by around 10–20% – at least for the brief time that they are able to maintain the high level of concentration.

When individuals aspire to improve their typing speed, typing teachers recommend that they set aside 15–20 minutes a day to type at the faster levels. The first benefit of typing faster than normal is that it reveals weaknesses and problem areas, such as certain letter combinations that are prone to errors or hesitations and thus require longer time to complete. Once problem areas have been identified, the typists can design special training activities to speed up those particular letter combinations. They tend to start working on the problematic letter combinations in isolation, then embed them in increasingly complex typing contexts with representative text as mastery improves.

The second benefit of typing faster than normal is that it forces the typist to try to anticipate upcoming words and their associated key presses. Whenever a finger involved in a future key press is not engaged in typing other letters, it can be moved toward its intended target in advance, and be ready to press the key. As I already noted in the section on the structure of expert typing, individual differences in typing speed have been closely related to how far ahead a typist looks in the text while typing. Increasing the speed of typing will push the typist to look farther ahead to allow superior preparation and optimization of typing movements.

When individuals engage in deliberate practice activities that are specially designed to improve performance, such as setting time aside to increase typing speed with full concentration, they usually find them too demanding to be playful or inherently enjoyable (Ericsson et al., 1993). This type of practice involves actively pushing performance beyond its reliable limits, and it often leads to mistakes as old habits are broken. In fact, when individuals engage in deliberate practice, they often try to push their performance in order to produce impasses and breakdowns in performance (Newell, 1990; VanLehn, 1991). An impasse should be viewed as a problem that needs to be overcome in order to improve the structure of the current skill. The individual should first try to replicate the impasse to assess the nature of the problem. For example, a typist who has tentatively identified a problem must consider how his or her technique can be modified to eliminate it without introducing other problems into the typing performance. The modified typing procedure will then be the focus of special training, initially in isolation, and later during the typing of representative texts.

As typing speed becomes faster and is mediated by increasingly complex representations, it becomes harder to identify the source of impasses and find effective modifications. If typists attempt to expand how far they look ahead and prepare keystrokes, they have to make appropriate adjustments contingent on motor actions and coordination of concurrent actions that they have already mastered. Within this view of skill building, motor actions acquired early will take on a special importance because they provide the foundation for subsequent adjustments and set constraints for local adjustments made in the future. An extreme example of this is the individual discussed earlier in this section who becomes a skilled hunt-and-peck typist and never attains the more efficient method of typing by touch.

The fine details underlying the execution of keystrokes will make a difference when a series of movements have to be coordinated in rapid sequence at very high levels of performance. In many perceptual-motor domains, such as piano and ballet, it is critical for students to master the fundamental techniques correctly from the beginning. Mastery of the fundamental movements in ballet while maintaining the correct posture is far more difficult than executing them "naturally." Playing the piano with correct posture and execution requires far more attention and control then merely hitting the prescribed sequence of keys.

The real benefits of acquiring the correct fundamentals will be apparent only years later when pianists and dancers with poor technique reach a point in their training where further progress is delayed until the fundamentals are learned. Teachers and parents play a crucial role in motivating young performers to acquire methods of performance that anticipate and avoid problems that will become apparent only years later at much higher levels of performance.

Acquiring Mechanisms Mediating Expert Performance in Chess

It is easy to learn enough chess so one can select moves that follow the rules. The difference between chess players at different levels of skill lies in their ability to select a winning sequence of moves. The central problem for anyone wanting to learn chess is that there no algorithm for computing the best move or series of moves. Chess players can evaluate the general quality of their playing by assessing whether or not they won. However, winning against an unskilled player wouldn't necessary imply that they selected the best or even very good moves. According to deliberate practice, chess players have to find a challenge that exceeds their current skill. The most frequent method is to seek out players in the same chess club that are as strong or even a little bit stronger. How can a chess player who easily beats everyone in his or her club improve his or her skill and move selection?

From biographies and informal interviews with chess experts, Ericsson et al. (1993) found that they spent as much as 4–5 hours a day studying games between chess masters found in books and magazines. The players study each game move by move, and for each position they try to predict the next move. If the players selected a move that matched the one made by the masters, they would get confirmation that their selection was on par with the masters. If they selected a different move, they would need to study and analyze the position until they could understand the masters' selection. Most of the analysis would consist of planning the consequences of possible moves. By engaging in this process, they eventually understand the masters' reasoning.

The quality of generated moves is not fixed for a given chess player but varies as a function of situational factors; sometimes even chess experts make inferior moves or even mistakes (Saarilouma, 1992). The most important factor determining the quality of moves is the amount of analysis and planning a player does before making a final move selection. Consequently, by taking more time to analyze positions a chess player can improve the quality of his or her selected moves. De Groot (1966) suggested that less skilled players can achieve the insights generated by more skilled players by taking more time to analyze the same position. He even claimed that the characteristics of a chess position extracted after a brief view by a chess master could often be generated by a club level player in 10–15 minutes. Similarly, skilled players benefit by extended study of a chess master's move selections.

The process of analysis will change the player's representation of chess positions. If a player failed to notice some attribute of a move that turned out to be important in analysis of the position, he or she must identify the error in his or her representation of the original position or the intermediate positions generated during planning. Some modification of memory representations would always be necessary to avoid making a similar mistake in the future. Complex learning in chess is therefore to a large degree problem solving. When an analysis of a chess position fails to generate the best move, then the player would need to keep a record of the process that generated the inferior move. By comparing the processing trace of the failed analysis to one that would uncover the best move, it should be possible to assess the necessary modifications to eliminate the mistake without generating other mistakes for other situations.

The gradual refinement of the memory mechanisms supporting planning and reasoning about positions is evident when comparing chess players of different skill levels. More skilled chess players show greater ability to memorize and mentally manipulate chess positions, as reviewed earlier in this chapter. The chess experts' superior memory abilities are consistent with acquired skills developed to support the working memory demands of finding and selecting the best moves (Ericsson et al., 2000). The development is also consistent with Charness et al.'s (1996) finding that the activity most closely related to official ratings of chess skill is the amount of accumulated self-study of chess – deliberate practice.

Educational Systems Supporting the Development of Expert Performance in Music

Our civilization has a relatively long history of training children and adolescents to attain skills in reading, writing, and arithmetic, as well as in gaining general knowledge of other domains. The goal of this general education is to provide a large number of adults with acceptable levels of skill rather than developing exceptional levels of performance in a small number of elite performers (Ericsson, 1998a). The domains with the longest history of specialized training to produce expert performers are the arts, such as music and dance.

Training of musicians follows a fairly standardized curriculum for each instrument that is relatively similar across teachers, and even different countries. The basic curriculum spans 12 years of study at graduated levels of difficulty. This is followed by several more years at the conservatory level until organized education is typically completed for professional musicians. During these decades of training, the primary focus is on individualized training and mastery of music pieces incorporating specific techniques. Teachers assess the weaknesses and strengths of the student's current performance and select and design training accordingly. At weekly meetings the students receive instructions for their immediate assignments and the specific goals for training. During the intervening week, the student attempts to attain these goals during individualized practice. The teacher guides the student by setting appropriate and attainable goals and by providing feedback about the current level of mastery until students learn to do this for themselves.

When music students are first introduced to training they depend on the teacher not just to instruct them in the training activity and its goals, but also for help with monitoring performance and with assistance with problems. Teachers will diagnose the source of problems and design practice activities that will help overcome obstacles to progress. Successful students will gradually assume responsibility for monitoring their performance and generating methods to master difficult passages of music during practice (Glaser, 1996). With experience, the successful student will start to acquire representations for imaging the desired music performance, for monitoring the sound of the music as he or she produces it, and for identifying methods to correct mistakes or deviations from the desired music experience (Ericsson, 1998b). With further training the student becomes increasingly skilled at critiquing his or her own performance, and can thus anticipate the feedback given by teachers. Hence, training of music students as independent performers involves something more than just transmitting the skill and knowledge that has been accumulated in the domain. It includes teaching the problem-solving methods necessary for maintaining high levels of technical proficiency, attaining new levels of mastery, and extending knowledge in the domain to produce innovations and creative contributions (Ericsson, 1998b, 1999).

The music domain offers some of the best evidence for the distinction between practice and deliberate practice. As children, many people may have spent a lot of time practicing the piano with modest improvements, or known other people who did. When parents forced them to practice, many piano students would simply play the same piece repeatedly without full concentration on specific aspects of their performance. Under those circumstances the existing performance level becomes only more stable and "practice" makes it permanent. The relation between current level of performance and the number of hours of "practice" is weak for this type of beginner (Lehmann, 1997).

Successful practice requires identifying specific goals for how to change the performance. The student has to be able to focus on those changes while playing the music. This process requires a mental representation that allows the student to control which aspects of the performance are changed. Furthermore, the student needs to be able to monitor the result in order gradually to refine the performance. Students must incrementally develop these representations to attain control over the complex structure of music, such as patterns involving tempo and loudness and the coordination of overlapping movements by hands, fingers, feet, and bodily posture.

Most deliberate practice by music students is solitary as they attempt to master specific assignments, often new pieces of music selected by their teachers to be of an appropriate difficulty level. Musicians will encounter difficult passages while mastering a new piece of music. To achieve mastery, the musician first identifies the source of the problem, often by playing the passage in a slow tempo. There are frequently several different ways to produce a sequence of notes, and pianists often engage in problem solving to find the combination of finger movements that will work best.

With focused repetitions the pianist will generally reach mastery. Sometimes the pianist will still experience difficulties and work on specific exercises that eventually lead to desired changes. In music, there is a large body of training techniques that have been designed to help musicians develop control over performance and attain the desired speed and dexterity. The use of techniques designed to overcome weaknesses and increase control exemplifies the essence of deliberate practice.

CONCLUDING REMARKS

The central thesis of this chapter is that the acquisition of expert performance involves problem solving, and the study of expert performance provides insight into the most advanced levels of thinking and problem solving. Individual differences in performance in many domains of expertise were shown to be mediated by complex mechanisms that had been acquired for a dual purpose. First, these mechanisms allow the performer to master tasks that present problems and challenges for less skilled individuals. Second, the same mechanisms also allow the performers to monitor, evaluate, and analyze their own performance. These mechanisms are a prerequisite for the performer who will keep improving by identifying and overcoming weaknesses through deliberate practice.

The study of expert performance informs us about problem solving in two corresponding ways. First, individual differences in problem-solving ability can be better understood by contrasting how skilled individuals and experts in a domain efficiently generate their responses in challenging situations that are problematic for less skilled individuals. During the 1970s and 1980s, there was considerable optimism that discovery and identification of the experts' knowledge and strategies would allow expertise and problem-solving ability in a given domain to be taught in an effective manner. Some scientists even hoped that this form of instruction would dramatically reduce the many years necessary for individuals to become experts.

Now, several decades later, engineers have accumulated a lot of experience describing the rules and knowledge of experts in order to build computer-based expert systems. This knowledge has helped investigators understand that experts' consistently superior performance on representative tasks in their domains is mediated by very complex factors. They found that the relation between explicit knowledge and experience in a domain and performance on representative tasks in that domain is frequently weaker than expected.

As the review in this chapter has shown, once a sufficient level of experience and knowledge has been attained, the relation between additional experience and performance is weak. The current examination of the cognitive processes mediating experts' reliably superior performance showed that the mediating mechanisms were complex, entailing representations that support planning, reasoning, and evaluation of future courses of action. The central role played by these representations in experts' superior performance implies that any educational program designed to develop expert performance will have to address how these representations are acquired.

The second connection between problem solving and expert performance concerns the actual process by which a given individual improves performance by changing the mediating mechanisms. I have reviewed evidence showing how performance in a domain is gradually modified by challenges encountered while engaging in typical activities. One distinctive characteristic of future expert performers is that they intentionally avoid the natural tendency toward automatization, with its associated loss of control of many relevant aspects. They typically seek out instruction by teachers and they regularly engage in problem solving in the form of deliberate practice. They seek out situations in which they strive to reach higher levels of performance. They strain their current performance and seek to find ways to make improvements without altering the desirable characteristics of the current performance.

Future expert performers typically start the development of basic representations as soon as they start regular practice. With further development they internalize some of the monitoring functions of their teachers and eventually become able to evaluate their performance, diagnose weaknesses, and identify appropriate adjustments. These representations allow them to identify their desired goals, construct plans for achieving them, and develop methods for monitoring their performance. The representations are tightly integrated aspects of their acquired skills. Refinements in the representations often precede further improvements of performance. Deliberate practice is designed to push the limits of the current representations and lead to refinements and modifications through problem-solving efforts.

The view of problem solving presented in this chapter differs from the more traditional accounts of problem solving and its relation to skill acquisition and expertise. According to these traditional accounts, individuals active in the domain will incrementally build expertise by accumulation of pieces of knowledge and automation of procedures. The process of improvement is thus viewed as a passive consequence of additional experience, suggesting that individuals with similar abilities would eventually reach the same expert level as long as they remained active in the domain (see Ericsson and Lehmann, 1996, for further discussion). Differences among highly experienced individuals are, within this traditional perspective, assumed to reflect general unmodifiable abilities.

In contrast, the deliberate practice view proposes that performance improvements are linked to active efforts to build representations for planning and monitoring, a process that counteracts automation and allows continued problem solving and modification of the developing performance. Differences between individuals' performance are accounted for by the acquired mental representations that support performance and guide future improvements. Differences in the constructed representations may explain creative variability at the highest levels of performance (Ericsson, 1998b, 1999). Many of the remarkable abilities of expert performers, such as the ability to play "blindfold chess" or to anticipate the path of tennis balls before their opponents have struck the ball, can be better explained by deliberately acquired representations rather than innate abilities. Similarly, experts' superior ability to reason and to plan solutions mentally in their domain of expertise is shown to reflect acquired representations rather than pure problem-solving abilities or intelligence.

Investigating the problem-solving abilities of expert performers has taken us far from the original conception of problem solving as a pure capacity or a core mechanism that can be studied in the laboratory with puzzles and unfamiliar tasks that minimize the role of prior knowledge and experience. The challenge for expert performers is effective management of extensive knowledge and experience, not performance in the absence of it. How should one build a cognitive structure that allows for further refinements as the skill and knowledge increase? What kinds of control mechanisms need to be constructed to monitor continued modification and refinement? How can the development of control mechanisms and performance be coordinated while maintaining an integrated performance?

It is clear that expert performance and its mediating mechanisms are not constructed completely from scratch. When individuals, especially adults, initially enter any domain of expertise, they bring a range of related abilities and associated knowledge and experience. To build a complete theoretical framework it is necessary to describe in detail how individuals apply these existing skills and abilities to performance within a new domain. Only by describing these initial mechanisms and how they are later modified and refined by deliberate practice will it be possible to account for the full range of development of expert performance. Within such a general theoretical framework it will be possible to integrate studies of traditional problem solving with laboratory studies of problem solving and to gradually refine our understanding of the mechanisms mediating high levels of achievement.

REFERENCES

Abernethy, B. (1987). Selective attention in fast ball sports. II. Expert-novice differences. *Australian Journal of Science and Medicine in Sports, 19*, 7–16.

Abernethy, B. (1991). Visual search strategies and decision-making in sport. *International Journal of Sport Psychology, 22*, 189–210.

Anderson, J. R. (1982). Acquisition of cognitive skill. *Psychological Review, 89*, 369–406.

Anderson, J. R. (1987). Skill acquisition: Compilation of weak-method problem situations. *Psychological Review, 94*(2), 192–210.

Atwood, M. E., Masson, M. E., & Polson, P. G. (1980). Further explorations with a process model for water jug problems. *Memory & Cognition, 8*, 182–192.

Barker, R. (1978). *Ecological psychology.* Stanford: Stanford University Press.

Bloom, B. S. (1985). Generalizations about talent development. In B. S. Bloom (Ed.), *Developing talent in young people* (pp. 507–549). New York: Ballantine Books.

Bourne, L. E., Jr., Goldstein, S., & Link, W. E. (1964). Concept learning as a function of availability of previously presented information. *Journal of Experimental Psychology, 67*, 439–448.

Bronfenbrenner, U. (1979). *The ecology of human development.* Cambridge, MA: Harvard University Press.

Brunswik, E. (1943). Organismic achievement and environmental probability. *Psychological Review, 50*, 255–272.

Calderwood, R., Klein, G. A., & Crandall, B. W. (1988). Time pressure, skill and move quality in chess. *American Journal of Psychology, 101*, 481–493.

Charness, N. (1981). Search in chess: Age and skill differences. *Journal of Experimental Psychology: Human Perception and Performance, 7*, 467–476.

Charness, N. (1991). Expertise in chess: The balance between knowledge and search. In K. A. Ericsson & J. Smith (Eds.), *Toward a general theory of expertise: Prospects and limits* (pp. 39–63). New York: Cambridge University Press.

Charness, N., Krampe, R. Th., & Mayr, U. (1996). The role of practice and coaching in entrepreneurial skill domains: An international comparison of life-span chess skill acquisition. In K. A. Ericsson (Ed.), *The road to excellence: The acquisition of expert performance in the arts and sciences, sports, and games* (pp. 51–80). Mahwah, NJ: Erlbaum.

Chase, W. G., & Ericsson, K. A. (1981). Skilled memory. In J. R. Anderson (Ed.), *Cognitive skills and their acquisition* (pp. 141–189). Hillsdale, NJ: Lawrence Erlbaum Associates.

Chase, W. G., & Ericsson, K. A. (1982). Skill and working memory. In G. H. Bower (Ed.), *The psychology of learning and motivation* (Vol. 16, pp. 1–58). New York: Academic Press.

Chase, W. G., & Simon, H. A. (1973). The mind's eye in chess. In W. G. Chase (Ed.), *Visual information processing* (pp. 215–281). New York: Academic Press.

Clark, R. W. (1983). *Benjamin Franklin: A biography*. New York: Random House.

Coltheart, V. (1971). Memory for stimuli and memory for hypotheses in concept identification. *Journal of Experimental Psychology, 89*, 102–108.

Cowley, M. (Ed.). (1959). *Writers at work: The Paris Review interviews*. New York: Viking.

Dawes, R. M. (1994). *House of cards: Psychology and psychotherapy built on myth*. New York: Free Press.

de Groot, A. D. (1966). Perception and memory versus thought: Some old ideas and recent findings. In B. Kleinmuntz (Ed.), *Problem solving: Research, method and theory* (pp. 19–50). New York; John Wiley & Sons.

de Groot, A. D. (1946/1978). *Thought and choice and chess*. The Hague: Mouton.

Donders, F. C. (1868/1969). On the speed of mental processes. *Acta Psychologica, 30*, 412–31. (Translated by W. G. Koster from "Over de snelheid can psychishe processen." Onzoekingen gedann in het Physiologisch Laboratorium der Utrechtsche Hoogeschool, 1868, Tweede reeks, 2, 92–120.)

Drake, C., & Palmer, C. (2000). Skill acquisition in music performance: relations between planning and temporal control. *Cognition, 74*, 1–32.

Duncker, K. (1926). A qualitative (experimental and theoretical) study of productive thinking (solving of comprehensible problems). *Pedagogical Seminary, 33*, 642–708.

Duncker, K. (1945). On problem solving. *Psychological Monographs, 58*(5, Whole No. 270).

Ericsson, K. A. (1988). Analysis of memory performance in terms of memory skill. In R. J. Sternberg (Ed.), *Advances in the psychology of human intelligence* (Vol. 4, pp. 137–179). Hillsdale, NJ: Erlbaum.

Ericsson, K. A. (1996). The acquisition of expert performance: An introduction to some of the issues. In K. A. Ericsson (Ed.), *The road to excellence: The acquisition of expert performance in the arts and sciences, sports, and games* (pp. 1–50). Mahwah, NJ: Erlbaum.

Ericsson, K. A. (1998a). Commentary on J. R. Anderson's, L. Reder's and H. A. Simon's paper "Radical constructivism, mathematics education and cognitive psychology." In D. Ravitch (Ed.), *Brookings papers on educational policy 1998* (pp. 255–264). Washington, DC: Brookings Institution Press.

Ericsson, K. A. (1998b). The scientific study of expert levels of performance: General implications for optimal learning and creativity. *High Ability Studies, 9*, 75–100.

Ericsson, K. A. (1999). Creative expertise as superior reproducible performance: Innovative and flexible aspects of expert performance. *Psychological Inquiry, 10*(4), 329–333.

Ericsson, K. A. (2001). Attaining excellence through deliberate practice: Insights from the study of expert performance. In M. Ferrari (Ed.), *The pursuit of excellence in education* (pp. 21–55). Hillsdale, N.J.: Erlbaum.

Ericsson, K. A., & Charness, N. (1994). Expert performance: Its structure and acquisition. *American Psychologist, 49*, 725–747.

Ericsson, K. A., & Crutcher, R. J. (1991). Introspection and verbal reports on cognitive processes – Two approaches to the study of thought processes: A response to Howe. *New Ideas in Psychology, 9*, 57–71.

Ericsson, K. A., & Delaney, P. F. (1999). Long-term working memory as an alternative to capacity models of working memory in everyday skilled performance. In A. Miyake & P. Shah (Eds.), *Models of working memory: Mechanisms of active maintenance and executive control* (pp. 257–297). Cambridge, UK: Cambridge University Press.

Ericsson, K. A., & Kintsch, W. (1995). Long-term working memory. *Psychological Review, 102*, 211–245.

Ericsson, K. A., & Kintsch, W. (2000). Shortcomings of generic retrieval structures with slots of the type that Gobet (1993) proposed and modeled. *British Journal of Psychology, 91*, 571–588.

Ericsson, K. A., Krampe, R. Th., & Heizmann, S. (1993). Can we create gifted people? In CIBA Foundation Symposium 178, *The origin and development of high ability* (pp. 222–249). Chichester, UK: Wiley.

Ericsson, K. A., Krampe, R. Th., & Tesch-Römer, C. (1993). The role of deliberate practice in the acquisition of expert performance. *Psychological Review, 100*, 363–406.

Ericsson, K. A., & Lehmann, A. C. (1996). Expert and exceptional performance: Evidence on maximal adaptations on task constraints. *Annual Review of Psychology, 47*, 273–305.

Ericsson, K. A., & Lehmann, A. C. (1999). Expertise. In M. A. Runco & S. Pritzer (Eds.), *Encyclopedia of creativity* (Vol. 1, pp. 695–707). San Diego, CA: Academic Press.

Ericsson, K. A., & Oliver, W. (1988). Methodology for laboratory research on thinking: Task selection, collection of observation and data analysis. In R. J. Sternberg & E. E. Smith (Eds.), *The psychology of human thought* (pp. 392–428). Cambridge, UK: Cambridge University Press.

Ericsson, K. A., Patel, V. L., & Kintsch, W. (2000). How experts' adaptations to representative task demands account for the expertise effect in memory recall: Comment on Vicente and Wang (1998). *Psychological Review, 107*, 578–592.

Ericsson, K. A., & Simon, H. A. (1984). *Protocol analysis: Verbal reports as data*. Cambridge, MA: Bradford Books/MIT Press.

Ericsson, K. A., & Simon, H. A. (1993). *Protocol analysis: Verbal reports as data* (Rev. ed.). Cambridge, MA: MIT Press.

Ericsson, K. A., & Smith, J. (1991). Prospects and limits in the empirical study of expertise: An introduction. In K. A. Ericsson & J. Smith (Eds.), *Toward a general theory of expertise: Prospects and limits* (pp. 1–38). Cambridge: Cambridge University Press.

Ericsson, K. A., & Staszewski, J. (1989). Skilled memory and expertise: Mechanisms of exceptional performance. In D. Klahr & K. Kotovsky (Eds.), *Complex information processing: The impact of Herbert A. Simon* (pp. 235–267). Hillsdale, NJ: Erlbaum.

Fitts, P., & Posner, M. I. (1967). *Human performance.* Belmont, CA: Brooks/Cole.

Frensch, P. A., & Sternberg, R. J. (1989). Expertise and intelligent thinking: When is it worse to know better? In R. J. Sternberg (Ed.), *Advances in the psychology of human intelligence* (pp. 157–188). Hillsdale, NJ: Erlbaum.

Gagne, R. H., & Smith, E. C. (1962). A study of the effects of verbalization on problem solving. *Journal of Experimental Psychology, 63,* 12–18.

Gibson, E. J. (1969). *Principles of perceptual learning and development.* Englewood Cliffs, NJ: Prentice-Hall.

Gibson, J. J. (1979). *An ecological approach to visual perception.* Boston: Houghton-Mifflin.

Glaser, R. (1996). Changing the agency for learning: Acquiring expert performance. In K. A. Ericsson (Ed.), *The road to excellence: The acquisition of expert performance in the arts and sciences, sports, and games* (pp. 303–312). Mahwah, NJ: Erlbaum.

Glaser, R., & Chi, M. T. H. (1988). Overview. In M. T. H. Chi, R. Glaser, & M. J. Farr (Eds.), *The nature of expertise* (pp. xv–xxviii). Hillsdale, NJ: Erlbaum.

Gobet, F., & Simon, H. A. (1996a). Recall of rapidly presented random chess positions is a function of skill. *Psychonomic Bulletin & Review, 3,* 159–163.

Gobet, F., & Simon, H. A. (1996b). The roles of recognition processes and look-ahead search in time-constrained expert problem solving: Evidence from grand-master-level chess. *Psychological Science, 7,* 52–55.

Gobet, F., & Simon, H. A. (1996c). Templates in chess memory: A mechanism for recalling several boards. *Cognitive Psychology, 31,* 1–40.

Gould, S. J. (1996). *Full house: The spread of excellence from Plato to Darwin.* New York: Harmony Books.

Greeno, J. G., & Simon, H. A. (1988). Problem solving and reasoning. In R. C. Atkinson, R. J. Herrnstein, G. Lindsey, & R. D. Luce (Eds.), *Stevens' handbook of experimental psychology* (2nd ed., Vol. 2, pp. 589–672). New: John Wiley.

Gruber, H., & Strube, G. (1989). Zweierlei Experten: Problemisten, Partiespieler und Novizen beim Lösen von Schachproblemen [Two types of experts: The solution of chess problems by expert solvers of "chess problems," expert tournament players, and beginners]. *Sprache & Kognition, 8,* 72–85.

Helsen, W. F., Starkes, J. L., & Hodges, N. J. (1998). Team sports and the theory of deliberate practice. *Journal of Sport and Exercise Psychology, 20,* 12–34.

Hodges, N. J., & Starkes, J. L. (1996). Wrestling with the nature of expertise: A sport specific test of Ericsson, Krampe and Tesch-Römer's (1993) theory of "Deliberate Practice." *International Journal of Sport Psychology, 27,* 400–424.

Hunt, E. B. (1978). Mechanics of verbal ability. *Psychological Review, 85,* 109–130.

Karat, J. A. (1982). Model of problem solving with incomplete constraint knowledge. *Cognitive Psychology, 14,* 538–559.

Karpov, A. (1995). Grandmaster musings. *Chess Life,* November, pp. 32–33.

Kliegl, R., Smith, J., Heckhausen, J., & Baltes, P. B. (1987). Mnemonic training for the acquisition of skilled digit memory. *Cognition and Instruction, 4,* 203–223.

Koltanowski, G. (1985). *In the dark.* Coraopolis, PA: Chess Enterprises.

Krampe, R. Th., & Ericsson, K. A. (1996). Maintaining excellence: Deliberate practice and elite performance in young and older pianists. *Journal of Experimental Psychology: General, 125,* 331–359.

Lehman, H. C. (1953). *Age and achievement.* Princeton, NJ: Princeton University Press.

Lehmann, A. C. (1997). Acquisition of expertise in music: Efficiency of deliberate practice as a moderating variable in accounting for sub-expert performance. In I. Deliege & J. A. Sloboda (Eds.), *Perception and cognition of music* (pp. 165–191). Hillsdale, NJ: LEA.

Lehmann, A. C., & Ericsson, K. A. (1993). Sight-reading ability of expert pianists in the context of piano accompanying. *Psychomusicology, 12,* 182–195.

Lehmann, A. C., & Ericsson, K. A. (1995). *Expert pianists' mental representation of memorized music.* Poster presented at the 36th Annual meeting of the Psychonomic Society, Los Angeles, CA, November 10–12.

Lehmann, A. C., & Ericsson, K. A. (1996). Music performance without preparation: Structure and acquisition of expert sight-reading. *Psychomusicology, 15,* 1–29.

Lehmann, A. C., & Ericsson K. A. (1997). Expert pianists' mental representations: Evidence from successful adaptation to unexpected performance demands. *Proceedings of the Third Triennial ESCOM Conference* (pp. 165–169). Uppsala, Sweden: SLU Service/Reproenheten.

Lehmann, A. C., & Ericsson K. A. (1998). The historical development of domains of expertise: Performance standards and innovations in music. In A. Steptoe (Ed.), *Genius and the mind* (pp. 67–94). Oxford, UK: Oxford University Press.

Lerner, T. (1915). An audience is the best teacher. In H. Brower (Ed.), *Piano mastery: Talks with master pianists and teachers* (pp. 38–46). New York: Frederick A. Stokes Company.

Levin, H., & Addis, A. B. (1979). *The eye-voice span.* Cambridge, MA: MIT Press.

Lindworsky, J. (1931). *Experimental methodology.* New York: Macmillan.

Logan, G. D. (1983). Time, information, and the various spans in type writing. In W. E. Cooper (Ed.), *Cognitive aspects of skilled typing* (pp. 197–224). New York: Springer Verlag.

Maier, N. R. F. (1931). Reasoning in humans: II. The solution of a problem and its appearance in consciousness. *Journal of Comparative Psychology, 12,* 181–194.

Morgan, C. L. (1894). *An introduction to comparative psychology.* London: Walter Scott Ltd.

Müller, G. E., & Pilzecker, A. (1900). Experimentelle Beiträge sur Lehre vom Gedächtniss [Experimental contributions to the theory of memory]. *Zeitschrift für Psychologie, Ergänzungs Band, 1,* 1–288.

Müller, G. E., & Schumann, F. (1894). Experimentelle Beiträge zur Untersuchung des Gedächtnisses [Experimental contributions to the study of memory]. *Zeitschrift für Psychologie, 6,* 81–190.

Neisser, U. (1976). *Cognition and reality: Principles and implications of cognitive psychology.* San Francisco: W. H. Freeman and Company.

Newell, A. (1990). *Unified theories of cognition.* Cambridge, MA: Harvard University Press.

Newell, A., & Rosenbloom, P. S. (1981). Mechanisms of skill acquisition and the law of practice. In J. R. Anderson (Ed.), *Cognitive skills and their acquisition* (pp. 1–55). Hillsdale, NJ: Erlbaum.

Newell, A., & Simon, H. A. (1972). *Human problem solving*. Englewood Cliffs, NJ: Prentice-Hall.

Norman, D. A., & Rumelhart, D. E. (1983). Studies of typing from the LNR research group. In W. E. Cooper (Ed.), *Cognitive aspects of skilled typing* (pp. 45–65). New York: Springer Verlag.

Norman, G. R., Trott, A. D., Brooks, L. R., & Smith, E. K. M. (1994). Cognitive differences in clinical reasoning related to postgraduate training. *Teaching and Learning in Medicine, 6*, 114–120.

Patel, V. L., & Groen, G. J. (1991). The general and specific nature of medical expertise: A critical look. In K. A. Ericsson & J. Smith (Eds.), *Toward a general theory of expertise* (pp. 93–125). Cambridge, MA: Cambridge University Press.

Payne, J. W. (1976). Task complexity and contingent processing in decision making: An informational search and protocol analysis. *Organizational Behavior and Human Performance, 16*, 366–387.

Pfau, H. D., & Murphy, M. D. (1988). Role of verbal knowledge in chess skill. *American Journal of Psychology, 101*, 73–86.

Rapaport, D. (Ed.). (1951). *Organization and pathology of thought: Selected sources*. New York: Columbia University Press.

Rosson, M. B. (1985). The role of experience in editing. *Proceedings of INTERACT '84 IFIP Conference on Human-Computer Interaction* (pp. 45–50). New York: Elsevier.

Saariluoma, P. (1989). Chess players' recall of auditorily presented chess positions. *European Journal of Cognitive Psychology, 1*, 309–320.

Saariluoma, P. (1991). Aspects of skilled imagery in blindfold chess. *Acta Psychologica , 77*, 65–89.

Saariluoma, P. (1992). Error in chess: The apperception-restructuring view. *Psychological Research, 54*, 17–26.

Salthouse, T. A. (1984). Effects of age and skill in typing. *Journal of Experimental Psychology: General, 113*, 345–371.

Schneider, W. (1993). Acquiring expertise: Determinants of exceptional performance. In K. A. Heller, J. Mönks, & H. Passow (Eds.), *International handbook of research and development of giftedness and talent* (pp. 311–324). Oxford, UK: Pergamon Press.

Schulz, R., & Curnow, C. (1988). Peak performance and age among superathletes: Track and field, swimming, baseball, tennis, and golf. *Journal of Gerontology: Psychological Sciences, 43*, 113–120.

Shaffer, L. H. (1973). Latency mechanisms in transcription. In S. Kornblum (Ed.), *Attention and Performance* (Vol. 4, pp. 435–446). New York: Academic Press.

Shiffrin, R. M., & Schneider, W. (1977). Controlled and automatic human information processing: II. Perceptual learning, automatic attending and a general theory. *Psychological Review, 84*, 127–189.

Simon, H. A. (1975). The functional equivalence of problem solving skills. *Cognitive Psychology, 7*, 268–288.

Simon, H. A. (1976). The information-storage system called "human memory." In M. R. Rosenzweig & E.L. Bennett (Eds.), *Neural mechanisms of learning and memory*. Cambridge, MA: MIT Press.

Simon, H. A., & Chase, W. G. (1973). Skill in chess. *American Scientist, 61*, 394–403.

Simonton, D. K. (1997). Creative productivity: A predictive and explanatory model of career trajectories and landmarks. *Psychological Review, 104*, 66–89.

Sloboda, J. A. (1984). Experimental studies in music reading: A review. *Music Perception, 22,* 222–236.

Sloboda, J. A. (1996). The acquisition of musical performance expertise: Deconstructing the "talent" account of individual differences in musical expressivity. In K. A. Ericsson (Ed.), *The road to excellence: The acquisition of expert performance in the arts and sciences, sports, and games* (pp. 107–126). Mahwah, NJ: Erlbaum.

Sloboda, J. A., Clarke, E. F., Parncutt, R., & Raekallio, M. (1998). Determinants of finger choice in piano sight-reading. *Journal of Experimental Psychology: Human Perception & Performance, 24,* 185–203.

Stael von Holstein, C.-A. S. (1972). Probabilistic forecasting: An experiment related to the stock market. *Organizational Behavior and Human Performance, 8,* 139–158.

Starkes, J. L., & Deakin, J. (1984). Perception in sport: A cognitive approach to skilled performance. In W. F. Straub & J. M. Williams (Eds.), *Cognitive sport psychology* (pp. 115–128). Lansing, NY: Sport Science Associates.

Starkes, J. L., Deakin, J., Allard, F., Hodges, N. J., & Hayes, A. (1996). Deliberate practice in sports: What is it anyway? In K. A. Ericsson (Ed.), *The road to excellence: The acquisition of expert performance in the arts and sciences, sports, and games* (pp. 81–106). Mahwah, NJ: Erlbaum.

Sternberg, R. J. (1977). *Intelligence, information processing, and analogical reasoning: The componential analysis of human abilities.* Hillsdale, NJ: Erlbaum.

Sternberg. R. J. (1996). Costs of expertise. In K. A. Ericsson (Ed.), *The road to excellence: The acquisition of expert performance in the arts and sciences, sports, and games* (pp. 347–354). Mahwah, NJ: Erlbaum.

Svenson, O. (1979). Process descriptions of decision making. *Organizational Behavior and Human Performance, 23,* 86–112.

VanLehn, K. (1991). Rule acquisition events in the discovery of problem-solving strategies. *Cognitive Science, 15,* 1–47.

Varon, E. J. (1935). The development of Alfred Binet's psychology. *Psychological Monographs, 46* (Whole No. 207).

Watson, J. B. (1913). Psychology as the behaviorist views it. *Psychological Review, 20,* 158–177.

Watson, J. B. (1920). Is thinking merely the action of language mechanisms? *British Journal of Psychology, 11,* 87–104.

Watson, J. B. (1924). The place of kinesthetic, visceral and laryngeal organization in thinking. *Psychological Review, 31,* 339–347.

Wenger, M. J., & Payne, D. G. (1995). On the acquisition of mnemonic skill: Application of skilled memory theory. *Journal of Experimental Psychology: Applied, 1,* 194–215.

Woody, R. H., Lehmann, A. C., & Ericsson, K. A. (1998). *Evidence for mental representations mediating expert musicians' expressive performance.* Presentation given at the 39th Annual meeting of the Psychonomic Society, Dallas, TX, November 19–22.

AUTHOR NOTES

This research was supported by the Edward Conradi Endowment Fund of Florida State University Foundation. This article was prepared in part while the author was a Fellow at the Center for Advanced Study in the Behavioral Sciences. The author is grateful for the financial support provided by the John D. and Catherine T. MacArthur Foundation Grant no. 32005-0. The author thanks Elizabeth Kirk for her most valuable comments on several earlier drafts of this chapter. Furthermore, helpful comments on the final draft are gratefully acknowledged.

PART II

RELEVANT ABILITIES AND SKILLS

3

Is Success or Failure at Solving Complex Problems Related to Intellectual Ability?

Dorit Wenke and Peter A. Frensch

INTRODUCTION

Imagine you are elected mayor of a town and are given absolute power over all town resources. You may hire workers for the local factory, raise taxes, have schools built, and close down local businesses. The one goal you are to strive for is to make certain that the town prospers.

A situation like this, simulated on a computer, was used in the early 1980s by Dietrich Dörner and his colleagues (e.g., Dörner & Kreuzig, 1983; Dörner, Kreuzig, Reither, & Stäudel, 1983) in Bamberg, Germany, to study individual differences in the human ability to solve complex problems. Dörner was interested in understanding why some of his research participants were much more successful in building prosperous towns than were others. One of his rather striking and hotly debated conclusions was that individual differences in the ability to govern the simulated town were not at all related to the individuals' IQs. Rather, an individual's ability to turn the town into a prosperous community seemed to be related to his or her extroversion and self-confidence.

In this chapter we are concerned with the question of what determines individual differences in complex problem-solving competence. The answer to this question may be traced from many different viewpoints: cognitive, social, biological, and evolutionary, to name just a few. Here, we focus on the contribution of cognitive psychology to providing an answer to the question. More specifically, we discuss to what extent, if indeed at all, complex problem-solving competence can be traced, both theoretically and empirically, to an individual's intellectual ability.

The chapter is divided into three main sections. In the first section, we provide definitions for *problem,* and because our focus is on complex problem solving, for *complex problem solving* as well. In addition, we define what we mean when we use the term *intellectual ability* within the tradition of cognitive psychology, and we discuss what it means to state that an individual's problem-solving competence is due to intellectual ability. In the second and third sections, we review much of the existing empirical work that relates complex problem-solving competence to some measure of intellectual ability. We distinguish two forms of complex problem solving. In the second section, we focus on explicit problem solving, that is, problem solving that is controlled by a problem solver's intentions. In the third section our focus is on implicit, that is, automatic or nonconscious, complex problem solving. Our main argument throughout the chapter is that there exists, thus far, no convincing empirical evidence that would support a causal relation between any intellectual ability, on the one hand, and complex, implicit or explicit, problem-solving competence, on the other hand. To be clear from the outset on what exactly it is that we are arguing for and what we are not arguing for, the reader should note that our argument is one that is based on a lack of evidence, not necessarily a lack of theoretical relation. That is, we do not deny the possibility that a causal relation between intellectual ability and complex problem-solving competence might exist; we argue only that there exists no convincing empirical evidence as of yet that would support such a relation.

DEFINITIONS AND CLARIFICATIONS

As pointed out by Frensch and Funke (1995), among many others, researchers in the area of human problem solving are often quite inconsistent in their use of terms such as *heuristic, problem, problem solving,* and *intellectual ability.* Although perhaps understandable, the different uses of the same terms seriously undermine scientific progress. Because the definition of terms affects the choice of experimental tasks and methods, and thus, ultimately affects the conclusions to be drawn (Frensch & Funke, 1995), we make an attempt in this section to delineate what exactly we mean when we talk about (a) *problems* in general and *complex problems* in particular, and (b) *intellectual ability.* In addition, we discuss what it means to state that there may be a relation between intellectual ability and complex problem-solving competence and outline our criteria for evaluating the empirical soundness of the proposed relation.

Simple and Complex Problems

In our daily lives we are confronted with all sorts of problems. For example, in the morning we need to decide what to wear and how to combine different clothes. Some problems have clearly defined goals, whereas others don't. Some problems require many "mental steps," whereas others are rather easy and quick to solve. Hence, problems differ widely in terms of their requirements, and, not surprisingly, there exist literally dozens of ways to meaningfully define and classify problems. In this chapter, we advance a "gap" definition of problem solving and classify problems according to where in the problem space gaps exist and how large the gaps are. Gap definitions have been proposed by many researchers, for instance, Lüer and Spada (1998), who hold that a problem exists

> whenever a person perceives and represents properties of the task environment and, in doing so, recognizes that the internal representation contains one or more unsatisfactory gaps. Consequently, the problem solver experiences a barrier between the current state and the goal state. (Lüer & Spada, 1998, p. 256; translation by the authors)

The "unsatisfactory gaps" proposed by Lüer and Spada can be of many different types and sizes, depending on the properties of the task. For example, a task may be stated in a way that leads to gaps in the representation of the problem state and in the relations among the elements of the problem state. Alternatively, a gap may exist in the representation of potential operators or of (external) constraints on the combination of operators, or in the representation of goal states.

What "gap definitions" make abundantly clear is that "problems" are due to the interaction between a problem solver and a task. The type and the size of the gaps depend (a) on characteristics of the problem solver, such as the amount of preexisting knowledge and, possibly, intellectual ability, as well as (b) on task characteristics such as the problem state and/or the goal state.

In the remainder of the chapter, we concentrate on problems at the high end of the "gap continuum," that is, on problems that consist of several and/or large gaps in the problem representations of most problem solvers, and that have more resemblance to real-world problems than to traditional laboratory problems such as the Tower of Hanoi. There are at least two reasons for why we focus on the relation between intellectual ability and complex, rather than simple, kinds of problem solving. First, there already exist several first-rate reviews of the relation between intellectual ability and simple problem-solving competence such as is displayed when typical laboratory problems are solved (e.g., Sternberg, 1982). The nutshell conclusion from these reviews appears to be that if there is indeed a relation between intellectual ability and problem-solving competence, then it is probably quite modest in size (i.e., correlations around .30). By comparison, the potential relation between intellectual ability and complex problem-solving competence has been rarely discussed and reviewed in detail thus far.

Second, and perhaps more important, the external validity of the artificial laboratory tasks that are typically used to study the relation between intellectual ability and problem-solving competence is highly questionable. The tasks have little resemblance to the problem-solving situations typically encountered by humans.

Following the work of Dietrich Dörner and his colleagues (e.g., Dörner, Kreuzig, Reither, & Stäudel, 1983), we define "complex problem solving" as occurring

> to overcome barriers between a given state and a desired goal state by means of behavioral and/or cognitive, multi-step activities. The given state, goal state, and barriers between given state and goal state are complex, change dynamically during problem solving, and are intransparent. The exact properties of the given state, goal state, and barriers are unknown to the solver at the outset. Complex problem solving implies the efficient interaction between a solver and the situational requirements of the task, and involves a solver's cognitive, emotional, personal, and social abilities and knowledge. (Frensch & Funke, 1995, p. 18)

Note that the term *complex problem*, according to the above definition, is not identical to the term *ill-specific problem*, a term frequently encountered in the problem-solving literature. Although "complex" problems can be experienced as "ill-specified" by problem solvers, "complex" problems have additional properties (such as, for instance, the dynamic change of the problem situation) that are not needed for a problem to be called "ill-specified."

As will become apparent later in the chapter, we distinguish complex problem solving that is dependent on the intended actions of a problem solver (i.e., explicit problem solving) and problem solving that occurs, more or less, outside the realm of intention (i.e., implicit problem solving). For both types of problem solving, we ask to what extent individual differences in problem-solving competence might be based on individual differences in intellectual ability.

Intellectual Ability

> What actually is an ability? That is partly an unanswerable question, or if there is an answer it has to be something unhelpful like, "It depends on the kind of ability concept that we happen to be using." (Howe, 1996, p. 41)

When we say about Aristotle that he possessed an outstanding reasoning ability, do we mean to state that he was a philosopher who could reason remarkably well, or are we proposing that his reasoning ability made him an outstanding philosopher? While we do not differentiate much between the descriptive and the explanatory use of the ability concept in our everyday life and language, in scientific contexts we need to do so in order to avoid circularity.

Our definition of an "intellectual ability" is strongly guided and constrained by two considerations. First, we focus on the explanatory, rather than descriptive, use of the concept. That is, when we use the term *intellectual ability*, we are referring to a concept that potentially explains problem-solving behavior and success. The adoption of the explanatory meaning of "intellectual ability" has strong implications for the assumed properties of the concept. We strongly believe that an explanatory concept of "intellectual ability" makes sense only if it is assumed that intellectual abilities (a) support performance on a wide variety of tasks and task domains, (b) are possessed by most if not all people, albeit to varying degrees, and (c) are relatively stable over time. We therefore tentatively define "intellectual ability" as a cognitive disposition that affects performance on a wide variety of tasks, is not modifiable by experience, and is possessed by all persons.

The second consideration influencing our understanding of "intellectual ability" is that we are taking the perspective of cognitive psychology when discussing the relation between intellectual ability and problem-solving competence. Thus, we do not consider possible biological, physiological, or neurological interpretations of "intellectual ability." We also do not consider sociological, behavior-genetic, or cultural attempts to qualify the nature of intellectual ability.

What does it mean, then, to take the perspective of cognitive psychology when defining the term *intellectual ability*? *Cognitive psychology* may be defined as "a general approach to psychology emphasizing the internal, mental processes. To the cognitive psychologist behavior is not specifiable simply in terms of its overt properties but requires explanations at the level of mental events, mental representations, beliefs, intentions, etc." (Reber, 1995, p. 135). Thus, by asking what an *intellectual ability* might be, we are asking which mental processes and/or representations or which properties of mental processes and/or representations might be ultimately responsible for problem-solving behavior. Consequently, in the remainder of this chapter the term *intellectual ability* is used to refer to "basic cognitive faculties, processes, and mechanisms that differ in degree among persons, affect performance on a wide variety of tasks, and are not modifiable by experience."

The reader should note that this definition does not necessitate that an intellectual ability be a concept that is semantically wider than the concept it potentially explains, namely, problem-solving competence. Although general intelligence and its various subfactors identified and measured in many contemporary intelligence tests (e.g., Wechsler Adult Intelligence Scale, WAIS; Wechsler, 1982) are perhaps prototypical examples of intellectual abilities in the sense of cognitive faculties, other much narrower concepts qualify also. To provide an example: Some cognitive psychologists have argued that the capacity of working memory is relatively constant (over time and demands) in a person but differs among persons. Thus, it is at least conceivable that better problem solvers might differ from not-so-great problem solvers primarily in terms of their working-memory capacity. In other words, working-memory capacity is one of many possible intellectual abilities that might explain problem-solving behavior and success.

The reader should also note that our definition of "intellectual ability" is meant to exclude (a) knowledge per se, although forms and processes of knowledge acquisition, organization, and application might qualify as intellectual abilities; (b) purely peripheral processes (e.g., motor programs); (c) motivational factors (e.g., self efficacy); and (d) biological/neurological substrates possibly underlying problem-solving behavior. Note also that our definition of intellectual ability is not restricted to intentionally applied processes, strategies, and the like. Rather, we consider all information-processing characteristics of the cognitive system as potential intellectual abilities. In this regard, we differ from Jensen, who defines "mental abilities" as "some particular, conscious, voluntary behavioral act that can be assessed as meeting (or failing to meet) some clearly defined standard" (Jensen & Weng, 1994, p. 236).

Evaluation Criteria

In keeping with our focus on the explanatory aspect of intellectual ability, we strongly believe that any theoretical and/or empirical approach arguing for a relation between intellectual ability and problem-solving competence must meet a number of criteria in order to be taken seriously. Below, we describe three criteria that we use to assess and evaluate the various approaches considered. We argue that each of the three criteria must be met before it can truly be maintained that any particular intellectual ability affects problem-solving competence.

CRITERION 1. *Both the intellectual ability presumably underlying problem-solving competence and problem-solving competence itself need to be explicitly defined and must not overlap at theoretical and/or operational levels.* At a theoretical level, this criterion implies that both intellectual ability and problem-solving competence need to be defined explicitly and, more important, independently of each other. If the latter is not the case, then any attempt to explain problem-solving competence in terms of an underlying intellectual ability is necessarily circular and redundant. At the operational level, Criterion 1 implies that independent and reliable measures need to be used to assess the respective constructs. When overlapping measures (e.g., items that appear on a questionnaire used to measure intellectual ability also appear on a questionnaire used to measure problem-solving competence) are used, then empirically observed correlations may reflect methodological artifacts rather than theoretically relevant relations.

CRITERION 2. *The presumed relation between intellectual ability and problem-solving competence must have a theoretical explanation.* This criterion demands that some theory or model exists that specifies the proposed relation between complex problem-solving competence and the hypothesized intellectual ability. Without an understanding of the theoretical foundation linking the two concepts, no explanation of problem-solving competence is acceptable.

CRITERION 3. *The direction of the presumed causality must be demonstrated empirically.* As noted earlier, we understand and use the term *intellectual ability* in its explanatory sense. After all, the scientifically interesting question is whether there exist intellectual abilities that cause better or worse problem-solving competence. Because a direct experimental manipulation of degree of intellectual ability is not feasible, indirect assessments of the direction of causality are required. Acceptable approaches are (a) to use longitudinal research designs and (b) to experimentally manipulate the use of particular abilities by varying either instructions or task properties, whereby potential third variables that possibly modulate empirically observed relations are controlled for.

Of course, criteria other than those described above are both thinkable and plausible. We believe nevertheless that the mentioned criteria are quite useful for evaluating the approaches discussed in this chapter.

In the next section we discuss theoretical ideas and empirical research that are relevant for exploring the relation between explicit, intention-driven, problem-solving competence for complex problems, on the one hand, and relatively stable and domain-general processing characteristics of the cognitive system, on the other hand.[1] In the third section we focus on intellectual abilities that potentially underlie implicit, that is, nonintentional problem solving.

INDIVIDUAL DIFFERENCES IN COMPLEX EXPLICIT PROBLEM SOLVING

Perhaps the most obvious intellectual ability potentially underlying complex explicit problem solving is general intelligence. In this part, we therefore review, first, some of the research – mostly European – on the relation between complex explicit problem solving (CEPS) and intellectual ability as, for example, assessed by traditional intelligence tests or specific subtests thereof. The assumption underlying this approach is, of course, that a

---

[1] This does not imply that we are searching for a unitary and "true" intellectual ability that might underlie all sorts and aspects of complex problem-solving competence. On the contrary, we agree with Hunt (1980), who noted with regard to explaining intelligence-test performance by underlying cognitive abilities that "the search for a 'true' single information-processing function underlying intelligence is as likely to be successful as the search for the Holy Grail" (Hunt, 1980, p. 457). Therefore, we sample from the intellectual abilities that have been proposed to be involved in complex problem solving and evaluate them according to the criteria described below.

person's IQ score reflects some more or less global and relatively stable intellectual ability that might potentially be associated with CEPS. With few exceptions, the tasks used to assess CEPS competence consist of dynamic scenarios presented on a computer, with the number of independent exogenous and interconnected endogenous variables ranging from 3 to about 2000. The scenarios are described to research participants with the more or less clearly specified goal being to optimize some aspects of the scenario's output.

CEPS and Global Intelligence

It is very common, even for psychologists, to assume that a person's intelligence is closely related to the person's ability to solve complex problems. The higher a person's intelligence, so the assumption, the better the person's problem-solving skills. (Beckmann & Guthke, 1995, p. 178).

It is perhaps surprising that empirical support for the popular belief described by Beckmann and Guthke (1995) is rather poor. Typically, the reported correlations are low or even zero, at least when the problem situation is not transparent and/or the goal to be achieved is poorly specified (for detailed reviews, see Kluwe, Misiak, & Haider, 1991, as well as Beckmann & Guthke, 1995). The probably best known study producing zero correlations has been conducted by Dörner and colleagues (1983) using the LOHHAUSEN system. Participants' task was to "take care of the future prosperity" of a small town called LOHHAUSEN over a simulated 10-year period. About 2000 variables were involved in this system (e.g., number of inhabitants and earnings of the industry). Participants had to derive subgoals for themselves, and interacted with the system through an experimenter. Problem-solving competence on this task did not correlate with the Raven's Advanced Progressive Matrices (APM; Raven, Court, & Raven, 1980) scores, nor did it correlate with scores on the Culture Fair Intelligence Test (CFT, Cattell & Weiss, 1980).

Results such as the ones described above have been interpreted and discussed quite controversially by different "camps" of researchers. One camp of researchers (e.g., Dörner & Kreuzig, 1983; Putz-Osterloh, 1983) has been arguing that zero correlations between problem-solving competence and general intelligence reflect the fact that traditional IQ measures tend to be ecologically less valid than CEPS measures. More specifically, these researchers claim that in dynamic scenarios (a) the goals are often ill specified, (b) information needs to be actively sought after, and (c) semantic/contextual embeddedness (i.e., a meaningful cover story) is almost always present, and that traditional intelligence tests do not measure the intellectual abilities (such as the so-called operative intelligence, Dörner,

1979) required for successful problem-solving performance in highly complex and ecologically valid environments.

According to a second camp of researchers (e.g., Funke, 1983, 1984; Kluwe et al., 1991), low correlations between IQ and CEPS are due to methodological and conceptual shortcomings. First, it has been pointed out (e.g., Kluwe et al., 1991) that it is impossible to derive valid indicators of problem-solving performance for tasks that are not formally tractable and thus do not possess a mathematically optimal solution. Indeed, when different dependent measures are used in studies using the same scenario (i.e., TAILORSHOP; e.g., Funke, 1983; Putz-Osterloh, 1981; Süß, Kersting, & Oberauer, 1991), then the conclusions frequently differ.

Second, the reliability of the performance indices may often be low (e.g., Funke, 1983, 1984; Kluwe et al., 1991). Few studies report reliabilities, and those reported are usually not very high (test-retest reliabilities ranging between .2 to .7, depending on the dependent variable used).[2] Other quite serious methodological criticisms concern the narrow sampling of IQ in most of the studies mentioned above (e.g., Funke, 1991), and the ecological validity of the scenarios.

However, the empirical picture is far more complicated and less clear than might have been suggested thus far. Although zero correlations between test intelligence and complex problem-solving competence are frequently obtained, this is not always the case. For example, Putz-Osterloh (1981; Putz-Osterloh & Lüer, 1981) has argued that the relation between global intelligence and complex problem-solving competence is mediated by the *transparency* of the problem-solving task. Like Dörner et al. (1983), Putz-Osterloh (1981) failed to find significant correlations between problem-solving competence and the Raven's APM in an intransparent experimental condition with the TAILORSHOP scenario, a scenario simulating a small company in which shirt production and sale had to be controlled by purchasing raw materials and modifying the production capacity in terms of number of workers and machines. Participants' goal was to maximize the company's profit, either under a transparent condition, in which they had access to a diagram depicting the relations between the system variables, or under an intransparent condition in which no diagram was shown.

However, Putz-Osterloh (1981, see also Putz-Osterloh & Lüer, 1981; Hörmann & Thomas, 1989) found a statistically reliable relation (Tau = .22) between IQ and problem-solving competence (operationalized by the number of months with increasing capital assets) in the transparent experimental condition (but see Funke, 1983, for different results).

---

[2] A remarkable exception is reported by Müller (1993). Müller used a mathematically defined abstract complex system consisting of "parallel" subsets with identical problem structure. Reliability estimates in his studies were about .9.

A different moderator variable affecting the link between global intelligence and complex problem-solving competence has been suggested by Strohschneider (1991). The author, using the MORO system in which participants are asked to improve the living conditions of nomads in the Sahel zone, manipulated the *specificity of the to-be-attained goals*. In the specific-goal condition, participants had to reach specified values on critical variables (e.g., number of cattle or number of inhabitants). In the unspecific-goal condition, the participants' task was to take actions that guarantee long-term improvements of the MORO living conditions.

Interestingly, in the unspecific-goal condition, problem-solving performance did not correlate with general intelligence as measured by the Berlin Intelligence Structure test[3] (BIS, Jäger, 1982), whereas substantial correlations (up to $r = -.59$) were found in the specific-goal condition.

Yet another variable affecting the relation between global intelligence and complex problem-solving ability may be the *semantic context* of a problem-solving task. Hesse (1982) investigated the impact of the semantic embeddedness of the problem-solving task on the relation between IQ and CEPS. In the semantic condition, participants were asked to solve the DORI problem, a computerized system involving ecological variables and relations. In the semantic-free condition, a system with an isomorphic problem structure but without the cover story and without meaningful variable names was presented to the participants. In addition, transparency was manipulated as in the Putz-Osterloh (1981) experiment described above. Hesse (1982) obtained moderate correlations between problem-solving performance and APM scores only in the semantic-free condition ($r = .38$ and $r = .46$ for the transparent and the intransparent condition, respectively).

On the whole, the empirical findings described above do not support a strong link between general intelligence and complex problem-solving competence when *goal specificity* and *transparency* are low and the *semantic content* is rich; the link appears to be somewhat stronger when the intelligence-testing conditions more closely resemble the problem-solving testing conditions. We agree with Kluwe et al. (1991) that, on the basis of the present results, it cannot be determined whether low correlations are due to invalid intelligence testing (i.e., their failure to assess real-world intellectual abilities necessary for dealing with complexity) or to a lack of reliability of the CEPS measures. The heterogeneity of the scenarios and IQ tests used further complicates the interpretation of the existing results.

---

[3] According to the BIS, operative factors, such as speed of processing, processing capacity/reasoning ability, creativity, and memory are distinguished with respect to verbal, numeral, and figural contents. The "g"-factor is determined as performance across tasks and contents.

Evaluation of Approach

CRITERION 1. *Both the intellectual ability presumably underlying problem-solving competence and problem-solving competence itself need to be explicitly defined and must not overlap at theoretical and/or operational levels.* Because independent tasks are typically used to assess problem-solving competence and intellectual ability, the measures do not overlap at an operational level. However, the fact that significant correlations between complex problem-solving competence and IQ are obtained when goal specificity is high and/or semantic embeddedness is missing suggests an overlap at the level of task requirements.

Even more disturbing is the fact that the potential theoretical overlap between intelligence and CEPS can be evaluated only on the basis of their respective definitions. Since neither CEPS nor intelligence seem to be particularly well defined, the obtained correlations may well be due to conceptual overlap. As Robert J. Sternberg has put it, "whatever intelligence may be, reasoning and problem solving have traditionally been viewed as important subsets of it" (Sternberg, 1982, p. 225). Thus, even when substantial correlations are obtained, there is good reason to believe that explaining CEPS in terms of intelligence may be circular because intelligence and problem-solving ability might be one and the same (cf. Howe, 1988).

CRITERION 2. *The presumed relation between intellectual ability and problem-solving competence must have a theoretical explanation.* Apart from general statements such as Sternberg's (1982), it is not obvious exactly how intelligence should contribute to CEPS. This is so because (a) to date, researchers have not agreed on the nature of intelligence (see, e.g., Kray & Frensch, 2002, for an overview of different accounts of the nature of "g"), and (b) no models exist that theoretically link intelligence to specific aspects of problem-solving behavior. The latter problem probably partly stems from the difficulty to define an objective problem space for mathematically intractable scenarios.

CRITERION 3. *The direction of the presumed causality must be demonstrated empirically.* To our knowledge, no longitudinal or training designs have been used to assess the direction of causality. Some empirical studies have manipulated task properties such as transparency, but only Funke (1983) used a between-group design (sampling from the extremes of the IQ distribution). Furthermore, it is questionable whether potential moderator variables have been adequately controlled for. For instance, when both semantic embeddedness and transparency are varied, as was the case in the study by Hesse (1982), then transparency does not affect problem-solving performance in the semantic-free condition. Hence, the direction of causality (if any exists) remains unclear.

To summarize, correlating global IQ scores with complex problem-solving performance does not seem to be particularly useful if the goal is to understand the role of intellectual ability in complex problem-solving competence. Our main concern with this approach relates to a lack of theoretical explanation. In the next part, we review research that goes beyond correlating global IQ with CEPS performance in that it singles out individual components of intelligence that may affect problem-solving competence.

CEPS and Specific Intelligence Components

In the research reviewed below, either IQ subtests such as the ones that are inherent in the BIS or learning-test scores have been correlated with complex problem-solving performance.

Süß et al. (1991; see also Hussy, 1991), for example, had problem solvers work on an intransparent version of the TAILORSHOP. The authors hypothesized that in order to successfully control this system, problem solvers need to infer the relations among critical variables and to deduce meaningful goals and actions. Therefore, reasoning ability, as assessed by the *BIS-factor K* (processing capacity, capturing the ability to recognize relations and rules and to form logical inferences in figure series, number series, and verbal analogies) should be the single most predictive ability of problem-solving ability. This is indeed what the authors found. Overall problem-solving performance correlated substantially with K ($r = .47$). In addition, *knowledge* (specific system knowledge as well as general economic knowledge) was found to be an important predictor of problem solving.

Similar findings have been reported by Hörmann and Thomas (1989), who administered the TAILORSHOP under two different transparency conditions. When problem solvers' system knowledge, as assessed by a questionnaire, was high, then the *K-factor* ($r = .72$) and the *G-factor* (indicating memory performance, $r = .54$) correlated with CEPS performance in the intransparent condition, whereas the *B-factor* (processing speed) was the best predictor in the transparent condition. However, when system knowledge was not considered, then significant correlations emerged only in the transparent condition.

Hussy (1989), on the other hand, found the *K-factor* to be the single most predictive operative factor, regardless of transparency condition and system knowledge. However, the scenario used by Hussy was the LUNAR LANDER, a mathematically well-defined system with only six variables and a very specific goal, which makes it difficult to compare this study directly to those using the TAILORSHOP. Nevertheless, it is interesting to note that Hussy (1989) also found the *G-factor* (memory) to be significantly correlated with problem-solving performance in the intransparent condition. This finding is similar to that of Hörmann and Thomas (1989) and points to the possibility that intransparent problems may pose particularly high memory demands when problem solvers attempt to develop internal models of the task (cf. Buchner, 1995).

In general, these results appear to be inconsistent with Strohschneider's (1991, see previous section) finding of high correlations between almost all BIS-operative factors and problem-solving performance in the specific-goal condition of the MORO system. But then again, Strohschneider's study differs substantially in terms of task demands, such as system complexity and operationalization of goal specificity, from the studies above, making direct comparisons difficult.

A different "componential" approach has been taken by Beckmann (1995; for a comprehensive overview, see Beckmann & Guthke, 1995). Beckmann and colleagues argue that successful problem-solving performance involves the *ability to learn from success and failure*. They therefore use learning tests[4] (e.g., Guthke, 1992) that assess problem solvers' learning potential, in addition to the reasoning subtests of traditional intelligence tests (Intelligence Structure Test, IST; Amthauer, Brocke, Liepmann, & Beauducel, 1973; and Learning Test Battery "Reasoning," LTS 3, Guthke, Jäger, & Schmidt, 1983) to predict problem-solving performance and knowledge acquisition. Diagrams for which the relevant relations have to be filled in assess the latter. The authors' six-variable system is based on a linear equation system, and was administered in either an abstract "machine" version or in a semantically meaningful version (CHERRYTREE, for which water supply, warmth, etc. had to be manipulated in order to control the growth of cherries, leaves, and beetles).

In the abstract version, problem solvers acquired substantial system knowledge, and learning-test scores correlated substantially with the system knowledge measure as well as with problem-solving performance measures, whereas traditional intelligence subtest scores correlated (albeit to a smaller degree) only with problem-solving performance. In contrast, in the CHERRYTREE version, problem solvers did not demonstrate system knowledge, nor did test scores (regardless of type) correlate with problem-solving performance (see also Hesse, 1982). It is interesting that the two experimental groups (i.e., abstract version vs. CHERRYTREE) did not differ in terms of the quality of their problem solving-performance, that is, in their control of the system. This and similar results have led several researchers (e.g., Berry & Broadbent, 1984) to propose different modes of learning and of problem solving. (We return to this issue in the third section when we discuss implicit problem solving.)

To summarize, when specific intelligence components are correlated with problem-solving performance in complex systems and when goals are specified, then moderate to substantial correlations are obtained, even under intransparent task conditions. The most important intelligence

---

[4] The tradition of using learning tests is based on Vygotzky's concept of the proximal zone of development and holds that problem solvers' intellectual abilities mainly show under conditions where they are required to learn from feedback, prompts, and the like.

components predicting problem-solving competence appear to be *processing capacity/reasoning ability* and *learning potential. Semantic content* appears to be an important mediator of the relation between abilities and CEPS (e.g., Hesse, 1982), implying that the content may activate prior knowledge and affect the problem representation. Furthermore, inconsistent results have been obtained regarding the relation between *system knowledge* (i.e., knowledge about the relations among variables) and problem-solving performance.

Evaluation of Approach

CRITERION 1. *Both the intellectual ability presumably underlying problem-solving competence and problem-solving competence itself need to be explicitly defined and must not overlap at theoretical and/or operational levels.* Regarding operational overlap, much the same can be said as in the previous section. There is little reason to expect much overlap at the operational level, although task requirements may overlap to some extent. Concerning theoretical overlap, the situation is even more satisfying. Learning and reasoning are better defined than is global intelligence, and the overlap between the theoretical concepts appears to be low.

CRITERION 2. *The presumed relation between intellectual ability and problem-solving competence must have a theoretical explanation.* Although interesting with regard to hypothesis generation, the approach discussed above suffers from a lack of theoretical explanation. Demonstrating that a person possesses reasoning ability, for instance, does not tell us much about the specific reasoning processes and representations that may be required for successful problem solving. Thus, the theoretical foundation of the link between the proposed ability and problem-solving performance remains rather unclear at the level of mechanisms. A closer task analysis (plus the use of mathematically tractable tasks) as well as a more systematic variation of task properties may be needed in order to better understand how specific intelligence components might be related to complex problem-solving competence.

CRITERION 3. *The direction of the presumed causality must be demonstrated empirically.* Largely the same conclusions can be drawn regarding this criterion as in the first part of the present section. In our view, a causal link between intellectual ability and specific intelligence components has not been demonstrated within this line of research. In fact, there has not even been an attempt to do so.

Taken together, the approach of correlating specific intelligence components with CEPS performance is theoretically much more interesting than correlating CEPS performance with global IQ. However, to theoretically understand CEPS in terms of the underlying intellectual abilities, we need (a) more detailed models of knowledge acquisition processes in CEPS situations, (b) more detailed theoretical accounts of the links between the proposed abilities and CEPS performance, as well as (c) research designs that allow inferences about the direction of causality.

Global Intelligence and Expertise

Instead of assessing complex problem-solving competence with the aid of computerized systems, researchers have also explored the relation between intellectual ability and problem-solving competence in a more natural context, namely, by correlating global intelligence with expertise. Arguably the best-known work in this regard has been performed by Steve Ceci and his colleagues (e.g., Ceci & Liker, 1986a, 1986b; Ceci & Ruiz, 1992, 1993), who claim that expertise is unrelated to global IQ. Ceci and Liker (1986a, 1986b), for instance, compared experts and novices in terms of their ability to handicap races and in the *cognitive complexity* underlying their handicapping performance. Furthermore, the relation between expertise and IQ, as measured by the WAIS, as well as between cognitive complexity and IQ was examined.

Experts differed from novices in terms of their ability to correctly predict posttime odds for the top three horses in 10 actual races on the basis of a priori factual information about the horses, although the two groups were comparable in terms of their factual knowledge about races (as assessed by a screening questionnaire), years of track experience, years of education, and, most important, IQ. That is, both groups contained high-IQ as well as low-IQ individuals.

Experts as well as novices subsequently handicapped 50 experimentally contrived races, in which an "experimental" horse had to be compared with a "standard" horse. For the former, values on potentially important variables (such as lifetime speed, claiming price, and trace surface condition) were systematically varied.[5] To model how experts and novices arrived at their odds predictions, Ceci and Liker used multiple-regression analyses.

The results of the study can be summarized as follows: First, the modeling results showed that a simple additive model was not sufficient to predict performance, at least not for experts. Rather, quite complicated interactive terms needed to be included. Second, experts gave more weight to higher-order interactions than did novices, suggesting a higher degree of cognitive complexity in their reasoning. Third, the weight of the

---

[5] Thus, the task used here differs from the dynamic-systems approach in that (a) the task or "system" is not dynamic (i.e., problem solvers predict posttime odds at a trial-to-trial basis), and (b) all variables are endogenous (i.e., cannot be altered by problem solvers' inputs). However, the two approaches also share certain commonalities. For example, both types of task contain a large number of highly interconnected variables and a high level of intransparency. That is, problem solvers need to find out which variables are important and what kinds of relations hold among them in order to derive meaningful action plans. Furthermore, both are typically semantically rich.

higher-order interactions correlated highly with handicapping ability, but did not correlate with IQ. The latter finding is particularly important because it suggests that global intelligence is unrelated to cognitive complexity in real-life complex problem solving such as handicapping races.

Interestingly, similar results have been obtained in very different areas of expertise. For example, in their recent work on practical intelligence (i.e., situational-judgment tests that present work-based problems for participants to solve), Sternberg and colleagues have repeatedly found no correlations between performance and IQ. In their most recent article, Sternberg et al. (2001) describe work that was done with 85 children between the ages of 12 and 15 in a rural village in western Kenya. The main dependent variable of interest was children's scores on a test of tacit knowledge for natural herbal medicines used to fight illnesses. Sternberg et al. found that scores on the tacit knowledge correlated trivially or even significantly negatively with measures of IQ and achievement, even after controlling for socioeconomic status.

Even if it is true that global intelligence is not related to expertise, it might still be related to the acquisition of expertise, however. To explore the latter possibility, Ceci and Ruiz (1992, 1993) conducted a follow-up case study in which they investigated the acquisition of expertise on a novel task of two race-handicapping experts with different IQ levels. The new task was constructed such that it had the same underlying "problem structure" as the race-handicapping task. That is, the authors constructed a "stock market game" that included just as many variables as were included in the handicapping task. In the new task, an experimental stock had to be compared with a standard stock. The two handicapping experts were asked to decide which of the two stocks would yield a better future price-earnings ratio. Experimental trials were constructed such that the equation modeling handicapping performance held for a subset of the stock market variables.

The results of this study showed that the two experts did not spontaneously transfer the "handicapping" rule to the new task before they were informed that the task-relevant variables could be weighed and combined in the same manner as they had done in predicting posttime odds. After receiving this hint, performance increased considerably for both experts. Modeling indicated that the experts had not developed a model as complex as the equation they used for handicapping. Rather, they appeared to work with models containing only lower-order interactions. Consequently, performance never reached impressive levels, although both experts managed to perform above chance. Most important, the high- and low-IQ experts differed neither in their performance nor in terms of the cognitive complexity they brought to bear on the new task.

Ceci and colleagues interpret their results as indicating (a) that intelligence always manifests itself as an interaction between underlying intellectual abilities and experience in particular domains, and is therefore context/content dependent, (b) that multiple intelligences exist, and (c) that IQ tests measure only a specific type of intelligence, namely, one developed in academic settings.

The Ceci studies have not remained without criticism. Detterman and Spry (1988; see also Ceci & Liker, 1988, for a reply), for instance, argued that sampling procedure, sample size, and questionable reliabilities (but see Ceci & Liker, 1988) might have led to an underestimation of the "true" correlations. Ceci and Ruiz (1993) themselves made the point that the difficulty of the novel task might have prevented transfer from occurring.

Regardless of the validity of the criticisms, it is important to acknowledge that the Ceci and Liker and Ceci and Ruiz studies are two of the very few studies that have related global intelligence to expertise and to the acquisition of problem-solving competence. The empirical result is both consistent with the European research reviewed earlier and intriguing: IQ does not seem to predict expertise (i.e., complex problem-solving competence) nor does it predict the acquisition of complex problem-solving competence.

Evaluation of Approach

CRITERION 1. *Both the intellectual ability presumably underlying problem-solving competence and problem-solving competence itself need to be explicitly defined and must not overlap at theoretical and/or operational levels.* Except for possibly similar task demands, no overlap appears to exist at the operational level. That is, the measures used to assess level of expertise and global intelligence differ. In addition, the reliability of the prediction performance scores may be better than has been pointed out by critics (e.g., Detterman & Spry, 1988). First, we agree with Ceci and Liker (1988) in that it makes sense to assess reliability for the sample as a whole for which the authors report a Kuder-Richardson reliability of $KR_{20} = .88$. Second, the prediction scores on the diagnostic 10 real races correlated substantially with the complexity indicators determined via modeling.

The argument Ceci and colleagues are pushing is that global intelligence and expert problem-solving competence do not overlap theoretically. As for separately defining expertise and global intelligence, some effort has been made to define critical (cognitive) characteristics of expertise. The problem concerning the nature of "g" discussed in the first part of the present section remains unsolved, however.

CRITERION 2. *The presumed relation between intellectual ability and problem-solving competence must have a theoretical explanation.* While an overall correlation between global intelligence and expertise was not expected, Ceci and Liker (1986a) state that "each of us possesses innate potentialities for achievement in abstract reasoning, verbal analysis, creative expression, quantification, visual-spatial organization, and so on" (Ceci & Liker, 1986a,

p. 139) that are funneled into specific expressions of intelligence according to experience and motivation. Thus, a more stringent test of the existence of independent context-specific manifestations of intelligence would have been to correlate prediction performance/complexity with (IQ) subtest scores. For example, it would be interesting to see whether or not people with different learning test scores differ regarding learning and transfer on the stock market task.

CRITERION 3. *The direction of the presumed causality must be demonstrated empirically.* Because a number of potential moderator variables, such as age, years of experience, and preexisting knowledge have been taken into account, the Ceci and Ruiz training study can be considered a first step in demonstrating the lack of a causal relation between IQ and the acquisition of complex problem solving. Of course, methodological shortcomings such as small sample size and possible floor effects regarding learning and problem-solving performance demand replication of the study. Moreover, the empirically demonstrated lack of a global IQ effect does not tell us much about (a) whether more specific abilities would have had predictive value, or (b) how much overlap in content is required for two "ability measures" to be correlated.

Taken together, Ceci and colleagues have undertaken an impressive attempt to demonstrate that expertise, defined as people's ability to reason complexly in one domain (i.e., race handicapping), is independent of general intelligence. Expertise has been relatively clearly defined, and an attempt has been made to study the cognitive processes involved in successful performance by careful task analysis. Moreover, the training study is the first attempt at assessing causality. However, as has been amply discussed above, correlating global intelligence with CEPS is not particularly informative as to the exact nature of the intellectual abilities underlying problem solving.

Task and Subject Properties Affecting Complex Explicit Problem Solving

In light of the fact that all empirical attempts to causally relate intellectual abilities (i.e., global intelligence and specific subcomponents of intelligence) to complex problem-solving competence can be said to have failed or produced null results, it seems only natural that researchers would turn to a research question that more directly asks which abilities might underlie CEPS. That is, instead of correlating all conceivable intellectual abilities with complex problem-solving competence, a more fruitful approach might be to directly examine which ability may be needed to successfully solve complex problems. This is the approach we turn to next.

Researchers interested in this approach often use mathematically well-defined problems for which optimal interventions can be specified that can be compared with the interventions selected by problem solvers. The general strategy relies on careful task analyses and tests hypotheses about the intellectual processes and knowledge that are required for successful problem solving by (a) systematically varying system variables and / or task instructions, and (b) assessing system knowledge separately from problem-solving performance. The specific processes and knowledge identified as required for successful problem solving then, in a second step – such at least is the idea – can be tied to intellectual abilities.

The general methodological approach has been to let participants explore some unknown system for a number of "trials" first, then to assess their structural knowledge by means of a causal diagram analysis, and subsequently to have them steer the system toward a specified target state (i.e., have them control the system).

Semantic Embeddedness

Funke (1992a, 1992b) showed that semantic context can activate existing knowledge and lead to a specification of model parameters before learning even starts. The author used an eight-variable dynamic ecological linear equation system that was developed on the basis of expert knowledge. The relations among the system variables largely corresponded to problem solvers' a priori beliefs about the domain, as was demonstrated in a pilot study, in which participants were asked to draw causal diagrams without having interacted with the system. In the experiment, half of the participants controlled the original system, whereas for the other half the signs of two of the relations were reversed. This rather subtle modification had detrimental effects on both system knowledge and problem-solving performance. Regarding problem-solving performance, Funke's results appear to differ from Beckmann's (1995), discussed above. Beckmann found in the semantic (CHERRYTREE) condition (a) that problem solvers did not tap into relevant prior system knowledge (as assessed by a diagram analysis before interacting with the system), but (b) that problem-solving performance was unaffected by the lack of an appropriate model.

Time Lag and Feedback Delay

A number of studies has been conducted that explore the effects of delayed feedback and time-lagged effects of inputs on problem-solving performance. The general picture that emerges from this research seems to be that feedback delay negatively affects structural knowledge as well as problem-solving performance. For example, Brehmer and Allard (1991; for a recent review on Brehmer's work on feedback delay, see Brehmer, 1995), using a rather complex FIRE FIGHTING[6] scenario, found that feedback

---

[6] In the fire-fighting scenario, fire-fighting units must be deployed in a way that allows minimizing the number and the impact of unpredictably emerging fires.

delay (reporting back of the fire fighting units) had a disastrous effect on problem-solving performance: Virtually no improvement took place during problem solving.

Likewise, Dörner and Preussler (1990), using a very simple predator-prey system, found a negative effect of feedback delay on problem-solving performance. Funke (1985), using a six-variable ecological system, demonstrated a negative effect of time delay on structural knowledge, suggesting that problem solvers do not develop any truly predictive model of the system under delay conditions. It is surprising, however, that in the Funke (1985) study, problem-solving performance was not affected as much as was structural knowledge by feedback delay. Clearly, more work is needed regarding the effects of feedback delay on structural knowledge and problem-solving performance before valid statements can be inferred.

Intervention vs. Observation

Funke and Müller (1988) hypothesized that active interaction with a system should be an important determinant of structural knowledge acquisition and problem-solving performance because only active exploration allows problem solvers to systematically test specific assumptions about the system. In their experiment, the authors manipulated whether participants were allowed to actively explore the SINUS system (a foreign planet linear equation system containing semantic-free variable names) in the learning phase, or had to simply observe the exploration behavior of an "experimental twin." The second (orthogonal) manipulation required half of the participants to predict the next system state after each input. Funke and Müller expected that prediction should lead to better models, and thus to better problem-solving performance.

The path-analytic results only partially confirmed the hypotheses. Active intervention was a significant predictor of problem-solving performance but affected system knowledge negatively (see Berry, 1991, for a similar dissociation). System knowledge, in addition, was a good predictor of problem-solving performance, but in the path analysis, prediction of the next system state had an unexpected negative effect on the quality of system knowledge. It is possible that this latter negative effect was an artifact of the path analysis, however, because the means for predictors' and nonpredictors' quality of knowledge scores were in the right direction (see Funke, 1993). It is interesting that neither the quality of knowledge nor the problem-solving performance of experimental twins who "saw" the same problem states and transitions during the learning phase were correlated, indicating a high degree of interindividual variability.

The impact of other system variables, such as the number of side effects, autonomous growth or decline, connectivity of variables, and presentation format (analog vs. numerical), has also been studied. On the whole, studies manipulating task characteristics and assessing structural knowledge independently from problem-solving performance show (a) that the quality of mental models of the task seems to affect problem-solving performance, and (b) that subtle changes of task demands can affect knowledge acquisition and problem-solving performance, whereby effects on system knowledge do not always accompany effects on problem-solving performance and vice versa. This suggests that the quality of structural knowledge may not be the only determinant of problem-solving performance.

Strategies

Vollmeyer, Burns, and Holyoak (1996) argue that rule induction in the context of complex problem solving is much like scientific reasoning. Based on Klahr and Dunbar's (1988; Simon & Lea, 1974) model of scientific reasoning and hypothesis testing, the authors reason that in order to acquire structural knowledge in complex problem solving, problem solvers need to search through two distinct problem spaces, namely, a hypothesis space (rule space) and an experiment space (instance space). The latter contains instances of encountered states and transitions as well as states predicted by particular hypotheses. The search through instance space involves directly comparing a given state to a goal state. The search through hypothesis space, on the other hand, consists of generating and modifying hypotheses about the structure of the system. These hypotheses and rules cannot be tested directly against a goal state, however. Instead, hypotheses testing requires problem solvers to internally set up "experiments" that generate states in instance space. Setting up clever experiments, in turn, requires the strategic ability to systematically vary system inputs.

Vollmeyer et al. (1996, first experiment) hypothesized that the strategies problem solvers adopt during the exploration phase (involving an eight-variable linear equation system simulating a BIOLOGY LAB with various water quality variables influencing the reproduction of different sea animals) should determine how much structural knowledge (again assessed by causal diagram analysis) is acquired, which in turn should affect problem-solving performance in the second phase of the experiment. Problem solvers' exploration strategies were classified according to their systematicity. More systematic strategies (such as varying one variable value at a time while holding the other constant) were assumed to lead to better knowledge and performance than more unsystematic hypothesis testing. As expected, Vollmeyer et al. found a significant effect of strategy systematicity on structural knowledge and on problem-solving performance, the latter effect being somewhat smaller (for comparable results, see Putz-Osterloh, 1993). Moreover, structural knowledge was correlated with problem-solving performance. On the whole, these results suggest that the use of efficient hypothesis-testing strategies is indeed a requirement for the acquisition of structural knowledge.

Fritz and Funke (1988) compared pupils with minimal cerebral dysfunctions (MCD) and matched controls in terms of their problem-solving
performance on a six-variable ecosystem scenario. MCD subjects and controls differed markedly in terms of the systematicity of the strategy they
employed. Surprisingly, however, the two groups did not differ with regard to the resulting structural knowledge, nor did they differ in terms of
their problem-solving success.

On the whole, the attempt to better understand the relation between intellectual ability and problem-solving competence by systematically varying task and subject characteristics has been quite successful in unearthing
a whole variety of variables that affect problem-solving competence. However, thus far, these variables have not been linked to underlying intellectual abilities at all nor has it been possible to discover specific intellectual
abilities that might explain the obtained empirical relations.

Evaluation of Approach

CRITERION 1. *Both the intellectual ability presumably underlying problem-
solving competence and problem-solving competence itself need to be explicitly
defined and must not overlap at theoretical and/or operational levels.* In most
studies, causal diagram analysis has been used to assess the acquisition of
structural knowledge in the exploration phase, whereas problem-solving
performance has been defined in terms of a deviation from a specified goal
state in the system control phase. One might argue that these measures
are reasonably independent, as are the various other measures employed.
Also, in the Vollmeyer et al. (1996) study, strategies have been operationalized independently of structural knowledge and performance measures.
As for the theoretical overlap, one may object that it is a truism that one
needs structural knowledge in order to control a complex system. However, given the dissociations between the quality of structural knowledge
and problem-solving performance in some studies (e.g., Beckmann, 1995;
Funke & Müller, 1988; also see next section), we believe that it is an empirical question worthy of pursuing.

It is somewhat disappointing that none of the studies reviewed in this
section reports any reliabilities. Thus, we have some concerns regarding the
reliability and validity of structural knowledge assessment, particularly for
semantically rich problems. As has been pointed out by Funke (1991; see
also Shanks & St. John, 1994), it may well be that problem solvers apply or
develop "incorrect" models that can nevertheless be useful for successful
problem solving within a restricted range of values.

CRITERION 2. *The presumed relation between intellectual ability and problem-
solving competence must have a theoretical explanation.* Funke's approach is to
derive hypotheses about mental representations on the basis of formal task
analyses. As Buchner (1995) has argued, this approach is very similar to
early experimental work on deductive reasoning that rested heavily on

the assumption that human deductive reasoning could best be described and explained in close analogy to formal logic. While such an approach demonstrates that system knowledge is a predictor of problem-solving performance, and helps us to understand how certain task characteristics constrain the process of knowledge acquisition, it does not tell us much about the underlying abilities leading to adequate structural knowledge and successful problem solving. As already mentioned earlier, knowledge by itself is not an intellectual ability.

Things are somewhat different with regard to Vollmeyer's approach, however. In our view, Vollmeyer et al. (1996) were indeed able to identify intellectual abilities involved in acquiring mental models of a task. It would be interesting to see whether problem solvers who differ in terms of certain cognitive characteristics (e.g., working memory capacity or learning ability) would also be able to learn and use systematic strategies to different degrees (see Fritz & Funke, 1988, for a promising start on this particular line of research).

CRITERION 3. *The direction of the presumed causality must be demonstrated empirically.* The only causal influence that has been demonstrated thus far is the link from task characteristics to structural knowledge. This assertion holds also for the Vollmeyer et al. study (but see their Experiment 2, next section), in which strategies have been identified in a post hoc manner. To demonstrate a causal influence, experimental manipulation of strategy use would be necessary, possibly in combination with between-group comparisons and training.

IMPLICIT PROBLEM SOLVING

Some findings in the domains of artificial grammar learning, sequence learning, and complex problem solving suggest that people acquire knowledge that allows them to successfully solve problems, although they are not able to express their knowledge. Such findings have led some researchers (e.g., Berry & Broadbent, 1984, 1987; Nissen & Bullemer, 1987; Reber, 1967, 1969) to propose independent learning systems, namely, explicit and implicit learning. The former is thought to be based on deliberate hypothesis testing, is selective with respect to what is being learned, and leads to consciously accessible and verbalizable knowledge. Implicit learning,[7] on the other hand, has been characterized as involving "the unselective and passive aggregation of information about the co-occurrence of environmental events and features" (Hayes & Broadbent, 1988, p. 251). Thus, it has been assumed that implicit learning takes place irrespective of the intention to learn, does not rely on hypothesis testing, and leads to implicit (tacit)

[7] This is only one characterization of implicit learning. For a collection of definitions, see, e.g., Frensch (1998).

knowledge that cannot or can be only partially accessed. Furthermore, it has been argued (Reber, Walkenfield, & Hernstadt, 1991; see also Anderson, 1998) that implicit learning shows less interindividual variability because it is an evolutionary older, less variable, and more robust ability.

In this section, we review empirical findings concerning the existence and the potential characteristics of such an implicit learning ability in the domain of complex problem solving. To this end, we first describe the tasks that are typically used in this type of research. We then highlight some of the results that have initially led researchers to propose two differing learning mechanisms, as well as research that relates implicit learning to intellectual ability. Next, we turn to results that question the original assumptions, and discuss alternative accounts of the main findings. Finally, we consider factors that might mediate the acquisition of different (e.g., explicit and implicit) types of knowledge.

The Tasks

The dynamic system most often used in the studies reported below consists of a simple linear equation relating one input variable to an output variable, also taking into account the previous output. In addition, in most studies a random component is added on two thirds of the trials, such that on these trials the system changes to a state one unit above or below the state that would be correct according to the deterministic equation. The system is frequently used in one or both of two semantic versions: the SUGAR FACTORY and the COMPUTER PERSON. When controlling the SUGAR FACTORY, problem solvers are required to reach and maintain specified levels of sugar output by varying the number of workers employed. In case of the COMPUTER PERSON, problem solvers enter attitude adjectives (e.g., "friendly" or "polite") from a fixed adjective set in order to get the computer person to display a specified behavior (e.g., "very friendly").

A second frequently used task is the CITY TRANSPORTATION system. This task is similar to the linear equation systems described in the previous section in that two variables (free parking slots and number of people taking the bus) need to be adjusted by varying two exogenous variables (time schedule for buses and parking fee). In the majority of studies problem solvers are asked to control the system from the beginning (i.e., there is no exploration phase). In addition, instructions and/or system features are varied. After controlling the system for a while, problem solvers are probed for their structural knowledge. This is usually done with the help of multiple-choice questionnaires that require problem solvers to predict outcomes, given a specified previous output and novel input. The experimental approach thus differs from the standard procedure of the studies discussed in the previous section in that (a) the systems are usually less complex in terms of the underlying variables and relations, (b) problem solvers are typically not allowed to explore the system before they are asked to reach specified target values, and (c) problem solvers are usually not probed for their structural knowledge before they have completed the experiment.

Empirical Evidence

Empirical evidence supporting the existence of two independent learning systems mainly comes from two types of dissociations, namely, (a) dissociations between problem-solving performance and questionnaire answers, and (b) differential effects on problem-solving performance when systems are controlled that are assumed to engage the different learning systems.

For instance, Berry and Broadbent (1984), using both the SUGAR FACTORY and the COMPUTER PERSON task, found that problem-solving performance improved with practice (two vs. one block of practice), but that structural knowledge was unaffected. Furthermore, correlations between problem-solving performance and knowledge tended to be negative. In contrast, informing problem solvers about the principles of the system after the first practice block improved structural knowledge but did not affect performance. Again, no positive correlations between problem-solving performance and knowledge emerged.

Berry and Broadbent (1987, 1988) demonstrated that this type of dissociation critically depends on the *salience* of the relations among variables. In their 1988 study, salience was manipulated by varying feedback delay in the COMPUTER PERSON task. In the salient version, the output depended on the input of the current trial. In contrast, in the nonsalient version, the output was determined by the problem solver's input on the preceding trial. Berry and Broadbent assumed that nonsalient tasks would induce implicit learning, whereas the easier salient task would be learned explicitly. The authors reported that performance improved with practice for both task versions, although performance on the salient task was generally better than on the nonsalient task. More interesting is that instructions to search for systematic relations between variables improved performance for the group working on the salient task, but impaired performance in the nonsalient group. Moreover, structural knowledge scores were higher in the salient group than in the nonsalient group, and correlations between knowledge and problem-solving performance tended to be somewhat higher in the salient group (yet none of the correlations reached significance).

The nature of the underlying relations also seems to affect the ability to transfer knowledge to novel situations (Berry & Broadbent, 1988; Hayes & Broadbent, 1988). Hayes and Broadbent found that a change of the equation after an initial learning phase impaired problem-solving performance in the nonsalient condition of the COMPUTER PERSON, but not in the salient condition. More dramatic, however, is that this pattern of results reversed when problem solvers worked under dual-task conditions (i.e., when they performed a concurrent random-letter generation task). That is, when a secondary task had to be performed concurrently, relearning was impaired in the salient, but not in the nonsalient condition. Based on these and similar results, Berry and Broadbent concluded that two independent learning systems exist, and that the unselective and unintentional implicit-learning mechanism is particularly well suited to dealing with highly complex situations in which deliberate hypothesis testing has little chance to be successful.

Implicit Learning and Intellectual Ability

If indeed an unintentional implicit-learning mechanism exists that might affect complex problem-solving performance, then it is at least conceivable that the efficiency with which this mechanism operates might be related to intellectual ability (e.g., IQ). In short, implicit learning might be related to intellectual ability. Unfortunately, there do not seem to exist any empirical studies that have explored this potential relation directly. However, there exist at least two studies that have explored the relation in a somewhat indirect manner.

Reber et al. (1991), for example, compared participants' performance on an "explicit" letter series completion task (i.e., requiring an explicit search for underlying rules) with implicit learning (i.e., a well-formedness judgment) following an artificial grammar learning task. During the learning phase of the artificial grammar learning task, participants were instructed to memorize letter strings produced by a finite state grammar. They were informed about the existence of rules underlying the strings only after the learning phase had ended, that is, before the test phase took place. During the test phase, participants were asked to judge whether a given string corresponded to the rules or not (i.e., well-formedness task). To ensure a common metric for the series completion task and the well-formedness task, performance on the series completion task was assessed via two-choice response alternatives. In addition, participants were required to explain their choices.

Reber et al. found relatively small individual differences on the well-formedness task as compared with much larger individual differences on the series completion task. This result could be corroborated by a reanalysis of former studies (e.g., Reber, 1976) in which implicit versus explicit learning was manipulated by varying the instruction for the artificial grammar task.

More to the point and much more interesting (although perhaps little surprising given that variance was lower in the implicit task) was the fact that Reber et al. (1991) could show that participants' WAIS scores correlated strongly with performance on the series completion task ($r = .69$), but only weakly and nonsignificantly with performance on the well-formedness task ($r = .25$). Thus, implicit learning did not correlate significantly with IQ.

A similar result was obtained by Zacks, Hasher, and Sanft (1982), who reported no differences in frequency encoding (an implicit-learning type test) between students from a university with median Scholastic Aptitude Test (SAT) scores of 610 and those from a school with median SAT scores of 471.

Although the implicit-learning task used by Reber and colleagues cannot be considered a complex problem-solving task, the null findings are nevertheless interesting because they point to the possibility that implicit and explicit problem-solving competence might rely on different intellectual abilities. Clearly, much research is needed in this particular area to explore the relation between cognitive abilities, on the one hand, and complex problem solving under different task conditions and instructions, on the other hand.

Doubts and Alternative Accounts

Unfortunately, not all researchers have empirically obtained such clear-cut dissociations between problem-solving performance and questionnaire answers supporting the existence of two independent learning systems as have Berry and Broadbent (1987, 1988), nor do all researchers agree with Berry and Broadbent's interpretation. For example, Green and Shanks (1993), in an attempt to replicate Hayes and Broadbent (1988), found that problem solvers in the salient and nonsalient conditions were similarly impaired by an equation reversal (transfer), as well as by an equation change under dual-task conditions. Moreover, under dual-task conditions, initial learning was better in the salient than in the nonsalient group. Green and Shanks concluded that feedback delay may simply influence *task difficulty* and hence the amount of knowledge acquired, instead of tapping into two functionally distinct learning systems. When problem solvers who learned nothing or very little during the initial learning phase were included in the analysis, Green and Shanks found that performance of nonlearners in the nonsalient/dual-task condition improved after the equation change. However, Berry and Broadbent (1995) reanalyzed the Hayes and Broadbent data and could not confirm this latter pattern in their data analysis. Instead, they raised the possibility that differences in instructions[8] may have contributed to these obviously contradictory results.

---

[8] Green and Shanks's (1993) instructions to both the salient and the nonsalient group included a search instruction similar to that used by Berry and Broadbent (1988).

Other studies, using slightly different manipulations and/or different indicators of verbalizable knowledge, also failed to find dissociations. For example, Stanley, Mathews, Buss, and Kotler-Cope (1989), who used both the original SUGAR FACTORY and the COMPUTER PERSON task, found that informing problem solvers about the underlying principles of the system did improve their performance relative to controls, which had not been the case in the Berry and Broadbent (1984) study. It is interesting, however, that other types of instructions, such as a memorization instruction (consisting of concrete examples), a simple heuristic instruction (e.g., "always select the response level half-way between the current production level and the target level"), or a pooled transcript of skilled problem solvers' explanations, all led to similar performance improvements, as did the "principles" instruction, suggesting that different kinds of *strategies* may lead to comparable levels of performance. Their explanation condition was derived from a different experiment, in which a separate group of problem solvers was asked to provide instructions on how to deal with the system after each block of practice. The informativeness of these instructions was assessed by the performance of yoked subjects requested to follow the transcribed instructions. Stanley et al.'s original learners' performance improved well before they were able to provide helpful instructions. This suggests that performance improves before helpful verbalizable knowledge emerges and that extended practice is needed to develop verbalizable structural knowledge (for a similar view, see Squire & Frambach, 1990).

On the other hand, Sanderson (1989) argued that high levels of practice might be necessary for verbal knowledge to show up because partially incorrect mental models that are induced by the semantic context need to be overcome. Sanderson, using mental model analysis techniques and questionnaires to assess verbal knowledge, found that verbalizable knowledge was associated with problem-solving performance on the CITY TRANSPORTATION system, and that changes in mental models preceded questionnaire improvement and accompanied performance improvement. However, the association between verbalizable knowledge and performance depended on the task demands. More specifically, the dissociation showed only after much practice when the *solution space* was enlarged by requiring problem solvers to enter decimal values instead of integer values. Sanderson argued that enlarging the problem space might render rule induction strategies more advantageous.

Results such as these have led researchers to doubt the existence of two truly independent and possibly antagonistic learning systems, and instead to focus more on describing the nature of the knowledge that is acquired and used under certain task demands, and to devise more refined measures of verbalizable knowledge.

Most researchers (e.g., Berry & Broadbent, 1988; Buchner, Funke, & Berry, 1995; Dienes & Fahey, 1995, 1998; Stanley et al., 1989) now seem to agree that complete and adequate structural knowledge (i.e., rule-based mental models) is not a necessary condition for successful problem solving in complex systems. Rather, in some conditions, problem solving may be predominantly memory-based.

For instance, Dienes and Fahey (1995), using a posttask prediction questionnaire that required problem solvers to determine the required input for unrelated new situations or old situations under a given target level without receiving feedback, demonstrated that problem solvers are better at answering posttask prediction questions consisting of old situations they have encountered when controlling the original SUGAR FACTORY or the nonsalient version of the COMPUTER PERSON task (especially those situations on which they have been correct) than answering questions that consist of novel situations. However, problem solvers who performed in the salient COMPUTER PERSON condition were also able to correctly answer novel-situation questions. Dienes and Fahey therefore concluded that problem solvers control nonsalient systems by retrieving old similar situations instead of by predicting subsequent states on the basis of abstract rules. In contrast, problem solvers in the salient condition may abstract rules that enabled them to successfully predict in novel situations.

Buchner et al. (1995) provided a similar account of the dissociation between problem-solving performance and performance on the traditional prediction task. The authors reasoned that good problem solvers (participants with many trials on target) experience fewer system transitions (situations) than do poor problem solvers who experience more specific situations, and are thus more likely to correctly answer more questions on the posttask questionnaire. As expected, Buchner et al. found that the number of trials necessary to "move" the system to a specified target state was negatively correlated with trials on targets, but was positively correlated with questionnaire performance. However, this correlational pattern emerged only when problem solvers had to reach one and the same target state in successive blocks. When problem solvers had to adjust the SUGAR FACTORY to a different target state in successive blocks and thus experienced a large number of different situations, then performance as well as questionnaire answering deteriorated. Furthermore, both problem-solving performance and prediction ability correlated negatively with the number of encountered state transitions. These results point to the possibility that under varied target conditions, reliance on a memory-based performance strategy is not effective, leading to a rule search strategy for some problem solvers. As pointed out by Sanderson (1989, see above), changes in learning-based mental models show up in questionnaire raw scores only after extended practice.

The studies reviewed thus far indicate that *task demands* and, possibly, *strategies* determine what is learned and how flexibly the acquired knowledge can be transferred to novel situations.

Vollmeyer et al. (1996) and Geddes and Stevenson (1997) investigated in more detail the mediating role of *strategies* adopted under different task demands. Vollmeyer et al. (1996) had their participants work on the linear equation system BIOLOGY LAB described in the previous section for three practice phases. In a first phase, participants were told to explore the system and to learn as much about it as possible, either under a nonspecific-goal condition (see previous section) or under a specific-goal condition in which they had to reach specific target states on several variables. Half of the participants in both groups were, in addition, instructed on how to use the optimal systematic strategy of varying only one variable at a time while holding the other variables constant.

When the exploration phase had been completed, system knowledge was assessed via causal diagram analysis. Based on Sweller's (e.g., Mawer & Sweller, 1982; Sweller, 1983, 1988) findings of impoverished rule knowledge in problem solvers who work under specific-goal instructions, Vollmeyer et al. expected that participants in the specific-goal condition would use a difference reduction strategy (i.e., reducing the distance between current state and goal state) and predominantly search instance space (Klahr & Dunbar, 1988; Simon & Lea, 1974; see previous section), leading to poor abstract system knowledge. In contrast, participants in the unspecific-goal condition do not have a specific target state for which a difference reduction strategy would be effective. Accordingly, Vollmeyer et al. expected participants in the nonspecific-goal condition to also search rule space and to proceed by hypothesis testing. This in turn should lead to a better understanding of the rules underlying system behavior, at least for those participants using systematic hypothesis-testing strategies. Vollmeyer et al. hypothesized that both groups of participants would be able to control the system in a subsequent experimental phase (phase 2) with comparable success in which the target states were the same as those given to the specific-goal group in the exploration phase. However, because knowledge in the specific-goal group should be tied to the goal participants had worked with in the exploration phase, the specific-goal group was expected to perform worse when transferred to a novel goal state (phase 3). The nonspecific-goal participants, on the other hand, should be able to use their system knowledge to perform reasonably well on the transfer task. After finishing the control task, all participants received a prediction task that was similar to that used by Berry and colleagues.

The results can be summarized as follows: (a) Exploring the system with an unspecific goal led to significantly better structural knowledge (causal diagram and prediction); (b) nonspecific-goal and specific-goal participants performed comparably well when controlling the system in the second phase, but (c) only nonspecific-goal participants were able to keep performance at a high level when the goal state was changed. Performance of the specific-goal group deteriorated considerably in the transfer phase; (d) both initial problem-solving performance and transfer as well as structural knowledge were affected by the strategy instruction, whereby separate strategy analyses show that instructed specific-goal participants tended to switch to a difference reduction strategy in the course of the exploration phase, whereas the nonspecific-goal participants benefited from the strategy instruction and stayed with their strategy throughout the exploration phase. These results illustrate that strategies are powerful mediators of what is learned under different task demands, and that comparable performance in some conditions (i.e., phase 2) may be achieved by different types of knowledge, namely, rule knowledge versus knowledge about specific transitions (see also Stanley et al., 1989).

Geddes and Stevenson (1997), following a line of reasoning similar to that of Vollmeyer et al., investigated the influence of goal specificity on instance versus rule learning using the nonsalient version of the COMPUTER PERSON task. In their study, there were three groups of participants: (1) those who explored the system without a specific goal (nonspecific-goal group working under search instruction), (2) a group with a specific goal but without the instruction to discover underlying rules (specific-goal group), and (3) a group with both a search instruction and a specific goal (dual group). All participants were then given a goal state different from that of the specific goal groups in the exploration phase (i.e., a transfer test in Vollmeyer et al.'s sense) before they were asked to answer post-task prediction questions of the kind used by Dienes and Fahey (1995, see above).

Transfer performance was best in the nonspecific-goal group, second best in the specific-goal group, and worst in the dual group. Moreover, participants in the specific-goal group and the dual group were better at predicting old than novel situations on the posttask questionnaire, whereas the nonspecific-goal group also correctly predicted novel situations, indicating that only the nonspecific-goal group acquired abstract rule knowledge.

In addition, the quality of performance correlated with prediction scores only in the nonspecific-goal group, suggesting that they could use their knowledge to control the system. It is interesting, however, that the dual group was even worse than the specific-goal group on the prediction task in that the dual group could master only old correct situations (see Dienes & Fahey, 1995), whereas the specific-goal group was good at predicting previously correct as well as incorrect situations.

Geddes and Stevenson interpret this result as indicating that problem solvers in the specific-goal condition might have engaged in some sort of goal-oriented hypotheses testing. However, because strategies have not been assessed directly, this conclusion is rather speculative. Whereas Geddes and Stevenson replicated the Vollmeyer et al. result that specific-goal groups are impaired on transfer tests involving novel goal states, a study by Haider (1992) also showed that the purely specific-goal and purely nonspecific-goal problem solvers do not necessarily differ when required to adjust the system to the "old" goal state. In her study, too, system knowledge was correlated with performance in the nonspecific-goal group only.

Taken together, these studies provide convincing illustrations of how task demands determine the way problem solvers approach a complex problem-solving task and what they learn while controlling the system. The studies do not, however, address the issue of whether and how problem solvers become aware of underlying rules when salient rules are used (e.g., Dienes & Fahey, 1995), when solution space is enlarged (e.g., Buchner et al., 1995; Sanderson, 1989), and/or after extended periods of practice (e.g., Sanderson, 1989; Stanley et al., 1989).

What are the implications of all this with regard to the effect of intellectual ability on complex problem-solving competence? We believe that the studies discussed do not provide firm evidence in support of two functionally dissociable learning systems, one being selective and intentional, resulting in explicit verbalizable knowledge, the other being passive, unconscious and leading to nonverbalizable knowledge. Rather, we agree with Whittlesea (e.g., Whittlesea & Dorken, 1993; Wright & Whittlesea, 1998) that people simply adapt to task demands and that learning is a consequence of the processing engaged in when trying to meet task demands. As Wright and Whittlesea propose, this may have little to do with unconsciousness about what is being learned (but see Dienes & Fahey, 1998):

> We claim that people directly acquire information only about those stimulus aspects they are required to process, under the demands of the task, but in doing so acquire the potential to respond along unanticipated dimensions. They are learning without awareness, but without awareness of the consequences of their current behavior, not of what they are currently learning, or their current intentions, or the demands under which they learn. They have learned something that makes them sensitive to implicit properties, but to call that "implicit learning" is parallel to referring to the act of winning a lottery as "implicit spending." (Wright & Whittlesea, 1998, p. 418)

We do not mean to say, however, that the processing, and hence the required intellectual abilities, are identical under different task conditions and instructions. Rather, we believe that the strategies employed to meet particular task demands play a major role with respect to what is learned and how flexibly this knowledge can be applied to novel situations. Furthermore, different strategies may be associated with different levels of interindividual variability, as was demonstrated by Reber et al. (1991) in the study discussed above in which problem solvers' performance on an "explicit" letter series completion task was compared with implicit learning on a different implicit learning task (artificial grammar learning). Reber et al. were able to show that series completion, but not implicit learning, was associated with global intelligence.

While goal specificity has been shown to be associated with different strategies, the role of semantic context (and, consequently, of activated prior knowledge), as well as of salience of underlying rules and practice, needs to be investigated further, possibly using mental model analysis techniques (e.g., Sanderson, 1989) and more refined assessments of verbalizable knowledge (e.g., Dienes & Fahey, 1995).

Evaluation of Approach

CRITERION 1. *Both the intellectual ability presumably underlying problem-solving competence and problem-solving competence itself need to be explicitly defined and must not overlap at theoretical and/or operational levels.* In most studies, structural knowledge has been assessed separately from problem-solving performance. However, using more sensitive measures of explicit knowledge (e.g., Dienes & Fahey, 1995) also renders the prediction task more similar to the problem-solving task. Especially when subjects are asked to predict old situations, the two tests can be regarded as overlapping, although the format of the tasks differs. Nevertheless, the systematic use of prediction tasks has led to insights about the flexibility of the application of acquired knowledge (i.e., whether knowledge can be transferred to novel situations), thus theoretically justifying this type of explicit test. Also, the mental model analysis techniques used by Sanderson (1989) are promising and appear to have little empirical overlap with the problem-solving task. Concerning theoretical independence, the concepts of implicit and explicit learning have been defined independently of each other; thus, one may argue that – at least according to the original assumptions – no theoretical overlap exists.

Unfortunately, none of the studies reviewed in the present section reports any reliabilities, neither for performance indicators nor for the questionnaires. Given the assumptions regarding the nature of the two learning mechanisms and the evidence regarding changes in learning/knowledge with practice, it would not make much sense to assess retest reliability. There is indirect evidence, however, that parallel-test reliability may not be very high. For example, several researchers (e.g., Stanley et al., 1989) have reported that problem solvers were better at controlling the COMPUTER PERSON than the SUGAR FACTORY task, although the structure of the two tasks is identical. This again points to the impact of semantic embedding and of prior knowledge that is brought to the task, which may differ across individuals and domains.

CRITERION 2. *The presumed relation between intellectual ability and problem-solving competence must have a theoretical explanation.* The proposal that an implicit learning mechanism might contribute to complex problem solving and is functionally dissociable from explicit learning is an exciting one because most work on abilities and individual differences has exclusively concentrated on explicit/conscious cognition. Unfortunately, however, convincing evidence for truly independent learning mechanisms does not exist. Rather, recent work on task demands and strategy use suggests that what differs is not learning per se, but the processing of study episodes when working with particular systems. It may well be the case that different strategies are associated with different levels of interindividual variability (e.g., Reber et al., 1991) and that the processing induced by different task demands correlates with different subtests of traditional intelligence tests and/or learning tests. Clearly, better definitions of critical task-related concepts such as "salience" and more thorough accounts of which processing requirements and abilities are afforded by certain task characteristics are needed in order to gain a better understanding of the abilities underlying implicit complex problem solving. Vollmeyer et al.'s as well as Geddes and Stevenson's work on strategies can be regarded as a first step in the right direction.

CRITERION 3. *The direction of the presumed causality must be demonstrated empirically.* Evidence for a causal influence of an implicit learning mechanism on complex problem solving is weak. However, some work (e.g., Geddes & Stevenson, 1997; Stanley et al., 1989; Vollmeyer et al., 1996) suggests that task demands encourage use of particular strategies, which in turn affect what is being learned. Particularly noteworthy in this regard is the study by Vollmeyer et al., who directly manipulated strategy use. Of course, more work including experimental strategy induction as well as training, in combination with between group designs, is necessary to gain a more complete understanding of strategic abilities. In addition, these studies should address the issues of (a) semantic embeddedness and its influence on the mental models problem solvers bring to the task, and (b) factors that lead to potential strategy shifts in the course of practice (e.g., chunking) or when working with enlarged solution spaces.

SUMMARY AND CONCLUSIONS

The main goal of the present chapter was to discuss to what extent, if indeed at all, differences in complex problem-solving competence can be traced to differences in an individual's intellectual ability. In the first section of the chapter we provided definitions of *complex problem solving* and of *intellectual ability* and described what it means to state that an individual's problem-solving competence is due to intellectual ability. In the second and third sections, we evaluated much of the empirical work that relates complex problem-solving competence to some measure of intellectual ability with regard to three evaluation criteria. Two forms of problem solving were distinguished. In the second section, we focused on explicit problem solving, that is, problem solving that is controlled by a problem solver's intentions. In the third section, our focus was on implicit, that is, automatic or nonconscious complex problem solving.

Our two main conclusions are as follows: First, there exists no convincing empirical evidence that would support a causal relation between any intellectual ability, on the one hand, and complex explicit or implicit problem-solving competence, on the other hand. It is important to emphasize, again, that this conclusion is one that is based on a lack of evidence, not necessarily a lack of theoretical relation. That is, we do not deny the possibility that a causal relation between intellectual ability and complex problem-solving competence might exist; we argue only that there exists no convincing empirical evidence as yet that would support such a relation.

The conclusion has two important consequences. First, because the intellectual abilities investigated thus far are much too coarse, general, and abstract to allow a prediction of interindividual differences in complex problem-solving competence, what is clearly needed in future research is a focus on much more specific and narrow intellectual abilities (e.g., working-memory capacity) that more closely capture the cognitive system's architecture and functioning.

Second, from the empirical evidence that is currently available it appears that the relation between intellectual ability and complex problem-solving performance might be moderated by a complex interaction among subjects, tasks, and situations. With restricted range in subjects, the empirically obtained correlations attenuate. With unreliable measurement, the correlations attenuate. With certain kinds of problem-solving tasks, the correlations attenuate. Thus, the future task may be to find not whether there is a correlation, but when.

Our second main conclusion is that there does, however, exist good evidence that differences in complex problem-solving competence, both explicit and implicit, are tied to differences in task knowledge and strategy. Whether or not differences in strategy and in the structure and acquisition of task knowledge may, in turn, be due to differences in specific intellectual abilities is, as yet, an open empirical question.

REFERENCES

Amthauer, R., Brocke, B., Liepmann, D. & Beauducel, A. (1973). *Intelligence Structure Test (IST 70)*. Göttingen: Hogrefe.

Anderson, M. (1998). Individual differences in intelligence. In K. Kirsner, C. Speelman, M. Maybery, A. O'Brien-Malone, M. Anderson, & C. MacLeod (Eds.), *Implicit and explicit processes* (pp. 171–185). Mahwah, NJ: Erlbaum.

Beckmann, J. F. (1995). *Lernen und komplexes Problemlösen: Ein Beitrag zur Validierung von Lerntests* [Learning and problem solving: A contribution to validate learning potential tests]. Bonn, Germany: Holos.

Beckmann, J. F., & Guthke, J. (1995). Complex problem solving, intelligence, and learning ability. In P. A. Frensch & J. Funke (Eds.), *Complex problem solving: The European perspective* (pp. 3–25). Hilldale, NJ: Erlbaum.

Berry, D. C. (1991). The role of action in implicit learning. *Quarterly Journal of Experimental Psychology, 43A,* 881–906.

Berry, D. C., & Broadbent, D. E. (1984). On the relationship between task performance and associated verbalizable knowledge. *Quarterly Journal of Experimental Psychology, 36A,* 209–231.

Berry, D. C., & Broadbent, D. E. (1987). The combination of explicit and implicit learning processes in task control. *Psychological research, 49,* 7–15.

Berry, D. C., & Broadbent, D. E. (1988). Interactive tasks and the implicit-explicit distinction. *British Journal of Psychology, 79,* 251–272.

Berry, D. C., & Broadbent, D. E. (1995). Implicit learning in the control of complex systems. In P. A. Frensch & J. Funke (Eds.), *Complex problem solving: The European perspective* (pp. 3–25). Hilldale, NJ: Erlbaum.

Brehmer, B. (1995). Feedback delays in complex decision tasks. In P. A. Frensch & J. Funke (Eds.), *Complex problem solving: The European perspective* (pp. 103–130). Hillsdale, NJ: Erlbaum.

Brehmer, B., & Allard, R. (1991). Dynamic decision making: The effects of task complexity and feedback delay. In J. Rasmussen, B. Brehmer, & J. Leplat (Eds.), *Distributed decision making: Cognitive models for cooperative work* (pp. 319–334). New York: Wiley.

Buchner, A. (1995). Basic topics and approaches to the study of complex problem solving. In P. A. Frensch & J. Funke (Eds.), *Complex problem solving: The European perspective* (pp. 27–63). Hillsdale, NJ: Erlbaum.

Buchner, A., Funke, J., & Berry, D. (1995). Negative correlations between control performance and verbalizable knowledge: Indicators for implicit learning in process control tasks? *Quarterly Journal of Experimental Psychology, 48A,* 166–187.

Cattell, R. B. & Weiss, R. H. (1980). *Culture Fair Intelligence Test, Scale 3 (CFT3).* Göttingen: Hogrefe.

Ceci, S. J., & Liker, J. K. (1986a). Academic and nonacademic intelligence: An experimental separation. In R. J. Sternberg & R. K. Wagner (Eds.), *Practical intelligence* (pp. 119–142). Cambridge, MA: Cambridge University Press.

Ceci, S. J., & Liker, J. K. (1986b). A day at the races: A study of IQ, expertise, and cognitive complexity. *Journal of Experimental Psychology: General, 115,* 255–266.

Ceci, S. J., & Liker, J. K. (1988). Stalking the IQ-expertise relation: When critics go fishing. *Journal of Experimental Psychology: General, 117,* 96–100.

Ceci, S. J., & Ruiz, A. (1992). The role of general ability in cognitive complexity: A case study of expertise. In R. R. Hoffmann (Ed.), *The psychology of expertise: Cognitive research and empirical AI* (pp. 218–230). New York: Springer.

Ceci, S. J., & Ruiz, A. (1993). Transfer, abstractness, and intelligence. In D. K. Detterman & R. J. Sternberg (Eds.), *Transfer on trial: Intelligence, cognition, and instruction* (pp. 168–191). Norwood, NJ: Ablex Publishing.

Detterman, D. K., & Spry, K. M. (1988). Is it smart to play the horses? Comment on "A day at the races: A study of IQ, expertise, and cognitive complexity" (Ceci & Liker, 1986). *Journal of Experimental Psychology: General, 117,* 91–95.

Dienes, Z., & Fahey, R. (1995). The role of specific instances in controlling a dynamic system. *Journal of Experimental Psychology: Learning, Memory, & Cognition, 21,* 848–862.

Dienes, Z., & Fahey, R. (1998). The role of implicit memory in controlling a dynamic system. *Quarterly Journal of Experimental Psychology, 51A,* 593–614.

Dörner, D. (1979). Kognitive Merkmale erfolgreicher und erfolgloser Problemlöser beim Umgang mit sehr komplexen Systemen [Cognitive properties of successful and less successful problem solvers interacting with highly complex systems]. In H. Ueckert & D. Rhenius (Eds.), *Komplexe menschliche Informationsverarbeitung* (pp. 185–195). Bern, Switzerland: Hans Huber.

Dörner, D., & Kreuzig, H. W. (1983). Problemlösefähigkeit und Intelligenz [Problem solving and intelligence]. *Psychologische Rundschau, 34,* 185–192.

Dörner, D., Kreuzig, H. W., Reither, F., & Stäudel, T. (1983). *Lohhausen: Vom Umgang mit Unbestimmtheit und Komplexität* [Lohhausen: On dealing with uncertainty and complexity]. Bern, Switzerland: Hans Huber.

Dörner, D., & Preussler, W. (1990). Die Kontrolle eines einfachen ökologischen Systems [Control of a simple ecological system]. *Sprache & Kognition, 9,* 205–217.

Frensch, P. A. (1998). One concept, multiple meanings. On how to define the concept of implicit learning. In M. A. Stadler & P. A. Frensch (Eds.), *Handbook of implicit learning* (pp. 47–104). Thousand Oaks: Sage Publications.

Frensch, P. A., & Funke, J. (1995). Definitions, traditions, and a general framework for understanding complex problem solving. In P. A. Frensch & J. Funke (Eds.), *Complex problem solving: The European perspective* (pp. 3–25). Hillsdale, NJ: Erlbaum.

Fritz, A., & Funke, J. (1988). Komplexes Problemlösen bei Jugendlichen mit Hirnfunktionsstörungen [Complex problem solving by children with cerebral dysfunctions]. *Zeitschrift für Psychologie, 196,* 171–187.

Funke, J. (1983). Einige Bermerkungen zu Problemen der Problemlöseforschung oder: Ist Testintelligenz doch ein Prädiktor? [Some remarks on the problems of problem solving research or: Does test intelligence predict control performance?]. *Diagnostica, 29,* 283–302.

Funke, J. (1984). Diagnose der westdeutschen Problemlöseforschung in Form einiger Thesen [Assessment of West German problem solving research]. *Sprache & Kognition, 3,* 159–172.

Funke, J. (1985). Steuerung dynamischer Systeme durch Aufbau und Anwendung subjektiver Kausalmodelle [Control of dynamic sytems through development and application of subjective causal models]. *Zeitschrift für Psychologie, 193,* 443–465.

Funke, J. (1991). Solving complex problems: Exploration and control of complex systems. In R. J. Sternberg & P. A. Frensch (Eds.), *Complex problem solving: Principles and mechanisms* (pp. 185–222). Hillsdale, NJ: Erlbaum.

Funke, J. (1992a). Dealing with dynamic systems: Research strategy, diagnostic approach and experimental results. *German Journal of Psychology, 16,* 24–43.

Funke, J. (1992b). *Wissen über dynamische Systeme: Erwerb, Repräsentation und Anwendung* [Knowledge about complex dynamic systems: Acquisition, representation, and use]. Berlin: Springer.

Funke, J. (1993). Microworlds based on linear equation systems: A new approach to complex problem solving and experimental results. In G. Strube & K. F. Wender (Eds.), *The cognitive psychology of knowledge* (pp. 313–330). Amsterdam: Elsevier.

Funke, J., & Müller, H. (1988). Eingreifen und Prognostizieren als Determinanten von Systemidentifikation und Systemsteuerung [Active control and prediction as determinants of system identification and system control]. *Sprache & Kognition, 7*, 176–186.

Geddes, B. W., & Stevenson, R. J. (1997). Explicit learning of a dynamic system with a non-salient pattern. *Quarterly Journal of Experimental Psychology, 50A*, 742–765.

Green, R. E., & Shanks, D. R. (1993). On the existence of independent explicit and implicit learning systems: An examination of some evidence. *Memory & Cognition, 21*, 304–317.

Guthke, J. (1992). Learning tests – The concept, main research findings, problems, and trends. *Learning and Individual Differences, 4*, 137–152.

Guthke, J., Jäger, C. & Schmidt, I. (1983). *LTS: Learning Test Battery "Reasoning."* Berlin: Humboldt-Universität zu Berlin, Institut für Psychologie.

Haider, H. (1992). Implizites Wissen und Lernen. Ein Artefakt? [Implicit knowledge and learning. An artifact?]. *Zeitschrift für Experimentelle und Angewandte Psychologie, 39*, 68–100.

Hayes, N. A., & Broadbent, D. E. (1988). Two modes of learning for interactive tasks. *Cognition, 28*, 249–276.

Hesse, F. W. (1982). Effekte des semantischen Kontexts auf die Bearbeitung komplexer Probleme [Effects of semantic context on problem solving]. *Zeitschrift für Experimentelle und Angewandte Psychologie, 29*, 62–91.

Hörmann, J. J., & Thomas, M. (1989). Zum Zusammenhang zwischen Intelligenz und komplexem Problemlösen [On the relationship between intelligence and complex problem solving]. *Sprache & Kognition, 8*, 23–31.

Howe, M. J. (1988). Intelligence as an explanation. *British Journal of Psychology, 79*, 349–360.

Howe, M. J. A. (1996). Concepts of ability. In I. Dennis & P. Tapsfield (Eds.), *Human abilities: Their nature and their measurement* (pp. 39–48). Mahwah, NJ: Erlbaum.

Hunt, E. (1980). Intelligence as an information-processing concept. *British Journal of Psychology, 71*, 449–474.

Hussy, W. (1989). Intelligenz und komplexes Problemlösen [Intelligence and complex problem solving]. *Diagnostica, 35*, 1–16.

Hussy, W. (1991). Problemlösen und Verarbeitungskapazität [Complex problem solving and processing capacity]. *Sprache & Kognition, 10*, 208–220.

Jäger, A. O. (1982). Mehrmodale Klassifikation von Intelligenzleistungen [Multimodal classification of intelligent performance]. *Diagnostica, 28*, 195–225.

Jensen, A. B., & Weng, L. J. (1994). What is a good g? *Intelligence, 8*, 231–258.

Klahr, D., & Dunbar, K. (1988). Dual space search during scientific reasoning. *Cognitive Science, 12*, 1–55.

Kluwe, R. H., Misiak, C., & Haider, H. (1991). Systems and performance in intelligence tests. In H. Rowe (Ed.), *Intelligence: Reconceptualization and measurement* (pp. 227–244). Hillsdale, NJ: Erlbaum.

Kray, J., & Frensch, P. A. (2002). A view from cognitive psychology: "g" – (G)host in the correlation matrix? In R. J. Sternberg & E. E. Grigorenko (Eds.), *The general factor of intelligence: Fact or fiction?* (pp. 183–222). Hillsdale, NJ: Erlbaum.

Lüer, G., & Spada, H. (1998). Denken und Problemlösen [Thinking and problem solving]. In H. Spada (Ed.), *Lehrbuch Allgemeine Psychologie* (2nd ed., pp. 189–280). Bern: Hans Huber.

Mawer, R. F., & Sweller, J. (1982). Effects of subgoal density and location on learning during problem solving. *Journal of Experimental Psychology: Learning, Memory, & Cognition, 8,* 252–259.

Müller, H. (1993). *Komplexes Problemlösen: Reliabilität und Wissen* [Complex problem solving: Reliability and knowledge]. Bonn, Germany: Hobos.

Nissen, M. J., & Bullemer, P. (1987). Attentional requirements of learning: Evidence from performance measures. *Cognitive Psychology, 19,* 1–32.

Putz-Osterloh, W. (1981). Über die Beziehung zwischen Testintelligenz und Problemlöseerfolg [On the relationship between test intelligence and success in problem solving]. *Zeitschrift für Psychologie, 189,* 79–100.

Putz-Osterloh, W. (1983). Kommentare zu dem Aufsatz von J. Funke: Einige Bermerkungen zu Problemen der Problemlöseforschung oder: Ist Testintelligenz doch ein Prädiktor? [Comments on J. Funke's paper: Some remarks on problems of problem solving research or: Does test intelligence predict control performance?]. *Diagnostica, 29,* 303–309.

Putz-Osterloh, W. (1993). Strategies for knowledge acquisition and transfer of knowledge in dynamic tasks. In G. Grube & K. F. Wender (Eds.), *The cognitive psychology of knowledge.* Amsterdam: Elsevier.

Putz-Osterloh, W., & Lüer, G. (1981). Über die Vorhersagbarkeit komplexer Problemlöseleistungen durch Ergebnisse in einem Intelligenztest [On the predictability of complex problem solving performance by intelligence test scores]. *Zeitschrift für Experimentelle und Angewandte Psychologie, 28,* 309–334.

Raven, J. C., Court, J. & Raven, J., Jr. (1980). *Advanced Progressive Matrices* (APM). Weinheim: Beltz.

Reber, A. S. (1967). Implicit learning of artificial grammars. *Journal of Verbal Learning and Verbal Behavior, 77,* 317–327.

Reber, A. S. (1969). Transfer of syntactic structure in synthetic languages. *Journal of Experimental Psychology, 81,* 115–119.

Reber, A. S. (1976). Implicit learning and tacit knowledge. *Journal of Experimental Psychology: Human Learning and Memory, 2,* 88–94.

Reber, A. S. (1995). *The Penguin dictionary of psychology* (2nd ed.). New York: Penguin Books, Inc.

Reber, A. S., Walkenfield, F. F., & Hernstadt, R. (1991). Implicit and explicit learning: Individual differences and IQ. *Journal of Experimental Psychology: Learning, Memory, & Cognition, 17,* 888–896.

Sanderson, P. M. (1989). Verbalizable knowledge and skilled task performance: Association, dissociation, and mental models. *Journal of Experimental Psychology: Learning, Memory, & Cognition, 15,* 729–747.

Shanks, D. R., & St. John, M. F. (1994). Characteristics of dissociable human learning systems. *Behavioral and Brain Sciences, 17,* 367–447.

Simon, H. A., & Lea, G. (1974). Problem solving and rule induction: A unified view. In L. W. Gregg (Ed.), *Knowledge and cognition.* Hillsdale, NJ: Erlbaum.

Squire, L. R., & Frambach, M. (1990). Cognitive skill learning in amnesia. *Psychobiology, 18,* 109–117.

Stanley, W. B., Mathews, R. C., Buss, R. R., & Kotler-Cope, S. (1989). Insight without awareness: On the interaction of verbalization, instruction, and practice in a simulated process control task. *Quarterly Journal of Experimental Psychology, 41A,* 553–577.

Sternberg, R. J. (1982). Reasoning, problem solving, and intelligence. In R. J. Sternberg (Ed.), *Handbook of human intelligence* (pp. 225–307). Cambridge, MA: Cambridge University Press.

Sternberg, R. J., Nokes, C., Geissler, P. W., Prince, R., Okatcha, F., Bundy, D. A., & Grigorenko, E. L. (2001). The relationship between academic and practical intelligence: A case study in Kenya. *Intelligence, 29,* 401–418.

Strohschneider, S. (1991). Problemlösen und Intelligenz: Über die Effekte der Konkretisierung komplexer Probleme [Complex problem solving and intelligence: On the effects of problem concreteness]. *Diagnostica, 37,* 353–371.

Süß, H. M., Kersting, M., & Oberauer, K. (1991). Intelligenz und Wissen als Prädiktoren für Leistungen bei computersimulierten komplexen Problemen [Intelligence and knowledge as predictors of performance in solving complex computer-simulated problems]. *Diagnostica, 37,* 334–352.

Sweller, J. (1983). Control mechanisms in problem solving. *Memory and Cognition, 11,* 32–40.

Sweller, J. (1988). Cognitive load during problem solving: Effects on learning. *Cognitive Science, 12,* 257–285.

Vollmeyer, R., Burns, B. D., & Holyoak, K. J. (1996). The impact of goal specificity on strategy use and the acquisition of problem structure. *Cognitive Science, 20,* 75–100.

Wechsler, D. (1982). *Wechsler Adult Intelligence Scale – Revised (WAIS-R).* New York: The Psychological Corporation.

Whittlesea, B. W., & Dorken, M. D. (1993). Incidentally, things in general are particularly determined: An episodic-processing account of implicit learning. *Journal of Experimental Psychology: General, 122,* 227–248.

Wright, R. L., & Whittlesea, B. W. (1998). Implicit learning of complex structures: Active adaptation and selective processing in acquisition and application. *Memory & Cognition, 26,* 402–420.

Zacks, R. T., Hasher, L., & Sanft, H. (1982). Automatic encoding of event frequency: Further findings. *Journal of Experimental Psychology: Learning, Memory, & Cognition, 8,* 106–116.

4

Creativity: A Source of Difficulty in Problem Solving

Todd I. Lubart and Christophe Mouchiroud

Many problems can be solved by accessing stored knowledge or by applying pre-established, "algorithmic" procedures to reach a solution. Such problems are the bread and butter of problem solving; from kindergarten to the university, students accumulate a great deal of experience with these "canned" problems. Difficulties arise, however, when people need to solve problems that do not fit the mold, that require some innovative thinking. Guilford (1967) proposed that "real" problem solving involved actively seeking, constructing new ideas that fit with constraints imposed by a task or more generally by the environment. In other words, in most instances "real" problem solving involves creative thinking (see Mayer, 1983). One well-known example of an unpredictable yet vital problem that was solved successfully is illustrated by the epic return flight of the Apollo 13 space mission (King, 1997). Preserving the lives of the crew members required a cascade of operations, each involving creative thinking, as the explosion of the ship's main oxygen supply was not the kind of problem that the flight crew expected to encounter, and thus they had no specific training, no preestablished procedure to follow.

NECESSITY IS THE MOTHER OF INVENTION

The world in which we live can be characterized as a rapidly evolving, technology- and information-oriented one in which creative problem solving skills are increasingly valued (Sternberg & Lubart, 1996). According to some theorists, such as Romer (1994), future economic growth will be driven by innovative products and services that respond to societal needs and problems rather than by providing established products and services more efficiently (see Getz & Lubart, 2001).

We would argue, therefore, that "real" problem solving as opposed to "canned" problem solving is a topic of growing interest. A "problem" can be conceived broadly as encompassing any task that an individual seeks to accomplish in which one's goal state is not equal to one's current state. Thus, scientists who seek to understand a complex phenomenon, artists who seek to express an idea, and people who seek to solve conflicts in their everyday lives can all be considered to be engaged in problem solving (see Runco & Dow, 1999).

Finding solutions to "real" problems – new ideas that fit with task constraints – is difficult for two main reasons. First, a diverse set of cognitive and conative factors is necessary. Second, in order to be effective, these abilities and traits must be called into play at appropriate points in the problem-solving process. We consider each of these points. Finally, we discuss a rather different (and even opposite) point of view on the relation between problem solving and creativity.

COGNITIVE AND CONATIVE FACTORS FOR CREATIVE THOUGHT

During the last twenty years, a multivariate approach to creativity has developed. In this perspective, creativity requires a particular combination of cognitive and conative factors whose expression is influenced by environmental conditions. The nature of the proposed factors and their interaction varies according to different theorists (see Feldhusen, 1995; Lubart, 1999a, 2000–2001; Runco, Nemiro, & Walberg, 1998). For example, Amabile (1996) proposed a componential model in which creativity stems from domain-relevant skills (e.g., knowledge, technical skills), creativity-relevant skills (e.g., ability to break mental set, heuristics for idea generation, and conducive work style), and task motivation (interest and commitment to the task). Feldman, Csikszentmihalyi, and Gardner (1994; Csikszentmihalyi, 1988, 1999) advanced a systems approach that focuses on interactions between individuals (with their cognitive and conative factors), domains (culturally defined bodies of knowledge), and fields (e.g., people who control or influence a domain by evaluating and selecting novel ideas). Other proposals include Woodman and Schoenfeldt's (1990) interactionist model and Runco and Chand's (1995) two-tier componential model. We base our presentation on Sternberg and Lubart's (1991, 1995) multivariate model, which proposes that creativity draws on specific aspects of intelligence, knowledge, cognitive styles, personality, and motivation operating within an environmental context.

From a cognitive point of view, certain information-processing abilities are particularly important (Sternberg & O'Hara, 1999), but one's knowledge base and cognitive styles also play a role (see Cropley, 1999; Finke, Ward, & Smith, 1992; Mumford, Baughman, Maher, Costanza, & Supinski, 1997; Mumford, Supinski, Baughman, Costanza, & Threlfall, 1997; Ward, Smith, & Finke, 1999). For example, the intellectual abilities considered as essential consist of identifying the problem to be solved, redefining it, noticing in the environment information in connection with the problem (broad attention [Kasof, 1997] and selective encoding [Davidson & Sternberg, 1984]), observing similarities between different fields that clarify the problem (analogy, metaphor, selective comparison [Davidson & Sternberg, 1984; Sternberg & Davidson, 1995]), combining various elements of information that, joined together, will form a new idea (e.g., selective combination [Davidson & Sternberg, 1984; Sternberg & Davidson, 1995], Janusian thinking [Rothenberg, 1996]), generating several alternative ideas (divergent thinking), and evaluating one's progress toward the solution of the problem. These capacities thus concern at the same time synthetic intelligence and analytic intelligence (Sternberg, 1985). One can also note that practical or social intelligence plays a role in the presentation of an idea in a form that will be accepted by one's audience.

The relationship between knowledge and creative problem solving is not as simple as it may seem at first glance (Weisberg, 1999). On the one hand, knowledge relevant to a problem is the raw material on which intellectual processes operate. According to many authors, a certain level of knowledge is required to be creative. Knowledge allows the comprehension of a problem and assures that already existing ideas will not be reinvented. In addition, knowledge helps one to profit from events observed by chance and to focus on new aspects of a task because the basics of the task are mastered and perhaps automatized. On the other hand, sometimes knowledge can have negative effects on creative thought. In a historiometric study of eminent creators, the level of formal education was found to have an inverted-U relation with creativity (Simonton, 1984). Several studies on expertise show that a high level of knowledge is sometimes associated with mental rigidity in the use of this knowledge. For example, Frensch and Sternberg (1989) found that experts in the game of bridge adapted less well than novices when key rules for bidding on cards were changed. Similarly, novices outperformed expert accountants when new information on tax laws modified how to handle standard deductions (Marchant, Robinson, Anderson, & Schadewald, 1991). Finally, Wiley (1998) examined how knowledge about a topic can influence idea generation, causing set effects and fixation on readily available but inappropriate information; in a series of studies, people with high and low knowledge levels about baseball solved remote associate problems (Mednick, 1962), in which one seeks a concept that relates to three given terms (blue, knife, cottage; the response is "cheese"). Certain misleading items used some baseball terms but the response was not related to baseball (e.g., plate, broken, shot; response = glass, incorrect baseball-guided association = home). Wiley (1998) found that these items were especially difficult (in terms of correct responses and response latency) for people with a high level of baseball knowledge compared with those without much baseball knowledge. The remote associate task has often been regarded as creativity-relevant; it involves generating associations and selectively combining information.

Taken together, the results of studies on expertise suggest that high levels of domain knowledge can sometimes bias problem solving, limiting the search space to readily available ideas. The paradox is that this internally generated knowledge set effect is often efficient because many problems can be solved with "canned" knowledge. One of the hallmarks of creative problems, however, is that they tend to involve breaking away from what already exists.

Research on cognitive styles – individual differences in preferences for perceiving, organizing, and processing information – suggests that certain styles may facilitate creative problem solving more than others (Martinsen, 1995, 1997; Martinsen & Kaufmann, 1999). For example, work based on Jung's typology suggests that a preference for an intuitive style (internally oriented information search based often on memory, emotions, idiosyncratic experiences) will be conducive to creativity compared with a "sensing" style (which focuses on information gathered externally with the five senses). A number of studies on samples of artists, scientists, architects, and others show that preference for the intuitive style (measured by the Myers-Briggs Type Indicator, a self-report questionnaire) is positively correlated with measures of creative performance. In our own research with adults from the community and university student samples, we found also that intuitive style measured by the MBTI and by a set of hypothetical scenarios (which allowed for "intuitive" or "logical reason–based" modes of information seeking) was correlated positively with creativity in a range of tasks (e.g., story writing, drawing; Lubart & Sternberg, 1995; Raidl & Lubart, 2000–2001).

In addition to the possibility of certain creativity-relevant cognitive styles, some recent work suggests that individuals who can switch easily from one style to another or those without strong style preferences are the most creative. For example, Sternberg (1997) discusses a "global style" that characterizes people who prefer to concentrate on the general aspects of a task, and a "local style" that describes those who prefer to focus their thought on the details of the task. Both styles are hypothesized to play a role in finding creative solutions (Sternberg & Lubart, 1991, 1995); the initial part of the creative process involves working on the problem as a whole, and in later phases of creative work, attention to details is necessary to produce an elaborated and efficient solution. Thus, having balanced preferences for the global-local styles may be best for creativity. With regard to other style dimensions, Noppe (1996) examined the field dependence-independence styles (Witkin, Dyk, Faterson, Goodenough, and Karp, 1962) and found that subjects who could adapt to the task demands were more creative than subjects with fixed style preferences. In a similar vein, Guastello, Shissler, Driscoll, and Hyde (1998) measured eight creativity-relevant cognitive styles (e.g., dreamer, synthesizer, modifier, critic, planner). Based on biographical self-reports of creative activities, they found that people who identified themselves as using several styles tended to be more creative than those that reported preferences for a single style.

With regard to conative factors that play a key role in creative problem solving, we focus on personality traits and motivation. During the past fifty years, numerous studies have sought to identify a set of traits that distinguish highly creative people from those who show relatively little creativity. In these studies, either contrasted groups (high vs. low creativity) are formed and mean differences in personality are examined or correlations are calculated for an entire sample of people assessed on measures of personality and creativity. MacKinnon (1962) conducted one of the landmark studies in this area; he compared the personality traits of three groups of architects: (a) peer-nominated highly creative architects, (b) competent architects who were not nominated for creativity but were matched closely to the creative ones on diverse criteria, and (c) "average" architects. The results showed that creative architects were more assertive, independent, individualistic, nonconformist, and spontaneous and lower on socialization (e.g., self-control, good impression) than their less creative peers. Dudek and Hall (1991) conducted a follow-up study of the same architects twenty-five years after the original study, in which 70 of the 83 surviving architects participated. They found that, in general, the differences in personality profiles and creativity (overall career achievement) still existed, suggesting long-term stability of links between certain traits and creativity.

Several authors have provided conceptual reviews of the personality-creativity literature, suggesting a set of traits that is important for creative work across disciplines (Barron & Harrington, 1981; Dellas & Gaier, 1970; Mumford & Gustafson, 1988; Sternberg & Lubart, 1995). Traits such as risk taking, individuality, openness to new experiences, perseverance (to overcome obstacles during creative work), and tolerance of ambiguity (coping with uncertainty and avoiding a premature, nonoptimal solution) have often been highlighted.

In our own work concerning an investment approach to creativity, we developed the idea that creative people must "defy the crowd" and take risks on advancing new ideas that have potential but may ultimately fail (Sternberg & Lubart, 1995). Most people are risk-averse, which limits their creative potential. In one of our studies, we evaluated the link between risk taking and creativity, having participants complete domain-specific measures of risk taking and creativity tasks in artistic and literary domains (Lubart & Sternberg, 1995). In particular, risk taking was measured by a questionnaire of hypothetical scenarios as well as by other methods. In the questionnaire we asked participants to indicate how they would proceed in situations in which a proposed behavior involved risk. The risk-taking situations concerned artistic activities, literary activities and everyday life situations. Creativity was measured by two tasks, one artistic (producing drawings) and the other literary (producing short stories); the creativity of the productions was evaluated by 15 peer judges. The results showed a significant correlation ($r = 0.39$) between the tendency to take risks in the artistic field and artistic creativity. In contrast, risk taking in literary situations and everyday life situations was not related to artistic creativity, indicating a specificity in the link between taking risk and creativity. For the story-writing task, the stories of participants having a high level of risk taking in the literary field were significantly less conventional than those of participants having a low level of risk taking (but the creativity of the stories was not significantly related to literary risk taking, because of some stories that went against popular political opinions or social mores).

Recently, Feist (1998, 1999) conducted the first quantitative meta-analysis of empirical studies of personality and creativity, focusing on scientific and artistic domains. This work examined effect sizes in 95 samples totaling more than 13,000 participants. Specifically, Feist compared personality traits between scientists and nonscientists, more creative scientists and less creative scientists, as well as artists and nonartists. Comparisons were made of studies in which traits relevant to the Five-Factor Model were measured, and each factor – Extraversion (E), Agreeableness (A), Conscientiousness (C), Neuroticism (N), and Openness (O) – was divided into its positive and negative poles. The overall results suggested that creative people are open to new experiences, self-confident, self-accepting, less conventional, impulsive, ambitious, driven, dominant, and hostile. In addition, studies using personality inventories such as the California Personality Inventory (CPI; Gough, 1987), the Sixteen Personality Factor Questionnaire (16PF; Cattell, Eber, & Tatsuoka, 1970), and the Eysenck Personality Questionnaire (EPQ; Eysenck & Eysenck, 1975) indicated that certain specific traits (which are not part of the Big Five model) were relevant to creativity in artistic and scientific samples. For example, the trait of psychoticism has been found to be positively related to rare responses in association tasks and may be at the origin of certain links between creativity and psychopathology (Eysenck, 1994, 1995).

Contrasts between artistic and scientific samples revealed some differences, however. For example, scientists were found to be more conscientious than artists, who were more emotionally unstable and less socialized in terms of accepting group norms (Feist, 1998). Of particular interest, comparisons of personality traits for highly creative scientists and less creative scientists showed that within this specific domain of endeavor, a high level of creativity was associated with traits of dominance, confidence, and openness.

In terms of specificity in the link between personality and creativity, Helson (1999) suggested that within a domain there are often nuances concerning how personality traits differentiate more and less creative samples, depending on the specific creative activity and the comparison group used. Other work suggests that the links between creativity and personality may depend on the specific kind of processing involved in the task; Mumford, Costanza, Threlfall, and Baughman (1993) investigated the links between personality and problem finding in a task that required participants to construct new matrix problems for an intelligence test. Traits such as self-awareness, tolerance of ambiguity, self-esteem, and openness were particularly relevant. It was proposed that this combination of traits led to a "self-initiated discovery" profile, and it was not the isolated traits but rather their conjunction that was important for creative performance in the task studied. Finally, Csikszentmihalyi (1999) proposed that creative people are possibly those who do not have strongly fixed personality traits but rather can adopt various profiles according to the phase of the creative process in which they are involved (e.g., extroverted when gathering information or communicating results, introverted when incubating or searching for solutions).

Creative problem-solving abilities are useless if one lacks the desire to solve the problem. Thus, motivation can be considered as another essential ingredient to creative behavior. Investigators in this field distinguish usually between intrinsic and extrinsic motivation. Intrinsic motivation is characterized by a focus on the task and the enjoyment derived from solving the problem. In contrast, extrinsic motivation focuses on external reward, for example, material goods, money, awards, or praise. In this case, the person is behaving to get reinforcement. As a result, the need is satisfied by the reward that follows task completion. Extensive work has been devoted to the study of the differential effects of intrinsic and extrinsic motivators on creativity (Amabile, 1983, 1996, 1997; Baer, 1998; Collins & Amabile, 1999; Eisenberger & Armeli, 1997; Gerrard, Poteat, & Ironsmith, 1996; Hennessey & Amabile, 1998; Mehr & Shaver, 1996; Ruscio, Whitney, & Amabile, 1998). In most of this research we see that intrinsic motivation is positively associated with creative performance.

A relationship between creativity and extrinsic motivation also exists but seems less straightforward. Some well-known cases of creative accomplishment indicate that extrinsic motivators can foster creative work, whereas others suggest that it is detrimental. Recent theoretical and empirical work in both laboratory and field settings (e.g., entrepreneurial creativity) indicate that, in fact, extrinsic motivation may facilitate certain phases of creative work, and that intrinsic and extrinsic motivators may work together to keep work progressing (Amabile, 1996, 1997).

In studies with children, Eisenberger and his colleagues have found that rewards can positively affect ideational productivity and creativity, when only creative behavior is rewarded (Eisenberger & Armeli, 1997; Eisenberger & Cameron, 1996, 1998). Experiments done by Amabile and associates have shown that extrinsic motivators do indeed foster creativity when children are specifically trained to maintain their intrinsic motivation (Hennessey, Amabile, & Martinage, 1989; Hennessey & Zbikowski, 1993). In a study of 7- to 10-year-olds who made a collage, Gerrard et al. (1996) found a main effect of reward on creativity ratings, with the highest mean ratings for the group of children that had followed intrinsic motivation training as opposed to a control training program. Additionally, certain individual difference variables, such as skill level in a domain, may influence the link between motivation and creativity. For example, low-skilled participants may be more positively affected than high-skilled ones by extrinsic motivators (Amabile, 1996; Baer, 1998).

Sternberg and Lubart (1995) proposed that the key to motivating creative problem solving is to keep a person focused on resolving the task. For intrinsic motivators, work on the task provides the "reward" by itself. For extrinsic motivators, some people are able to remain task-focused (which facilitates creativity), whereas others become "reward-focused" and hence distracted from their task. In line with this interpretation, Ruscio et al. (1998) examined how intrinsic motivation influenced creative task performance by observing participants as they worked. They found that intrinsic motivation was associated with specific behaviors indicating "involvement," or absorption in the task, and this "involvement" was, in turn, predictive of creativity. It is also interesting to note that some forms of motivation that are not purely intrinsic or extrinsic, such as achievement motivation, involving both internal rewards (e.g., a sense of accomplishment) and external rewards (e.g., social recognition), have been linked to creativity (Sternberg & Lubart, 1995).

ENVIRONMENT

Physical surroundings, family environment, school or work settings, and cultural climate can all have an impact on creative problem-solving (Amabile, 1997; de Alencar & Bruno Faria, 1997; Lubart, 1999b; Simonton, 1984; Tesluk, Farr, & Klein, 1997). Studies show, for example, that a stimuli-rich physical environment or contact with diverse cultural centers promotes creative thinking, whereas time constraints, competition, and external evaluation during problem solving tend to have negative effects (Amabile, 1996; Shalley & Oldham, 1997). A review of creativity across cultural settings suggests that social environments tend to allow or encourage creativity in certain activities (such as art) and restrict it in others (such as religion; Lubart, 1999b). Regardless of the domain of activity, the social environment is not always receptive to creative ideas because these ideas diverge from well-known, traditional ways of approaching an issue, which although nonoptimal are familiar and "comfortable" to the audience. People may even have vested interests in maintaining the status quo because a change could reduce their own status, acquired knowledge, or expertise in a domain. Thus, creative problem solving that stems from individuals' cognitive and conative resources may be facilitated or hindered by the environment within which an individual operates.

PUTTING TOGETHER COGNITIVE AND CONATIVE FACTORS

Concerning the combination of these components, the level of creativity of a given subject does not result from the simple additive combination of the various components. If somebody has a level close to zero for a given component, the probability is very low that creative work will emerge. For example, if one knows nothing in nuclear physics, one has essentially no chance to be creative in this field, even if one is at the optimal level for all the other components of creativity. But one can imagine that there is partial compensation for the weakest components if they satisfy a required minimum level. Thus, for example, a high degree of perseverance may partly compensate for relatively low levels on certain cognitive abilities. Finally, it is possible that the various components interact between themselves in a multiplicative way to support creativity.

We undertook a study to test the multivariate approach, involving 48 adult subjects (average age 33 years) who completed eight measures of creativity: two drawings, two short stories, two television commercials, and two science-fiction problems (Lubart & Sternberg, 1995). Also, the participants completed a series of tests and questionnaires measuring the cognitive and conative aspects considered important for creativity (from which we created scores for creativity-relevant cognitive abilities, task-relevant knowledge, cognitive styles, relevant personality traits, and motivation). Fifteen peer judges evaluated the creativity of the productions using a consensual assessment procedure (see Amabile, 1996). The alpha coefficients of homogeneity of the judgments ranged between 0.70 and 0.80 according to the task.

Multiple regression analyses indicated that a noteworthy, significant percentage of the variance on creativity was "explained" by the cognitive and conative variables; for example, for the story generation task, 63% of the variance in creativity scores was modeled. In our study, cognitive abilities and domain-relevant knowledge constituted the most important predictors of creative performance (the short, laboratory nature of the creativity tasks undoubtedly decreased the influence of the conative aspects, such as perseverance and motivation). Moreover, we observed an interaction between intelligence and knowledge, such that additional variance in creative performance was explained when specific combinations of participants' levels on intelligence and knowledge were considered. The results support the idea that interindividual differences in creative problem solving are due to a diverse set of cognitive and conative factors. Similar conclusions about the multivariate components necessary for creative problem solving were reached in research conducted on Amabile's componential model (Conti, Coon, & Amabile, 1996).

Concerning the range of creative performance from everyday levels to eminent creativity, the multivariate model suggests that these different levels can be explained by the same cognitive and conative factors (Sternberg & Lubart, 1991, 1995). The fact that the cognitive and conative factors may combine interactively, coupled with the low probability that a high level of all the components for creativity will be found simultaneously in a given person, explains why eminent levels of creativity are quite rare and why creative problem solving is in general difficult.

With a multivariate approach, we can also understand why a given person may be able to solve problems creatively in one domain but not another. Creativity can be observed in virtually any domain, including arts, science, mathematics, social problem solving, business, teaching, and everyday life. Research with adults shows that creativity is moderately but not completely domain-specific (Baer, 1991; Lubart & Sternberg, 1995; Runco, 1987), with correlations typically ranging from .20 to .30. Similarly, creativity research on task-specificity also shows, at best, moderate intertask correlations. Consistent with these findings, studies of eminent creators seem also to lead to a domain specificity hypothesis. Gray (1966) found that 17% of his sample of historically significant creators had made a contribution to more than one field, and that only 2% accomplished a creative work in disparate domains (e.g., painting and writing). Within the multivariate perspective, each person presents a particular profile on the various cognitive and conative factors. This profile will tend to correspond better to the requirements of a task concerned with a certain field rather than another. Thus, observed weak-to-moderate correlations between various tasks of creativity are expected (Conti et al., 1996; Lubart & Sternberg, 1995). As most research on the question of field specificity has concerned scientific, artistic, and verbal domains, we explored this issue further by observing creative performance in social problem solving tasks (Mouchiroud & Lubart, 2000, 2002). For example, we asked children, adolescents, and adults to generate ideas for tasks such as convincing a peer to play a specified game or reducing people's aggressive behavior when driving their cars. The results suggest that social creativity may form a unitary construct, whereas the strength of the link between social and other nonsocial, more object-oriented tasks (such as generating ideas for using a box) varies developmentally, showing the strongest correlations for 11- to 12-year-olds, after which creative capacities seem to become more and more specific.

COGNITION AND CONATION IN ACTION: THE CREATIVE PROCESS

Simply having the cognitive abilities, knowledge, cognitive style, personality traits, and motivation that are relevant to creative thinking is not enough. These resources must be put into action appropriately during problem solving.

In the literature on creativity, one of the key topics is the creative process – the sequence of thoughts and actions that leads to a novel and adaptive production (Lubart, 2000–2001). Based on introspective accounts, Wallas (1926) identified the following stages: (a) preparation, (b) incubation, (c) illumination, and (d) verification. For many researchers, this four-stage model (or one of its variants) still constitutes the basis for describing the creative process (Busse & Mansfield, 1980; Cagle, 1985; Goswami, 1996; Ochse, 1990; Osborn, 1953; Stein, 1974; Taylor, 1959; Taylor, Austin, & Sutton, 1974). For example, Amabile (1996) described the creative process in the following way: (a) identification of the problem or the task, (b) preparation (collection and reactivation of suitable information), (c) generation of response (search and production for possible solutions), (d) validation and communication of the response (including critical examination of the possible response), and (e) a final phase concerning the decision to continue or not (a person may stop because the task was completed or because there was failure, or may return to one or more phases of the creative process and start working again). Based on her componential model of creativity mentioned earlier, Amabile suggested that individual differences in task motivation influence particularly the problem identification and response generation phases; that domain-relevant skills influence the preparation and response-validation phases; and that creativity-relevant processes influence the response generation phase.

Some work (e.g., using an observational method and/or interviews with artists and writers) suggests, however, another vision of the creative process. It involves a dynamic combination of several mutually reinforcing subprocesses (Ebert, 1994; Lubart, 2000–2001). For example, in a study of artists, Cawelti, Rappaport, and Wood (1992) found evidence for the simultaneity of processes such as centering on a topic, generating new ideas, expanding ideas, and evaluating one's work. Israeli (1962, 1981) described the creative process as a series of quick interactions between productive and critical modes of thought, with some planning and compensatory actions. According to Finke et al.'s Geneplore model (1992; Ward et al., 1999), generative processes (e.g., knowledge retrieval, idea association, synthesis, transformation) that lead to preinventive structures combine in cyclical sequences with exploratory processes (e.g., examination, elaboration) that develop nascent ideas. Brophy's (1998) creative problem-solving model emphasizes the interplay between divergent (ideation) and convergent (evaluative) modes of thought in creativity, and predicts that highly creative products are scarce, in part, due to the difficulties that most people have with alternating between these two cognitive processes.

Based on this view, research has examined in some detail the nature of certain subprocesses involved in creativity, such as the formulation or definition of a problem, divergent thinking, synthesis, the use of heuristics, remote association, the reorganization of information, as well as evaluation and analysis of information (see Lubart, 2000–2001; Mumford, Mobley, Uhlman, Reiter-Palmon, & Doares, 1991). For example, the subprocess of forming remote associations may involve spreading activation through previously established links in semantic memory (Mednick, 1962), random chance-based connections that lead to coherent idea configurations (Simonton, 1988), or emotional resonance (Lubart & Getz, 1997). According to the emotional resonance model, each person has stored in memory a diverse set of emotional experiences associated with objects, places, people, and situations that have been encountered. These emotional traces, called endocepts, are activated during problem solving and may resonate with each other, thereby activating cognitively remote but emotionally related concepts in memory. A person may, in turn, notice the simultaneously activated concepts and form an association that is perhaps more idiosyncratic, and unusual in the population, than those formed through cognitive paths. Empirical tests of this model show that the emotional richness with which a concept is characterized explains significant variance of originality in associative thinking tasks based on the concept, beyond that explained by rich cognitive descriptions of the same concept (Getz & Lubart, 2000).

Beyond the growing body of work concerning subprocesses involved in creativity, few studies have specifically addressed how the creative process as a whole differs from the noncreative or barely creative process. For example, are certain subprocesses present in very creative problem solving and absent or reduced in less creative problem solving? Do different orders of the subprocesses lead to differences in the creative level of the outcome?

Mumford et al. (1991) suggested that the creative problem solving process and the "canned," noncreative process differ in four main ways. First, creative problem solving involves ill-defined problems more than routine problem solving. This places an emphasis on the problem construction phase in creative work. Second, in the creative process people must generate new, alternative solutions that involve divergent and convergent thinking. In routine problem solving, people apply previously acquired procedures, search for ready-made solutions, and tend to satisfice, all of which involve mainly convergent thinking (see also Mayer, 1999). Third, the creative process involves active, attention-demanding processing with multiple cycles of divergent and convergent thought, whereas the "standard" process proceeds in an "additive fashion" with more direct activation, generation, and application. Fourth, in the creative process existing information is restructured, reorganized, or combined. In routine, noncreative problem solving, information is recalled and understood using existing categories. Thus the subprocesses of combination and reorganization of category information as well as problem construction differentiate creative and standard problem solving. Within the creative process, different levels of creativity result, in part, from the skill or quality with which each of the involved subprocesses is executed.

Consider now some studies that begin to address how differences in the process as a whole contribute to the individual differences in creativity. For example, Getzels and Csikszentmihalyi (1976) observed art students as they made a drawing based on a set of objects that were provided (e.g., a manikin, a book, a hat, a glass prism). A panel of expert judges rated the originality of the drawings. All the art students handled the objects to set up their still-life composition. However, some students manipulated only a few objects and did not examine much these objects, whereas other students explored in detail many of the proposed objects. Furthermore, some students rearranged the still-life composition after having begun to draw what they had initially set up. The number of objects manipulated and the extent to which each object was explored in detail correlated significantly ($r > .50$) with originality, as did problem formulation behaviors during the drawing phase. Thus, differences in the quality and quantity of problem finding as well as when it occurred during the drawing task were related to originality.

Using a think-aloud methodology, Goor and Sommerfeld (1975) examined differences in the subprocesses used by "creative" and "noncreative" students preselected based on performance on divergent thinking tasks. The students thought aloud while solving three insight-type problems (making four triangles with six matches, killing a tumor without destroying healthy cells, solving a problem concerning the selection of colored pebbles by chance). Problem-solving protocols were divided into brief intervals, and seven categories of verbal behavior were noted (e.g., generating new information or hypotheses, self-reference or self-criticism, silence). The high creative group spent more time than the low creative group on generating new information or hypotheses, working on these hypotheses, and self-reference or self-criticism. There were also some group differences on the sequences of activities. For example, following self-reference or self-criticism, the high creative group tended to engage in generating new information or developing hypotheses, whereas the low creative group entered a period of silence.

Finally, Lubart (1994) examined the nature of the creative process, by looking at the role of idea evaluation. The evaluation of the strengths and weaknesses of potential ideas and problem solutions under development serves as a filter in creative work. In natural work situations, we find that some people auto-evaluate their ideas early on in their work. Others tend to make later auto-evaluations. Finally, there are those who engage in auto-evaluations at regular intervals. Based on these interindividual differences, two studies using an experimental methodology were conducted with university student participants.

In the first study, the students composed short stories and created drawings based on provided objects; the creativity of these two types of productions was judged by graduate-level teaching assistants in, respectively, literary composition and studio art. During their work, the students were briefly stopped at various times and instructed to evaluate for themselves their production in progress. The moment and the quantity of these auto-evaluations were controlled. There were groups of subjects that carried out their auto-evaluations relatively early in the work, relatively late in the work, or at regular intervals throughout the work. Additionally, there was a control group that engaged in other activities at the indicated times and that was not explicitly encouraged to auto-evaluate. For the writing composition task, the results showed that early auto-evaluations were the most effective for creativity, in comparison with late auto-evaluations or auto-evaluations at regular intervals, and with the results of the control group.

In a second study, these results were replicated, in general, with various methods for inducing auto-evaluations and with a different story-writing composition task. For the drawing task, no clear effect of the synchronization of auto-evaluations was found. This may be due to the fact that last-minute changes to a drawing could greatly influence its overall appearance, whereas the story task tended to be more linear, increasingly constrained as one progresses in elaborating the plot ("surprise" endings invented at the last minute tended to be inadequate). Finally, for the various tasks (short stories and drawings), no effect of the quantity of auto-evaluations was observed.

These results indicate that differences in the sequence of cognitive activities can influence the level of creativity observed, at least for certain tasks. Thus, creative problem-solving seems to depend on having certain cognitive-conative resources *and* using them at appropriate points in the problem-solving process. It may well be that some potentially creative people who have relevant capacities and traits do not produce creative ideas because they fail to put their resources into action during the problem-solving process, with the optimal use of these resources being domain or task specific.

CREATIVITY AS A SOURCE OF DIFFICULTY IN PROBLEM SOLVING: ANOTHER LOOK

Up to this point, we have developed the idea that creativity is a source of difficulty in problem solving because some problems require original solutions and these solutions are not easy to generate. They require a set of cognitive and conative factors that are used at appropriate moments in the course of problem solving. In this final section, we consider briefly a rather different way in which creativity is a source of difficulty in problem solving.

Consider the following case that a physics professor submitted to his colleague, whom he requested to be an impartial judge: The physics professor asked on an exam how one could measure the height of a building using a barometer. The student replied that one could take the barometer to the top of the building, attach it to a cord, slowly let the barometer down along the side of the building and once the barometer was on the ground, bring it back up and measure the length of the cord to determine the height of the building. This answer was given a zero; it did not use any of the formulas taught in class. However the student claimed that the answer deserved full credit.

The impartial colleague of the student's professor decided to give the student a second chance and asked the student to respond to the question using his knowledge of physics. After several minutes without any response the impartial professor asked the student if he had found a solution. The student said that he had several and was trying to choose the best one. Soon after, he proposed putting the barometer on the roof and dropping it from the building. The height of the building can be found by applying a formula that takes into account the time it took the barometer to reach to ground and the gravitational constant. The impartial professor decided that this response deserved full credit.

Seeing how the student had considered several answers, the impartial professor was curious to know what were the others. The student explained that one could put the barometer in the sun and measure its shadow as well as the building's shadow, and then compare the two using a simple proportion. He noted several other solutions as well, such as one in which the barometer could be used as part of a pendulum with measures taken at the top and bottom of building. Finally, the student proposed that one could offer the building's superintendent a barometer as a gift if he would give the height of the building.

At the end of this exam, the impartial professor asked the student whether he knew which answer his professor had expected. The student replied that he did but he was fed up with having to spit back information to get a good grade. The student, by the way, was Niels Bohr, who went on to win the Nobel Prize in physics. The impartial professor was Ernest Rutherford.

Ogden Nash, the modern American poet, summed up the point of the story in his work entitled *Reflections on Ingenuity*: "Sometimes too clever is dumb." In other words, being creative can get one into trouble if "canned" problem solving is requested. Every year there are cases of students who claim that they deserve credit for their creative answers to test items, because their responses are valid but do not correspond to the designated correct answer. In this vein, Cropley (1996) described the case of a teacher who asked his class of 5-year-olds to provide examples of "workers in wood." Several answers were proposed, such as cabinet maker or carpenter. Then, one child proposed "termites." The teacher became angry at the child and told him to be silent if he was not able to propose a valid answer. Employing creative thinking when a canned problem solving mode is requested can be, itself, a problem.

Using the Ideal Child Checklist, which consists of a series of 66 traits to be evaluated as desirable or not for an ideal child, studies by Kaltsounis (1977a, 1977b) and Torrance (1975) have compared the teachers' opinions with those of a panel of experts in the field of creative personality. The results were striking: The traits characterizing an ideal student for elementary school teachers were not at all similar to creativity experts' descriptions of an ideal creative child's profile. For example, teachers favored traits such as "considerate of others" or "doing work on time," whereas creativity experts saw "courage in convictions," "curiosity," and "independent thinking" as the most valuable characteristics. Kaltsounis reported that there was only 4% of shared variance between the rankings given by teachers and creativity researchers. Another study involving student teachers showed that they valued highly "obedience/submission to authority" and did not value "unwillingness to accept things on mere say-so," which are obviously antithetical to creativity. Such findings suggest that at least some school settings do not particularly emphasize creative problem solving, and may even sanction it. Thus, we see how the environment is important for providing a setting that favors or inhibits creative problem solving.

CONCLUSION

All problem solving is not creative problem solving. Although we have contrasted "creative" and "canned" problem solving, there exists a continuum between the two extremes; some problem solving relies heavily on existing procedures but requires some novelty, some enhancements to existing structures (Sternberg, 1999). In any case, the ability to come up with new and useful ideas applies to a wide range of problem situations ("creative" and "partially canned" ones) and represents one of the most valuable human assets. At the level of the individual, creativity relates to coping abilities, leadership, self-actualization, and psychological health (Carson & Runco, 1999). At the societal level, creative solutions contribute to major cultural advancements.

Why is creative problem solving often difficult? First, because creative thinking involves a large set of cognitive and conative factors. Second, these factors must be used appropriately during task completion, the problem solving process. Third, some environments are hostile toward new ideas and may even view creative thinking as a hindrance. Identifying difficulties associated with creative problem solving is one thing, overcoming these difficulties is another. Both of these endeavors should be pursued because, in our view, there is much to problem solving beyond "canned" solutions.

REFERENCES

Amabile, T. M. (1983). *The social psychology of creativity*. New York: Springer-Verlag.

Amabile, T. M. (1996). *Creativity in context*. Boulder, CO: Westview.

Amabile, T. M. (1997). Entrepreneurial creativity through motivational synergy. *Journal of Creative Behavior, 31*(1), 18–26.

Baer, J. (1991). *Creativity and divergent thinking: A task-specific approach*. Hillsdale, NJ: Erlbaum.

Baer, J. (1998). Gender differences in the effects of extrinsic motivation on creativity. *Journal of Creative Behavior, 32*(1), 18–37.

Barron, F., & Harrington, D. M. (1981). Creativity, intelligence, and personality. *Annual Review of Psychology, 32*, 439–476.

Brophy, D. R. (1998). Understanding, measuring, and enhancing individual creative problem-solving efforts. *Creativity Research Journal, 11*(2), 123–150.

Busse, T. V., & Mansfield, R. S. (1980). Theories of the creative process: A review and a perspective. *Journal of Creative Behavior, 14*(2), 91–103.

Cagle, M. (1985). A general abstract-concrete model of creative thinking. *Journal of Creative Behavior, 19*(2), 104–109.

Carson, D. K., & Runco, M. A. (1999). Creative problem solving and problem finding in young adults: Interconnections with stress, hassles, and coping abilities. *Journal of Creative Behavior, 33*(3), 167–190.

Cattell, R. B., Eber, H. W., & Tatsuoka, M. M. (1970). *The handbook for the Sixteen Personality Factor (16PF) Questionnaire*. Champaign, IL: Institute for Personality and Ability Testing.

Cawelti, S., Rappaport, A., & Wood, B. (1992). Modeling artistic creativity: An empirical study. *Journal of Creative Behavior, 26*(2), 83–94.

Collins, M. A., & Amabile, T. M. (1999). Motivation and creativity. In R. J. Sternberg (Ed.), *Handbook of creativity* (pp. 297–312). Cambridge: Cambridge University Press.

Conti, R., Coon, H., & Amabile, T. M. (1996). Evidence to support the componential model of creativity: Secondary analyses of three studies. *Creativity Research Journal, 9*(4), 385–389.

Cropley, A. J. (1996). Recognizing creative potential: An evaluation of the usefulness of creativity tests. *High Ability Studies, 7*(2), 203–219.

Cropley, A. J. (1999). Creativity and cognition: Producing effective novelty. *Roeper Review, 21*(4), 253–260.

Csikszentmihalyi, M. (1988). Society, culture, and person: A systems view of creativity. In R. J. Sternberg (Ed.), *The nature of creativity: Contemporary psychological perspectives* (pp. 325–339). New York: Cambridge University Press.

Csikszentmihalyi, M. (1999). Implications of a systems perspective for the study of creativity. In R. J. Sternberg (Ed.), *Handbook of creativity* (pp. 313–335). Cambridge: Cambridge University Press.

Davidson, J. E., & Sternberg, R. J. (1984). The role of insight in intellectual giftedness. *Gifted Child Quarterly, 28,* 58–64.

de Alencar, E., & Bruno Faria, M. (1997). Characteristics of an organizational environment which stimulate and inhibit creativity. *Journal of Creative Behavior, 31*(4), 271–281.

Dellas, M., & Gaier, E. L. (1970). Identification of creativity: The individual. *Psychological Bulletin, 73,* 55–73.

Dudek, S. Z., & Hall, W. B. (1991). Personality consistency: Eminent architects 25 years later. *Creativity Research Journal, 4*(3), 213–231.

Ebert, E. S. (1994). The cognitive spiral: Creative thinking and cognitive processing. *Journal of Creative Behavior, 28*(4), 275–290.

Eisenberger, R., & Armeli, S. (1997). Can salient reward increase creative performance without reducing intrinsic creative interest? *Journal of Personality and Social Psychology, 72*(3), 652–663.

Eisenberger, R., & Cameron, J. (1996). Detrimental effects of reward: Reality or myth? *American Psychologist, 51*(11), 1153–1166.

Eisenberger, R., & Cameron, J. (1998). Reward, intrinsic interest, and creativity: New findings. *American Psychologist, 53*(6), 676–679.

Eysenck, H. J. (1994). Creativity and personality: Word association, origence, and psychoticism. *Creativity Research Journal, 7*(2), 209–216.

Eysenck, H. J. (1995). *Genius: The natural history of creativity*. Cambridge: Cambridge University Press.

Eysenck, H. J., & Eysenck, S. B. G. (1975). *Manual of the Eysenck Personality Questionnaire*. London: Hodder & Stoughton.

Feist, G. J. (1998). A meta-analysis of personality in scientific and artistic creativity. *Personality and Social Psychology Review, 2*(4), 290–309.

Feist, G. J. (1999). The influence of personality on artistic and scientific creativity. In R. J. Sternberg (Ed.), *Handbook of creativity* (pp. 273–296). Cambridge: Cambridge University Press.

Feldhusen, J. F. (1995). Creativity: A knowledge base, metacognitive skills, and personality factors. *Journal of Creative Behavior, 29*(4), 255–268.

Feldman, D. H., Csikszentmihalyi, M., & Gardner, H. (1994). *Changing the world: A framework for the study of creativity*. Westport, CT: Praeger.

Finke, R. A., Ward, T. B., & Smith, S. M. (1992). *Creative cognition: Theory, research, and applications*. Cambridge, MA: MIT Press.

Frensch, P. A., & Sternberg, R. J. (1989). Expertise and intelligent thinking: When is it worse to know better? In R. J. Sternberg (Ed.), *Advances in the psychology of human intelligence* (Vol. 5, pp. 157–188). Hillsdale, NJ: Erlbaum.

Gerrard, L. E., Poteat, G. M., & Ironsmith, M. (1996). Promoting children's creativity: Effects of competition, self-esteem, and immunization. *Creativity Research Journal, 9*(4), 339–346.

Getz, I., & Lubart, T. I. (2000). An emotional-experiential perspective on creative symbolic-metaphorical processes. *Consciousness & Emotion, 1*(2), 89–118.

Getz, I., & Lubart, T. I. (2001). Psychologie, economie et créativité: Exploration de leurs interactions [Psychology, economics and creativity: Exploration of their interactions]. *Psychologie Française, 46*(4), 365–378.

Getzels, J., & Csikszentmihalyi, M. (1976). *The creative vision: A longitudinal study of problem-finding in art*. New York: Wiley-Interscience.

Goor, A., & Sommerfeld, R. E. (1975). A comparison of problem-solving processes of creative students and noncreative students. *Journal of Educational Psychology, 67*(4), 495–505.

Goswami, A. (1996). Creativity and the quantum: A unified theory of creativity. *Creativity Research Journal, 9*(1), 47–61.

Gough, H. G. (1987). *California Psychological Inventory: Administrators' guide.* Palo Alto, CA: Consulting Psychologists Press.

Gray, C. E. (1966). A measurement of creativity in western civilization. *American Anthropologist, 68,* 1384–1417.

Guastello, S. J., Shissler, J., Driscoll, J., & Hyde, T. (1998). Are some cognitive styles more creatively productive than others? *Journal of Creative Behavior, 32*(2), 77–91.

Guilford, J. P. (1967). *The nature of human intelligence.* New York: McGraw-Hill.

Helson, R. (1999). A longitudinal study of creative personality in women. *Creativity Research Journal, 12*(2), 89–101.

Hennessey, B. A., & Amabile, T. M. (1998). Reward, intrinsic motivation, and creativity. *American Psychologist, 53*(6), 674–675.

Hennessey, B. A., Amabile, T. M., & Martinage, M. (1989). Immunizing children against the negative effects of reward. *Contemporary Educational Psychology, 14,* 212–227.

Hennessey, B. A., & Zbikowski, S. (1993). Immunizing children against the negative effects of reward: A further examination of intrinsic motivation training techniques. *Creativity Research Journal, 6,* 297–308.

Israeli, N. (1962). Creative processes in painting. *Journal of General Psychology, 67*(2), 251–263.

Israeli, N. (1981). Decision in painting and sculpture. *Academic Psychology Bulletin, 3*(1), 61–74.

Kaltsounis, B. (1977a). Middle Tennessee teachers' perception of ideal pupils. *Perceptual and Motor Skills, 44,* 803–806.

Kaltsounis, B. (1977b). Student teachers' perceptions of ideal pupils. *Perceptual and Motor Skills, 44,* 160.

Kasof, J. (1997). Creativity and breadth of attention. *Creativity Research Journal, 10*(4), 303–315.

King, M. J. (1997). Apollo 13 creativity: In-the-box innovation. *Journal of Creative Behavior, 31*(4), 299–308.

Lubart, T. I. (1994). *Product-centered self-evaluation and the creative process.* Unpublished doctoral Dissertation, Yale University, New Haven, CT.

Lubart, T. I. (1999a). Componential models. In M. A. Runco & S. R. Pritsker (Eds.), *Encyclopedia of creativity* (Vol. 1, pp. 295–300). New York: Academic Press.

Lubart, T. I. (1999b). Creativity across cultures. In R. J. Sternberg (Ed.), *Handbook of creativity* (pp. 339–350). Cambridge: Cambridge University Press.

Lubart, T. I. (2000–2001). Models of the creative process: Past, present and future. *Creativity Research Journal, 13*(3–4), 295–308.

Lubart, T. I., & Getz, I. (1997). Emotion, metaphor, and the creative process. *Creativity Research Journal, 10,* 285–301.

Lubart, T. I., & Sternberg, R. J. (1995). An investment approach to creativity: Theory and data. In S. M. Smith, T. B. Ward, & R. A. Finke (Eds.), *The creative cognition approach* (pp. 271–302). Cambridge, MA: MIT Press.

MacKinnon, D. W. (1962). The nature and nurture of creative talent. *American Psychologist, 17*, 484–495.

Marchant, G., Robinson, J. P., Anderson, U., & Schadewald, M. (1991). Analogical transfer and expertise in legal reasoning. *Organizational Behavior and Human Decision Processes, 48*(2), 272–290.

Martinsen, O. (1995). Cognitive styles and experience in solving insight problems: Replication and extension. *Creativity Research Journal, 8*, 291–298.

Martinsen, O. (1997). The construct of cognitive style and its implications for creativity. *High Ability Studies, 8*(2), 135–158.

Martinsen, O., & Kaufmann, G. (1999). Cognitive style and creativity. In M. A. Runco & S. R. Pritsker (Eds.), *Encyclopedia of creativity* (Vol. 1, pp. 273–282). New York: Academic Press.

Mayer, R. (1999). Problem solving. In M. A. Runco & S. R. Pritzker (Eds.), *Encyclopedia of creativity* (Vol. 2, pp. 437–447). New York: Academic Press.

Mayer, R. E. (1983). *Thinking, problem solving, cognition.* New York: Freeman.

Mednick, S. A. (1962). The associative basis of the creative process. *Psychological Review, 69*, 220–232.

Mehr, D. G., & Shaver, P. R. (1996). Goal structures in creative motivation. *Journal of Creative Behavior, 30*(2), 77–104.

Mouchiroud, C., & Lubart, T. I. (2000). *The development of social creativity: Analysis of its specificity in children.* Paper presented at the XVIth Biennal Meeting of the International Society for the Study of Behavioural Development, Beijing, China.

Mouchiroud, C., & Lubart, T. I. (2002). Social creativity: A cross-sectional study of 6- to 11-year-old children. *International Journal of Behavioral Development, 26*(1), 60–69.

Mumford, M. D., Baughman, W. A., Maher, M. A., Costanza, D. P., & Supinski, E. P. (1997). Process-based measures of creative problem-solving skills: IV. Category combination. *Creativity Research Journal, 10*(1), 59–71.

Mumford, M. D., Costanza, D. P., Threlfall, K. V., & Baughman, W. A. (1993). Personality variables and problem-construction activities: An exploratory investigation. *Creativity Research Journal, 6*(4), 365–389.

Mumford, M. D., & Gustafson, S. B. (1988). Creativity syndrome: Integration, application, and innovation. *Psychological Bulletin, 103*(1), 27–43.

Mumford, M. D., Mobley, M. I., Uhlman, C. E., Reiter-Palmon, R., & Doares, L. M. (1991). Process analytic models of creative capacities. *Creativity Research Journal, 4*(2), 91–122.

Mumford, M. D., Supinski, E. P., Baughman, W. A., Costanza, D. P., & Threlfall, K. V. (1997). Process-based measures of creative problem-solving skills: V. Overall prediction. *Creativity Research Journal, 10*(1), 73–85.

Noppe, L. D. (1996). Progression in the service of the ego, cognitive styles, and creative thinking. *Creativity Research Journal, 9*, 369–383.

Ochse, R. (1990). *Before the gates of excellence.* New York: Cambridge University Press.

Osborn, A. F. (1953). *Applied imagination.* New York: Charles Scribner's Sons.

Raidl, M.-H., & Lubart, T. I. (2000–2001). An empirical study of intuition and creativity. *Imagination, Cognition and Personality, 20*(3), 217–230.

Romer, P. M. (1994). The origins of endogenous growth. *Journal of Economic Perspectives, 8*, 3–22.

Rothenberg, A. (1996). The Janusian process in scientific creativity. *Creativity Research Journal, 9*(2–3), 207–231.

Runco, M. A. (1987). The generality of creative performance in gifted and non-gifted children. *Gifted Child Quarterly, 31,* 121–125.

Runco, M. A., & Chand, I. (1995). Cognition and creativity. *Educational Psychology Review, 7*(3), 243–267.

Runco, M. A., & Dow, G. (1999). Problem finding. In M. A. Runco & S. R. Pritsker (Eds.), *Encyclopedia of creativity* (Vol. 2, pp. 433–435). New York: Academic Press.

Runco, M. A., Nemiro, J., & Walberg, H. J. (1998). Personal explicit theories of creativity. *Journal of Creative Behavior, 32*(1), 1–17.

Ruscio, J., Whitney, D. M., & Amabile, T. M. (1998). Looking inside the fishbowl of creativity: Verbal and behavioral predictors of creative performance. *Creativity Research Journal, 11*(3), 243–263.

Shalley, C. E., & Oldham, G. R. (1997). Competition and creative performance: Effects of competitor presence and visibility. *Creativity Research Journal, 10*(4), 337–345.

Simonton, D. K. (1984). *Genius, creativity, and leadership.* Cambridge, MA: Harvard University Press.

Simonton, D. K. (1988). Creativity, leadership, and chance. In R. J. Sternberg (Ed.), *The nature of creativity: Contemporary psychological perspectives* (pp. 386–426). New York: Cambridge University Press.

Stein, M. I. (1974). *Stimulating creativity: Individual procedures.* New York: Academic Press.

Sternberg, R. J. (1985). *Beyond IQ: A triarchic theory of human intelligence.* New York: Cambridge University Press.

Sternberg, R. J. (1997). *Thinking styles.* Cambridge: Cambridge University Press

Sternberg, R. J. (1999). A propulsion model of types of creative contribution. *Review of General Psychology, 3*(2), 83–100.

Sternberg, R. J., & Davidson, J. E. (Eds.). (1995). *The nature of insight.* Cambridge, MA: MIT Press.

Sternberg, R. J., & Lubart, T. I. (1991). An investment theory of creativity and its development. *Human Development, 34,* 1–31.

Sternberg, R. J., & Lubart, T. I. (1995). *Defying the crowd: Cultivating creativity in a culture of conformity.* New York: Free Press.

Sternberg, R. J., & Lubart, T. I. (1996). Investing in creativity. *American Psychologist, 51*(7), 677–688.

Sternberg, R. J., & O'Hara, L. A. (1999). Creativity and intelligence. In R. J. Sternberg (Ed.), *Handbook of creativity* (pp. 251–272). Cambridge: Cambridge University Press.

Taylor, I. A. (1959). The nature of the creative process. In P. Smith (Ed.), *Creativity: An examination of the creative process* (pp. 51–82). New York: Hastings House Publishers.

Taylor, I. A., Austin, G. A., & Sutton, D. F. (1974). A note on "instant creativity" at CPSI. *Journal of Creative Behavior, 8*(3), 208–210.

Tesluk, P. E., Farr, J. L., & Klein, S. R. (1997). Influences of organizational culture and climate on individual creativity. *Journal of Creative Behavior, 31*(1), 27–41.

Torrance, E. P. (1975). *Ideal Child Checklist.* Athens, GA: Georgia Studies of Creative Behavior.

Wallas, G. (1926). *The art of thought*. New York: Harcourt, Brace.

Ward, T. B., Smith, S. M., & Finke, R. A. (1999). Creative cognition. In R. J. Sternberg (Ed.), *Handbook of creativity* (pp. 189–212). Cambridge: Cambridge University Press.

Weisberg, R. W. (1999). Creativity and knowledge: A challenge to theories. In R. J. Sternberg (Ed.), *Handbook of creativity* (pp. 226–250). Cambridge: Cambridge University Press.

Wiley, J. (1998). Expertise as mental set: The effects of domain knowledge in creative problem solving. *Memory and Cognition, 26*(4), 716–730.

Witkin, H. A., Dyk, R., Faterson, H. F., Goodenough, D. R., & Karp, S. A. (1962). *Psychological differentiation*. New York: Wiley.

Woodman, R. W., & Schoenfeldt, L. F. (1990). An interactionist model of creative behavior. *Journal of Creative Behavior, 24*(4), 279–291.

5

Insights about Insightful Problem Solving

Janet E. Davidson

Many years ago, I tried to go night skiing with some friends. We were driving to the mountain wishing we had checked the ski report to find out whether there would be snow, when suddenly we found ourselves in a blizzard. Cars were skidding off the road and getting stuck in large snowdrifts. The car I was in also went off the road, but the driver, who had never before driven in a blizzard, somehow managed to get it back on course. (I cannot tell you how he did this because I had my eyes closed.)

A similar situation occurs when people try to solve nonroutine problems. Nonroutine problems can be difficult because we do not possess preexisting procedures for solving them (Mayer, 1995). This difficulty is compounded when the givens, goals, and obstacles in the problems are not well specified. Under these conditions, there are times when we all go off track. Some people manage to get on course and successfully solve the problem; others remain stuck. In this chapter I claim that the ability to get on track when solving nonroutine problems often involves conceptual change and insight. In addition, getting on track in one's problem solving, after being off course, is frequently accompanied by a feeling of suddenly knowing what to do.

Insight has long been associated with creative thoughts and products. For example, Graham Wallas (1926) proposed four stages involved in the creative process. These stages are (1) preparation, where the problem solver gathers relevant information and begins conscious work on a problem; (2) incubation, which is a period of time away from consciously working on the problem; (3) illumination or insight, when the problem solver suddenly "sees" or knows how to solve the problem; and (4) verification, where the solution is worked out and checked for accuracy. Many important contributions to the world have been attributed to the third stage, where insight or illumination occurs (Gruber, 1981). If major, or even minor, accomplishments do stem from insightful problem solving, then it seems important to understand the nature of these seemingly sudden realizations. In addition, our general understanding of how successful problem solving occurs would be incomplete if we did not consider the role, if any, of insight.

But what exactly is insight? This surprisingly controversial question has been around since the early 1900s, and several different approaches have tried to answer it. Four of these approaches are discussed in this chapter. Each approach has its own goals and methodology, and each one tells a different part of the story of insight. First, the Gestalt approach sets the historical context for the later approaches. Gestalt psychologists introduced the concept of insightful problem solving, and many aspects of it that are still being studied today. Second, the nothing-special approach tests the null hypothesis that insight does not actually exist. This approach examines some of the Gestaltists' assumptions and attempts to illustrate how nonroutine problems could be solved using routine processes. Third, the puzzle-problem approach uses perplexing riddles and mathematical problems to examine empirically the mental processes and subjective feelings involved in insight. Finally, the great-minds approach analyzes, usually retrospectively, the commonalties in societally recognized demonstrations of insight. In the concluding section of this chapter, these approaches are critiqued and integrated to highlight what is and is not known about insightful problem solving.

HISTORICAL CONTEXT FOR INSIGHT: THE GESTALT APPROACH

Our story of insightful problem solving begins with the Gestalt psychologists. Prior to this time, problem solving was thought to begin with trial and error applications of preexisting responses. It was believed that people automatically form associations during trial and error learning and that these associations result in reproductive thinking. When problem solvers receive a routine problem, they simply reproduce a solution that they have previously associated with success on the problem (Thorndike, 1911). When faced with a novel problem, they extend or modify their associations. In other words, nothing completely new is ever created.

In sharp contrast to this associationist view, the Gestaltists felt that insightful problem solving occurs through productive thinking. In productive thinking, the problem solver goes beyond old associations and views a problem in a completely new way (Kohler, 1925; Wertheimer, 1945/1959). A novel solution is produced, often preceded by an "Aha!" experience or a feeling of suddenly knowing what needs to be done. In other words, insight occurs when a problem solver moves from not knowing how to reach a problem's goal to a deep understanding of the problem and its solution (Maier, 1940).

The Gestaltists were interested in the conditions that do and do not promote insight. They believed that people's inability to produce an insightful solution for a problem is often due to their fixation on past experience and associations. For example, in what is now seen as a classic insight problem, Karl Duncker (1945) gave people three small cardboard boxes, candles, matches, and thumbtacks. The participants' task was to mount a candle vertically on a screen so that it could serve as a reading lamp. The solution is to light a candle, melt wax onto the top of a box, stick the candle into the wax, and tack the box to the screen. Individuals who were given boxes filled with tacks, matches, and candles had much more difficulty solving the problem than did people who received the same supplies outside of the boxes. According to Duncker, seeing a box serve the typical function of a container made it difficult for problem solvers also to view the box as a structural support. This phenomenon became known as functional fixedness and has been replicated in a variety of studies (e.g., Adamson, 1952, Adamson & Taylor, 1954; DiVesta & Walls, 1967; Scheerer, 1963.)

According to the Gestalt view, functional fixedness is not the only type of fixation, or mental block, that interferes with insightful problem solving. Fixation on previous solution procedures can also inhibit insightful thinking. For example, Luchins (1942; Luchins & Luchins, 1950) had subjects use three hypothetical water jugs of varying capacity to obtain precise quantities of water. Problems within a set all required the same solution procedure. When a new problem was introduced that could be solved using either a new, simple solution procedure or the complicated one that had been established, Luchins found that most participants did not notice the simple solution. In other words, fixation can keep people from changing their problem-solving strategies, even when old procedures are not as relevant to the present situation. The Gestaltists speculated that breaking fixations, or mental blocks, allows problem solvers to view a situation in a new way and, therefore, reach an insightful solution.

Richard Mayer (1995) derived four other sources of insightful problem solving, in addition to the source of overcoming fixation, that were introduced by Gestalt psychologists. For example, in the early 1900s, Otto Seltz proposed that insightful problem solving could occur when the problem solver discovers how to complete a mental schema for a problem. Complete schemas are important because they allow the problem solver to fill in gaps between the given elements and the goals of a problem, thus making the path to solution more obvious. Seltz (see Frijda & de Groot, 1982) provided empirical support for his view by asking problem solvers to think aloud as they solved word-association problems, such as naming a superordinate of newspaper (e.g., publication) or a subordinate of the tool category (e.g., ax). Selz found that problem solvers did not solve these problems simply by generating a series of word associations. Instead, they performed goal-directed cognitive operations in an attempt to create a coherent, integrated structure (or schema) for the given elements and desired outcome imbedded in a problem.

According to Mayer (1995), another Gestalt source of insightful problem solving involves the spontaneous restructuring of visual information
related to a problem's goal. This view highlights the relationship between
Gestalt views of problem solving and Gestalt principles of perception.
Sudden changes in how information is perceived are similar to figure-
ground reversals where "elements at one moment are seen as one unity, at
the same moment, another unity appears with the same elements" (Ellen,
1982, p. 324). For example, Wolfgang Kohler (1925) observed a chimpanzee
trying unsuccessfully to reach a bunch of bananas hung above his reach.
Fortunately, the chimpanzee was able to view the crates in his cage as the
makings of a set of stairs. By stacking the crates and climbing the finished
structure, he successfully reached the bananas. Kohler concluded that the
chimpanzee's cognitive reorganization of information in his visual field
allowed him to reach an insightful solution.

A third source of insight that was introduced by the Gestalt psychologists involves the reformulation, or restructuring, of a problem's components so that the problem is viewed in a new way. Reformulation can
occur multiple times as an individual moves from general to specific mental
representations of a problem. It can also occur in one of two parts of a problem. A suggestion from above involves the reformulation of a problem's
goal or desired outcome. Although this view is most often attributed to
Duncker (1945), Max Wertheimer provides a simple example (1945/1959,
pp. 169–181). Suppose two boys of different ages played multiple games
of badminton and the older boy consistently beat the younger one. The
younger, less talented player refuses to play again, even though the older
boy desperately wants to continue. How can the older boy get the younger
one to play? One possible solution would be for him to change the goal of
the game from a competition to a cooperative effort. In other words, the
boys could now focus on keeping the badminton bird in play as long as
possible, counting their number of consecutive hits. As their proficiency
increased, they could move to more difficult shots.

A suggestion from below involves reformulating, in a productive way,
the given elements of a problem. Consider, for example, the two-string
problem used by Maier (1930, 1931, 1970), where the problem solver is
asked to tie together two strings that are hanging from the ceiling. Because the strings are too far apart to be held at the same time, one of
them needs to be reformulated as a potential pendulum. The solution
is to tie a moderately heavy object to one of the strings, set it into motion, and then grasp the other string. When the pendulum is caught on
its upswing, the two strings can be tied together. Reformulations of a
problem's given elements can occur if the problem solver spontaneously
views them in a new way or if external hints are provided. For example,
Maier found that most participants solved the two-string problem when
the experimenter bumped into one of the strings and set it into motion.

Interestingly, these problem solvers were usually unaware that a hint had been provided.

Finally, according to the Gestalt psychologist Max Wertheimer (1945/1959), insight can occur when a problem solver finds an analogue to a problem he or she is trying to solve. Unlike fixation, where one has to overcome a reliance on prior experience, here the problem solver capitalizes on his or her prior knowledge and experience. In other words, a connection is seen between the structural organization of a familiar situation and the structural organization of a new problem. This connection allows the problem solver to understand the new problem's solution.

Wertheimer (1945/1959) provided empirical support for his view of problem formulation in part through the use of problems requiring students to find the area of parallelograms. First, he gave students one of two types of training. One type focused on the formula for finding a parallelogram's area, but not on a conceptual understanding of the structural nature of the problem. The second type of training capitalized on students' prior knowledge about finding the area of rectangles. Students were shown how to remove the triangle found at each end of a parallelogram and to combine these two triangles into a rectangle. By computing the areas of the two rectangles that comprise a parallelogram and adding them together, they would have the parallelogram's total area. When students were given transfer problems that were somewhat different from the ones used during training, Wertheimer found that type of training influenced problem-solving performance. Most students who were merely taught the formula were unable to solve the transfer problems; they did not know where to begin. In contrast, the students who understood the structural relationship between a parallelogram and a rectangle successfully applied their knowledge to the new problems.

The Gestalt approach raised important questions about insightful problem solving but provided few answers about exactly what insight is and how it occurs. Gestalt descriptions of insight as resulting from accelerated mental processes, a short-circuiting of conventional reasoning, or unconscious leaps in thinking, for example, are vague and do not specify what insight is or precisely how it takes place (Perkins, 1981). In other words, no coherent, falsifiable theory of insightful problem-solving developed from this approach. In addition, the research has been criticized for not being scientifically rigorous or representative of problem-solving situations (Ohlsson, 1984a, 1984b; Weisberg, 1986). Only one problem was used in some of the studies and it was presented under artificial circumstances.

It should be emphasized, however, that the Gestalt psychologists left behind a powerful legacy. They introduced many of the ideas about insight being studied today and they created some of the "insight" problems that are still being used. In addition, and perhaps most important, the

Gestalt approach led us to consider whether nonroutine problems are solved in a different manner than routine ones.

THE NOTHING-SPECIAL APPROACH

As mentioned earlier, the prevailing view prior to the Gestalt approach was that all problem solving occurs through reproductive, associative thinking. Just as the Gestaltists left behind a legacy, associationism influenced a current approach to insight that is sometimes called the nothing-special approach (Davidson & Sternberg, 1984; Sternberg & Davidson, 1982) or the memory position (Finke, Ward, & Smith, 1992). In contrast to the Gestalt approach, the nothing-special view of insight proposes that insightful problem solving is basically the same as routine problem solving (Langley & Jones, 1988; Perkins, 1981; Weisberg, 1986). What we think of as insights, according to the nothing-special view, are merely significant products that come from ordinary mental processes. This would mean that "insight" problems, such as the candle problem and the two-string problem mentioned above, are inaccurately named. Such problems mostly measure the retrieval and application of problem-specific prior knowledge. For example, Robert Weisberg and Joseph Alba (1981) asked participants to solve "classic" insight problems, such as the "nine-dot" problem.

In the nine-dot problem, individuals are each given a 3 × 3 matrix of nine equally spaced dots and asked to connect the nine dots with four straight lines without lifting their pencils from the paper. What was unusual about Weisberg and Alba's experiment was that participants were given a crucial clue that is needed to solve the problem: They were told that the problem could be solved only by drawing the lines beyond the implicit boundaries formed by the dots. Unlike Maier's two-string experiment (1930, 1931, 1970), where participants benefited from an external clue, Weisberg and Alba's hint did not help their participants. Even when problem solvers were essentially told how to reformulate the nine-dot problem's elements, they had difficulty finding the answer. However, they were much better at solving it after they had been trained on highly similar problems.

From their results, Weisberg and Alba conclude that the retrieval of relatively specific prior knowledge about a problem, rather than insightful thinking, is the key to successful problem solving. Therefore, according to their view, the terms *fixation* and *insight* do not belong in theories of problem solving. Weisberg and Alba (1982) do note, however, differences in how prior knowledge is applied to routine and nonroutine problems.

> Retrieval of problem-specific past experience is only the first step in solving a problem; the problem solver then attempts to apply this experience to the new problem. To the degree that the present problem is novel, solutions to previous problems will not completely solve

it. Therefore, the problem solver will be confronted with mismatches between past experience and the present problem. These mismatches serve as the basis for further searches of memory in the same way as the initial presentation of the problem initiated a memory search. These mismatches between the old solution and the new problem are new problems to be solved. The person attempts to solve these mismatch problems through further memory search, which may result in retrieval of information that will enable the person to eliminate the mismatch. This would result in a modification of the old solution in such a way as to solve the new problem. (p. 328)

In other words, multiple memory searches and the resulting variety of solution attempts can lead problem solvers to restructure nonroutine problems. However, this type of restructuring does not involve the spontaneous reorganization of previously unrelated experiences that the Gestaltists proposed.

Weisberg and Alba's claim that the retrieval of prior knowledge has a major influence on successful problem solving is similar to conclusions that have been drawn about how and why experts in a domain differ from novices. Several researchers (e.g., Chase & Simon, 1973; Chi, Feltovich, & Glaser, 1981; Larkin, McDermott, Simon, & Simon, 1980) have found that large, well-organized knowledge structures, rather than unique mental processes, allow experts to outperform novices when they solve standard domain-specific problems.

In addition, Perkins (1981) and Weisberg (1986) argue that the solution of nonroutine problems, as well as routine ones, takes place in incremental steps, rather than through spontaneous reformulations of the problems or leaps of insight. As support for this view, Perkins analyzed individuals' retrospective reports of how they solved the following problem:

A dealer in antique coins got an offer to buy a beautiful bronze coin. The coin had the emperor's head on one side and the date 554 B.C. on the other. The dealer examined the coin, but instead of buying it, he called the police. Why?

Very few problems solvers reported "Aha!" experiences, where they suddenly realized that the date was impossible because the coin's maker could not anticipate when, or even if, Christ would be born. The majority of participants verbalized a series of incremental steps involving ordinary understanding and reasoning skills. Partly based on this analysis, Perkins is skeptical of the Gestalt notion that solutions to novel problems are based on special mental processes that cannot be verbalized.

Further support for the nothing-special view comes from a set of computer programs that reproduced major scientific discoveries in a variety of domains (Langley, Simon, Bradshaw, & Zytkow, 1987). What is intriguing about these programs is that they used the same recognition processes that are used to solve routine problems. No special processes were needed for these computer-generated creative discoveries.

In sum, arguments for the nothing-special view are essentially arguments by default: Because insight processes have not been found, they must not exist. After repeated failures to identify a construct empirically, ascribing the failure to the nonexistence of the construct seems like a natural response. Such a response has two potential benefits. First, theories of problem solving are more parsimonious if the same mental processes can be used to explain performance on a variety of problems. Second, researchers who believe that insightful problem solving does differ from other types of problem solving are challenged to provide concrete empirical support for their view. Vague descriptions, anecdotal evidence, and lack of scientific rigor associated with the Gestalt approach cannot counteract the arguments and alternative explanations proposed by the nothing-special theorists.

There are, however, some methodological weaknesses connected with the nothing-special approach. Finding no differences between insightful and routine problem solving does not mean that significant differences do not exist. Consider, for example, the computer programs developed by Langley et al. (1987) to replicate important scientific discoveries. Writing computer programs that reproduce already known discoveries might well require processes that differ from those used by the scientists who originally defined the problems, created mental representations for them, and searched for and found the novel solutions (Kuczaj, Gory, & Xitco, 1998; Sternberg & Davidson, 1999).

Furthermore, some researchers have questioned Weisberg and Alba's interpretation of the results from their experiment using the nine-dot problem (e.g., Davidson & Sternberg, 1986; Dominowski, 1981; Ellen, 1982; Lung & Dominowski, 1985; Ohlsson, 1984a). These critics argue (a) that some problems, such as the nine-dot problem, may require more than one insight or restructuring, and (b) that Weisberg and Alba oversimplified the Gestalt notions of fixation and insight, then rejected these notions by asserting the null hypothesis (see Weisberg, 1993, for additional discussion).

Finally, recent research (e.g., Siegler, 2000; Siegler & Stern, 1998; Smith & Kounios, 1996) does not support David Perkins's (1981) view that solutions to novel problems occur in incremental steps that can be described by problem solvers. Robert Siegler and Elsbeth Stern, for example, found that the majority of second graders in their study abruptly generated an arithmetic insight at an unconscious level before they were able to verbalize it.

THE PUZZLE-PROBLEM APPROACH

Unlike the Gestalt approach, the puzzle-problem approach tends to use several constrained riddles and problems that are administered to a large number of participants in well-controlled settings. Several aspects of the Gestalt view of insight have been tested using this empirical approach. These aspects include fixation, incubation, and subjective feelings of suddenness associated with insight. In addition, the puzzle-problem approach has been used to identify specific mental processes involved in insightful problem solving.

To avoid problems of inconsistency found in past research, puzzle problems should meet certain criteria when they are used to study insight (Weisberg, 1995). First, their solutions must not be obvious to the people solving them. In fact, these puzzles are often nonroutine problems that are disguised as routine ones; they are designed to mislead solvers into taking incorrect solution paths. Consider the following problem:

> You have blue stockings and red stockings mixed in a dresser drawer in the ratio of 4 to 5. How many stockings must you remove in order to guarantee that you have a pair that is the same color?

Many people incorrectly assume that this is a ratio problem and, therefore, that they must compute the answer using the 4 : 5 information.

The second criterion is that the puzzle problems cannot be solved simply through a careful reading of the problems. An example of a problem not conducive to insight would be the following one about eggs. "Is it more correct to say the yolk is white or the yolk are white? " For a problem to foster insight, its solution must result from the formation of a new mental representation of the problem, not simply a careful reading of it. Consider a problem that is conducive to insight:

> Water lilies double in area every 24 hours. At the beginning of the summer, there is one water lily on a lake. It takes 30 days for the lake to become completely covered with water lilies. On what day is the lake half covered?

Most problem solvers attempt to solve this problem by working forward from the first day. To reach the correct solution of day 29, they must switch to a mental representation of the problem that involves working backward from the last day.

The final criterion is that solution of the problems cannot be dependent on labor-intensive computations or domain-specific prior knowledge. The puzzles should be solved when problem solvers change their mental representations of the givens, goals, and obstacles found in the problems, rather than through the application of knowledge that might be available only to individuals of certain ages, cultures, or educational backgrounds.

Mental Processes

If changes in the mental representations of problems are crucial for insightful problem solving, how do these changes occur? According to the three-process theory of insight (Davidson, 1995; Davidson & Sternberg, 1986), the mental processes of selective encoding, selective combination, and selective comparison are used to restructure one's mental representations. When individuals do not have a routine set of procedures for solving a problem, they often search through a space of alternative ways of solving it (Newell & Simon, 1972). Selective encoding, selective combination, and selective comparison help guide this search and lead to a change in the internal representation of the givens, the relations among the givens, or the goals found in a problem. Each of the three processes are discussed in turn.

Selective Encoding

Insightful encoding occurs when a person finds in a stimulus, or set of stimuli, one or more elements that previously have been nonobvious. Significant problems generally present an individual with large amounts of information, only some of which is relevant to problem solution. Selective encoding contributes to insight by restructuring one's mental representation so that information that was originally viewed as being irrelevant is now seen as relevant for problem solution. Also, information that was originally seen as relevant may now be viewed as irrelevant.

The problem of the two colors of stockings mixed in the ratio of 4 to 5 that was mentioned above illustrates how selective encoding can occur. Some individuals first try to use the ratio information and realize their computations lead to an absurd answer. They then review the problem and realize the ratio information is irrelevant. By focusing on the relevance of the two colors, they can imagine what would happen if they took stockings out of the drawer one at a time. After two drawings, they may not have a matching pair but the third drawing guarantees that they will have two stockings of the same color.

Ignaz Semmelweis's discovery of the importance of asepsis is a famous example of a selective encoding insight in science. While on the staff of the general hospital in Vienna, Semmelweis noticed that more women on the poor ward were dying from infection during childbirth than were women on the rich ward. He encoded that doctors, even if they came straight from working on cadavers, seldom washed their hands before they had contact with the poor women, and he realized the relevance that this had for spreading puerperal fever. Unfortunately, Semmelweis was ridiculed for this insight and committed suicide before others accepted the relevance of his discovery.

Selective Combination

Insightful combination occurs when an individual discovers a previously nonobvious framework for the relevant elements of a problem situation. In many problems, even when the relevant features have been identified, it is often difficult (a) to know that these features should be combined and (b) to find a procedure to combine them appropriately. Consider the following example:

> Using six matches, make four equilateral triangles with one complete match making up the side of the triangle.

Most problem solvers initially try to build a two-dimensional structure with the matches. When this fails to meet the problems' requirements, some individuals discover that they can combine the matches to form the three-dimensional structure of a tetrahedron.

Kary Mullis's Nobel prize–winning invention of polymerase chain reaction (PCR) seems to have involved an insight of selective combination. "There was not a single unknown in the scheme. Each step involved had been done already" (Mullis, 1998, p. 9). While driving his car and thinking about science, Mullis suddenly realized that the steps could be combined to replicate short sequences of DNA. He was surprised that the majority of his colleagues did not see the relevance his combination would have for producing abundant supplies of specific DNA sequences.

Selective Comparison

Insightful comparison occurs when one suddenly discovers a nonobvious connection between new information and prior knowledge. It is here that analogies, metaphors, and models are used to solve problems. (Selective comparison is related to Wertheimer's [1945/1959] view, mentioned earlier, that insight can occur when the structural organization of one problem is used to solve a new problem.) The person having an insight suddenly realizes that new information is similar to old information in some ways and then uses this similarity better to understand the newly acquired information. Consider the following problem:

> A jar contains 3 different sizes of buttons; there are 15 small buttons, 20 medium buttons, and 10 large buttons. You need 3 buttons of the same size. How many buttons must you take out of the jar in order to make sure that you will have 3 small, 3 medium, or 3 large buttons?

If individuals know how to solve the "two colors of stockings" problem mentioned earlier and see its relation to this new problem, they will ignore the quantities of each size button and imagine the longest sequence of drawings needed to ensure three of the same size (i.e., 7).

Archimedes's theory of "specific gravity" is a famous example of a selective comparison insight. While trying to determine whether silver had been put into King Hiero's crown, Archimedes supposedly took a bath. He noticed that the amount of water that was displaced in the bathtub was equal to the volume of his body that was under water. By drawing an analogy between his bath and the problem with the crown, Archimedes suddenly knew how to determine the purity of the crown. He could compute the crown's volume by placing it in water and measuring the amount of displaced water. The crown could then be weighed against an equal volume of gold. (But first, according to legend, he was compelled to run naked through the streets of Syracuse shouting "Eureka!")

In sum, these three processes form the basis for a theory of insightful problem solving. Selection and relevance are important to all three of these mental processes. In encoding, one is selecting elements from the often numerous possible elements that constitute the problem situation; the key is to select the relevant elements. In combination, an individual is selecting one of many possible ways in which elements of information can be combined or integrated; the key is to select a relevant way of combining the elements in a given situation. Selective comparison involves selecting one (or more) of numerous possible old elements of information to which to relate new information. There is any number of relations that might be drawn; the key is to select the relevant comparison or comparisons to make for one's purposes.

Note, however, that not every instance of selective encoding, selective combination, or selective comparison is an insight. To be referred to as insightful, the relevant selections must not occur to people immediately upon presentation of a problem. After individuals reach an impasse, they must spontaneously search for and discover previously overlooked relevant elements, methods for combining elements, or connections between prior knowledge and the problem situation. Also, successful search for this relevant information must result in an abrupt change in the problem solver's mental representation of the problem. In contrast, routine encodings, combinations, and comparisons do not require the self-management of a nonobvious search nor do they lead to a restructuring of one's mental representation of a problem. In other words, the proposed theory is process, rather than product, oriented. Nonroutine problems are more likely than routine problems to elicit insightful problem solving. However, one individual may correctly solve a nonroutine problem by having an insight, whereas another individual may solve the same problem correctly without having an insight. The difference between these two individuals lies in the nature of the processes they use, rather than in the outcome.

In studies conducted with children and adults, it was found that selective encoding, selective combination, and selective comparison play an important role in the solution of nonroutine problems and in individual differences in intelligent behavior. More specifically, individuals who solved the puzzle problems correctly were more likely than those who solved the problems incorrectly (a) to have above average intelligence, (b) to apply spontaneously the three insight processes, (c) to switch mental representations as a result of these processes, and (d) to take longer to solve the problems (Davidson, 1986, 1995; Sternberg & Davidson, 1982). The last finding supports the view that successful insights can require a great deal of preparation time and verification (Wallas, 1926). In addition, it was found that insightful problem solving can be trained on the basis of the three mental processes, and that the training effects are transferable and durable (Sternberg & Davidson, 1989).

It should be noted that individuals who correctly solved routine problems were also more likely than those who solved them incorrectly to have above average intelligence. In fact, intelligence test scores were more highly correlated with performance on routine problems than with performance on nonroutine problems, probably because standard tests of general intelligence emphasize routine problem solving. However, very little restructuring of mental representations occurred while participants were solving the routine problems, and restructuring was not related to accuracy. In addition, correct and incorrect solutions for routine problems took approximately the same length of time (Davidson, 1995).

In sum, insightful problem solving, unlike other types of problem solving, involves searching for and selecting previously overlooked relevant encodings, combinations, and comparisons of information and then restructuring one's mental representation of the problem based on this search. Highly intelligent individuals are better at this search and restructuring than individuals of average intelligence.

The Roles of Incubation

According to Wallas's four stages of creative problem solving described earlier, incubation often precedes illumination or insight. To understand how incubation can lead to insight, it helps to understand why novel problems are often difficult for us to solve. There are at least two reasons for their difficulty (Kaplan & Davidson, 1988). One reason is stereotypy. In this case, the problem solver becomes fixated on an incorrect solution procedure. As mentioned earlier, a property of many novel, nonroutine problems is that, on the surface, they appear to be routine ones. Unfortunately, applying routine procedures leads to obvious, but incorrect, solutions. Even when problem solvers realize that they are approaching a problem incorrectly, they often cannot break their focus on this approach in order to develop a more worthwhile plan for solution. In other words, fixation keeps individuals from changing their problem-solving strategies, even when they know that old procedures are not relevant to the current situation.

The other main source of problem difficulty involves the inability to generate any paths to solution. If a problem is sufficiently novel or complex, the solver may not know where to begin. For example, consider the task of cutting a hole in a 3 × 5 index card of sufficient size to put one's head through. If problem solvers do not have the insight to cut a spiral out of the card, they often cannot generate any strategies for solving this problem

(Davidson, 1995). In research using a range of problems, Schooler and Melcher (1995) found that problem solvers gave more statements about reaching an impasse on "insight" problems than on analytic problems. In other words, these individuals could generate more strategies for the analytic problems.

The role of incubation, or a break in conscious problem solving that results in illumination, has been tested in two ways using the puzzle-problem approach. One method, related to stereotypy, is to examine when a break in problem solving does and does not reduce fixation and lead to insightful solutions. The other method is to examine whether information provided during an incubation period helps the problem solver generate new strategies for solving a problem and, therefore, overcome an impasse. Each of these methods is discussed in turn.

Forgetting

According to Woodsworth (1938), "incubation consists in getting rid of false leads and hampering assumptions so as to approach the problem with an open mind" (p. 823). In other words, a break in problem solving allows unproductive fixations to weaken and more useful associations to surface. This implies that problem solvers must first have a sufficient period of preparation time on a problem, where incorrect assumptions can be formed and false solution paths pursued. If an incubation period occurs too early, individuals may not have adequately encoded the problem, let alone attempted its solution. A premature interruption would, therefore, hinder problem solving if elements of the problem, rather than false leads and assumptions, were forgotten. Similarly, if individuals are already pursuing a productive solution path, an interruption may hinder problem solving by causing them to lose track of this path (Murray & Denny, 1969). However, if individuals become fixated on incorrect solution procedures, a break from problem solving allows them to forget their fixations and approach the problem in a new way (Smith, 1995).

For example, Smith and Blankenship (1989) used rebus problems (picture-word puzzles) to examine the relationship between fixation and incubation. Correct solutions to rebuses are common phrases or idioms that fit the situation depicted in a problem. For example, the solution to "*timing tim ing*" is "*split second timing*" because the second word in the problem is divided into two parts. Misleading cues, such as "clock," were given along with the rebuses in order to block problem solvers' access to the correct solution. Smith and Blankenship found that relatively long incubation periods decreased individuals' memory of the misleading cues and increased their chances of accessing the correct solutions.

The explanation that an incubation period provides an opportunity for problem solvers to forget their fixation on incorrect procedures can account for some improvements in individuals' performance after they have had time away from a problem (Mednick, Mednick, & Mednick, 1964; Smith & Blankenship, 1989, 1991). However, forgetting cannot explain how incubation effects occur when no incorrect procedures are pursued during initial exposure to a problem. How can a break in problem solving help individuals generate paths to a problem's solution?

Opportunistic Assimilation

According to Colleen Seifert and her colleagues (Seifert, Meyer, Davidson, Patalno, & Yaniv, 1995), when motivated problem solvers cannot generate a path or strategy for solving a problem, their long-term memory systems store "failure indices" that mark the problem as unsolved. These individuals then move from the preparation stage of problem solving to the incubation stage, where they no longer consciously work on the problem. However, the "failure indices" in long-term memory cause them unconsciously to process the environment in light of the unsolved problem. Information that might be relevant to solving the problem now receives special attention, whereas this same information might have been ignored prior to the problem-solving impasse. If a piece of relevant information provides a potential solution path, problem solvers move from the incubation stage to the illumination (or insight) stage of problem solving.

Seifert et al. (1995) used two different paradigms to test the opportunistic-assimilation model of insight. In one, participants were exposed to target items and asked to judge whether the items were words or nonwords. They were not told that, at times, the target items would be related to general information questions they attempted to answer earlier. When old and new general information questions were given to participants a day later, the relevant target items helped them answer the questions they had previously failed. However, neither mere passage of time nor prior exposure to target items that were related to new general information questions improved problem-solving performance. In a memory-for-problems paradigm, participants were more likely later to remember puzzle problems when they had reached an impasse in solving them than when they had reached successful solutions or been interrupted prior to reaching an impasse. Results from both paradigms are consistent with the opportunistic-assimilation model of insightful problem solving: Impasse on a problem causes a failure index to be stored in long-term memory, and this index allows new information to be assimilated and used to overcome the impasse.

The Role of Affect

Insight is often defined as a sudden realization of a problem's solution (e.g., Duncker, 1945; Kaplan & Simon, 1990; Kohler, 1969; Worthy, 1975). In support of this definition, Janet Metcalfe (1986a, 1986b; Metcalfe & Weibe,

1987) found that steady increases in feelings of confidence (or warmth) that one is nearing a solution negatively predict correct solution of insight problems but positively predict correct solution of routine, algebra problems. In other words, individuals who felt they were gradually getting closer to solving insight problems tended to arrive at incorrect solutions, whereas individuals who felt they were far from solving the insight problems and then suddenly felt they knew the answers tended to give correct solutions. Metcalfe concludes that insight problems are correctly solved by a subjectively catastrophic process rather than by incremental processes.

In a follow-up to Metcalfe's work, Davidson (1995) asked adults to solve puzzle problems requiring selective encoding, selective combination, and selective comparison, and routine problems that had clear paths to their solution. In some cases, participants were given cues pointing to solution-relevant information in the problems. In addition to objective performance measures, Metcalfe's (1986a) subjective measure of problem solvers' feelings of confidence about nearing solution was used. Results showed that sudden, dramatic increases in confidence ratings coincided with the selection of appropriate information on the uncued insight problems. Sometimes searching for and finding the relevant information was sufficient for problem solvers immediately to know the answer to a problem. In these cases, a dramatic increase in confidence ratings was immediately followed by the correct solution. At other times, especially on problems requiring selective combination, an abrupt increase in confidence ratings was followed by a gradually increasing (incremental) pattern of ratings. The abrupt increase occurred when participants changed their mental representations and discovered a path to solution; the incremental ratings were given as problem solvers followed the path and worked out the answer. This last finding agrees with the view that verification or further work often follows illumination (Dominowski & Dallob, 1995; Wallas, 1926).

In contrast, participants showed an incremental pattern of confidence ratings when they were explicitly given cues about the relevant encodings, combinations, and comparisons in the insight problems. Apparently, feelings of sudden realization occur only when problem solvers need to search for and select relevant information that will change their mental representations and help them solve the problems. Similarly, incremental patterns of confidence ratings preceded incorrect solutions on the insight problems and both correct and incorrect solutions for routine problems.

In sum, the puzzle-problem approach uses a range of challenging problems in well-controlled settings to test various theories about insight. This approach has allowed researchers to move beyond the anecdotes, vague descriptions, and methodological weaknesses associated with the Gestaltist psychologists and empirically examine the mental processes, individual differences, and subjective feelings related to insightful problem solving. The resulting research indicates that insight is a multifaceted phenomenon.

It can come from a variety of mental processes, such as the selective encoding, selective combination, and selective comparison of nonobvious relevant information. A break in problem solving can enhance the use of these processes by allowing problem solvers to forget their fixation on irrelevant information or opportunistically assimilate new information. These seemingly sudden changes in what information is and is not used allow individuals to restructure their mental representations of a problem and, therefore, approach the problem in a new way. Furthermore, the restructuring of a mental representation is often accompanied by sudden, subjective feeling of confidence that one is reaching solution. In contrast, routine problem solving usually does not involve the same restructuring of representations and is often accompanied by incremental feelings that one is nearing solution.

Even though the puzzle-problem approach has increased our knowledge about insightful problem solving, it has at least two weaknesses. First, the views are mainly descriptive and do not fully explain how insight occurs. For example, the three-process theory of insight (Davidson, 1995; Davidson & Sternberg, 1986) does not specify how individuals search for relevant elements, combinations, and prior knowledge and distinguish them from irrelevant information. It also does not establish whether the three processes constitute three independent sources of individual differences or are interrelated because of their derivation from one or more higher-order processes. Similarly, Smith's (1995) intriguing view of forgetting does not specify how a break in problem solving allows the activation of misleading information to decay or how this decay changes one's mental context for, and representation of, the problem. Also, the opportunistic-assimilation model of insight (Seifert et al., 1995), though highly plausible and supported by data, does not establish exactly how, or by what mechanism, individuals detect the relevant information that moves them from the incubation stage of problem solving to the illumination phase. In other words, future in-depth work needs to be conducted on the specific mechanisms problem solvers use to search for nonobvious information, to distinguish this information from irrelevant material, and to apply this relevant information to their mental representations and reformulations of problems.

The second weakness to this approach, oddly enough, originates from advantages found in the empirical use of puzzle problems. Among the advantages are that the puzzles come in a variety of forms (e.g., spatial, verbal, and numerical), do not require specialized prior knowledge on the part of the problem solver, and lend themselves to cuing and other forms of manipulation. As a consequence, solving these puzzles probably does not require the same motivation, social interaction, preparation time, restructuring, and solution procedures that individuals need to solve significant, real-world problems. In addition, the puzzle-problem approach provides problem solvers with ready-made problems; no information is obtained on how individuals find new problems or how the discovery of a problem might influence insightful problem solving. At some point, the three-process theory and other theories of insight need to be tested using more consequential nonroutine problems, and research participants need to be given opportunities to find their own problems.

THE GREAT-MINDS APPROACH

Unlike the puzzle-problem approach, the great-minds approach does examine how significant insights occur in the real world. Structured interviews, case studies, and observations take us beyond an experimental context and provide perspective on insightful problem solving that society recognizes as valuable. Some common themes about insight come out of in-depth examinations of creative, accomplished problem solvers. Three of these themes are discussed here: intrinsic motivation, identification of an impasse, and social interaction.

Intrinsic Motivation

Most individuals who have significant insights also have the motivation to acquire relevant knowledge, overcome numerous obstacles, and persist in the face of problem impasses. One reason that persistence is important is that, unlike solving puzzle problems in laboratory experiments, major breakthroughs typically require about ten years of preparatory work in at least one domain (Hayes, 1989). As Dean Simonton notes (1995, p. 479), even someone as talented as Mozart did not compose masterpieces until he spent ten years writing music.

However, the length of preparation is not the same for all types of insights. Mihaly Csikszentmihalyi and Keith Sawyer (1995) make an important distinction between insights that occur when individuals solve problems that are given to them and insights that first involve finding a previously unknown problem. (The Gestalt, nothing-special, and puzzle-problem approaches focus on presented problem-solving insights.) From their interviews with 91 accomplished individuals in a wide range of domains, Csikszentmihaly and Sawyer found that presented problem-solving insights involve a relatively short amount of preparation time in a single domain. Short periods of incubation, illumination, and elaboration follow the preparation period. In contrast, problem-finding insights, which tend to be more revolutionary than presented problem-solving insights, involve a relatively extended preparation period and are characterized by the synthesis of information from more than one domain. For this type of insight to occur, individuals must (a) acquire knowledge of one or more domains, (b) become immersed in a field that practices the domain, (c) focus on a problematic situation in the domain and internalize information relevant to this situation, (d) use parallel processing to let the relevant information interact at a subconscious level with information from other domains, (e) recognize a new configuration emerging from this interaction of information that helps solve the problem, and (f) evaluate and elaborate the resulting insight in ways that are valued and understood by colleagues (Csikszentmihalyi & Sawyer, 1995, pp. 358–359). The problem-solving cycle for problem-finding insights can take a year or longer.

A second reason that intrinsic motivation is important is that real-world insights often involve many failures before an insight is achieved. Because the correct approach to a significant nonroutine problem is not obvious, multiple solution paths are often followed before the correct one is found (Csikszentmihalyi & Sawyer, 1995; Simonton, 1995). In his in-depth study of Darwin's accomplishments, Howard Gruber (1981) points out that the best predictor of great discoveries is a prolonged and passionate dedication to a subject. Individuals must have enough devotion to endure ambiguity and initial problem-solving failures.

Closely related to intrinsic motivation is the ability to maintain intense concentration and undivided attention while working on a problem. Mihaly Csikszentmihalyi (1996) refers to this highly focused state of consciousness as "flow." Individuals who have experienced periods of flow often report being completely immersed in what they are doing and losing track of time. Csikszentmihalyi and his colleagues (Csikszentmihalyi, 1996; Csikszentmihalyi, Rathunde, & Whalen, 1993) found that creative adolescents and adults often achieved flow states while working in domains that match their interests and abilities. These flow states increase the likelihood that material within a domain will be mastered and insights will occur. Individuals who achieve flow tend to be curious, sensitive to sensory information, and open to new experience.

Identification of an Impasse

Unfortunately, intrinsic motivation alone does not lead to insight. In fact, persistence can be harmful if one is pursuing an incorrect solution. However, conceptual change and insightful solutions often occur not long after problem solvers realize that they, or the field in which they are working, are on an unproductive path for solving a particular problem. For example, Kevin Dunbar (1995, 2001) found that experienced scientists usually abandoned their hypotheses after obtaining inconsistent or unexpected evidence that indicated they were on the wrong track. Immediately after the unexpected results were deemed valid, these scientists often made major shifts in their reasoning. Similarly, problem-finding insights occur when individuals identify an impasse within a domain and then recognize a new reconfiguration that overcomes it (Csikszentmihalyi & Sawyer, 1995).

How does recognition of an impasse lead to conceptual change? While observing scientists at a wide range of laboratories, Dunbar (2001) found that these individuals often turn to analogies to help them understand and move beyond obstacles in problem solving. For example, after obtaining a series of unexpected results, molecular biologists and immunologists often draw analogies to different types of models and mechanisms. These analogies are still within the same general domain of the research but involve connections to work conducted by other laboratories studying different organisms.

In contrast, Csikszentmihalyi and Sawyer (1995) propose that revolutionary problem-finding insights involve the random convergence of ideas from different symbolic domains. Impasses are processed serially using conscious attention, and then a semiconscious filter determines which relevant information will enter a subconscious network. Unlike the serial nature of conscious processing, subconscious processing allows connections between ideas to be generated and tested in parallel. Insights occur when a new configuration of ideas from different domains emerges from the subconscious and enters consciousness.

Social Interaction

The Gestalt, nothing-special, and puzzle-problem approaches treat insight as a solitary, cognitive event. Research participants are given problems and asked to solve them independently, without interacting with other problem solvers. However, findings from the great-minds approach indicate that significant insights are embedded within an important social context. Even though the actual insights usually occur when people are alone, the preparation, evaluation, and elaboration stages surrounding the insights depend on interaction with, and input from, one's colleagues. According to Csikszentmihalyi and Sawyer (1995, pp. 334–335), "Although the moment of creative insight usually occurs in isolation, it is surrounded and contextualized within an ongoing experience that is fundamentally social, and the insight would be meaningless out of that context."

Csikszentmihalyi (1988) adopts a "systems" model that takes into account both social and cognitive factors related to creativity. According to this model, creativity involves a positive interaction among an individual, a domain, and a field. It occurs when (a) an individual's knowledge, talents, and interests are a good match for the particular domain to which the individual contributes and (b) knowledgeable judges in the larger field, or context, of the domain favorably evaluate the individual's contributions.

Similarly, Dunbar (1995) found that the social structure of weekly laboratory meetings plays a crucial role in conceptual change and scientific insights. Questions from colleagues during these meetings seem to be particularly important. For example, conceptual change often occurs when scientists are asked questions that cause their thinking to move from one level to another. In addition, researchers often consider alternative explanations that can lead to insights when the interpretations of their results are challenged or even when they face the prospect of publicly admitting an impasse. According to Dunbar, the most constructive laboratory meetings occur when group members have different backgrounds and sources of knowledge.

In sum, the great-minds approach provides information about the cognitive and social mechanisms that foster significant insights in real-world settings. This approach, unlike the other three discussed here, focuses on a wide range of factors that influence insight but that cannot easily be studied in an experimental setting. In particular, the in-depth examination of great thinkers indicates that prolonged hard work and social interactions within one or more domains provide an important foundation for insightful problem solving.

However, the great-minds approach does not permit the controls and empirical manipulations that play an integral part in experimental research. Even though some of the findings are followed up in laboratory experiments (Dunbar, 2001), it is not clear how far the results from the great-minds approach generalize to other populations. In addition, it is not yet obvious how to incorporate the findings into existing models of insight. For example, current theories of insight cannot account for the social factors that influence insight.

CONCLUSIONS

Four approaches to insightful problem solving were reviewed in this chapter. On the surface, these approaches seem quite different from each other because each one has its own goals and methodologies. The Gestalt approach attempted to demonstrate productive thinking by using novel problems that need to be viewed and solved in new ways. The emphasis was on the interpretation and reinterpretation of a problem's components and structure, rather than on the mental mechanisms or processes used to achieve a reinterpretation. The nothing-special approach, by showing that nonroutine problems can be solved using knowledge retrieval and routine procedures, focuses on the null hypothesis that insight does not exist as a distinct cognitive construct. The puzzle-problem approach empirically tests theories and models of insight by examining the selection, retrieval, and application of relevant information related to puzzle problems. Finally, the great-minds approach focuses on the insight processes used by accomplished thinkers in the context of their work. This view obtains "real-world" information on all four stages of the creative process: preparation, incubation, illumination, and verification.

There are, however, some common themes that have come out of these different approaches. For example, all four attach some degree of importance to the retrieval and application of prior knowledge. The Gestaltists proposed that the application of previously learned analogues is one source of insight; insightful problem solving can occur when the structural organization of an old situation is used to understand and solve a new problem. Proponents of the nothing-special view use knowledge retrieval and its application as evidence that solving "insight" problems requires routine information and procedures, rather than insight. The puzzle-problem researchers address the retrieval and application of prior knowledge in several ways. One way is through the mental process of selective comparison, where one successfully searches for old information that is similar in some way to new information and then uses this similarity to solve a problem. Another is through the view that incubation allows problem solvers to forget fixations that are blocking their access to relevant information that they have in memory. Similarly, the opportunistic-assimilation model of insight proposes that failure indices in long-term memory allow us to assimilate and remember information that is related to problem solving impasses. Finally, researchers who focus on great thinkers have found that large amounts of knowledge within and across domains play a crucial role in real-world instances of insightful problem solving. In other words, findings from these four approaches indicate that old knowledge can help individuals view problems in new, insightful ways.

Another common theme is that the restructuring of mental representations, or conceptual change, plays an important role in the solution of nonroutine problems. Impasses in problem solving often lead problem solvers to search for new ways of approaching a problem. Research generated by all four approaches has found that prior knowledge and its match (or mismatch) with new information can lead to the restructuring of a nonroutine problem. Research from three of the approaches – the Gestalt, the puzzle-problem, and the great-minds approaches – has found that other factors also influence changes in problem solvers' mental representations. In addition, researchers using these three approaches propose that reformulations of a problem are related to insight and to the subjective feeling of suddenly understanding how to solve a problem. Insight does not require unique mental processes but does involve using mental processes in novel ways in order to create new mental representations.

If these approaches have one common weakness, it is that they all lack sufficient specification. The Gestalt approach never went beyond labels and rather vague descriptions of insightful behavior. As Mayer (1995) points out, the Gestaltists asked difficult questions without having the knowledge and technology we have today to answer them completely. The nothing-special approach does not specify what type of evidence, if any, could firmly establish that insightful problem solving does not exist. Showing that special processes are not needed to solve classic insight problems does not mean that special processes are never used. As mentioned earlier, the puzzle-problem approach does not specify exactly how relevant information is distinguished from irrelevant information, how irrelevant information is forgotten, and how mental processes are used to restructure the problem and change the context of solving it. The great-minds approach does not specify how current models of insight should incorporate the social factors related to insightful problem solving.

Given this common weakness, how insightful are these approaches to insightful problem solving? If one's definition of insight includes the restructuring of a problem (Dominowski & Dallob, 1995; Duncker, 1945; Wertheimer, 1945/1959), then the answer is that they are quite insightful. The Gestaltists provided many questions about insight but few of the answers. When impasses were reached and these questions about insight could not be addressed in their original form, the form was changed. For example, the nothing-special approach turned the question of what is insight into the question of whether insight exists as a distinct, cognitive phenomenon. This reformulation of the question generated new research and a conflict in the answers. In some cases, different conclusions were drawn from evidence that was collected using the same stimuli (Weisberg, 1995). This conflict in interpretations has prompted some researchers to examine insight as a multifaceted construct, rather than a singular one, and to study individual differences in insightful-thinking skills. In other words, reformulations of the questions about insightful problem solving have moved the field forward in constructive directions.

However, if one's definition of insight includes the sudden realization of a solution (Duncker, 1945; Kaplan & Simon, 1990; Kohler, 1969; Worthy, 1975), then these four approaches, even in combination, have not yet insightfully discovered the full nature of insight. There are still questions about how insight occurs and what role it plays in problem solving. But the search for answers about insight is well under way, and these approaches have narrowed the space of possible solutions.

REFERENCES

Adamson, R. E. (1952). Functional fixedness as related to problem solving: A repetition of three experiments. *Journal of Experimental Psychology, 44,* 288–291.

Adamson, R. E., & Taylor, D. W. (1954). Functional fixedness as related to elapsed time and set. *Journal of Experimental Psychology, 47,* 122–216.

Chase, W. G., & Simon, H. A. (1973). The mind's eye in chess. In W. G. Chase (Ed.), *Visual information processing* (pp. 215–281). New York: Academic Press.

Chi, M. T. H., Feltovich, P., & Glaser, R. (1981). Categorization and representation of physics problems by experts and novices. *Cognitive Science, 5,* 121–152.

Csikszentmihaly, M. (1988). Society, culture, and person: A systems view of creativity. In R. J. Sternberg (Ed.), *The nature of creativity* (pp. 325–339). Cambridge, U.K.: Cambridge University Press.

Csikszentmihaly, M. (1996). *Creativity: Flow and the psychology of discovery and invention.* New York: Harper Collins Publishers.

Csikszentmihalyi, M., Rathunde, K., & Whalen, S. (1993). *Talented teenagers: The roots of success and failure.* New York: Cambridge University Press.

Csikszentmihaly, M., & Sawyer, K. (1995). Creative insight: The social dimension of a solitary moment. In R. J. Sternberg, & J. E. Davidson (Eds.), *The nature of insight* (pp. 329–363). New York: Cambridge University Press.

Davidson, J. E. (1986). Insight and intellectual giftedness. In R. J. Sternberg & J. E. Davidson (Eds.), *Conceptions of giftedness* (pp. 201–222). New York: Cambridge University Press.

Davidson, J. E. (1995). The suddenness of insight. In R. J. Sternberg, & J. E. Davidson (Eds.), *The nature of insight* (pp. 125–155). New York: Cambridge University Press.

Davidson, J. E., & Sternberg, R. J. (1984). The role of insight in intellectual giftedness. *Gifted Child Quarterly, 28,* 58–64.

Davidson, J. E., & Sternberg, R. J. (1986). What is insight? *Educational Horizons, 64,* 177–179.

DiVesta F. J., & Walls, R. T. (1967). Transfer of object-function in problem solving. *American Educational Research Journal, 63,* 596–602.

Dominowski, R. L. (1981). Comment on "An examination of the alleged role of 'fixation' in the solution of 'insight' problems." *Journal of Experimental Psychology: General, 110,* 199–203.

Dominowski, R. L., & Dallob, P. (1995). Insight and problem solving. In R. J. Sternberg, & J. E. Davidson (Eds.), *The nature of insight* (pp. 33–62). New York: Cambridge University Press.

Dunbar, K. (1995). How scientists really reason: Scientific reasoning in real-world laboratories. In R. J. Sternberg, & J. E. Davidson (Eds.), *The nature of insight* (pp. 365–395). New York: Cambridge University Press.

Dunbar, K. (2001). The analogical paradox: Why analogy is so easy in naturalistic settings, yet so difficult in the psychological laboratory. In D. Gentner, K. J. Holyoak, & B. Kokinov (Eds.), *The analogical mind: Perspectives from cognitive science.* Cambridge, MA: MIT Press.

Duncker, K. (1945). On problem solving. *Psychological Monographs, 58*(5), Whole No. 270.

Ellen, P. (1982). Direction, past experience, and hints in creative problem solving: Reply to Weisberg and Alba. *Journal of Experimental Psychology: General, 111,* 316–325.

Finke, R. A., Ward, T. B., & Smith, S. M. (1992). *Creative cognition: Theory, research and applications.* Cambridge, MA: MIT Press.

Frijda, N. H., & de Groot, A. D. (Eds.). (1982). *Otto Selz: His contribution to psychology.* The Hague: Mouton.

Gruber, H. E. (1981). On the relation between "Aha! experiences" and the construction of ideas. *History of Science, 19,* 41–59.

Hayes, J. R. (1989). *The complete problem solver* (2nd ed.). Hillsdale, NJ: Erlbaum.

Holyoak, K. J. (1984). Analogical thinking and human intelligence. In R. J. Sternberg (Ed.), *Advances in the psychology of human intelligence* (Vol. 2, pp. 199–230). Hillsdale, NJ: Erlbaum.

Kaplan, C. A., & Davidson, J. E. (1988). Hatching a theory of incubation effects. *Technical Report*, CIP No. 472, Carnegie-Mellon University.

Kaplan, C. A., & Simon, H. A. (1990). In search of insight. *Cognitive Psychology, 22,* 374–419.

Kohler, W. (1925). *The mentality of apes* (2nd ed.). New York: Harcourt Brace.

Kohler, W. (1969). *The task of Gestalt psychology.* London: Routledge & Kegan Paul.

Kuczaj, S. A. II, Gory, J. D., & Xitco, M. J. (1998). Using programs to solve problems: Imitation versus insight. *Behavioral and Brain Sciences, 21,* 695–696.

Langley, P., & Jones, R. (1988). A computational model of scientific insight. In R. J. Sternberg (Ed.), *The nature of creativity: Contemporary psychological perspectives* (pp. 177–201). New York: Cambridge University Press.

Langley, P., Simon, H. A., Bradshaw, G. L., & Zytkow, J. M. (1987). *Scientific discovery: Computational explorations of the creative process.* Cambridge, MA: MIT Press.

Larkin, J. H., McDermott, J., Simon, D. P., & Simon, H. A. (1980). Expert and novice performance in solving physics problems. *Science, 208,* 1335–1342.

Luchins, A. S. (1942). Mechanization in problem solving. *Psychological Monographs, 54*(6), Whole No. 248.

Luchins, A. S., & Luchins, E. S. (1950). New experimental attempts at preventing mechanization in problem solving. *Journal of General Psychology, 42,* 279–297.

Lung, C., & Dominowski, R. L. (1985). Effects of strategy instructions and practice on nine dot problem solving. *Journal of Experimental Psychology: Learning, Memory, and Cognition, 11,* 804–811.

Maier, N. R. F. (1930). Reasoning in humans: I. On direction. *Journal of Comparative Psychology, 12,* 115–143.

Maier, N. R. F. (1931). Reasoning in humans: II. The solution of a problem and its appearance in consciousness. *Journal of Comparative Psychology, 12,* 181–194.

Maier, N. R. F. (1940). The behavior mechanisms concerned with problem solving. *Psychological Review, 47,* 43–53.

Maier, N. R. F. (1970). *Problem solving and creativity.* Belmont, CA: Brooks/Cole.

Mayer, R. E. (1995). The search for insight. In R. J. Sternberg, & J. E. Davidson (Eds.), *The nature of insight* (pp. 3–32.) New York: Cambridge University Press.

Mednick M. T., Mednick, S. A., & Mednick, E. V. (1964). Incubation of creative performance and specific associative priming. *Journal of Abnormal Psychology, 69,* 84–88.

Metcalfe, J. (1986a). Feeling of knowing in memory and problem solving. *Journal of Experimental Psychology: Learning, Memory, and Cognition, 12,* 288–294.

Metcalfe, J. (1986b). Premonitions of insight predict impending error. *Journal of Experimental Psychology: Learning, Memory, and Cognition, 12,* 623–634.

Metcalfe, J., & Weibe, D. (1987). Intuition in insight and noninsight problem solving. *Memory & Cognition, 15,* 238–246.

Mullis, K. (1998). *Dancing naked in the mind field.* New York: Vintage Books.

Murray, H. G., & Denny, J. P. (1969). Interaction of ability level and interpolated activity (opportunity for incubation) in human problem solving. *Psychological Reports, 24,* 271–276.

Newell, A. & Simon, H. A. (1972). *Human problem solving*. Englewood Cliffs, NJ: Prentice-Hall.

Ohlsson, S. (1984a). Restructuring revisited: I. Summary and critique of the Gestalt theory of problem solving. *Scandinavian Journal of Psychology, 25,* 65–68.

Ohlsson, S. (1984b). Restructuring revisited: II. An information processing theory of restructuring and insight. *Scandinavian Journal of Psychology, 25,* 117–129.

Perkins, D. (1981). *The Mind's Best Work.* Cambridge, MA: Harvard University Press.

Scheerer, M. (1963). Problem solving. *Scientific American, 208,* 118–128.

Schooler, J. W., & Melcher, J. (1995). The ineffability of insight. In S. Smith, T. Ward, & R. Finke (Eds.), *The creative cognition approach* (pp. 97–133). Cambridge: MIT Press.

Seifert, C. M., Meyer, D. E., Davidson, N., Patalno, A. L., & Yaniv, I. (1995). Demystification of cognitive insight: Opportunistic assimilation and the prepared-mind perspective. In R. J. Sternberg & J. E. Davidson (Eds.), *The nature of insight* (pp. 65–124). New York: Cambridge University Press.

Siegler, R. S. (2000). Unconscious insights. *Current Directions in Psychological Science, 9,* 79–83.

Siegler, R. S., & Stern, E.(1998). Conscious and unconscious strategy discoveries: A microgenetic analysis. *Journal of Experimental Psychology: General, 127,* 377–397.

Simon, H. A. (1986). The information processing explanation of Gestalt phenomena. *Cognitive Psychology, 2,* 241–255.

Simon, H. A., Newell, A., & Shaw, J. C. (1979). The process of creative thinking. In H. A. Simon (Ed.), *Models of thought* (pp.144–174). New Haven: Yale University Press.

Simonton, D. K. (1995). Foresight in insight? A Darwinian answer. In R. J. Sternberg, & J. E. Davidson (Eds.), *The nature of insight* (pp. 465–494). New York: Cambridge University Press.

Smith, R. W., & Kounios, J. (1996). Sudden insight: All-or-none processing revealed by speed-accuracy decomposition. *Journal of Experimental Psychology: Learning, Memory, and Cognition, 22,* 1443–1462.

Smith, S. M. (1995). Getting into and out of mental ruts. In R. J. Sternberg, & J. E. Davidson (Eds.), *The nature of insight* (pp. 229–251). New York: Cambridge University Press.

Smith, S. M., & Blankenship, S. E. (1989). Incubation effects. *Bulletin of the Psychonomic Society, 27,* 311–314.

Smith, S. M. & Blankenship, S. E. (1991). Incubation and the persistence of fixation in problem solving. *American Journal of Psychology, 104,* 61–87.

Sternberg, R. J., & Davidson, J. E. (1982). The mind of the puzzler. *Psychology Today, 16,* 37–44.

Sternberg, R. J., & Davidson, J. E. (1989). A four-prong model for intellectual skills development. *Journal of Research and Development in Education, 22,* 22–28.

Sternberg, R. J., & Davidson, J. E. (1999). Insight. In M. Runco (Ed.), *Encyclopedia of creativity.* San Diego, CA: Academic Press.

Thorndike, E. L. (1911). *Animal intelligence: Experimental studies.* New York: Macmillan.

Wallas, G. (1926). *The art of thought.* New York: Harcourt, Brace.

Weisberg, R. W. (1986). *Creativity: Genius and Other Myths.* New York: W. H. Freeman & Co.

Weisberg, R. W. (1993). *Creativity: Beyond genius and other myths.* New York: Freeman.

Weisberg, R. W. (1995). Prolegomena to theories of insight. In R. J. Sternberg, & J. E. Davidson (Eds.), *The nature of insight* (pp. 157–196). New York: Cambridge University Press.

Weisberg, R. W. & Alba, J. W. (1981). An examination of the alleged role of "fixation" in the solution of "insight" problems. *Journal of Experimental Psychology: General, 110,* 169–192.

Weisberg, R. W. & Alba, J. W. (1982). Problem solving is not like perception: More on Gestalt theory. *Journal of Experimental Psychology: General, 111,* 326–330.

Wertheimer, M. (1945/1959). *Productive thinking.* Chicago: University of Chicago Press. (Original work published 1945.)

Woodsworth, R. S. (1938). *Experimental psychology.* New York: Henry Holt.

Worthy, M. (1975). *Aha! A puzzle approach to creative thinking.* Chicago: Nelson Hall.

6

The Role of Working Memory in Problem Solving

David Z. Hambrick and Randall W. Engle

The combination of moment-to-moment awareness and instant retrieval of archived information constitutes what is called the working memory, perhaps the most significant achievement of human mental evolution. (Goldman-Rakic, 1992, p. 111)

Working memory plays an essential role in complex cognition. Everyday cognitive tasks – such as reading a newspaper article, calculating the appropriate amount to tip in a restaurant, mentally rearranging furniture in one's living room to create space for a new sofa, and comparing and contrasting various attributes of different apartments to decide which to rent – often involve multiple steps with intermediate results that need to be kept in mind temporarily to accomplish the task at hand successfully. (Shah & Miyake, 1999, p. 1)

More than 25 years ago, Baddeley and Hitch (1974) lamented, "Despite more than a decade of intensive research on the topic of short-term memory (STM), we still know virtually nothing about its role in normal information processing" (p. 47). The primary concern for Baddeley and Hitch was the presumed centrality of limited-capacity short-term memory in contemporary models of memory, including Atkinson and Shiffrin's (1968) "modal model." For example, Baddeley and Hitch described a patient with brain-damage (K.F.) who exhibited grossly deficient performance on tests of short-term memory but normal performance on long-term learning tasks. Logically, this could not occur if information passes from short-term memory to long-term memory. Baddeley and Hitch also reported a series of experiments in which participants performed various reasoning tasks while concurrently performing a task designed to place a load on short-term memory. For example, in one experiment, the task was to verify sentences purporting to describe the order of two letters (e.g., *A is not preceded by B–AB*) while repeating the word "the," a predictable sequence of digits, or a random sequence of digits. Surprisingly, short-term memory load had very little effect on reasoning.

How could these findings be reconciled with the view that short-term memory is the central bottleneck in information processing? Baddeley and Hitch (1974) proposed that short-term memory is not a single, capacity-limited store, but rather a more complex system consisting of three components: two "slave" systems – the *phonological loop* and *visuospatial sketchpad*, devoted to temporary storage and maintenance of information – and a *central executive* responsible for control processes such as reasoning, planning, and decision making. This model could easily handle empirical results that Atkinson and Shiffrin's (1968) modal model could not. For example, K.F. exhibited deficient performance on short-term memory tasks but normal long-term learning, because only the phonological loop component of his working memory system was impaired. K.F.'s central executive was intact. Similarly, in the experiments described by Baddeley and Hitch, decrements in reasoning performance emerged only when the storage load imposed by the secondary task exceeded the capacity of the phonological loop. Otherwise, the limited resources of the central executive could be devoted exclusively to reasoning. Thus, Baddeley and Hitch demonstrated that short-term memory is merely one component of an information processing system involving not only storage limitations but processing limitations as well.

THE GOAL AND ORGANIZATION OF THIS CHAPTER

As the quotations at the beginning of this chapter suggest, working memory has emerged as one of the most important and intensively researched constructs in cognitive psychology. However, we believe that there is still much to be learned about the role of working memory in real-world cognitive functioning. Indeed, one might conclude that despite nearly three decades of intensive research, we still know relatively little about the role of working memory in "normal information processing." For example, a literature search revealed only 12 publications devoted to working memory and problem solving during the 25-year period from 1975 through 1999. Furthermore, in a recent review, Kintsch, Healy, Hegarty, Pennington, and Salthouse (1999) noted that tasks studied by researchers interested in working memory are often simple and artificial, and cannot be considered what Hutchins (1995) termed "cognition in the wild" – complex cognitive tasks encountered in everyday settings.

Thus, the goal of this chapter is to speculate about the role of working memory in problem solving. The chapter is organized into three major sections. In the first section, we establish the scope of the chapter by considering the question, "What is a problem?" Research on problem solving is sometimes viewed as a narrow area of scientific inquiry restricted to "toy" tasks such as Tower of Hanoi, but we suggest that many cognitive tasks and activities can be considered examples of problem solving in the sense that they involve purposeful, goal-directed behavior. Or as Anderson (1985) observed: "It seems that all cognitive activities are fundamentally problem solving in nature. The basic argument . . . is that human cognition is always purposeful, directed to achieving goals and to removing obstacles to those goals" (pp. 199–200).

In the second section of the chapter, we examine the role of working memory in various cognitive tasks. Evidence from two traditions of working memory research is considered. The first tradition is associated with work in Europe, primarily by Baddeley and his colleagues, and concerns the role of the phonological loop and visuospatial sketchpad "slave" systems in cognitive performance. The second tradition has been pursued by researchers, primarily in North America, interested in individual differences in working memory capacity and their relation to cognitive performance. In the third section, we consider the question of *when* working memory capacity should be expected to play an important role in problem solving.

WHAT IS A PROBLEM?

A *problem* is often defined as a goal that is not immediately attainable. For example, Duncker (1945) proposed that "a problem exists when a living organism has a goal but does not know how this goal is to be reached" (p. 2). Consistent with this definition, problem-solving research has traditionally focused on so-called insight problems. The Tower of Hanoi task is a prototypical example. In the version of this task illustrated in Figure 6.1, there are three pegs (1, 2, and 3) and three disks (A, B, and C). The initial state is that the disks are set on Peg 1, with the smallest disk (Disk A) on the top and the largest disk (Disk C) on the bottom. The goal is to move the disks from Peg 1 to Peg 3, but the rules state that only one disk can be moved at a time, that only the top disk can be moved, and that a disk can never be placed on a smaller disk. Once the target configuration of pegs is achieved, the problem is solved.

Perhaps the most salient aspect of tasks such as Tower of Hanoi is that the solution must be *discovered*. That is, although the initial state and the goal state are clear, how to transform the initial state into the goal state is unclear. By contrast, proficiency in more routine problem-solving tasks involves execution of well-learned skills and procedures. For example, success in a reading comprehension task depends not so much on figuring out the most effective way to read the material, but rather on the efficiency and effectiveness of processes already in place. As another example, how one should proceed in order to mentally calculate the answer to an arithmetic problem such as $1,356 - 234 = ?$ is probably clear for any educated adult. The

Tower of Hanoi

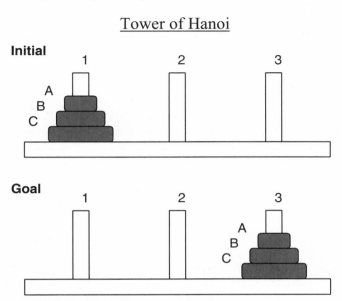

FIGURE 6.1. The Tower of Hanoi problem.

solution *1,122* is not discovered; rather, it is derived. In short, as Anderson (1993) noted, "Some activities, like solving a Tower of Hanoi problem or solving a new kind of physics problem, feel like problem solving, whereas other more routine activities, such as using a familiar computer application or adding up a restaurant bill, do not" (p. 39).

Working Memory as a Unifying Construct

How, though, are tasks such as Tower of Hanoi and other cognitive tasks similar, and how can they be compared at a theoretical level? Our view is that success in many tasks is predicated on the *ability to maintain goals, action plans, and other task-relevant information in a highly activated and accessible state, and when necessary, to inhibit activation of irrelevant or distracting information.* For example, during performance of the Tower of Hanoi task, what one must keep active are the rules of the task and subgoals created en route to the solution. In addition, discovery of a solution may depend on the ability to activate information from multiple, unsuccessful solution attempts, and to maintain that activation until the information is integrated. Similarly, a fundamental requirement of understanding the meaning of a difficult passage about an unfamiliar topic is the ability to maintain some representation, either verbatim or gist, from clause to clause, sentence to sentence, and paragraph to paragraph (Kintsch & van Dijk, 1978). Finally, in a mental arithmetic task, intermediate sums must be kept active in order to compute the correct answer. To sum up, the argument is that working memory is a fundamental determinant of proficiency in a wide range of tasks.

Working Memory and Problem Solving

Research on working memory has proceeded along two theoretical paths during the past 25 years. Working memory research in Europe has concentrated primarily on the slave systems of the Baddeley-Hitch model. More specifically, what is the role of the phonological loop and the visuospatial sketchpad in working memory, and how are they involved in performance of tasks such as reasoning and comprehension? In contrast, working memory research in North America has focused primarily (although not exclusively) on the central executive component of working memory. More specifically, what is the nature of individual differences in central executive functioning, and how are they related to individual differences in performance of various cognitive tasks? Scholars from the European and North American traditions of working memory research have also tended to rely on different methodological approaches. Generally, working memory research in Europe is experimental, whereas working memory research in North America is more often correlational.

Theoretical and methodological differences aside, results from both traditions of research are informative about the role of working memory in higher level cognition. We review a subset of these findings in the context of the Baddeley-Hitch model of working memory. To review, Baddeley and Hitch (1974) conceptualized the phonological loop as a store for holding speech-based information and a subvocal rehearsal process responsible for reinstantiating or refreshing the information. Similarly, the visuospatial sketchpad refers to a memory store for holding visual or spatial information and a mechanism responsible for reinstantiating the information (Logie, 1995). The third component of the model, the central executive, is a general-purpose, attention-based entity responsible for control processes such as planning, reasoning, decision making, and coordination of the slave systems.

This organizational scheme provides a context for the discussion, given that much of the research that is reviewed below concerns the Baddeley-Hitch model. However, an important difference between the view of working memory set forth in this model and our view is that we conceptualize working memory as a system in which phonological and spatial formats are but two of many ways of representing information (see, e.g., Engle, Kane, & Tuholski, 1999). More specifically, we assume that working memory consists of two primary components. The first component – *short-term memory* – refers to long-term memory representations activated above threshold as a means of temporary maintenance. Long-term memory representations can become activated through an external event or because an internal event (i.e., a thought) spreads activation to the representation. Furthermore, representations can be maintained in many different formats, including not only phonological and visual or spatial, but also orthographic, lexical, semantic, tactile, and so forth. Therefore, the phonological loop and the visuospatial sketchpad are different representational formats and not distinct storage modules (see Cowan, 1995, for a similar view). Finally, periodic attention to the representations is necessary to keep them active above a threshold, below which the information would have to be retrieved from long-term memory. In many circumstances, this is not a problem if retrieval can be carried out quickly and with little chance of error. By contrast, maintenance of information in the active state above threshold is particularly important under conditions in which retrieval from long-term memory is slow or error prone because of interference.

The second component of our model – *working memory capacity* – is a concept that has emerged from a synthesis of a number of ideas. For example, working memory capacity corresponds to individual differences in the capability of the central executive of Baddeley and Hitch's (1974) model. Therefore, it is assumed to play an important role in a wide range of tasks. In addition, it is similar to Kahneman's (1973) notion of effortful processing. That is, working memory capacity refers to a limited-supply cognitive resource that can be allocated flexibly depending on the demands of the task at hand. Finally, working memory capacity is reminiscent of what Cattell (1943) termed *fluid intelligence*, because it is thought to reflect a general and relatively stable cognitive ability. *However, the specific function of working memory capacity is to bring memory representations into the focus of attention, and to maintain these representations in a highly activated and accessible state.* Thereby, working memory capacity underlies what Horn and Masunaga (2000) recently described as the ability to maintain focused concentration. Working memory capacity may also be called on when it is necessary to suppress, inhibit, or otherwise remove memory representations from the focus of attention (see Hasher & Zacks, 1988, for a somewhat similar view).

The Slave Systems

One way that the so-called slave systems have been studied is through use of concurrently performed secondary tasks thought to interfere with the slave system believed to be important to the primary task. That is, participants perform a primary task (e.g., reasoning) while concurrently performing a secondary task designed to prevent storage of information in either the phonological loop or the visuospatial sketchpad. For example, a phonological secondary task might involve repeating a predictable sequence of digits (e.g., 1 to 6) or the word "the," whereas a visuospatial secondary task might require tracking a visual target. If performance of the primary task is impaired in the secondary task condition relative to a no-interference control condition, then involvement of the targeted slave system is suggested.

Of course, a fundamental problem with this technique is the problem inherent in all methodological approaches that rely on subtractive logic (Donders, 1868/1969) to isolate the role of a component process (e.g., the action of a slave system) in performance of a complete task. To be exact, when a secondary task produces a decrement in primary task performance, one cannot be sure that this decrement reflects involvement of only the targeted slave system. For example, even a very simple task such as repeating the word "the" may require some level of central executive resources, in addition to the slave system in question. Despite this limitation, research using a secondary task approach has contributed to the theoretical understanding of working memory. A brief review of this research follows.

Comprehension

Comprehension – the ability to understand the larger meaning of a set of events or words – is a fundamental aspect of cognitive functioning. For example, a person would have little hope of success in a task such as Tower of Hanoi unless he or she first comprehended the instructions. Indeed, Kintsch (1998) proposed that comprehension is fundamental for understanding many different types of cognition. What, then, is the role of the slave systems in comprehension? Not surprisingly, much of the research germane to this question has focused on storage of speech-based information in the phonological loop. For example, Baddeley, Elridge, and Lewis (1981) found that a phonological secondary task interfered with participants' ability to detect errors of word order in sentences such as: *We were to that learn he was a very honest person, even though he loved money.* Waters, Caplan, and Hildebrandt (1987) replicated this result and also found that the detrimental effect of articulatory suppression was greater for sentences with multiple propositions than for sentences with a single proposition. Finally, Baddeley, Vallar, and Wilson (1987) found that patients with brain damage who had deficits in phonological processing had difficulty comprehending long sentences but not shorter ones.

Much less is known about the role of the visuospatial sketchpad in comprehension, but there is some evidence to suggest that this slave system contributes to comprehension of high-imagery prose. For example, in a study by Glass, Eddy, and Schwanenflugel (1980), participants read and verified sentences that were either concrete and highly imageable (e.g., *The star of David has six points*) or abstract (e.g., *Biology is the study of living matter*). In addition, for half of the trials, participants concurrently maintained a visual pattern and indicated whether it matched a pattern presented after the sentence. Glass et al. found that, although maintaining the visual pattern did not selectively disrupt verification of the high-imagery sentences, verification of the high-imagery sentences impaired pattern matching. Thus, Glass et al. concluded that comprehension of the high-imagery sentences involved the visuospatial sketchpad.

Reasoning

The contribution of the phonological loop and the visuospatial sketchpad to reasoning has been investigated in a number of studies. For example, using a phonological secondary task similar to the one described above, Evans and Brooks (1981), Halford, Bain, and Maybery (1984), and Toms, Morris, and Ward (1993) found no evidence for involvement of the phonological loop in a conditional reasoning task in which participants evaluated conclusions for rules stated in the form "if p then q" – for example, *If I eat haddock, then I do not drink gin. I drink gin. I do not eat haddock.* Toms et al. also reported that reasoning was unimpaired by concurrent performance of a spatial secondary task. Similarly, Gilhooly, Logie, Wetherick, and Wynn (1993) found no effect of either phonological or spatial secondary tasks on syllogistic reasoning. Thus, in contrast to comprehension, there is little evidence to suggest that the slave systems play an important role in reasoning.

Insight Tasks

The preceding review indicates that the slave systems may play a limited role in comprehension, but perhaps play no role at all in reasoning. What is the role of the slave systems in tasks, such as Tower of Hanoi, traditionally studied in research on problem solving? One possibility already mentioned is that the phonological loop influences performance of such tasks through comprehension of instructions. Furthermore, for tasks such as choosing a move in a chess game, it seems reasonable to suggest that the visuospatial sketchpad may contribute to performance, at least when a spatial visualization strategy is used. Consistent with this speculation, in a study of chess, Robbins et al. (1996) found that a spatial secondary task (pressing keys in a repetitive counterclockwise fashion) had a detrimental effect on performance in a "choose-a-move" task in which chess players were shown an unfamiliar chess position and attempted to generate an optimal move.

But how important are the slave systems for tasks such as Tower of Hanoi or choosing a move in a chess game? This question can be considered in light of evidence concerning reasoning already considered. More specifically, reasoning about the potential effectiveness of different ways to approach a task can probably be considered a critical aspect of performance in many complex tasks, at least when immediate retrieval of a solution from long-term memory is not possible. If this is true, then the slave systems might be expected to play a minor role in tasks such as Tower of Hanoi relative to the third component of the Baddeley-Hitch model – the central executive. That is, a consistent finding is that secondary tasks designed to tap the central executive impair reasoning. For example, Gilhooly et al. (1993) and Klauer, Stegmaier, and Meiser (1997) found that reasoning suffered when participants performed a putative central executive secondary task in which they were asked to generate random numbers (e.g., from the set 1–9) at a constant rate. Similarly, Robbins et al. (1996) found that chess players were virtually unable to perform the aforementioned chose-a-move task while concurrently performing a random-letter-generation task. Summarized, our speculation is that the processes subsumed by the central executive represent one important determinant of success in a wide range of problem-solving tasks. The next section discusses research that has investigated this claim from an individual-differences perspective.

The Central Executive

In North America, interest in working memory gained momentum in the early 1980s with the development of a reliable measure of *working memory capacity*, the Daneman and Carpenter (1980) reading span task. Consistent with Baddeley and Hitch's (1974) conception of the central executive, this task was designed to emphasize simultaneous storage and processing of information. Briefly, the goal of the reading span task is to read a series of sentences while remembering the final word from each sentence. Working memory capacity (or "span") is then operationalized as the number of sentence-final words recalled. Hence, the reading span task is actually a dual task because the subject must read sentences while trying to remember the word following each sentence. The goal of a similar task, called operation span (Turner & Engle, 1989), is to solve a series of arithmetic questions and to remember a word following each for recall.

Measures of working memory capacity, such as operation span and reading span, predict performance in a wide range of tasks, including language comprehension (Daneman & Merikle, 1996), learning to spell (Ormrod & Cochran, 1988), math (Adams & Hitch, 1997), following directions (Engle, Carullo, & Collins, 1991), vocabulary acquisition (Daneman & Green, 1986), and writing (Benton, Kraft, Glover, & Plake, 1984). Clearly, then, working memory tasks "work" in the sense that they exhibit predictive validity. But why do they work? In other words, as illustrated in Figure 6.2, what accounts for the correlation between individual differences in working memory capacity and individual differences in various cognitive tasks?

The premise of what we have labeled the *task-specific hypothesis* is that measures of working memory capacity capture acquired skills involved in performance of the criterion task. For example, according to

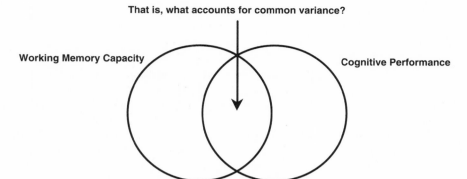

FIGURE 6.2. Why do measures of working memory capacity work?

this hypothesis, the reading span task predicts reading comprehension because both tasks involve reading. Consequently, a key prediction of the task-specific hypothesis is that a working memory task will exhibit predictive validity only when it captures the specific skills involved in the criterion task. By contrast, the basic idea of the *general capacity hypothesis* is that measures of working memory capacity capture domain-general information-processing capabilities that can be brought to bear on many tasks. Therefore, a key prediction of the general capacity hypothesis is that operations unique to a particular working memory task (e.g., reading sentences) are largely unimportant in accounting for the relationship between working memory capacity and cognitive performance. Instead, working memory tasks are thought to be imperfect indicators of a construct involved in the execution of a wide range of tasks.

Comprehension

Daneman and Carpenter (1980) were the first to demonstrate a relationship between central executive functioning and individual differences in comprehension. Their participants read a series of narrative passages and then answered different types of questions. For example, the final sentence of each passage contained an ambiguous pronoun, and the participants' task was to supply the referent, which occurred at some earlier point in the passage. Daneman and Carpenter found a strong positive correlation between reading span and this index of comprehension, particularly when several sentences separated the pronoun and referent. There were positive correlations between reading span and other indexes of comprehension as well, including memory for facts and verbal SAT score. Daneman and Carpenter argued that the relationship between reading span and reading comprehension occurs simply because both measures capture reading skill. That is, by virtue of more efficient and automatic reading strategies, participants with high levels of reading skill were able to devote more working memory resources to remembering the sentence-final words.

Thus, Daneman and Carpenter (1980) argued that reading span is a consequence of reading skill. The results of a large number of subsequent studies from our laboratory run counter to this argument. We describe the results of two such studies. Turner and Engle (1989) reasoned that if the correlation between working memory span and reading comprehension reflects the fact that both measures index reading skill, then the strength of the relationship between the two measures should vary depending on the nature of the processing component of the span task. Following this logic, participants completed four working memory tasks in which the processing task was either reading sentences or solving arithmetic equations. The measures of reading comprehension were scores on the Nelson-Denny reading test and verbal SAT. Turner and Engle found that the processing component manipulation (sentences vs. equations) had little effect on the relationship between working memory span and reading comprehension.

Engle, Cantor, and Carullo (1992) conducted a more systematic investigation of the relationship between working memory capacity and reading comprehension. In a series of experiments, participants performed either the operation span task or the reading span task using a moving window technique in which each equation-word (operation span) or sentence-word (reading span) stimulus was presented one element at a time. The time required to advance through the equation or sentence was used as an index of skill in executing the processing component of the task; verbal SAT served as a measure of comprehension. Engle et al. reasoned that if skill in the processing component of the span tasks accounted for the correlation between working memory capacity and verbal SAT, then controlling for processing skill would eliminate the correlation. This was not the case: Controlling for processing skill had *no effect* on the correlation between working memory capacity and comprehension.

One possible interpretation of the evidence reviewed thus far is that working memory capacity reflects a domain-general capability instead of skills and procedures applicable to a particular task or class of tasks. Recently, however, Ericsson and Kintsch (1995) and Kintsch (1998) suggested a viewpoint more in line with the task-specific hypothesis. In particular, they suggested that what the reading span task measures is the efficiency of comprehension. For example, Kintsch stated, "What the reading span measures is the efficiency with which readers can comprehend sentences and hence store them in long-term memory" (p. 239). To support their claim, Ericsson and Kintsch reviewed evidence suggesting that long-term memory contributes to performance in the reading span task. For example, using a version of the reading span task, Masson and Miller (1983) found a positive correlation between recall of the sentence-final words and cued recall of words from earlier in the sentences. There were also positive correlations of each measure with reading comprehension. Assuming that participants could not maintain all of the sentences in temporary storage, it seems clear that the sentences were stored in long-term memory.

Nevertheless, a critical point about the original Daneman and Carpenter (1980) reading span task, and the version of this task used by Masson and Miller (1983), is that the sentence-final "span" words were not *separate* from the sentences themselves. The problem with this task is that it is not possible to disentangle working memory capacity and reading skill. Indeed, recall of the sentence-final words may in part reflect the efficiency with which readers can comprehend sentences and store them in long-term memory (Kintsch, 1998). By contrast, in the version of the reading span task used by Engle et al. (1992), the span words were separate from the sentences. Hence, it was possible to examine effects of reading span on comprehension controlling for skill in the processing component of the task. To reiterate, reading skill did *not* account for the relationship between working memory capacity and comprehension. Based on this evidence, we believe that the findings cited by Ericsson and Kintsch (1995) are important, but they are not sufficient to falsify the claim that measures of working memory capacity reflect a general capacity that transcends task-specific skills.

Multiple Working Memory Capacities?

A study by Shah and Miyake (1996) is also relevant to the present discussion. The major question of this study was whether working memory capacity represents a single cognitive resource or whether domain-specific pools of working memory resources can be distinguished. To investigate this issue, Shah and Miyake had participants perform two working memory tasks, one verbal and one spatial. The Daneman and Carpenter (1980) reading span task served as the verbal working memory task. The spatial working memory task involved simultaneous maintenance and processing of spatial information. For each trial, participants indicated whether the orientation of a letter was normal or mirror-imaged. Then, after a number of trials, the objective was to recall the orientation of each letter. Verbal SAT score was used as a measure of verbal ability, and spatial visualization tests were used to measure spatial ability. Shah and Miyake (1996) found that the spatial working memory measure correlated moderately with spatial ability, but near zero with verbal SAT. Conversely, the verbal working memory measure correlated moderately with verbal SAT, but near zero with spatial ability. In addition, the correlation between the two working memory measures was weak ($r = .23$). The same basic pattern of results was replicated in a second study. Shah and Miyake therefore concluded, "The predictive powers of the two complex memory span tasks seem to be domain specific . . ." (p. 11).

Nevertheless, the results of these studies should be evaluated in light of two potential methodological limitations. First, the sample sizes were very small for individual differences research (i.e., $N = 54$ for Study 1 and $Ns = 30$ for Study 2). This is problematic not only from the standpoint of low statistical power, but also from the standpoint of the replicability of the results. Second, given that the participants were college students from two selective universities, it seems likely that the score ranges on the working memory tasks (and other ability tests) were quite restricted. Therefore, it is possible that Shah and Miyake (1996) found evidence for separable working memory resources simply because variability due to a domain-general working memory capacity was effectively controlled, or at least reduced relative to what might be expected within more heterogeneous samples. To sum up, our view is that Shah and Miyake's suggestion of separable verbal and spatial working memory resource pools is intriguing, but should be investigated using larger and more diverse samples.

Reasoning and Fluid Intelligence

Research examining the relationship between working memory capacity and the broad aspect of cognitive functioning referred to as *fluid intelligence* provides additional evidence for claims about the domain-generality of working memory capacity. Fluid intelligence refers to aspects of cognition that are at least somewhat independent of prior knowledge and experience (Cattell, 1943), and it is typically measured with tests of abstract reasoning and spatial visualization that emphasize solution of novel problems. For example, in one commonly used test of fluid intelligence, Raven's Progressive Matrices, each item contains a series of abstract figures arranged in a 3×3 matrix. One figure is always missing, and the task is to identify which of eight alternatives completes the matrix.

Using a latent variable approach, Kyllonen and Christal (1990) found a strong positive correlation ($r = .90$) between working memory capacity and fluid intelligence. Furthermore, Kyllonen (1996) also reported high positive correlations between fluid intelligence and latent variables representing working memory capacity in three content areas: verbal ($r = .94$), spatial ($r = .96$), and numerical ($r = .95$). Kyllonen summarized his research as follows:

> We have observed in study after study, under a variety of operationalizations, using a diverse set of criteria, that working memory capacity is more highly related to performance on other cognitive tests, and is more highly related to learning, both short-term and long-term, than is any other cognitive factor. *This finding of the centrality of the working memory capacity factor leads to the conclusion that working memory capacity may indeed be essentially Spearman's g* [italics added, p. 73].

Engle, Tuholski, Laughlin, and Conway (1999) sought to better understand the nature of the relationship between working memory capacity and fluid intelligence. Working memory capacity was measured with tasks similar to the span tasks described earlier; short-term memory capacity was measured with simple memory span tasks (e.g., word recall); and fluid intelligence was measured with two nonverbal tests of abstract reasoning ability. Engle et al. predicted that latent variables representing working memory capacity and short-term memory capacity would correlate, given that some of the same domain-specific skills and procedures are captured by both. For example, skill in encoding information into long-term memory could contribute to performance in both the reading span task and a word recall task. However, Engle et al. also predicted that once this correlation was taken into account, the residual variance in working memory capacity would reflect the controlled attention component of the working memory system. Therefore, the working memory capacity residual would predict fluid intelligence, whereas the short-term memory capacity residual would not. As illustrated in Figure 6.3, the data were consistent with

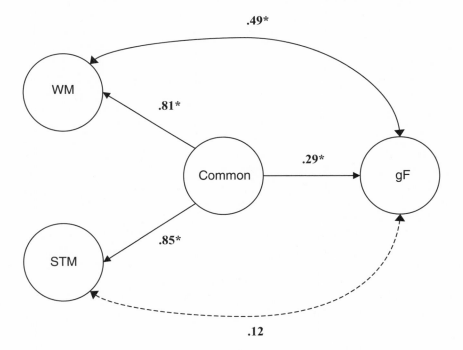

*p < .01

FIGURE 6.3. Structural equation model with the variance in common to the short-term memory (STM) and working memory (WM) capacity variables removed as common. The curved lines represent correlations between fluid intelligence (gF) and the residual for short-term memory and working memory capacity. Dashed line indicates nonsignificant relation.

this prediction. Working memory capacity and short-term memory capacity were correlated, as evidenced by the fact that they loaded onto a single common factor. However, only the working memory capacity residual variance was a significant predictor of fluid intelligence.

Insight Tasks

Relatively little is known about the role of this capability in insight tasks such as Tower of Hanoi. In fact, we could find only one relevant study. However, this study serves as a good example of how working memory capacity might affect performance in this type of task. Welsh, Satterlee-Cartmell, and Stine (1999) reported positive correlations between two measures of working memory capacity and performance on the Tower of London task, a variant of the Tower of Hanoi task in which the goal is to move a set of colored balls across different-sized pegs to match a target configuration. In fact, the two measures of working memory capacity accounted for a substantial proportion of the variance in solving the Tower of London problem (25% and 36%). Another interesting finding was that processing speed showed no correlation with solution success.

Welsh et al.'s (1999) finding adds to the body of evidence suggesting that working memory capacity plays an important role in many different types of problem solving. Furthermore, the finding that working memory capacity predicted Tower of London performance, whereas information processing speed did not, suggests to us that working memory capacity may even be the *primary* determinant of proficiency in cognitive domains, at least when the influence of prior knowledge and experience is minimal. But what specific functions might working memory capacity support in the context of problem solving? One possibility, alluded to before, is based on Hebb's (1949) proposal that a connection between two ideas is formed only when representations of those ideas are held together in an activated state. More specifically, the ability to maintain information in a highly activated state via controlled attention may be important for integrating information from successive problem-solving attempts in insight tasks such as Tower of Hanoi. A similar view of the importance of the coincident representation of events for subsequent connection between them is proposed by computational models of cognition such as Anderson's ACT-R (Anderson, 1983).

Problem Solving Difficulties
Working memory capacity may also be involved in a number of well-documented problem solving "difficulties," including *functional fixedness* and *negative set*. Functional fixedness refers to the inability to use a familiar concept or object in a novel manner. To illustrate, in the Duncker (1945) candle problem, the subject is given three items – a box of thumbtacks, a

matchbook, and a candle – and the task is to mount the candle on the wall. The solution is to empty the box of thumbtacks, tack the box to the wall, and mount the candle in the box. Hence, the box must be thought of as a platform instead of as a container. Similarly, negative set – or *Einstellung* – occurs when a person rigidly continues to use one effective solution approach when a simpler (and also effective) approach is possible. For example, in a study by Luchins (1942), participants were given the task of measuring out a particular quantity of water using three jugs, each with a different capacity. In addition, the trials were sequenced so that the first five problems required a lengthier solution than problems encountered later (i.e., the 6th and the 10th problems). Luchins found that the majority of participants (80%) failed to notice the simpler solution for the latter problems when they had already used the lengthier solution.

How might working memory capacity be involved in problem-solving difficulties such as functional fixedness and negative set? One possibility stems from the view that working memory capacity represents the capability for controlled attention, which in our view is responsible for not only maintenance of information in a highly activated state, but also for suppression or inhibition of irrelevant or misleading information (see also Hasher & Zacks, 1988). For example, according to this view, functional fixedness might occur because of an inability to suppress retrieval of some salient feature of an object or concept, and *Einstellung* occurs because of an inability to suppress previously retrieved solutions. Indirectly, evidence also suggests that working memory capacity may be particularly critical when it is necessary to suppress a solution that has been retrieved many times in previous solution attempts. For example, Rosen and Engle (1997, 1998) found that participants high in working memory capacity were able to prevent retrieval of previously recalled items in a word fluency task, whereas participants with lower levels of working memory capacity were less able to do so and thus suffered from many more intrusions.

More generally, inhibitory functions of working memory capacity may be critical for what Frensch and Sternberg (1989a) termed *flexibility in thinking* – "the ability to change one's mode or direction of thinking as a function of changing task or situational constraints . . ." (p. 163) – and may underlie differences in the extent to which people experience difficulties in problem solving. Of course, a prediction that follows naturally from this speculation is that people with high levels of working memory capacity should be less susceptible to problem-solving difficulties than those with lower levels of working memory capacity. This possibility has not yet been investigated, but Miller (1957) found a negative correlation between general intelligence and problem solving rigidity in the water jar problem, such that low ability participants exhibited greater *Einstellung* than high ability participants. Given the strong relationship between working memory capacity and fluid intelligence, an interesting question for future research would be whether, and to what extent, working memory capacity predicts the incidence of *Einstellung*.

Adult Age and Problem-Solving Difficulties

Studies of adult aging provide additional evidence for the potential importance of working memory capacity in problem solving. Research on aging and cognition has established that working memory capacity decreases across the adult portion of the life span (see Salthouse, 1992a, 1996, for reviews). In addition, such decreases appear to be partly responsible for concomitant decreases in more complex aspects of cognition, such as text comprehension (e.g., Hultsch, Hertzog, & Dixon, 1990; Stine & Wingfield, 1990) and reasoning (e.g., Babcock, 1994; Bors & Forrin, 1995; Salthouse, 1992b). Finally, there is some evidence to suggest that older adults are more susceptible to problem-solving difficulties than are young adults. For example, using a task modeled after the Luchins (1942) water-jar paradigm, Heglin (1956) found that older adults were more prone to *Einstellung* than were young adults. Similarly, using a concept identification task, Rogers, Keyes, and Fuller (1976) found that older adults had difficulty shifting from one solution rule to another. The hypothesis that problem-solving difficulties in older adults are attributable to age-related decreases in working memory capacity, in general, and to the inability to inhibit previous solutions, in particular, has apparently not been tested. However, it seems plausible in light of the finding that older adults may be less effective than younger adults in inhibiting extraneous and no-longer-relevant information from the focus of attention (e.g., Hasher, Quig, & May, 1997; Hasher, Zacks & May, 1999; Zacks, Hasher, & Li, 2000).

Summary and Conclusion

Why do working memory tasks work? That is, what accounts for the predictive power of working memory tasks? Our answer to this question is that they capture a domain-general aspect of cognition corresponding to the capability for controlling attention. Nevertheless, the evidence for this claim presented thus far is indirect. For example, although the finding of a strong positive relationship between working memory capacity and fluid intelligence seems difficult to reconcile with the view that working memory tasks tap task-specific skills, the idea that controlled attention underlies this relationship is speculative. The research discussed in the next section provides more direct evidence for this idea.

WHEN IS WORKING MEMORY CAPACITY IMPORTANT?

Common observation suggests that although everyday tasks can often be performed with little effort and concentration, there are times when maximal attention is demanded. For example, consider how difficult it is to read a scientific journal article while trying to ignore a distracting conversation, or while trying to avoid worrisome thoughts about an upcoming medical exam. Consistent with this type of everyday experience, an important tenet of our model of working memory is that working memory capacity should correlate with cognitive performance *only* when controlled processing is demanded because task-relevant information must be maintained in a highly activated state under conditions of distraction or interference, or because distracting information must be inhibited. An implication of this idea is that performance can proceed with little or no involvement of working memory capacity in the absence of these conditions. Consequently, working memory capacity is *not always* important, and hence should *not always* correlate positively with performance. Unlike the research described in the preceding section, this hypothesis has been investigated using elementary cognitive tasks in which factors thought to moderate involvement of working memory capacity can be controlled. Three such tasks are described next.

Dichotic Listening Task

People are often very effective in attending to one aspect of the environment while ignoring other aspects. For example, in a series of experiments by Cherry (1953), participants were instructed to repeat a message presented in one ear and to ignore a message presented in the other ear. Cherry found that participants had little difficulty performing this task. To illustrate, they did not notice when the language of the unattended message was changed from English to German. Nevertheless, Moray (1959) demonstrated that content from an unattended message is not rejected completely. In particular, Moray found that a substantial number of participants (33%) heard their name when it was presented in the unattended message. By contrast, very few participants could recall a word that was repeated 35 times in the unattended ear. Moray concluded that only information important to the subject (e.g., his or her name) can break the "attentional barrier" evident in the dichotic listening task.

But why did only 33% of Moray's (1959) participants hear their own names? Why not 100%? Conway, Cowan, and Bunting (2001) made the somewhat counterintuitive prediction that if one function of working memory capacity is to inhibit distracting information, then people with high levels of working memory capacity (high-span participants) would be *less* likely to notice their names in an unattended message than people with lower levels of working memory capacity (low-span participants). To test this prediction, Conway et al. replicated Moray's (1959) experiment with participants classified as either low or high in operation span. The results were exactly as predicted: 65% of low-span participants heard their names in the unattended message, whereas only 20% of high-span participants did so. Furthermore, inconsistent with the argument that low-span participants adventitiously heard their names after letting attention drift to the unattended message, there were no span-related differences in shadowing errors immediately preceding or concurrent with name presentation. Conway et al. concluded that high-span participants were better able to inhibit information from the unattended message.

Antisaccade Task

Kane, Bleckley, Conway, and Engle (2001) investigated the effect of working memory capacity on control of attention using a visual-orienting paradigm that might be considered simpler than even the dichotic listening task. The goal of the "antisaccade task" is to detect onset of a visual cue and to use that cue to direct the eyes to a location that will contain a target stimulus. Once the target stimulus appears, a response is executed. In the Kane et al. experiment, both low-span and high-span participants performed the following version of this task. For each trial, a cue flashed on the screen, and then a target (the letter B, P, or R) appeared. The task was to press a key corresponding to the given target. There were two types of trial: In the antisaccade trials, the cue and the target always appeared in opposite locations on a monitor, whereas in the prosaccade trials, the cue and the target always appeared in the same location.

Kane et al. (2001) found that high-span participants were faster in target identification than low-span participants *only* in the antisaccade trials. Eye movement data revealed the source of this difference. Relative to high-span participants, low-span participants were more likely to make reflexive eye movements toward the cue (and hence away from the target). One possible interpretation of this finding is that high-span participants were better able to maintain activation of a task-relevant goal (e.g., *look away from cue*). Another possibility is that high-span participants were better able to inhibit the tendency to look toward the attention-attracting cue. Whatever the case, the results of the Kane et al. study suggest that individual differences in working memory capacity are related to the ability to control attention. This finding also reinforces the notion that the predictive power of working memory capacity seems to be limited to situations that place a high demand on control of attention.

WHEN IS WORKING MEMORY CAPACITY IMPORTANT?
A BROADER PERSPECTIVE

We believe that the preceding results are consistent with a controlled attention view of working memory capacity. But how important is working memory capacity in the performance of everyday problem-solving tasks, and does it contribute above and beyond other individual-difference characteristics? Consider, for example, the question of whether working memory capacity contributes to the prediction of cognitive performance above and beyond knowledge within a specific domain.

The Knowledge-Is-Power Hypothesis

Research on expertise leaves little doubt that domain knowledge is a potent predictor of success in cognitive domains. For example, Chase and Simon (1973) found that an expert chess player recalled more information from game positions than less skilled players. By contrast, there was no effect of chess skill on recall of random configurations of chess positions. Chase and Simon concluded that expertise in chess is predicated largely on a vast store of information about chessboard positions. The finding that domain knowledge facilitates memory for task-relevant information has since been replicated in numerous domains, including bridge (Charness, 1981), computer programming (Barfield, 1997), music (Meinz & Salthouse, 1998), dance (Allard & Starkes, 1991), and map reading (Gilhooly, Wood, Kinnear, & Green, 1988).

Of course, the facilitative effect of domain knowledge on cognitive performance is not limited to tasks involving episodic memory. For example, in a study by Voss, Greene, Post, and Penner (1983), three groups of participants (political scientists with expertise in Soviet affairs, chemists, and undergraduate students) were given a problem in which the goal was to increase crop productivity in the Soviet Union. The political scientists began by creating a representation of the problem using their knowledge about the history of low crop productivity in the Soviet Union. By contrast, the chemists and the undergraduate students proposed solutions without clear specification of the possible causes, and their solutions were both judged ineffective. Thus, what was important in problem-solving success was not general scientific training, but rather specialized knowledge.

But what about the *joint effects* of domain knowledge and working memory capacity on problem-solving performance? One possibility is suggested by a viewpoint often referred to as the *knowledge-is-power hypothesis.* The major idea of this viewpoint is that domain knowledge is the primary determinant of proficiency in cognitive domains, whereas capacity-limited aspects of the system play a less important role. Minsky and Papert (1974) alluded to this idea in the following passage:

> It is by no means obvious that very smart people are that way directly because of the superior power of their general methods – as compared with average people. Indirectly, perhaps, but that is another matter: a very intelligent person might be that way because of the specific

local features of his knowledge-organizing knowledge rather than because of global qualities of his "thinking" which ... might be little different from a child's. (p. 59)

In a similar vein, Feigenbaum (1989) articulated the basic argument of the knowledge-is-power hypothesis in a principle:

The Knowledge Principle states that a system exhibits intelligent understanding and action at a high level of competence primarily because of the specific knowledge that it can bring to bear.... A corollary of the KP is that reasoning processes of intelligent systems are generally weak and not the primary source of power. (p. 179)

Most people would agree that domain knowledge is "power." Clearly, within the domain of expertise, people with high levels of domain knowledge tend to outperform people with lower levels of knowledge. However, it is less clear what the knowledge-is-power hypothesis implies about the *interplay* between cognitive ability characteristics such as working memory capacity and domain knowledge. Three hypotheses are illustrated in Panels A to C of Figure 6.4.

Compensation Hypothesis
The first hypothesis is illustrated in Figure 6.4 (Panel A) and is based on the idea that domain knowledge is not only power, but also reduces, and may even eliminate, the effect of working memory capacity. Stated somewhat differently, high levels of domain knowledge can "compensate" for low levels of working memory capacity. Consistent with this idea, Ackerman and Kyllonen (1991) stated, "There is a relationship between knowledge and working memory capacity such that having specific knowledge can replace having to exercise working memory" (p. 216). In a similar vein, Frensch and Sternberg (1989b) observed that

beginners in any game seem to be relying on domain-general abilities, whereas experienced players utilize an extensive body of domain-relevant knowledge. One might expect, therefore, that measures of general intelligence would be related to novices' but not to experts' game playing ability. (p. 375)

Basic Mechanism Hypothesis
The second hypothesis is illustrated in Figure 6.4 (Panel B) and stems from the view that although domain knowledge is power, it is not *all-powerful*. Rather, working memory capacity is a basic mechanism underlying proficiency in cognitive domains and contributes to performance even at high levels of domain knowledge. For example, although it may be possible to overcome the limitations associated with working memory capacity in very specific situations, the limitations may reemerge in the domain

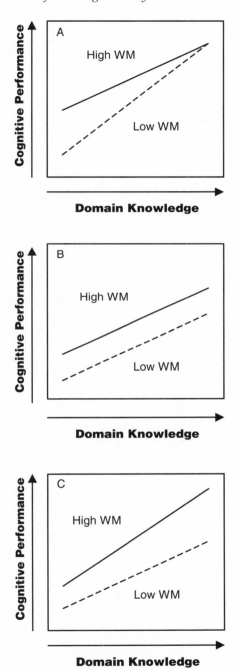

FIGURE 6.4. Possible effects of domain knowledge and working memory capacity on cognitive performance.

of expertise when the situation demands the maintenance of information in the highly active and accessible state under conditions of interference and/or distraction, or the suppression of interfering, competing, or irrelevant information.

Rich-Get-Richer Hypothesis

The third hypothesis concerning the interplay between domain knowledge and working memory capacity is illustrated in Figure 6.4 (Panel C). The basic argument of this model is that the "rich get richer" in the sense that the beneficial effect of domain knowledge on cognitive performance should be greater at high levels of working memory capacity than at lower levels. For example, to the extent that working memory capacity is related to the amount of information that can be maintained in a highly activated state during task performance, then people with high levels of working memory capacity may be able to draw on more domain knowledge than can those with lower levels. Furthermore, working memory capacity might be called on when a controlled search of long-term memory is necessary to determine which piece of preexisting domain knowledge is relevant to the current task or situation.

Relevant Evidence

Evidence concerning the predictions illustrated in Figure 6.4 is limited. For example, in studies of text comprehension, Haenggi and Perfetti (1992, 1994) found main effects of both domain knowledge and working memory capacity on measures of expository text comprehension. High levels of domain knowledge and high levels of working memory were associated with superior performance. Unfortunately, however, Haenggi and Perfetti did not evaluate the interaction between working memory capacity and domain knowledge. More recently, using structural equation modeling, Britton, Stimson, Stennett, and Gülgöz (1998) found that domain knowledge had a direct effect on expository text comprehension, whereas working memory did not. Britton et al. also did not evaluate the possibility of interactive effects of domain knowledge and working memory capacity.

Memory for Baseball Games

Recently, we conducted a study to better understand the joint effects of domain knowledge and working memory capacity on a task involving text comprehension and memory (Hambrick & Engle, 2002). The knowledge domain for this study was the game of baseball, and the criterion task involved listening to and then answering questions about simulated radio broadcasts of baseball games. The participants were 181 adults with wide ranges of working memory capacity and knowledge about baseball. The radio broadcasts were recorded by a baseball announcer for a local radio

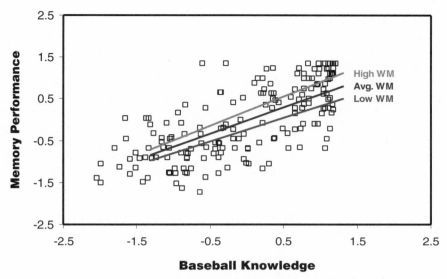

FIGURE 6.5. Effects of baseball knowledge and working memory capacity on memory for changes in game status. Values along the x-axis and the y-axis are z scores.

station and were realistic in presentation and content. (In fact, a number of participants mistook them for actual radio broadcasts of baseball games.) Baseball knowledge was assessed with paper-and-pencil tests, and working memory capacity was measured with tasks similar to those described earlier. Finally, memory for changes in the status of each game was evaluated after each broadcast. That is, participants answered questions about (a) which bases were occupied at the conclusion of each player's turn at bat and (b) the number of outs and number of runs scored during the inning.

For the analyses described next, composite variables were created for baseball knowledge, working memory capacity, and memory performance by averaging the z scores corresponding to each construct. Figure 6.5 depicts the effects of baseball knowledge and working memory capacity on memory for changes in game status. Perhaps the most striking feature of this figure is the magnitude of the knowledge effect. In fact, baseball knowledge accounted for over half of the reliable variance in memory performance (i.e., $R^2 = .56$). However, there was also a significant effect of working memory capacity above and beyond baseball knowledge (i.e., $R^2 = .06$). Furthermore, there was no evidence to suggest that baseball knowledge reduced, much less eliminated, the effect of working memory capacity on performance in this task. Therefore, although domain knowledge was clearly the most important predictor of performance, working memory capacity contributed as well.

Additional evidence concerning the interplay between domain knowledge and working memory capacity was reported by Wittmann and Süβ (1999). In an innovative series of studies, these researchers investigated the effects of domain knowledge and working memory capacity on performance in tasks designed to simulate complex work-related tasks. For example, in one task, the goal was to control the energy output of a coal-fired power plant by manipulating a number of variables (e.g., coal input). Another task involved managing the production of a garment manufacturing company. A consistent finding from this research was that task-specific knowledge (i.e., knowledge acquired during the simulations) was a strong predictor of final performance. However, Wittmann and Süβ also reported that working memory capacity was a significant predictor of performance above and beyond task-specific knowledge. Thus, both knowledge and working memory capacity contributed to performance differences in the simulated work tasks.

SUMMARY AND CONCLUSIONS

Baddeley and Hitch (1974) began their chapter by commenting on the dearth of evidence concerning the role of short-term memory in normal information processing. We end this chapter by asking whether the same can the same be said of working memory: After nearly three decades of research on working memory, have we made progress toward understanding the role of working memory in higher level cognition? The answer appears to be yes and no. First consider the "yes" part of the answer. There is a considerable amount of evidence concerning the role of working memory in comprehension and reasoning. For example, research suggests that the phonological loop and visuospatial sketchpad components of the Baddeley-Hitch model – or what we think of as maintenance of speech-based and imaginal information – play a limited, but not completely unimportant, role in tasks involving comprehension and reasoning. Moreover, the phonological loop may be especially important during reading or listening when sentences are long and complex, and the visuospatial sketchpad may be called on when comprehension depends on visualization. Furthermore, the central executive – or what we think of as working memory capacity – appears to be very important for certain tasks. That is, secondary tasks designed to tax the central executive usually result in a dramatic impairment in primary task performance, and working memory capacity predicts performance in various comprehension and reasoning tasks. The question of what accounts for this predictive relationship remains open, but our view is that the available evidence is consistent with the hypothesis that working memory capacity is a general information processing capability corresponding to controlled attention.

Now consider the "no" part of the answer. Very little is known about the role of working memory in tasks traditionally studied in research on problem solving. Nevertheless, we have both speculated about how working memory might contribute to performance in such tasks and pointed out directions for future research. For example, one way that the phonological loop (or maintenance of speech-based information) may play an important role in tasks such as the Tower of Hanoi is through comprehension of the instructions for the task. Furthermore, our theoretical view of working memory suggests that central executive functioning (or working memory capacity) should play a particularly important role in problem solving. To illustrate, one of the primary functions of working memory capacity is to maintain memory representations in a highly activated and accessible state. This function may be important when impasses in problem solving can be overcome by drawing together information from multiple problem-solving attempts. In addition, the ability to inhibit information from the focus of attention may be critical when one must shift from one way of solving a problem to another. Finally, research by Wittmann and Süβ (1999) suggests that working memory capacity contributes to performance in complex problem-solving tasks even when the effect of domain knowledge is taken into account. We believe that additional research concerning the interplay between domain knowledge and working memory capacity will prove particularly informative about the importance of working memory capacity in problem solving.

REFERENCES

Ackerman, P. L., & Kyllonen, P. C. (1991). Trainee characteristics. In J. E. Morrison (Ed.), *Training for performance: Principles of applied human learning* (pp. 193–229). Chichester, UK: John Wiley & Sons.

Adams, J. W., & Hitch, G. J. (1997). Working memory and children's mental addition. *Journal of Experimental Child Psychology, 67*, 21–38.

Allard, F., & Starkes, J. L. (1991). Motor-skill experts in sports, dance, and other domains. In K. A. Ericsson & J. Smith (Eds.), *Toward a general theory of expertise: Prospects and limits* (pp. 126–152). New York: Cambridge University Press.

Anderson, J. R. (1983). *The architecture of cognition.* Mahwah, NJ: Lawrence Erlbaum.

Anderson, J. R. (1985). *Cognitive psychology and its implications.* New York: Freeman.

Anderson, J. R. (1993). Problem solving and learning. *American Psychologist, 48*, 35–44.

Atkinson, R. C., & Shiffrin, R. M. (1968). Human memory: A proposed system and its control processes. In K. W. Spence & J. T. Spence (Eds.), *Advances in the psychology of learning and motivation research and theory* (Vol. 2, pp. 89–195). New York: Academic Press.

Babcock, R. L. (1994). Analysis of adult age differences on the Raven's Progressive Matrices Test. *Psychology and Aging, 9*, 303–314.

Baddeley, A. D., Elridge, M., & Lewis, V. (1981). The role of subvocalisation in reading. *Quarterly Journal of Experimental Psychology: Human Experimental Psychology, 33A*, 439–454.

Baddeley, A. D., & Hitch, G. J. (1974). Working memory. In G. H. Bower (Ed.), *The psychology of learning and motivation* (Vol. 8, pp. 47–89). New York: Academic Press.

Baddeley, A. D., Vallar, G., & Wilson, B. (1987). Sentence comprehension and phonological memory: Some neuropsychological evidence. In M. Coltheart (Ed.), *Attention and performance VII: The psychology of reading* (pp. 509–529). Hove, UK: Lawrence Erlbaum.

Barfield, W. (1997). Skilled performance on software as a function of domain expertise and program organization. *Perceptual & Motor Skills, 85*, 1471–1480.

Benton, S. L., Kraft, R. G., Glover, J. A., & Plake, B. S. (1984). Cognitive capacity differences among writers. *Journal of Educational Psychology, 76*, 820–834.

Bors, D. A., & Forrin, B. (1995). Age, speed of information processing, recall, and fluid intelligence. *Intelligence, 20*, 229–248.

Britton, B. K., Stimson, M., Stennett, B., & Gülgöz, S. (1998). Learning from instruction text: Test of an individual-differences model. *Journal of Education Psychology, 90*, 476–491.

Cattell, R. B. (1943). The measurement of adult intelligence. *Psychological Bulletin, 40*, 153–193.

Charness, N. (1981). Search in chess: Age and skill differences. *Journal of Experimental Psychology: Human Perception & Performance, 7*, 467–476.

Chase, W. G., & Simon, H. A. (1973). Perception in chess. *Cognitive Psychology, 4*, 55–81.

Cherry, C. E. (1953). Some experiments on the recognition of speech, with one and with two ears. *Journal of the Acoustical Society of America, 25*, 975–979.

Conway, A. R. A., Cowan, N., & Bunting, M. F. (2001). The cocktail party phenomenon revisited: The importance of working memory capacity. *Psychonomic Bulletin and Review, 8*, 331–335.

Cowan, N. (1995). *Attention and memory: An integrated framework.* Oxford: Oxford University Press.

Daneman, M., & Carpenter, P. A. (1980). Individual differences in working memory and reading. *Journal of Verbal Learning & Verbal Behavior, 19*, 450–466.

Daneman, M., & Green, I. (1986). Individual difference in comprehending and producing words in context. *Journal of Memory & Language, 25*, 1–18.

Daneman, M., & Merikle, P. M. (1996). Working memory and language comprehension: A meta-analysis. *Psychonomic Bulletin & Review, 3*, 422–433.

Donders (1868/1969). Over de snelheid van psychische processen. Onderzoekingen gedann in het Pysiologish Laboratorium der Utrechtsche Hoogeschool (W. G. Koster, Trans.). In W. G. Koster (Ed.), Attention and Performance II. *Acta Psychologica, 30*, 412–431. (Original work published in 1868.)

Duncker, K. (1945). On problem-solving. *Psychological Monographs, 58* (Whole No. 270).

Engle, R. W., Cantor, J., & Carullo, J. J. (1992). Individual differences in working memory and comprehension: A test of four hypotheses. *Journal of Experimental Psychology: Learning, Memory, & Cognition, 18*, 972–992.

Engle, R. W., Carullo, J. J., & Collins, K. W. (1991). Individual differences in working memory for comprehension and following directions. *Journal of Education Research, 84,* 253–262.

Engle, R. W., Kane, M. J., & Tuholski, S. W. (1999). Individual differences in working memory capacity and what they tell us about controlled attention, general fluid intelligence, and functions of the prefrontal cortex. In A. Miyake & P. Shah (Eds.), *Models of working memory: Mechanisms of active maintenance and executive control* (pp. 102–134). New York: Cambridge University Press.

Engle, R. W., Tuholski, S. W., Laughlin, J. E., & Conway, A. R. A. (1999). Working memory, short-term memory, and general fluid intelligence: A latent-variable approach. *Journal of Experimental Psychology: General, 128,* 309–331.

Ericsson, K. A., & Kintsch, W. (1995). Long-term working memory. *Psychological Review, 102,* 211–245.

Evans, J. St. B., & Brooks, P. G. (1981). Competing with reasoning: A test of the working memory hypothesis. *Current Psychological Research, 1,* 139–147.

Feigenbaum, E. A. (1989). What hath Simon wrought? In D. Klahr & K. Kotovsky (Eds.), *Complex information processing: The impact of Herbert A. Simon* (pp. 165–180). Hillsdale, NJ: Lawrence Erlbaum.

Frensch, P. A., & Sternberg, R. J. (1989a). Expertise and intelligent thinking: When is it worse to know better? In R. J. Sternberg (Ed.), *Advances in the psychology of human intelligence* (Vol. 5, pp. 157–188). Hillsdale, NJ: Lawrence Erlbaum.

Frensch, P. A., & Sternberg, R. J. (1989b). Skill-related differences in game playing. In R. J. Sternberg & P. A. Frensch (Eds.), *Complex problem solving: Principles and mechanisms* (pp. 343–381). Hillsdale, NJ: Lawrence Erlbaum.

Gilhooly, K. J., Logie, R. H., Wetherick, N. E., & Wynn V. (1993). Working memory and strategies in syllogistic-reasoning tasks. *Memory & Cognition, 21,* 115–124.

Gilhooly, K. J., Wood, M., Kinnear, P. R., & Green, C. (1988). Skill in map reading and memory for maps. *Quarterly Journal of Experimental Psychology: Human Experimental Psychology, 40,* 87–107.

Glass, A. L., Eddy, J. K., & Schwanenflugel, P. J. (1980). The verification of high and low imagery sentences. *Journal of Experimental Psychology: Human Learning & Memory, 6,* 692–704.

Goldman-Rakic, P. S. (1992). Working memory and the mind. *Scientific American, 267,* 110–117.

Haenggi, D., & Perfetti, C. A. (1992). Individual differences in reprocessing of text. *Journal of Educational Psychology, 84,* 182–192.

Haenggi, D., & Perfetti, C. A. (1994). Processing components of college-level reading comprehension. *Discourse Processes, 17,* 83–104.

Halford, G. S., Bain, J. D., & Mayberry, M. T. (1984). Does a concurrent memory load interfere with reasoning? *Current Psychological Research and Reviews, 3,* 14–23.

Hambrick, D. Z., & Engle, R. W. (2002). Effects of domain knowledge, working memory capacity, and age on cognitive performance. *Cognitive Psychology, 44,* 339–387.

Hasher, L., Quig, M. B., & May, C. P. (1997). Inhibitory control over no-longer-relevant information: Adult age differences. *Memory and Cognition, 25,* 286–295.

Hasher, L., & Zacks, R. T. (1988). Working memory, comprehension, and aging: A review and a new view. In G. H. Bower (Ed.), *The psychology of learning and motivation: Advances in research and theory* (Vol. 22, pp. 193–225). San Diego, CA: Academic Press.

Hasher, L., Zacks, & May, C. P. (1999). Inhibitory control, circadian arousal, and age. In D. Gopher & A. Koriat (Eds.), *Attention and performance XVII. Cognitive regulation of performance: Interaction of theory and application* (pp. 653–675). Cambridge, MA: MIT Press.

Hebb, D. O. (1949). *The organization of behavior: A neuropsychological theory.* New York: Wiley.

Heglin, H. J. (1956). Problem solving set in different age groups. *Journal of Gerontology, 38,* 71–76.

Horn, J. L., & Masunaga, H. (2000). New directions for research into aging and intelligence: The development of expertise. In T. J. Perfect & E. A. Maylor (Eds.), *Models of cognitive aging* (pp. 125–159). Oxford: Oxford University Press.

Hultsch, D. F., Hertzog, C., & Dixon, R. A. (1990). Ability correlates of memory performance in adulthood and aging. *Psychology and Aging, 5,* 356–368.

Hutchins, E. (1995). *Cognition in the wild.* Cambridge, MA: MIT Press.

Kahneman, D. (1973). *Attention and effort.* Englewood Cliffs, NJ: Prentice-Hall.

Kane, M. J., Bleckley, M. K., Conway, A. R. A., & Engle, R. W. (2001). A controlled attention view of working memory capacity. *Journal of Experimental Psychology: General, 130,* 169–183

Kintsch, W. (1998). *Comprehension: A paradigm for cognition.* Cambridge: Cambridge University Press.

Kintsch, W., Healy, A. F., Hegarty, M., Pennington, B. F., & Salthouse, T. A. (1999). Models of working memory: Eight questions and some general issues. In A. Miyake & P. Shah (Eds.), *Models of working memory: Mechanisms of active maintenance and executive control* (pp. 412–441). Cambridge: Cambridge University Press.

Kintsch, W., & van Dijk, T. A. (1978). Towards a model of text comprehension and production. *Psychological Review, 85,* 363–394.

Klauer, K. C., Stegmaier, R., & Meiser, T. (1997). Working memory involvement in propositional and spatial reasoning. *Thinking and Reasoning, 3,* 9–47.

Kyllonen, P. C. (1996). Is working memory capacity Spearman's g? In I. Dennis & P. Tapsfield (Eds.), *Human abilities: Their nature and measurement* (pp. 49–75). Mahwah, NJ: Lawrence Erlbaum Associates, Inc.

Kyllonen, P. C., & Christal, R. E. (1990). Reasoning ability is (little more than) working-memory capacity? *Intelligence, 14,* 389–433.

Logie, R. H. (1995). *Visuo-spatial working memory.* Hove, UK: Lawrence Erlbaum.

Luchins, A. S. (1942). Mechanization in problem solving. *Psychological Monographs, 54* (Whole No. 248).

Masson, M. E., & Miller, Jo A. (1983). Working memory and individual differences in comprehension and memory of text. *Journal of Educational Psychology, 75,* 314–318.

Meinz, E. J., & Salthouse, T. A. (1998). The effects of age and experience on memory for visually presented music. *Journals of Gerontology, 53B,* 60–69.

Miller, K. M. (1957). Einstellung rigidity, intelligence and teaching methods. *British Journal of Educational Psychology, 27,* 127–134.

Minsky, M. L., & Papert, S. (1974). *Artificial intelligence.* Eugene, OR: State System of Higher Education.

Moray, N. (1959). Attention in dichotic listening: Affective cues and the influence of instructions. *Quarterly Journal of Experimental Psychology, 11,* 56–60.

Ormrod, J. E., & Cochran, K. F. (1988). Relationship of verbal ability and working memory to spelling achievement and learning to spell. *Reading Research & Instruction, 28,* 33–43.

Robbins, T. W., Anderson, E. J., Barker, D. R., Bradley, A. C., Fearnyhough, C., Henson, R., Hudson, S. R., & Baddeley, A. D. (1996). Working memory in chess. *Memory & Cognition, 24,* 83–93.

Rogers, J. C., Keyes, B. J., & Fuller, B. J. (1976). Solution shift in the elderly. *Journal of Gerontology, 31,* 670–675.

Rosen, V. M., & Engle, R. W. (1997). The role of working memory capacity in retrieval. *Journal of Experimental Psychology: General, 126,* 211–227.

Rosen, V. M., & Engle, R. W. (1998). Working memory capacity and suppression. *Journal of Memory and Language, 39,* 418–436.

Salthouse, T. A. (1992). *Mechanisms of age-cognition relations in adulthood.* Hillsdale, NJ: Lawrence Erlbaum.

Salthouse, T. A. (1996). The processing speed theory of adult age differences in cognition. *Psychological Review, 103,* 403–428.

Shah, P., & Miyake, A. (1996). The separability of working memory resources for spatial thinking and language processing: An individual differences approach. *Journal of Experimental Psychology: General, 125,* 4–27.

Shah, P., & Miyake, A. (1999). Models of working memory: An introduction. In A. Miyake & P. Shah (Eds.), *Models of working memory: Mechanisms of active maintenance and executive control* (pp. 1–27). Cambridge, UK: Cambridge University Press.

Stine, E. A. L., & Wingfield, A. (1990). How much do working memory deficits contribute to age differences in discourse memory? *European Journal of Cognitive Psychology Special Issue: Cognitive Gerontology, 2,* 289–304.

Toms, M., Morris, N., & Ward, D. (1993). Working memory and conditional reasoning. *Quarterly Journal of Experimental Psychology: Human Experimental Psychology Special Issue: The cognitive psychology of reasoning, 46A,* 679–699.

Turner, M. L., & Engle, R. W. (1989). Is working memory capacity task dependent? *Journal of Memory & Language, 28,* 127–154.

Voss, J. F., Greene, T. R., Post, T. A., & Penner, B. C. (1983). Problem-solving skill in the social sciences. In G. H. Bower (Ed.), *The psychology of learning and motivation: Advances in research theory* (Vol. 17, pp. 165–213). New York: Academic Press.

Waters, G., Caplan, D., & Hildebrandt, N. (1987). Working memory and written sentence comprehension. In M. Coltheart (Ed.), *Attention and performance 12: The psychology of reading.* Hove, England: Lawrence Erlbaum.

Welsh, M. C., Satterlee-Cartmell, T., & Stine, M. (1999). Towers of Hanoi and London: Contribution of working memory and inhibition to performance. *Brain & Cognition, 41,* 231–242.

Wittmann, W. W., & Süß, H. (1999). Investigating the paths between working memory, intelligence, and complex problem-solving performances via Brunswik Symmetry. In P. L. Ackerman, P. C. Kyllonen, & R. D. Roberts (Eds.), *Learning and individual differences* (pp. 77–110). Washington, DC: American Psychological Association.

Zacks, R. T., Hasher, L., & Li, K. Z. H. (2000). Human memory. In T. A. Salthouse & F. I. M. Craik (Eds.), *The handbook of aging and cognition* (2nd ed., pp. 293–357).

Mahwah, NJ: Lawrence Erlbaum.

ACKNOWLEDGMENTS

We thank Russell Smith, Catherine Jamal, and Genie Addleton for help in preparing this chapter.

7

Comprehension of Text in Problem Solving

Shannon Whitten and Arthur C. Graesser

Imagine that on some unlucky weekday morning your coffee machine breaks down. For many of us, notably the authors of this chapter, this would be a serious problem. One way of solving this urgent problem is by physically fumbling with the broken machine, trying to fix it by using problem-solving heuristics or sheer trial and error. As an alternative, text would come to the rescue. You could read the manual that came with the machine. You could look in a book on household repairs. You could also consult the Internet. When you pursue any of these latter options, you must be able to comprehend the text and apply what you have learned. This chapter explores the factors that predict your success in solving problems such as the broken coffee machine after reading a text.

Whenever texts are successfully used to solve a problem, the solver must accurately represent both the problem and the messages presented in the texts. A *text representation* is a cognitive representation that has some reference to elements, features, or structural patterns in the explicit text. Many factors contribute to the construction of text representations. To put it simply, two classes of factors are properties of the text (such as its organization into topics, subtopics, and sentences) and properties of the reader (such as domain-specific knowledge and general reading skill). One of the central assumptions of this chapter is that text representations constrain problem solving. To clarify *how*, we need to discuss theories of text representation, how the representations are built, and how they are accessed and used.

We start by discussing five levels of text representation and the factors that contribute to successful representations at each level. Next, we present some evidence that forming a reliable representation from the explicit text is sometimes crucial to solving a problem. We subsequently discuss how text representations are accessed and used. The final section presents three classes of models that make radically different claims about text representation.

FIVE LEVELS OF TEXT REPRESENTATION

Most discourse psychologists agree that there are five levels of text representation (Graesser, Millis, & Zwaan, 1997; Kintsch, 1998). These five levels are (1) the surface code, (2) the textbase, (3) the referential situation model, (4) the communication level, and (5) the discourse genre. The *surface code* preserves the exact wording and syntax of the discourse. For example, this might include the verbatim sentence, "The coffee machine has five parts," if you were reading a text on repairing a coffee machine. If readers had a perfect memory of the surface code, they would distinguish the verbatim sentence from alternative paraphrases, such as "There are five components in the coffee machine." However, readers of technical texts rarely remember the surface code for more than 30 seconds or a few minutes. With rare exceptions, there is much better memory for the other four, *deeper* levels of text representation (Kintsch, 1998; Singer & Kintsch, 2001). It would be necessary for the reader to actively rehearse and recycle the verbatim information in working memory if the surface code was, for some reason, very critical for solving a problem. An accurate record of surface code is potentially helpful when the reader has low domain knowledge, the text is ambiguous, or subtle distinctions need to be made.

The *textbase* contains the meanings of the words in a propositional form, but ignores the exact wording and syntax. A *proposition* is the representation of a particular event, action, state, or goal expressed in the text. The linguistic format of a proposition consists of a *predicate* (e.g., verb, adjective, connective) plus one or more *arguments* (e.g., noun phrase, prepositional phrase, embedded proposition; Kintsch, 1998). The example sentence above would contain three propositions: HAS (MACHINE, PARTS), COFFEE (MACHINE), and FIVE (PARTS). The predicates are positioned to the left of the parentheses, whereas the arguments are positioned within the parentheses. The predicates specify how arguments are interrelated (e.g., parts are contained within the machine) or they ascribe properties to the arguments (the machine is a coffee machine). The textbase is not entirely limited to these explicit propositions. The textbase sometimes includes information that is essential for connecting explicit propositions. For example, in the sentence "The coffee machine has five parts, but the power adaptor is not normally needed," the bridging inference IS-A(ADAPTOR, PART) would be inserted for achieving text coherence even though it is not explicitly stated. The textbase also deletes some information that is not regarded as important, such as verb tense and quantifiers (e.g., "usually"). As one might expect, there have been some debates in discourse psychology as to the exact composition of the textbase, that is, what inferences get inserted, what information is deleted, what constitutes propositions, and indeed whether a propositional textbase is needed at all in a theory of text representation (Perfetti & Britt, 1995).

The *situation model* (or mental model) is the nonlinguistic, referential content of what the text is about (Graesser, Singer, & Trabasso, 1994; Johnson-Laird, 1983; Kintsch, 1998; Zwaan & Radvansky, 1998). The situation model contains component hierarchies (parts and subparts), causal chains, goal hierarchies, spatial regions, and other dimensions of reality. The situation model for a story would be a mental microworld with characters, settings, character traits, actions, and events that unfold in a plot, and the characters' emotional reactions to the episodes in the plot. The situation model for a technical expository text about a device would describe its components, how it works, and how it is used (Gentner & Stevens, 1983; Kieras & Bovair, 1984; Mayer, 1996; Millis, King, & Kim, 2000). Situation models are constructed through interactions between prior world knowledge and the explicit text (surface code and textbase). For example, you would infer that the power adaptor is needed for an electric energy source rather than it being a nutrient to add to the coffee. You would infer that the five parts must operate together in a coordinated fashion rather than being a mere collection of detached components. One of the hot debates in discourse psychology during the last decade addresses the question about what inferences are constructed in the situation model (Graesser et al., 1994; Lorch & O'Brien, 1995; McKoon& Ratcliff, 1992; Schank, 1999; Trabasso & Magliano, 1996). For example, the constructionist theory (Graesser et al., 1994) stipulates that one class of inferences that readers routinely construct are explanation-based inferences; these inferences specify *why* actions are performed (i.e., motives of characters and agents) and *why* events occur (i.e., causes of events). In contrast, readers do not routinely generate inferences during comprehension that refer to spatial layouts of objects (*where*), the manner in which events occur (*how*), and consequences that unfold causally in the distant future (*what if*).

The *communication* level captures the pragmatic context that frames the messages in the text (Beck, McKeown, Hamilton, & Kucan, 1997; Graesser, Bowers, Olde, & Pomeroy, 1999; Nystrand, 1986; Rosenblatt, 1994; Schraw & Bruning, 1996). Simply put, who is communicating to whom? What author is talking to what reader? Is there a narrator communicating to an addressee? Continuing with coffee machines, the reader represents the text rather differently when trying to repair the coffee machine, when trying to assemble a new coffee machine, or when deciding whether to purchase a coffee machine. On the flip side, a good technical writer anticipates whether the reader will be a repairman, an assembler, or a potential customer. The writer crafts the texts for these different purposes. There is a new program for improving reading comprehension called Questioning the Author (Beck et al., 1997). Children are trained to imagine the author of the text and to challenge what the author claims by asking pointed questions: "What evidence is there for claim X presented by the author?" and "Why did the author say X?" Elementary school children have a dramatic improvement in reading after being taught the Questioning the Author program for a few months.

Finally, the *genre* level assigns the text to one or more rhetorical categories (Biber, 1988) and uses the selected text genre to guide comprehension. Some examples of text genres at a basic level of classification are science textbooks, literary novels, repair manuals, comic books, and science fiction novels. The traditional general categories are narrative, expository, persuasion, and description (Brooks & Warren, 1972). If the sentence "The coffee machine has five parts" appeared in a detective novel, it might serve as a clue to the mystery. The identical sentence would clarify the composition of the coffee machine in a repair manual. Zwaan (1994) has reported that college students represent a narrative very differently when instructed that the narrative text is literature versus an article in a newspaper. When told the text is literature, more surface code is preserved in the memory representation, at the expense of having a less detailed situation model.

The reader's success at constructing each of the above five levels of representation depends on three aspects of the comprehension mechanism: *code*, *process*, and *skill*. These aspects are mutually constrained by both the text and the reader. The text needs to supply adequate fragments of the code to afford correct interpretations. For example, if the text is missing critical words and has improper syntactic composition, the surface code will not be well formed and there will be barriers to constructing the textbase. If the rhetorical organization of the text lacks organization and coherence, it will be difficult to construct the situation model and text genre. The textual code is necessary, but not sufficient for constructing the text representations. The code needs to be *processed* by *readers*. The processes include those of activating the relevant knowledge that is affiliated with each level of representation (through pattern recognition processes) and of manipulating the representations appropriately. For each level of code, the reader needs to have the skill and knowledge to process the code. For example, the reader will not be able to get past the surface code if the reader is an English speaker and the repair manual is in Spanish. A repair manual will be useless if reader's knowledge base lacks an understanding of the "diagnosis and repair" genre. Sometimes world knowledge can compensate for a text that is not fully fortified by a complete configuration of code. For example, most readers know that the first steps in coffee machine troubleshooting are making sure that the machine is plugged in and turned on. This is not explicitly mentioned in the text, so the reader is expected to infer it. Thus, world knowledge can help compensate by filling the gaps in explicit text. In the case of high-knowledge readers, the process of accessing the world knowledge about coffee makers is successfully completed and the relevant inferences are entered into the text representation. But these gaps in the text end up being risky for readers with low domain knowledge.

The formation of a useful cognitive representation from the explicit text is potentially important for solving a problem like the broken coffee machine, at least if the reader uses printed text. In this section, we have discussed five levels of text representation (surface code, textbase, situation model, communication, and genre). We have also discussed three aspects of the comprehension mechanism that contribute to a successful representation at each level (text code, process, and skill). If one imagines a matrix with 15 cells, i.e., 5 (levels of text representation) × 3 (aspects), one gains a broad landscape of potential problems with comprehension that may emerge for particular readers for particular problem solving contexts. It is beyond the scope of this chapter to document potential problems in each of these 15 cells, but we explore some of the deeper levels of text comprehension that affect problem solving.

THE IMPORTANCE OF TEXT REPRESENTATION FOR PROBLEM SOLVING

One of the central arguments in this chapter is that the ability to build an accurate and integrated representation of the text is crucial to problem solving. Kintsch and Greeno (1985) proposed that the process of solving word problems occurs in two phases. The first is the text comprehension phase that generates the mental representation of the problem. For example, a "COMBINE" representation might be generated from a problem that requires addition. The second is the problem-solving phase where solvers actually compute the answer. The second phase cannot take place without the first. Without the first, the reader will end up solving the wrong problem.

Lucangeli, Tressoldi, and Cendron (1998) investigated seven abilities related to success in solving word problems. These abilities were text comprehension, problem representation, problem categorization, solution estimate, planning the solution, procedure evaluation, and self-evaluation. For each ability, participants were given multiple-choice questions as they solved word problems. A multiple regression analysis revealed that text comprehension, problem representation, problem categorization, planning the solution, and self-evaluation were significant predictors of the accuracy of the solution. More interesting was that a path analysis revealed that text comprehension directly influenced the other four abilities. Thus, text comprehension is a fundamental component in problem solving in analyses that provide psychometric assessments of several processing components.

The distinction between the *superficial* and the *structural* similarity between problems is one property of text representation that has received a great deal of attention in the problem-solving literature. Obviously, the process of solving a target problem should be influenced by a similar problem that was previously solved (Gentner & Markman, 1997; Gick & Holyoak,

1980; Schank, 1999). Superficial similarity refers to shared surface code and to shared argument slots in the textbase. For example, "coffee mug" and "tea cup" are examples of objects that share superficial properties: They are both small containers with handles used to drink hot beverages. A coffee mug in one problem would be analogies to a teacup in another problem by virtue of superficial similarity. Two problems may also be similar from the standpoint of relational information. Relational similarity refers to shared complex propositions in a textbase or to shared structural configurations in the situation model. For example, the process of electrons revolving around the nucleus of an atom has a relational similarity to the process of planets revolving around the sun in the solar system. *Analogies* are defined according to structural similarity rather than superficial similarity, although it is important to acknowledge that the distinction between superficial and relational similarity is not entirely a crisp dichotomy (Gentner & Markman, 1997).

One empirical question addresses the extent to which new problems are solved by spontaneously accessing and using problems that have been previously solved. A *target* problem is defined as the problem that is currently being attended to, whereas a *source* problem is one that was solved sometime in the prior history of the participant in an experiment. *Spontaneously* means "incidentally," that is, without specific instructions or hints to look for similarities between the target problem and a source problem. Multiple steps need to be completed for spontaneous access to a source problem. The first step is forming an adequate representation of the target problem, as discussed above. Then the representation directs pattern recognition processes to access a relevant source problem from memory. Once the appropriate problem has been retrieved, the solver needs to accurately map or align the features of the target problem to features of the source problem. At that point, there has been a successful *transfer* from a source problem to a target problem. A potentially successful transfer can break down at any of these stages: problem representation, access processes, and alignment processes.

Gick and Holyoak (1980) conducted a landmark study that tested whether structural similarities were sufficient to provoke spontaneous analogical transfer. In that study, the authors presented college students with Duncker's (1945) "radiation problem" as a target. In the radiation problem, a doctor has a patient with a malignant tumor. The tumor is inoperable, but there is a type of ray can kill the tumor. However, one ray that is intense enough to kill the tumor will also kill any surrounding tissue, and therefore the patient. Alternatively, a ray that is not intense enough to kill the tissue will not kill the tumor. What should the doctor do? A solution would be to use several lower intensity rays aimed at the tumor. This is a difficult problem for most people to solve. Gick and Holyoak presented some participants with an analogous story, or source, before solving the difficult radiation problem. This story described a general of an army that wanted to attack a fortress. There were several roads leading to the fortress, but many were covered with mines. Thus, the army could not attack the fortress by traveling along one road or the general might lose his entire army. However, an attack by a small portion of the army would not succeed because the entire army was needed to invade the strong fortress. So, the general had several small groups travel along different roads toward the fortress. Participants were able to solve the target problem after receiving the analogous source story, but *only* when they were explicitly instructed to use the source problem to help them solve the target problem. This study demonstrated that readers can access an analogous source problem from memory, and also use this problem to solve a novel problem, but only when they knew to look for similarities. The results are interesting because they suggest that analogical transfer does not occur spontaneously.

Holyoak and Koh (1987) conducted a follow-up study that tested the role of superficial similarities between the source and the target problems. The authors hypothesized that differences in the superficial and structural similarities between the source and target problems may determine the circumstances under which spontaneous transfer occurs. That study again tested participants with Duncker's (1945) radiation problem as the target problem. In their study, however, the analog that was used as the source problem shared more superficial features with the radiation problem. When using this surface analog, spontaneous analogical transfer was facilitated. Therefore, spontaneous transfer is rare when only structural similarities are shared (Gick & Holyoak, 1980, 1983; Holyoak & Koh, 1987), but is more successful when the surface features also have correspondences. Readers do not spontaneously invoke a remote analog of a problem on the basis of relational structure alone. This result is compatible with the computational model of analogical reasoning that was developed by Forbus, Gentner, and Law (1994). Superficial similarity is critical for directing the initial pattern recognition processes for successful memory matches, whereas relational similarity is critical for directing the subsequent alignment processes. The world is kind when superficial similarity is correlated with relational similarity.

Catrambone, Jones, Jonicles, and Seifert (1995) demonstrated further that humans have a higher likelihood of using analogies when there are strong superficial cues to do so. To test this, they presented pictures of curved tubes to participants, who were asked to predict the path of a substance moving through that tube. Those participants who were explicitly reminded of a hose demonstrated a significant advantage over those who were not reminded of this analogy (on average, 75% to 39%).

The organization of the text into labeled goals and subgoals has been shown to facilitate problem solving. Catrambone (1996) reported that learning the Poisson distribution was facilitated when the text was organized in a series of subgoals, compared with having a single superordinate goal. Consider the following text as an example for the equation of the Poisson distribution: $P(X = x) = [e^{-\Lambda}(\Lambda^x)]/x!$, where Λ is the expected value of the random variable X.

A judge noticed that some of the 219 lawyers at City Hall owned more than one briefcase. She counted the number of briefcases each lawyer owned and found that 180 of the lawyers owned exactly one briefcase, 17 owned two briefcases, 13 owned 3 briefcases, and 9 owned 4 briefcases. Use the Poisson distribution to determine the probability of a randomly chosen lawyer at City Hall owning exactly two briefcases.

To solve this problem, the solver must first calculate the number of briefcases. Participants received one of the two organizational formats below.

SUPERORDINATE CONDITION Goal: Find Λ

Method:

1. Multiply each category by (e.g., owning exactly zero briefcases, owning exactly one briefcase, etc.) by its observed frequency.
2. Sum the results.
3. Divide the sum by the total number of lawyers to obtain the average number of briefcases per lawyer.

SUBGOAL CONDITION: Goal: Find Λ

Method:

1. Goal: Find total number of briefcases
   Method:
      a. Multiply each category by its observed frequency.
      b. Sum the results to obtain the total number of briefcases.
2. Divide the sum by the total number of lawyers to obtain the average number of briefcases per lawyer.

Catrambone found that subgoal condition facilitated transfer to a novel problem that includes the same subgoal, compared with the superordinate goal condition. Therefore, the representation of the problem can be significantly influenced by the organization and labeling of the text.

THE IMPORTANCE OF THE READER IN COMPREHENDING TEXT FOR PROBLEM SOLVING

Readers vary in their world knowledge and their ability to integrate this knowledge with text representations. Such individual differences end up influencing the likelihood of solving problems. The fact that world knowledge has a critical impact on these processes is not a particularly astute observation. However, researchers have documented some intriguing interactions between world knowledge and various processes. For example, when problem solvers have a rich base of relevant domain knowledge, they are less reliant on the integrity of the superficial code and coherence of the explicit text. In fact, as we shall learn below, sometimes it is better for a high-knowledge reader to be given texts with coherence gaps and a nonoptimal organization.

It is well documented in discourse psychology that world knowledge has a robust impact on text comprehension (Cote, Goldman, & Saul, 1998; Graesser et al., 1994, 1997; Kintsch, 1998; Voss & Silfies, 1996). The incoming information from the text is integrated with information from the reader's knowledge base. This knowledge base allows the readers to generate inferences that tie together or elaborate on the ideas described by the explicit text.

Most of the research on inferences in text comprehension has focused on narratives because the readers' knowledge base is much richer in the case of narratives than expository text. Prior knowledge about social situations, the order and duration of scripted action sequences, and the function of everyday objects guide the readers' understanding of narrative text. The major purpose of writing expository text, on the other hand, is to discuss and explain information on unfamiliar topics. Most adults do not understand the mechanics that underlie coffee machines, for example. So they need to consult expository text or to listen to their friends' stories about how they fixed their coffee machines. Two basic questions arise when exploring the role of world knowledge in guiding text comprehension during problem solving. How do problem solvers construct representations of novel problems? How do they access and use available information in memory during the problem-solving process?

Novick (1988) conducted a study that helps illuminate the importance of background knowledge in spontaneous analogical transfer. Novick hypothesized that experts and novices would differ in representing a problem. More specifically, she hypothesized that experts would represent the relational (structural) information in a problem, whereas novices would represent the superficial aspects of a problem. According to this hypothesis, only the experts would demonstrate positive, spontaneous, analogical transfer when the source and target problems shared exclusively relational similarities. Novices would demonstrate negative analogical transfer when the problems shared only superficial similarities, the relational similarities were critical, and there was no correlation between superficial and relational similarities.

To test this first hypothesis, experts and novices were selected and presented four word problems with the correct solution procedures. One of the source problems was a remote analog of the target problem that shared relational, but not superficial similarities. All participants tried to solve the same target problem of a high school band that needed to split up into even columns for the homecoming parade. If the columns contained 8 or 12 students, one student was always left alone in a column. Finally, the band director arranged the musicians in rows of five, and that worked. The critical question was how many students are in the band if the number is between 45 and 200. Some of the participants received an analogous source problem, which described a woman and her husband trying to arrange different types of plants in their garden. The solutions for the source problems were given. If this source problem were accessed and used, there should be positive transfer. A baseline condition was also included in which none of the four problems was related to the target. The results robustly supported the hypothesis. Whereas 56% of the experts generated the correct solution in the analog condition, only 6% did so in the baseline condition. This result clearly demonstrated spontaneous analogical transfer. In contrast, novices did not show any differences between the analog and baseline conditions.

Novick conducted another experiment that tested whether novices would be seduced by source problems that were superficially similar, but not similar at the level of relations. The same basic procedure was run as in experiment 1, except that the source problem was related to the target problem by only superficial features. This functioned as a distracter problem, because accessing this problem would not facilitate solving the target problem. Indeed, there should be negative transfer if the source problem were activated. The results of this experiment revealed that both novices and experts showed negative transfer. So even the experts were seduced by source problems that were superficially similar.

In a third experiment, both the relationally similar and the superficially similar problems were given prior to solving the target problem. This experiment was designed to test whether participants would demonstrate negative transfer if both types of problems were given. Positive transfer was found for the experts, but not the novices. That is, experts used the correct, structurally similar problem, but novices did not. Negative transfer was found in both groups, but was weaker for experts. So again, both groups attempted to use the incorrect, superficially similar problem. However, experts typically did not make more than one attempt to use the distracter problem.

Novick's study demonstrates three principles. First, background knowledge has a significant impact on the ability to adequately represent, access, and use an analogous problem. Second, superficial similarities robustly determine access to similar problems, for both novices and experts. Third, spontaneous analogical transfer is possible when there are only structural similarities between a source and target, but only for experts.

Chi, Feltovich, and Glaser (1981) have reported similar results in their studies of physics problems. The authors asked physics experts and novices to sort problems according to similarity. The physics majors sorted problems according to relational similarities, that is, general physics principles, whereas novices sorted problems on the basis of superficial similarities. The authors hypothesized that experts and novices categorize problems differently, and these different categories elicit different knowledge structures. For experts, these knowledge structures and categories are based on similar solution procedures.

Sometimes, the properties of the reader and the properties of the text interact in counterintuitive ways. McNamara, Kintsch, Songer, and Kintsch (1996) presented children with biology texts. Half of the children had high domain knowledge and half had low domain knowledge. The texts varied in degree of coherence. The high-coherence texts were more explicit in specifying the relational organization of the text. For example, the high-coherence texts contained full noun phrases instead of pronouns, titles and subtitles, elaborations, and more sentence connectives. The authors found an interaction between knowledge level and text coherence when they measured performance on tasks that required reasoning, problem-solving tasks, and the construction of deeper, situation models. As expected, participants with low knowledge performed better after receiving texts with high coherence than those with low coherence. Rather surprisingly, participants with high domain knowledge actually performed better after reading a low coherence text than a high-coherence text. This is a counterintuitive result. How is it possible that a less coherent text facilitates learning? McNamara et al. (1996) concluded that the low-coherence texts forced the high-knowledge readers to engage in active, effortful processing at the level of the situation model. High-knowledge readers can experience an illusion of comprehension, on automatic pilot, when the text is well written and they have a rich knowledge base. However, when there are text disfluencies, they need to recruit their world knowledge for effortful processing at the situation model; the consequence is better learning at deeper levels. In contrast, the low-knowledge readers need to build a situation model from scratch, and this is facilitated by coherent texts.

The McNamara et al. (1996) study also measured performance that tapped the surface and textbase levels of representation. Such measures include recognition memory and recall memory. There was an advantage of high-coherence texts over low-coherence texts for both groups of participants, although the differences were less pronounced for readers with high domain knowledge. The results of the McNamara et al. study underscore the importance of specifying the levels of text representation that are tapped in the measures of performance. The pattern of data for the surface code and textbase was very different from that of the situation model. There was a complex three-way interaction among the features of the text (i.e., manipulated coherence), the reader (i.e., domain knowledge), and the level of representation (surface code, textbase, or situation model).

Complex interactions among text, reader, and representation have been reported in a number of recent studies in discourse psychology (Cote et al., 1998; Goldman, Saul, & Cote, 1995; Graesser, Kassler, Kreuz, & McLain-Allen, 1998).

Mannes and Kintsch (1987) reported a similar study that supports the conclusion that it is critical to keep track of the level of representation when performance measures are reported. Instead of varying the coherence of the text itself, Mannes and Kintsch manipulated the composition of an *advanced organizer* (i.e., general outline), which was comprehended before the readers comprehended the text. The information in the advanced organizer was presented either in the same order as the subsequent text or in a different order. After receiving the organizer and the text, participants were tested with a sentence verification task. There were two types of statements to be verified by the participants. Verbatim statements contained an explicit excerpt from the text and therefore tested memory at the surface code and textbase levels. Inference statements contained information that needed to be inferred from the text and therefore tested deeper comprehension of material. Inference statements tapped the situation model level of representation. Mannes and Kintsch (1987) found that the participants who received the congruent outline did better on the verbatim memory statements. In contrast, those who received an organizer with an incongruent order performed better on the inference task. This suggests that readers with the incongruent organizer were reading the text at a deeper level.

According to the research presented in this section, an adequate theory of text comprehension requires researchers to dissect the linguistic properties of the text, the abilities of the reader, and levels of text representation that are involved. There are complex interactions among the three components, and the mechanisms sometimes generated counterintuitive results. In the next, final section of this chapter, we briefly describe three classes of models that have dramatically different views of comprehension mechanisms.

THREE CLASSES OF MODELS OF TEXT COMPREHENSION

Three classes of text comprehension models have dominated the field of discourse psychology during the last 20 years. These classes make radically different assumptions about the nature of the representations and the processes that shape comprehension. It is beyond the scope of this chapter to provide a comprehensive description of each model, but we do want to convey the distinctive highlights of each model and point out some of their implications for problem solving. We call these three classes of models the knowledge structure model, the construction integration model, and the embodied cognition model.

Knowledge Structure Models

The first class of models assumes that text representations and world knowledge have highly structured compositional formats (Gernsbacher, 1997; Graesser & Clark, 1985; Kintsch & vanDijk, 1978; Schank & Abelson, 1977; Trabasso & Suh, 1993). The representations normally consist of nodes (concepts, propositions) that are interrelated by a network of relations (such as Is-a, Has-as-parts, Cause, Reason, Outcome). The course of comprehension consists of building the text representations by creating, modifying, inserting, deleting, and reorganizing the nodes and relations. The process of constructing these structures is accomplished by accessing world knowledge from long-term memory and using this knowledge to guide the construction of a specific text representation. The world knowledge can either be generic knowledge or specific knowledge (e.g., a source problem in the present context of problem solving). All of these constructive activities take place in a limited capacity working memory.

World knowledge often comes in natural packages that organize its components. Scripts are one class of world knowledge packages that have received extensive attention (Graesser et al., 1998; Schank, 1999; Schank & Abelson, 1977). A script organizes frequently enacted activities that are performed in particular settings. For example, in a RESTAURANT script, a customer enters a restaurant, is seated, looks over the menu, orders food, and so on. There are typical props (e.g., table, chairs, menus), goals (customer wants to get food, waiter wants to get money), and results (customer is full). The goal-driven actions and events are at the heart of the scripts. The sequence of actions is so stereotypical that many of the actions do not have to be stated explicitly in order to be incorporated into the text representation at the level of the situation model. For example, readers may later remember that the "customer ate" even though this was inferred rather than explicitly stated. Scripts are generic packages of information that guide the readers' attention, expectations, inferences, and interpretations of explicit text.

Current theories of script representation assume that scripts are flexible and dynamic rather than being rigid action sequences (Schank, 1999). For example, if you go to the doctor's office and there is coffee available, you might note this information and later remember it. If there is always coffee available in the waiting room of the doctor's office, "COFFEE" ends up being part of your generic script. If there is also coffee routinely available in the waiting room of the dentist's office and the lawyer's office, then coffee ends up being part of your "WAITING ROOM" script.

There must be some way to access scripts. The way to access a script from memory is through indexing (Schank, 1999; Schank & Abelson, 1995). An index is any specific piece of information that distinctively colors the incoming information and associates it with a scripted memory representation. Breakdowns, salient contrasts, expectation violations, norm violations, and other unusual occurrences are good candidates for being indexes, but in principle an index can refer to objects, events, locations, beliefs, attitudes, or most other dimensions of reality. If we witness the event that John spilled coffee all over Sarah in a restaurant, then the particular restaurant and other information about the scene would be forever encoded in our memories, indexed by "the coffee spilling incident."

Scripts provide insight into building representations from narratives because most readers have the background knowledge to interpret a narrative. However, solving problems from text is often a different story. Usually, readers do not have the requisite script knowledge. In fact, that is often why most are reading in the first place. Furthermore, information is presented differently in expository and narrative texts. The goal in narrative is to violate scripts to make them interesting. Think of a story with a causal structure, but no conflict. For example, consider this literary artwork:

> Shannon slowly got out of bed and got dressed.
> She put on her blue jeans and flip-flops.
> She drove to school.
> She first had a meeting with Art.
> Art was late because he had to get some coffee.
> They talked about issues in problem solving.
> Then, Shannon had a class.

Stories in which all schemas are not violated and in which all goals are achieved and in which all predictable patterns are met are boring, unmemorable, and unenlightening. Similarly, we would not predict that a text on a working coffee machine will be particularly memorable for an adult (although it probably would be novel for children). However, in the case of adults, when the coffee maker breaks down, then a causal representation will be formed that it is hoped can be applied to other situations. Script theory assumes that learning really takes place when mistakes are made and prior scripts are violated (Graesser et al., 1998; Schank, 1999).

Another theory of text representation that applies to problem solving is the *structure and alignment* theory (Clement & Gentner, 1991). According to Clement and Gentner, the parts of two representations are put into alignment based on structural similarities. This theory predicts that people observe the systematicity principle: Systematic relations between two representations are preferred over individual superficial features. Therefore, inferences connected to the causal structure should be preferred over inferences that are not connected to the causal structure. According to this theory, it is the relational structure that is aligned, not the superficial features. This is supported by the fact that people find it easier to state differences between similar pairs of items, such as "kitten" and "cat" than nonsimilar pairs of items, such as "kitten" and "newspaper" (Gentner &

Markman, 1994). Also, people find it easier to generate category-based inferences when they are connected to the causal structure, rather than unconnected facts (Clement & Gentner, 1991; Lassaline, 1996; Wu & Gentner, 1998).

Wu and Gentner (1998) demonstrated that people prefer inferences that originate from an explicit causal structure, rather than inferences that originate from shared independent features. The authors asked participants to choose the stronger of two possible inferences from the following text:

The following facts are true of Animal A (the Attribute Base):
Has muscular forearms.
Has sensitive gums.
Has high risk for strokes.
The following facts are true of Animal B (the Causal Base):
Has an overactive thyroid.
Has an underdeveloped visual system.
An overactive thyroid causes an underdeveloped visual system.
The following facts are true about Animal C (the Target):
Has muscular forearms.
Has sensitive gums.
Has an overactive thyroid.

After reading this text, participants were given the following task:

Please infer only one property of Animal C:
Has high risk for strokes (Attribute Inference).
Has an underdeveloped visual system (Causal Inference).

Participants chose the causal inference significantly more than they chose the attribute inference. The findings of this study support the systematicity principle because participants were making inferences based on the causal structure rather than on the basis of superficial attributes or shared features.

A related model was introduced by Forbus, Gentner, and Law (1994), called the MAC-FAC (many are called, few are chosen) model. This model attempts to explain retrieval based on similar features. This model processes information in two phases. The first phase engages in a quick, gross pattern-matching search that produces candidate matches. The second phase uses a structure-mapping engine to detect structural similarities among the items retrieved in the first phase. This model accounts for the phenomena that structural commonalities are weighted as more important, yet superficial commonalities seem to be the basis of retrieval.

Another type of structural model is the *Situational Operator* model (Millis et al., 2001). According to this model, situation models are built in a piecewise fashion using basic operations, called *situational operators*. Some of the basic situational operators include MAKE, REVISE, COMPARE, MOVE/ADD, and, SHIFT. The Situational Operator model assumes that one or more of these operators are executed when each sentence in a text is comprehended. Each time one of these operators is executed, readers will update their situation model accordingly in working memory. Further, updating the situation model will take time and resources from the limited working memory. Consequently, working memory is taxed and processing time increases as a function of the number of operators that are needed to understand an incoming sentence. Millis et al. (in press) tested this model by presenting participants with texts that described a machine and collecting self-paced sentence reading times. The model was supported by the fact that as the number of operations increased, the reading times increased. In addition, the authors were able to show that these situational operators correlated with other variables previously demonstrated to correlate situation model construction. These variables included rereading the text, comprehension ability, the presence of a test, and the presence of a diagram. All of these variables were shown to be influenced by the number of situational operators.

Construction-Integration Model

In addition to structural models, there are *connectionist models* of text representation. The most well known of these models is the *construction-integration*, or CI model (Kintsch, 1998). Actually, the CI model is the best of both worlds, combining symbolic expressions with connectionist weights. The symbolic aspect of the model includes content words, explicit text propositions, and propositions about world knowledge and the situation model. In the sentence "The coffee machine has five parts," there are four content words (COFFEE, MACHINE, FIVE, PARTS) and three explicit text propositions: (1) HAS (MACHINE, PARTS), (2) COFFEE (MACHINE), and (3) FIVE (PARTS). One of the propositions in the situation model is WORK TOGETHER (PARTS).

According to a connectionist (neural network) model, each of the nodes above is a unit that is connected by weights. There are 8 units in total (4 content words + 3 explicit propositions + 1 world knowledge proposition). These 8 units collectively are connected by $8 \times 8 = 64$ weights, which have values that vary from negative to positive. To understand how the units are weighted, consider the explicit text propositions. Propositions 1 and 3 would have a strong positive weight because of *argument overlap*, or the degree to which two propositions share an argument; these propositions share the argument, PARTS. However, propositions 2 and 3 would not have a strong connection (with a value approaching 0) because they do not have a direct argument overlap. Propositions could also contradict each other and be connected by negative weights.

According to the CI model, a representation is formed from the text in two phases: the construction phase followed by the integration phase. The construction phase is a fast, dumb spreading activation process. During this phase, the propositions in the explicit text activate related information in memory, including relevant propositions from the previous text. For example, suppose your text read

The coffee machine has five parts.
The most frequently broken is the filter.

From these 13 words you may activate 130 concepts. These concepts may be only tangentially related, such as "hot" or "Starbucks" for the concept "coffee." In addition, concepts from the previous text can be reactivated and reinforced. Thus, the concept "filter" in the second sentence may reactivate the concept "coffee" or "part."

During the integration phase, a process of spreading activation occurs with the result of settling on a coherent meaning representation. In this phase, weights are assigned via strength of activation. For example, "filter" may have a strong weight, "hot" may have a medium weight, and "Starbucks" may have a very weak weight. The network settles on a coherent, integrated, stable representation after several cycles of spreading activation. The final activation of each node is an index of how strongly it has been encoded in the memory representation.

An important component of this model is the formation of macrostructures. The macrostructure refers to the global structure or topic structure of the text, as opposed to the local structure or microstructure. According to the CI model, the formation of a macrostructure is a normal part of text comprehension. A macrostructure is formed when the microstructures within the text are organized hierarchically as a result of the integration phase of processing.

The CI model of text representation is important because it accounts for a large number of empirical findings that reflect text representation and comprehension (Singer & Kintsch, 2001). For example, readers tend to recall those nodes that received the strongest level of activation as a result of comprehension. The model predicts that readers are likely to remember information at the situation model level to a greater extent than the textbase and surface code, with such differences being more pronounced after increasing retention intervals. The CI model predicts that some information in the explicit text is overlooked or suppressed during the reading of the text because it is contradictory to the macrostructure. For example, Otero and Kintsch (1992) conducted a study in which participants were presented with passages about superconductivity. Within the passage was an explicit contradiction: The passage first claimed that superconductivity has been achieved only through cooling certain materials. A few sentences later, the same paragraph claimed that superconductivity was achieved through increasing the temperature of particular materials. Forty percent of the participants in the study did not detect the contradiction, thus providing some support for the model's claims about suppression and negative weights. But more interesting, there were interactions between world knowledge and the likelihood of detecting contradictions. With more world knowledge, there are stronger connections within the situation model and to the situation model, so contradictions can be detected better. It should be noted that the CI model is the only model in discourse psychology that can account for the complex interactions among text features, the reader's world knowledge, and levels of representation (Graesser et al., 1998; Mannes & Kintsch, 1987; McNamara et al., 1996).

Embodied Cognition Model

A recent model of text representation is the *embodied cognition model* (Glenberg, 1997). According to this model, instead of representing concepts symbolically, we represent concepts according to what we can do with them within the constraints of our bodies. In one sense, this theoretical position is compatible with those that dissect the mechanism of situation model construction (Graesser, et al. 1994; Johnson-Laird, 1983; Millis et al., 2001): Readers construct representations of what the text *means* in the real world, not representations of the language itself. There is considerable evidence in discourse psychology that supports such a claim. Any model of text representation must account for the fact that situation models preserve not the surface code or syntax but the meaning message. What is unique about the embodied situation model is that it assumes that readers construct a very rich representation that incorporates details and constraints about bodies moving in the world. In contrast, the constructionist theory (Graesser et al., 1994) would not assume that these rich knowledge representations are constructed while readers are reading 250 to 400 words per minute, but might be made when there is extended study of the text and when the reader has reading goals that are pitched at such fine-grained embodiments.

According to Zwaan (1999), there are two points to be made in favor of an embodied model of text representation: (1) There is more involved in situation models than declarative knowledge, and (2) situation models themselves are analogical representations, not symbolic representations. Regarding the first point, it would be parsimonious to assume that the way we build situation models from text descriptions of objects and events is the same way we build representations of objects and events when we perceive and act in our environment. Thus, if a story describes a protagonist as being in the center of the room, those objects that are closest to the center will be more accessible (Franklin & Tversky, 1990). The second point addresses the implausibility of symbolic, amodal representations. Consider a text that reads "He spilled the scalding coffee all over his face." This would obviously be painful. You may have formed a very graphic depiction in your mind when reading this sentence, or even winced when the imaginary coffee touched your skin. This mental representation is so rich that it would possibly take thousands of propositions to construct it. Therefore, the more parsimonious explanation seems to be that the representation is amodal.

The embodiment model perhaps captures the core functions of language and cognition. According to Glenberg (1997), the purpose of memory is to serve action, which includes navigating through a dangerous world. By remembering that coffee is hot, one can prevent oneself from getting burned. Therefore, the memory of hot coffee guides one's actions: One may now pick it up gently by the handle rather than grabbing the base. Barsalou (1999) extends this idea to language comprehension. He hypothesizes that language evolved to support future situated action rather than to catalog facts.

Glenberg and Robertson (1999) reported a study that tested some of the claims about embodiment. They tested a specific hypothesis called the *indexical hypothesis.* That model assumes that experiential or perceptual components are crucial to language comprehension, and that most words, phrases, and propositions are indexed to objects, people, and events. To test this hypothesis, the authors had participants learn about using a compass and maps. There were four conditions. The first was a "listen only" condition in which the participants heard an explanation of the compass and map. The second was a "listen and picture" condition in which the participants listened to the tape and saw pictures of the objects (such as the compass) displayed on a screen. In the third condition, the "listen and read" condition, participants first listened to the audiotape and then were given the script of what they had just heard to read. The fourth condition was the "listen and index" condition in which not only did the participants receive a picture of the compass, but an agent's hand would point to the relevant parts and operations at the appropriate times during the audio.

The primary dependant variables were (1) a posttest, which tested general archival knowledge, and (2) performance on a transfer task, in which the participants had to utilize what they have learned. The transfer task had participants actually navigate an area with the tools introduced in the first phase and three step instructions for executing the task. The dependant measures of this task were the correct performance of each step of the instructions, the number of references the participant made to the script, and the time it took to complete the transfer task. If the participants in the reading and indexing condition performed better on the transfer task, support would be provided for the indexical hypothesis.

The important comparison is between the listen and read condition and the listen and index condition. There was no significant difference on the posttest between these two conditions. However, there were differences on performance of the transfer task. Participants in the listen and index condition referred to the script less than half as much as those in the listen and read condition, a statistically reliable difference. They also took 25% less time to read the transfer task. However, performance on the active transfer tasks were far superior. Although reading and indexing may not appear to have different effects on the standard, paper and pencil test, there are differences in the application of the material. When the incoming information can be indexed, participants are more likely to be able to apply that knowledge to real-world problems.

The embodiment model differs from a connectionist model or a structural model to the extent that it does not require a system of abstract symbols to represent concepts. Instead, all concepts are represented analogically in a fashion that caters to the constraints of the human body and the world. The model appears to solve many of the standard theoretical problems with the representation of concepts in memory (see Glenberg, 1997). However, it is too early in the testing phases of the model to know whether it can explain a large body of data that apparently can be explained by previous models. For example, Kintsch's CI model is able to account for some three-way interactions among text, readers, and representations, whereas it is not clear that the embodied theories will go the distance in providing comparable explanations. Also the theories need more specification, as in the recent perceptual symbol theory recently proposed by Barsalou (1999).

Much of the solutions to problems in everyday life is encoded in a text. Like the case of the broken coffee machine, most of us need to look to written instructions to guide our efforts in solving problems. Forming a representation of that text is the key to solving the problem. This chapter has reviewed the literature on text representation and models of building a representation from text. One of the future research directions is to provide more incisive tests between these theories in the context of solving real-world problems.

REFERENCES

Barsalou, L. W. (1999). Language comprehension: Archival memory or preparation form situated action? *Discourse processes, 28,* 61–80.
Barsalou, L. W. (1999). Perceptual symbol systems. *Behavior and Brain Sciences, 22,* 577–660.
Beck, I. L., McKeown, M. G., Hamilton, R. L., & Kucan, L. (1997). *Questioning the author: An approach for enhancing student engagement with text.* Delaware: International Reading Association.
Biber, D. (1988). *Variation across speech and writing.* Cambridge, MA: Cambridge University Press.
Brooks, C., & Warren, R. P. (1972). *Modern rhetoric.* New York: Harcourt Brace Jovanovich.
Catrambone, R. (1994). Improving examples to improve transfer t novel problems. *Memory & Cognition, 22,* 606–615.

Catrambone, R. (1996). Generalizing solution procedures learned from examples. *Journal of Experimental Psychology: Learning, Memory, and Cognition, 22,* 1020–1031.

Catrambone, R., Jones, C. M., Jonicles, J., & Seifert, C. (1995). Reasoning about curvilinear motions: Using principles or analogy. *Memory & Cognition, 23,* 368–373.

Chi, M. T. H., Feltovich, P. J., & Glaser, R. (1981). Categorization and representation of physics problems by experts and novices. *Cognitive Science, 5,* 121–152.

Clement, C. A., & Gentner, D. (1991). Systematicity as a selection constraint in analogical mapping. *Cognitive Science, 15,* 89–132.

Cote, N., Goldman, S. R., & Saul, E. U. (1998). Students making sense of informational text: Relations between processing and representation. *Discourse Processes, 25,* 1–53.

Duncker, K. (1945). On problem solving. *Psychological Monographs, 58.*

Forbus, K. D., Gentner, D., & Law, K. (1994). A model of similarity-based retrieval. *Cognitive Science, 19,* 141–205.

Franklin, N., & Tversky, B. (1990). Searching imagined environments. *Journal of Experimental Psychology: General, 119,* 63–76.

Gentner, D., & Markman, A. B. (1994). Structural alignment in comparison: No difference without similarity. *Psychological Science, 5,* 152–158.

Gentner, D., & Markman, A. B. (1997). Structure-mapping in analogy and similarity. *American Psychologist, 52,* 45–56.

Gentner, D., & Stevens, A. (1983). *Mental models.* Hillsdale, NJ: Erlbaum.

Gernsbacher, M. A. (1997). Two decades of structure building. *Discourse Processes, 23,* 265–304.

Gick, M. L., & Holyoak, K. J. (1980). Analogical problem solving. *Cognitive Psychology, 12,* 306–355.

Gick, M. L., & Holyoak, K. (1983). Schema induction and analogical transfer. *Congnitive Psychology, 15,* 1–38.

Glenberg, A. M. (1997). What memory is for. *Behavioral and Brain Sciences, 20,* 1–55.

Glenberg, A. M., & Robertson, D. A. (1999). Indexical understanding of instructions. *Discourse Processes, 28,* 1–26.

Goldman, S. R., Saul, E. U., & Cote, N. (1995). Paragraphing, reader, and task effects on discourse comprehension. *Discourse Processes, 20,* 273–305.

Graesser, A. C., Bowers, C., Olde, B., & Pomeroy, V. (1999). Who said what? Source memory for narrator and character agents in literary short stories. *Journal of Educational Psychology, 91,* 284–300.

Graesser, A. C., & Clark, L. F. (1985). *Structures and procedures of implicit knowledge.* Norwood, NJ: Ablex.

Graesser, A. C., Kassler, M. A., Kreuz, R. J., & McLain-Allen, B. (1998). Verification of statements about story worlds that deviate from normal conceptions of time: What is true about *Einstein's Dreams*? *Cognitive Psychology, 35,* 246–301.

Graesser, A. C., Millis, K. K., & Zwaan, R. A. (1997). Discourse comprehension. *Annual Review of Psychology, 48,* 163–189.

Graesser, A. C., Singer, M., & Trabasso, T. (1994). Constructing inferences during narrative text comprehension. *Psychological Review, 101,* 371–395.

Holyoak, K. J., & Koh, K. (1987). Surface and structural similarity in analogical transfer. *Memory & Cognition, 15,* 332–340.

Johnson-Laird, P. N. (1983). *Mental models.* Cambridge, MA: Harvard University Press.

Kieras, D., & Bovair, S. (1984). The role of a mental model in learning to operate a device. *Cognitive Science, 8,* 255–274.

Kintsch, W. (1998). *Comprehension: A paradigm for cognition.* Cambridge: Cambridge University Press.

Kintsch, W., & Greeno, J. G. (1985). Understanding and solving word arithmetic problems. *Psychological Review, 92,* 109–129.

Kintsch, W., & vanDijk, T. A. (1978). Towards a model of text comprehension and production. *Psychological Review, 85,* 363–394.

Lassaline, M. E. (1996). Structural alignment in induction and similarity. *Journal of Experimental Psychology: Learning, Memory, and Cognition, 22,* 754–770.

Lorch, R. F., & O'Brien, J. D. (1995). *Sources of coherence in reading.* Mahwah, NJ: Erlbaum.

Lucangeli, D., Tressoldi, P. E., & Cendron, M. (1998). Cognitive and metacognitive abilities involved in the solution of mathematical word problems: Validation of a comprehensive model. *Contemporary Educational Psychology, 23,* 257–275.

Mannes, S. M., & Kintsch, W. (1987). Knowledge organization and text organization. *Cognition and Instruction, 4,* 91–115.

Mayer, R. E. (1996). Learning strategies for making sense out of expository text: The SOI model for guiding three cognitive processes in knowledge construction. *Educational Psychology Review, 8,* 357–371.

McKoon, G., & Ratcliff, R. (1992). Inference during reading. *Psychological Review, 99,* 440–466.

McNamara, D. S., Kintsch, E., Songer, N. B., & Kintsch, W. (1996). Learning from text: Effect of prior knowledge and text coherence. *Discourse Processes, 22,* 247–288.

Millis, K. K, King, A., & Kim, H. J. (2000). Updating situation models from text: A test of the situational operator model. *Discourse Processes, 30,* 201–236.

Novick, L. R. (1988). Analogical transfer, problem similarity, and expertise. *Journal of Experimental Psychology: Learning, Memory, and Cognition, 14,* 510–520.

Novick, L. R. (1990). Representational transfer in problem solving. *Psychological Science, 1,* 128–132.

Nystrand, M. (1986). *The structure of written communication: Studies in reciprocity between readers and writers.* Norwood, NJ: Ablex.

Otero, J., & Kintsch, W. (1992). Failure to detect contradictions in text: What readers believe vs. what they read. *Psychological Science, 3,* 229–234.

Perfetti, C. A., & Britt, M. A. (1995). Where do propositions come from? In C. A. Weaver, S. Mannes, & C. R. Fletcher (Eds.), *Discourse comprehension: Essays in honor of Walter Kintsch* (pp. 11–34). Hillsdale, NJ: Erlbaum.

Rosenblatt, L. M. (1994). *The reader, the text, the poem: The transactional theory of the literary work.* Carbondale, IL: Southern Illinois University Press. (Original work published in 1978.)

Schank , R. P. (1999). *Dynamic memory revisited.* Cambridge: Cambridge University Press.

Schank, R. C., & Abelson, R. P. (1977). *Scripts, plans, goals, and understanding.* Hillsdale, NJ: Erlbaum.

Schank, R. C., & Abelson, R. P. (1995). In R. S. Wyer (Ed.) *Advances in social cognition: Vol. 8, Knowledge and memory: The real story* (pp. 1–85). Hillsdale, NJ: Erlbaum.

Schraw, G., & Bruning, R. (1996). Reader's implicit models of reading. *Reading Research Quarterly, 31*, 290–305.

Singer, M., & Kintsch, W. (2001). Text retrieval: A theoretical explanation. *Discourse Processes, 31*, 27–59.

Trabasso, T., & Magliano, J. P. (1996). Conscious understanding during comprehension. *Discourse Processes, 21*, 255–287.

Trabasso, T., & Suh, S. (1993). Understanding text: Achieving explanatory coherence through on-line inferences and mental operations in working memory. *Discourse Processes, 16*, 3–34.

Voss, J. F., & Silfies, L. N. (1996). Learning from history texts: The interaction of knowledge and comprehension skill with text structure. *Cognition and Instruction, 14*, 45–68.

Wu, M. L., & Gentner, D. (1998). Structure in category-based induction. *Proceedings of the twentieth annual conference of the cognitive science society,* 1154–1158.

Zwaan, R. A. (1994). Effects of genre expectations on text comprehension. *Journal of Experimental Psychology: Learning, Memory, and Cognition, 20*, 920–933.

Zwaan, R. A., & Radvansky, G. A. (1998). Situation models in language comprehension and memory. *Psychological Bulletin,*

Zwaan, R. A. (1999). Embodied cognition, perceptual symbols, and situation models. *Discourse Processes, 28*, 81–88.

PART III

STATES AND STRATEGIES

8

Motivating Self-Regulated Problem Solvers

Barry J. Zimmerman and Magda Campillo

Solving a complex problem requires more than mere knowledge; it requires the motivation and personal resourcefulness to undertake the challenge and persist until a solution is reached. Classical theories of problem solving have emphasized the role of discovery or illumination as a primary motive to learn, but contemporary research has uncovered an array of highly predictive task- and performance-related motivational beliefs, such as self-efficacy, outcome expectations, intrinsic task interest, and learning goal orientations. Unlike trait motivational constructs, such as the need for achievement, these motivational beliefs change during the course of problem solving, and a complete account of their role must describe their interrelation with metacognitive and motor learning processes. Self-regulation models of learning and performance have integrated metacognitive, motoric, and motivational aspects of problem solving within a cyclical structure. We discuss how these task- and performance-related motivational beliefs instigate problem-solving efforts, and reciprocally how these beliefs are modified based on the outcomes of self-regulated solution efforts.

This chapter begins with a description of the difficulties of problem solving in formal and informal contexts, with particular focus on motivational beliefs and associated behavioral processes. The limited conceptions of problem solving derived from research in formal contexts are discussed, and the need to broaden these conceptions to explain problem solving in informal contexts is emphasized. Methods of problem solving used by experts and their high levels of motivation are described, and a model of self-regulated problem solving is presented that cyclically integrates numerous motivation beliefs and self-regulatory processes. Self-regulation of problem solving in informal contexts, such as problem-based learning, is considered, and research on the importance of motivational beliefs and associated self-regulatory processes in learners' development of problem-solving skill is discussed. Finally, the instructional implications of a self-regulatory approach for enhancing problem solving are considered.

EXPANDING CONCEPTIONS OF PROBLEM SOLVING

Problem Solving in Formal and Informal Contexts

Historically, researchers have studied human problem solving in formal learning contexts, such as mathematical problems, verbal puzzles, or motoric games, such as the Towers of Hanoi. These types of problems involve a well-defined task with an exact solution, such as a crossword puzzle. All necessary information is typically given, such as word clues in crossword puzzles, and boundary conditions for solutions are carefully specified, such as the need to produce answers that are interdependent across rows and columns in crossword puzzles. In addition to their clear definition, formal problems are *structured* by their creators to be interesting, challenging, and soluble. Word clues that are mundane, obvious, or insoluble are eliminated. To become expert in solving formal problems, learners must become familiar with the imposed limitations of formal contexts and develop solution strategies that optimize performance within those contexts, such as using a dictionary or thesaurus to identify synonyms for word clues or for potential answers. Because these formal problems are prespecified, solution skills, such as problem sensitivity and self-definition, are not required (see example below). Furthermore, because anticipation problems are structured to be interesting and soluble, they are less dependent on noninterest sources of motivation, such as perceptions of efficacy, outcome expectations, and goal orientations, than are informal problems.

Unfortunately, formal contexts eliminate many processes that are essential for solving informal problems that arise during the course of normal human activity, such as problem anticipation, regulating open-ended task contexts, seeking necessary information, development of high levels of behavioral competence, and multiple sources of motivation to sustain long-term, recursive solution efforts. In informal contexts, a person may not be sensitive to the presence of a problem that is implicit or subtle, such as the first hint of a malfunctioning automobile. Often a person becomes aware of informal problems only after adverse outcomes occur, such as when a vehicle will not start. Problem anticipation is essential for navigating daily problems under conditions that often appear benign, such as detecting slight increases in ignition time to start the car. When solving problems in informal contexts, learners must be able to cognitively anticipate potential outcomes of various courses of action and behaviorally to restructure the immediate problem context into a more conducive one, such as by seeking out information that is missing. In the case of a malfunctioning car, this could involve testing the battery to see whether it was maintaining an electrical charge. Learners in informal problem contexts often must transcend initial boundary conditions before a solution can be attained, such as leaving the drivers' seat, opening the hood of a car, and checking for signs of malfunctioning.

In informal contexts, learners often eschew formal symbolic solutions to problems (Brown, Collins, & Duguid, 1989), such as attempting to see whether the gas gauge of an automobile was functioning properly by calculating the miles traveled since the last refueling. Instead, they use less cognitively demanding behavioral procedures in a recursive manner, such as trying various devices in the car's tank to find one that successfully measures the gas level. A high degree of motivation is required to solve problems in informal contexts because solutions require repeated physical efforts. Solution efforts must often be repeated many times in order to develop necessary behavioral skill. For example, fixing a malfunctioning water pump of a car may require not only getting advice about possible solutions but also developing motoric skills, such as using wrenches, to disconnect the old pump and reconnect a new pump. Low levels of these skills can require extended recursive efforts to solve the problem. For this reason, professional mechanics are given extensive training and practice in choice and use of wrenches. However, even skilled mechanics seldom solve various car problems purely cognitively but instead work their way through the problem behaviorally – testing various solutions until one works. In these informal problem contexts, learners' solution efforts depend on one's anticipation of strategy outcomes (an outcome expectation), on one's perceived competence (a self-efficacy belief), or on one's willingness to invest time and effort in learning new skills (a learning goal orientation). Intrinsic interest in knowing the details of an automobile's functioning may be low in a list of motivators to solve these problems.

Finally, it should be mentioned that with many informal problems, there is often no exact solution. Instead, they require continuing adjustment of one's approach to shifting conditions, such as when drivers must decide on how much pressure to apply to a brake pedal to stop a vehicle. The solution to this informal problem depends on the speed and weight of the vehicle, the quality of the tires, the wear on the brake pads, and road conditions, among other factors. In the informal problem context of driving an automobile, drivers do not formally measure and calculate the effects of these variables but instead use deceleration feedback from braking efforts to increase or decrease their pressure on the brake pedal (Powers, 1998). Thus, problem solving in informal contexts requires recursive behavioral efforts, accurate self-monitoring, and adaptive self-reactions.

These differences in problem solving between formal and informal contexts are summarized in Table 8.1. Most problem-solving tasks involve admixtures of formal and informal characteristics. Only the most formal of problems will adhere to all criteria in column 2, and only the most

TABLE 8.1. *Differences in problem-solving components in formal and informal contexts*

Problem-solving components	Problem	Contexts
	Formal (structured)	Informal (unstructured)
Problem source	Socially presented	Personally anticipated/defined
Boundary conditions	Constrained	Open-ended
Solution resources	Necessary information given	Necessary information sought
Types of solutions	Formal cognitive	Practical behavioral
Solution process	Exact	Recursive
Motivation source	Intrinsic interest	Self-efficacy, outcome expectations, goal orientation, intrinsic interest
Behavioral competence	Preexisting	To be developed

informal of problems will adhere to all criteria in column 3. Students who self-regulate their solution efforts benefit in both problem-solving contexts but especially in informal contexts where high levels of motivation and resourcefulness are needed.

Problem Solving by Experts and Novices

Some researchers have studied optimal problem solving by interviewing expert problem solvers who were identified by their accomplishments, high level of training, and/or teachers and coaches. In this research, experts' problem-solving performance in their area of specialty was compared with that of novices who had some familiarity with the tasks in question but had performed poorly. The findings were striking. First, experts possessed greater domain-specific knowledge about a task than novices (Elstein, Shulman, & Sprafka, 1978; Simon, 1979). Experts excelled mainly in their own domains and did not have greater knowledge of general problem-solving strategies. For example, an expert cab driver in one city will have no advantages in a different city where he or she lacks knowledge of back streets and alleys to avoid traffic jams. Clearly, the context-relatedness of one's knowledge is important in developing problem-solving expertise.

Second, experts perceived meaningful patterns in a problem that novices missed because these novices could not analyze the information appropriately. These experts redefined and classified problems that they encountered according to underlying principals, whereas novices classified problems on the basis of surface features of the task. For example, skilled judges and lawyers detect important principles in legal documents that are missed by novices (Lundeberg, 1987). There is evidence that experts perceive underlying patterns more effectively because they organize their knowledge more hierarchically than novices (Chi, Glaser, & Rees, 1982).

Third, experts performed very quickly with few errors. This occurred because they could use their domain-specific knowledge to take strategic short-cuts. Even if they could not solve the problem at the outset, their short-cuts enabled them to reach a solution much more quickly (Chase & Simon, 1973). Furthermore, the speed of problem-solving experts stemmed from their automatized implementation of solution strategies, which freed them to concentrate on the effectiveness of the strategies. Fourth, experts spent more time planning and analyzing problems than novices did (Moore, 1990). Rather than plunging into an impulsive solution, experts developed a plan reflectively that could fully address the problem. Fifth, experts redefined and reinterpreted a problem task, whereas novices responded to the task without modifying the structure to match their own existing knowledge (Resnick, 1985). Sixth, experts monitored their performance more carefully, and understood the value of strategy use better (Mayer, 1992). Experts used strategies to break a task into parts and to solve each part sequentially (Bruning, Schraw, & Ronning, 1995), and this allowed them to monitor their sequential progress more easily. By contrast, novices tried to deal with the task as a whole, which overloaded their working memory and led to piecemeal solution efforts. The superior self-monitoring by experts enabled them to determine whether their strategies were working or whether they needed more fine-tuning (Voss, Greene, Post, & Penner, 1983).

Finally, retrospective research studies of the development of expertise (Ericsson & Charnes, 1994) have shown that an enormous amount of study and practice time goes into the development of nationally recognized levels of expertise in a wide array of problem-solving skills, such as chess, music, dance, and athletics. Needless to say, high levels of motivation are necessary to sustain the many hours of daily practice that are needed to attain high levels of skill. Although most of the experts were attracted to their particular skill because of a childhood interest, their commitment to its development grew over time (Bloom, 1985). It is likely that additional sources of motivation emerged to help sustain them when their initial interest waned and fatigue or boredom occurred.

Pressley and McCormick (1995) have emphasized the role of self-regulation in the problem solving of experts. Despite receiving high-quality formal training from others, experts had to become ultimately their own teachers in order to succeed. They had to learn to keep themselves on task and to guide their thinking through regulation of complex sequences of procedures that are combined and coordinated with prior knowledge. When prior knowledge did not fit the current situation, experts made self-regulatory adjustments that produced new knowledge, which was then available for future purposes. "Self-regulated thinking builds on itself, with the self-regulated thinker always becoming a better thinker" (Pressley & McCormick, 1995, p. 108).

Clearly, experts display a distinctive profile of competencies when compared with novices. Experts display greater use of hierarchical knowledge when formulating strategic solutions, greater use and self-monitoring of strategies, more accurate self-evaluation, and greater motivation than novices. Much of this research emerged from retrospective interviews that included problem-solving practice and performance in informal contexts. The processes and motivational beliefs displayed by problem-solving experts appear remarkably similar to those described and studied by researchers investigating self-regulated learning processes, which we turn to next.

SELF-REGULATORY PROCESSES UNDERLYING PROBLEM SOLVING

Self-regulation models seek to explain students' proactive efforts to acquire knowledge and skill, which includes problem solving in formal and informal contexts where self-initiative and self-direction are paramount. Self-regulation refers to self-generated thoughts, feelings, and actions that are planned and cyclically adapted for the attainment of personal goals, such as solving a problem (Zimmerman, 1998). The cyclical nature of self-regulation stems from its reliance on feedback from prior performance efforts to make adjustments during current efforts. Self-regulatory formulations stress the importance of perceptions of personal agency to initially motivate and sustain problem solvers (Zimmerman, 1989). Unlike views of problem solving that focus exclusively on metacognitive knowledge states and deductive reasoning, self-regulatory views also stress the importance of motivational self-beliefs and affective self-reactions, such as optimism and fears (Zimmerman, 1996). For example, chess players may try to implement a well-known offensive strategy during a competitive match but may abandon it if their confidence falters. To understand the role of motivation as well as other self-regulatory processes underlying problem solving, we present a social cognitive model of self-regulation below and describe how self-regulatory processes and motivational beliefs guide problem solving in informal as well as structured settings.

We suggest that all efforts to learn a new skill on one's own involve a form of problem solving, even motor learning tasks such as dart throwing. Problem solving occurs with such tasks because self-regulated learners must discover from performance feedback a strategy that is optimally effective for them. In these informal problem contexts, exact solutions are seldom possible because problem solving usually focuses on continuing improvements rather than a final single outcome. For example, dart throwers who seek to develop high levels of expertise must constantly

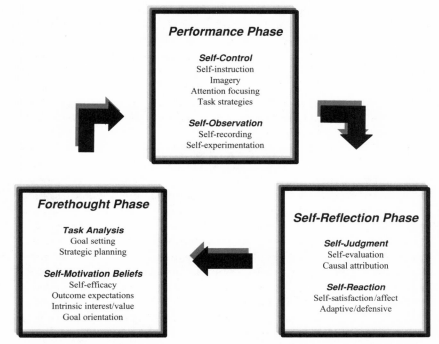

FIGURE 8.1. Phases and subprocesses of self-regulation.

refine their understanding of the task and must readjust their throwing strategy to changing contextual and self-related conditions, such as audience noise or anxiety (Zimmerman & Kitsantas, 1997).

From a social cognitive perspective (Zimmerman, 2000), problem-solving processes and accompanying beliefs fall into three cyclical self-regulatory phases: forethought, performance, and self-reflection (see Fig. 8.1). Forethought processes precede efforts to solve a problem and set the stage for it. Performance phase processes occur during solution efforts and influence attention and action, and self-reflection processes occur after solution performance efforts and influence a person's response to them. These self-reflections, in turn, influence forethought regarding subsequent solution efforts, thus completing a self-regulatory cycle. Because of its cyclical nature, this model can explain problem solving in informal contexts where problem solving is a continuing process, as well as in formal contexts.

Forethought Phase

Forethought processes fall into two major categories: (a) task analysis and (b) self-motivation belief. A key form of task analysis is *goal setting*, which refers to deciding on the intended outcomes of a solution effort, such as solving a group of division problems in mathematics during a study session (Locke & Latham, 1990). The goal systems of highly self-regulated individuals are organized hierarchically, such that strategy process and subprocess goals serve as proximal regulators of more distal outcome goals (Bandura, 1991). Carver and Scheier (2000) envision process (or sequence) goals as less abstract than outcome (or program) goals in their hierarchy. We already noted that expert problem solvers organize their task knowledge hierarchically (Chi, Glaser, & Rees, 1982).

A second form of task analysis is *strategic planning* (Weinstein & Mayer, 1986). For a problem to be solved, learners need to select or create methods that are appropriate for the task and setting. Solution strategies are systematic methods for solving problems. Appropriately selected problem-solving strategies enhance performance by aiding cognition, controlling affect, and directing motoric execution (Pressley, Woloshyn, et al., 1995). For example, using an analogy between the problem situation and a familiar situation is a commonly used problem-solving strategy. Students can solve a medical problem by comparing it to a military campaign, such as by containing, isolating, and destroying a tumor just like an enemy regiment (Gick and Holyoak, 1980, 1983). The planning and selection of strategies requires on-going adjustments due to cyclical feedback from earlier efforts, because no self-regulatory strategy will work optimally on all tasks or occasions. As a learner draws closer to a solution of a problem, the effectiveness of an initial strategy often declines to the point where another strategy becomes necessary, such as the use of a new analogy.

Problem-solving skills mean little if a person is not motivated to use them. Underlying forethought processes of goal setting and strategic planning are a number of key self-motivational beliefs: self-efficacy, outcome expectations, intrinsic interest or valuing, and goal orientation. Classical theories of problem solving have emphasized the role of discovery as an intrinsic motive to learn. This source of *intrinsic interest* refers to valuing a task for its own properties, rather than to valuing a task for its instrumental qualities in gaining other outcomes. An example of intrinsic interest is playing a piano for personal entertainment rather than for monetary rewards. Initially, a number of cognitive theorists (Deci, 1975; Lepper & Hodell, 1989) hypothesized that extrinsic sources of motivation, such as monetary rewards, would undermine the formation of intrinsic motivation; however, there is growing evidence that intrinsic and extrinsic sources additively improve motivation (Zimmerman, 1985). Both sources of motivation are included in the present formation (see outcome expectancies below). An additional source of motivation is *self-efficacy*, which refers to personal beliefs about having the means to learn or perform effectively (Bandura, 1997). Having knowledge and skill does not produce high-quality problem solving if people lack the self-assurance to use these personal resources. The more self-efficacious people believe themselves to be, the more effort and persistence they will display (Bandura, 1997; Schunk 1984a). This is especially important when people experience difficulty in attaining solutions. Those who are self-efficacious will increase their solution efforts, whereas those who are self-doubters will withdraw (Bandura & Cervone, 1986).

A closely related source of motivation is *outcome expectations*, which refer to beliefs about the ultimate ends of performance (Bandura, 1997). To illustrate their interrelationship using mathematical problems, self-efficacy refers to the belief that one can solve fraction problems on a test, and outcomes refer to expectations about the consequences these solutions will produce, such as social acclaim as being "smart" or derision as being a "geek." A person's willingness to engage and sustain his or her problem-solving efforts depends on his or her self-efficacy beliefs about achieving a solution.

Finally, students' *goal orientation* during problem solving is another source of self-motivation. A learning orientation (Dweck, 1988) – which has been also labeled as a mastery (Ames, 1992) or a task goal orientation (Nicholls, 1984) – measures problem solvers' focus on developing competence rather than optimizing short-term performance. With a learning goal, individuals are oriented toward developing new skills, trying to understand their work, improving their level of competence, and achieving a sense of mastery based on self-referenced standards. By contrast, *performance orientation* is concerned with being able in comparison to others and receiving public recognition for that ability (Ames, 1992). Learners with this goal orientation seek to demonstrate their superior ability by succeeding with little effort, surpassing others or normative-based standards. These learners firmly believe that learning is a means to an end, not an end in itself, and that their self-worth stems from their level of performance.

These motivational constructs are fundamentally social cognitive in form, although they are linked theoretically to affective reactions, such as satisfaction and anxiety. The constructs fall within the classic motivational domains of expectancy or value, such as outcome and self-efficacy expectancies and intrinsic interest and goal orientation values. Unlike achievement motivation theory, which also includes expectancy-value elements (McClelland, Atkinson, Clark, & Lowell, 1953), social cognitive theories have excluded static unconscious motivational traits, such as need for achievement. Because of their dynamic cognitive nature, social cognitive motivational constructs are closely related to metacognitive ones, such as planning and strategy use. These motivational constructs are predictive of persistence and effort during problem solving because they assess beliefs about personal competence and value, whereas metacognitive constructs are predictive of learning and solution methods because they assess solution knowledge. A primary purpose of a self-regulation view of problem solving is to integrate metacognitive processes, such as planning and strategy use, and social cognitive motives, such as self-efficacy, in a single comprehensive theoretical account.

Performance Phase

Performance phase processes have been grouped into two major classes: self-control and self-observation. Self-control processes, such as self-instruction, imagery, attention focusing, and task strategies, help learners and performers to focus on the physical task and optimize their solution effort. For example, *self-instruction* involves overtly or covertly describing how to proceed as one executes a task, such as "thinking aloud" when solving a mathematics problem, and research shows that such verbalizations can improve students' learning (Schunk & Rice, 1985). *Imagery*, or the forming of vivid mental pictures, is another widely used self-control technique to assist encoding and performance (Pressley 1977; Pressley & Levin, 1977). For example, sport psychologists have taught competitive skaters, divers, golfers, tennis players, and gymnasts to imagine successful executions of planned routines in order to guide their learning and performance efforts (Garfield & Bennett, 1985; Loehr, 1991).

A third form of self-control, *attention focusing*, is designed to improve one's concentration and screen out other covert processes or external events during problem solving. Expert performers report using a wide variety of techniques to improve their attentional control, such as environmental structuring to eliminate diversions or slow-motion executing to assist motor coordination (Mach, 1988). Volitional methods of control, such as ignoring distractions and avoiding ruminating about past mistakes, are effective in enhancing problem solving (Kuhl, 1985). *Task strategies* can assist problem solving by reducing a task to its essential parts and reorganizing them meaningfully. It will be recalled that expert problem solvers reported extensive use of analysis and synthesis strategies (Bruning et al., 1995).

The second major class of performance phase process is self-observation. This refers to a person's tracking of specific aspects of his or her own performance, the conditions that surround it, and the effects that it produces (Zimmerman & Paulsen, 1995). Self-observation often seems trivial when solving simple problems, because recall of prior attempts is easy. However, when solving complex problems, naive self-observers are often overwhelmed by the amount of information that must be tracked and remembered, and this can lead to disorganized or cursory self-monitoring. As was noted above, problem-solving experts are able to selectively track themselves, such as when chess experts encode their prior sequence of board positions and moves, and this enables them to make more fine-grained adaptations than novices (Voss et al., 1983). Problem solvers who set hierarchical process goals during forethought can self-observe more effectively during performance because these structurally limited goals provide greater focusing and reduce the amount of information that must be recalled (Zimmerman & Kitsantas, 1997).

A number of features of self-observation influence its effectiveness during problem solving. Feedback that is delayed in time precludes a person from taking corrective action in a timely fashion, such as chess players's monitoring the seconds of contemplation for each "move" during a match rather than after the match. Regarding the accuracy of self-observations, individuals who fail to encode and recall their prior solution efforts cannot adjust their strategies optimally. There is evidence that novice problem solvers are likely to misperceive or inaccurately remember their solution efforts (Voss et al., 1983). *Self-recording* can provide the learner with more accurate information regarding prior solution attempts, structure that information to be most meaningful, and give a longer database for discerning evidence of progress of problem solution efforts (Zimmerman & Kitsantas, 1996).

Self-observation of one's performance, especially in informal contexts, can lead to systematic self-discovery or *self-experimentation* (Bandura, 1991). When self-observation of natural variations in one's task performance does not provide decisive diagnostic information, people can engage in self-discovery by systematically varying certain aspects of their functioning. For example, tennis players who are struggling with their serves may increase their spin on the ball to see whether it will better clear the net and land within the service area. Langer (1989) has concluded that experts regularly vary even effective performances to enhance their concentration and creative solutions. She calls this experimental approach to optimal functioning "mindfulness."

Self-Reflection Phase

There are two major classes of self-reflection: self-judgments and self-reactions. Self-judgments involve self-evaluating one's problem-solving performance and attributing causal significance to the outcomes. *Self-evaluation* refers to comparing self-monitored outcomes with a standard or goal, such as when aspiring crossword-puzzle aficionados judge each day's newspaper puzzle–solving effort against their best previous effort. It is relatively easy to judge the adequacy of one's solution efforts when they produce a single exact outcome, such as the answer to a mathematical problem. However, high levels of evaluative expertise are needed when solution efforts produce recurring inexact outcomes, such as judging one's relative position to other swimmers at various points during a competition.

Being ahead at the wrong points in the race can be disadvantageous. Ultimately, the adaptive quality of people's problem solutions depends on the accuracy of their self-evaluations (Zimmerman & Paulsen, 1995), and knowing this, experts set challenging criteria for themselves (Ericsson & Lehman, 1996).

There are four main types of criteria that people use to evaluate their problem solving: mastery, previous performance, normative, and collaborative. Mastery criteria are absolute indices of a solution, such as comparing a crossword puzzle solution with the author's solution. Problem solving in formal contexts often involves a mastery criterion of success. An advantage of this criterion is it provides a consistent measure of personal learning to judge one's progress during problem solving. The use of process goal hierarchies predisposes a problem solver to adopt a mastery criterion for self-evaluation because this hierarchical specification of subgoals provides a ready index of mastery.

When solving problems in unstructured informal contexts, self-evaluation is more difficult. Under these circumstances, skilled learners must often rely on nonmastery standards, such as comparisons of their current performance with previous levels of performance, which are often vague or difficult to remember unless records are kept. Bandura has termed these standards self-criteria (Bandura, 1997). For example, crossword aficionados could judge their growing competence by comparing the number of errors in their current solution effort with the previous day's effort. Like mastery comparisons, self-comparisons involve within-subject changes in functioning, and as a result, they can highlight learning progress, which typically improves with repeated practice.

Normative criteria for self-evaluating one's problem solutions involve social comparisons with the performance of others, such as classmates or during a national competition. Awards are given at problem-solving competitions, such as a medal at a spelling bee, on the basis of the order of finishing. The winner is the person who comes in first regardless of whether he or she spelled the most difficult words in the dictionary. Among the drawbacks of using normative criteria for self-evaluation is that they heighten attention to social factors, which can distract from close attention to the task. Another shortcoming is that social comparisons often tend to emphasize negative aspects of functioning instead of the positive ones, such as when a student loses the spelling bee despite having improved his or her spelling skill in comparison to previous efforts. Coming in "second" in a competition can produce strong negative self-reactions even when the performance differences are trivial.

Finally, a collaborative criterion is used primarily in team problem-solving endeavors (Bandura, 1991). Under these common but more complex circumstances, success is defined in terms of fulfilling a particular role, such as serving as a member of an Academic Olympic team. The criterion of problem-solving success for a "science expert" on the team is different from that for a "humanities expert."

Self-evaluative judgments are linked to *causal attributions* about the results of solution efforts, such as whether a failure is due to one's limited ability or to insufficient effort. These attribution judgments are essential components of self-reflection, because attributions of errors to a fixed ability prompt learners to react negatively and discourage further solution efforts (Weiner, 1979). Attributions of errors to solution strategies are especially effective in sustaining motivation during periods of solution (e.g., Zimmerman & Kitsantas, 1996, 1997), because strategy attributions sustain perceptions of efficacy until all possible strategies have been tested. Thus, poorly self-regulated problem solvers attribute their errors to uncontrollable variables, and highly self-regulated problem solvers attribute errors to controllable variables. This emphasis on the controllability of causes represents a recent shift in attributional research and theory, which has historically emphasized internality and stability of causes (Weiner, 1985). Another emergent dimension in attribution research is intentionality (Weiner, 1986). Individuals who have the skill to solve a problem may not use this source of control intentionally, and as a result, they will not experience adverse affective self-reactions for poor results. Weiner (1986) has suggested that perceptions of high controllability over adverse outcomes can lead to a sense of guilt, whereas perceptions of low controllability can lead to a sense of shame. For example, if students fail to solve a problem despite intending to solve it, and if they attribute it to a lack of ability (which is uncontrollable), they will experience shame and dissatisfaction. This could lead to their withdrawal from further solution efforts.

Therefore, attributions are not automatic outcomes of favorable or unfavorable self-evaluations, but rather depend on prior motivational beliefs, such as perceptions of personal control (e.g., self-efficacy) or environmental conditions that affect outcome expectations (Bandura, 1991). For example, when basketball free-throw shooters miss a shot, those who are self-efficacious are more likely to attribute it to insufficient effort or a poor task strategy than those who are self-doubters (Cleary & Zimmerman, 2001). Task analysis processes also affect attribution judgments during problem solving. People who plan to use a specific solution strategy during forethought and implement its use during the performance phase are more likely to attribute failures to that strategy rather than to low ability, which can be devastating personally (Zimmerman & Kitsantas, 1997). Because strategies are perceived as correctable causes of error, strategy attributions protect problem solvers against negative self-reactions and lead to a strategically adaptive course of subsequent action.

There are two key forms of self-reactions to problem solution efforts: self-satisfaction and adaptive inferences. *Self-satisfaction* refers to perceptions of satisfaction or dissatisfaction and associated affect regarding one's performance. People will pursue courses of action that result in satisfaction and positive affect and will avoid those courses that produce dissatisfaction and negative affect, such as anxiety (Bandura, 1991). When learners condition their self-satisfaction on reaching their problem-solving goals, they can direct their actions and persist in their efforts much better (Schunk, 1983c). Thus, a person's motivation stems not from the problem goals themselves, but rather from self-evaluative reactions to solution efforts. A person's level of self-satisfaction also depends on the intrinsic value or importance of a problem task. For example, crossword aficionados will experience greater dissatisfaction and anxiety if they fail to solve a puzzle than will casual solvers.

The other form of self-reactions involves *adaptive or defensive inferences,* which are conclusions about how one needs to alter his or her problem-solving approach during subsequent efforts to reach a solution. Adaptive inferences direct people to new and potentially better solution efforts, such as by choosing a more effective strategy (Zimmerman & Martinez-Pons, 1992). When some problem solvers become too discouraged, they will resort to defensive inferences, which serve primarily to protect them from future dissatisfaction and aversive affect. Among the most insidious defensive self-reactions are helplessness, procrastination, task avoidance, cognitive disengagement, and apathy. These defensive reactions have been referred to as "self-handicapping" because, despite their intended protectiveness, they ultimately limit personal growth (Garcia & Pintrich, 1994).

Because of the cyclical nature of self-regulation, self-reactions to problem solution efforts influence forethought processes regarding further solution efforts. For example, positive self-satisfaction reactions strengthen self-efficacy beliefs about eventually solving the problem, enhance learning goal orientations (Schunk, 1996), and increase intrinsic interest in a task (Zimmerman & Kitsantas, 1997). These enhanced self-motivational beliefs form the basis for peoples' sense of personal agency about continuing their cyclical self-regulatory efforts and eventually reaching a solution. In contrast, self-dissatisfaction reactions reduce one's sense of efficacy and intrinsic interest in continuing problem solving further. Thus, a cyclical social cognitive model seeks to explain the persistence and sense of personal fulfillment of successful problem solvers as well as the avoidance and self-doubts of unsuccessful ones. From a cyclical social cognitive perspective, neither motivational beliefs nor self-regulatory processes has causal priority; rather, both are linked in bidirectional relationships (Schunk & Zimmerman, 1994). We suggest this bidirectional link between self-regulation and motivation is key to understanding the origins of self-enhancing and self-defeating cycles of problem solving.

Self-Regulation of Problem Solving in Informal Contexts

The role of self-regulation in problem solving has been studied in research on problem-based learning (Evensen & Hmelo, 2000). This form of learning, which has been used extensively in medical schools, involves presenting practitioner problems to solve, such as medical case studies, to small groups of students. Unlike medical students receiving traditional teacher-controlled instruction, problem-based learners are encouraged to select their own reference sources, tests to run, medicines to prescribe, and outcomes to monitor. Problem-based learning is generally informal in context, except perhaps for the problem source, which can be selected by the faculty (see Table 8.1). Problem-based learning researchers have studied three classes of self-regulatory processes: identifying learning goals or objectives, pursuing learning in a self-directed manner, and self-evaluating learning (Zimmerman & Lebeau, 2000). These classes of processes correspond, respectively, to the forethought, performance, and self-reflection phase processes of a cyclical model of self-regulation.

A cyclical phase analysis of problem solving in a medical practice can be illustrated using the case study of an 8-year-old boy with a "breathing" problem. In this informal context, the child's family physician must sense whether the child's symptoms are abnormal and, if so, define the medical problem clearly (e.g., when and where breathing problems occur). In terms of *forethought*, a hierarchy of possible causes must be considered as diagnostic goals, and an appropriate medication strategy must be selected. Regarding the physician's motivation, he or she will reject medical cases perceived to be beyond his or her level of self-efficacy and medical cases where treatment options are unlikely to work, such as psychosomatic causes. If the doctor tentatively diagnoses the disease as asthma, several drugs may be prescribed. In terms of the *performance phase*, the boy will be given the drugs and monitored daily using a peak flow meter, which assesses constricted breathing. In terms of *self-reflection*, declines in lung constriction must be evaluated by the doctor and attributed to the medications or to other factors, such as exposure to allergens. If the medications are not working satisfactorily, the physician must adapt them or, in extreme cases, may discontinue treatment and refer the patient to a specialist. By contrast, if the boy responds satisfactorily, the physician's sense of self-efficacy in managing the case will be strengthened, and the physician may even raise his or her expectations regarding the eventual outcomes of therapy. The physician's adaptive inferences will guide his or her forethought regarding improving the medication plan. Thus, solving problems in informal settings, such as a medical practice, depends on a physician's cyclical regulation of solution processes. It should also be noted that a patient's eventual control of a chronic disease, such as asthma, requires his or her assuming personal regulation of the same cyclical processes (Zimmerman, Bonner, Evans, & Mellins, 1999).

INVESTIGATING MOTIVATIONAL PROCESSES DURING PROBLEM SOLVING

As we noted, problem solving in informal contexts involves unique challenges, and as a result, learners must be motivated to develop additional cognitive and behavioral skills in order to succeed. This review focuses on the issue of how motivational beliefs lead to and depend on specific self-regulatory processes. Although these studies deal with problems having many formal features, such as teacher-presented mathematics or writing tasks, they focus primarily on students' methods of self-directed *practice*, such as the setting of goals. These practice contexts have many informal features, such as a focus on developing behavioral competence, strong self-efficacy beliefs, and recursive efforts to solve problems as a class of skills.

Goal Setting

There is evidence that students' goal setting is closely linked to key sources of self-motivation. Bandura and Schunk (1981) studied the impact of proximal goal setting during mathematical problem solving on students' perceptions of self-efficacy and intrinsic interest in solving these problems. Children were presented with sets of subtraction material, and one group pursued a proximal goal of completing one set of problems during each session. A second group was given a distal goal of completing all sets by the end of all sessions. A third group was given the general goal of working productively. Proximal goals increased persistence during problem solving and led to the highest posttest subtraction skill and self-efficacy. Proximal goals also increased the students' free choice of working on mathematical problems, which is a measure of intrinsic interest in this task. These outcomes show how proximal goal setting not only can enhance the quality and intensity of problem-solving performance but also can enhance self-efficacy and intrinsic interest beliefs in cyclical fashion.

   Schunk (1983b) also studied the relationship between goal challenge[1] and mathematical problem solving when training a group of students

---

[1] Schunk referred to the goal manipulation in this study as "goal difficulty," but we prefer the label "goal challenge" to emphasize the fact that the difficult goals in this study were attainable. Difficult goals are not expected to motivate students to exert greater effort unless they are perceived as challenging but attainable.

with deficient math skills. These students were assigned to one of two conditions – high goal challenge and low goal challenge – and were asked to solve several division problems. Students in the high goal challenge group were encouraged to solve more problems than students in the low goal challenge group. Half of the students in each goal group were given a social comparison criterion, and the other half were given a mastery criterion to self-evaluate their goal attainment. The social criterion specified that other students like the learner could solve 25 problems during a session, whereas the mastery criterion specified that 25 problems was an attainable goal. It was found that problem solvers in the high goal challenge group outperformed their peers in the low goal challenge group. These learners also displayed significantly higher perceptions of self-efficacy. Self-evaluative criteria interacted with goal setting such that students who set challenging goals and adopted a mastery criterion solved more problems and displayed higher self-efficacy than students in the other groups. This study suggests that goals by themselves do not automatically enhance performance and motivation. Rather, certain goal properties, such as proximity and challenge, influence problem-solving performance, self-reflection, and forethought self-motivation for subsequent problem-solving efforts (Bandura, 1991).

Researchers have also studied hierarchical relations among problem-solving goals. One such relation involves process and outcome goals. Process goals focus on task solution strategies, whereas outcome goals emphasize the final product of solution efforts (Schunk & Swartz, 1993). Zimmerman and Kitsantas (1999) studied high school girls' solution of writing-revision problems that involved summarizing a series of kernel sentences into a single sentence. For example, sentences such as, "The ball is red," "The ball is hard," and "The ball rolled across the room," could be rewritten to say: "The hard red ball rolled across the room." Although girls in the experimental groups were all taught an effective strategy for revising the sentences, they were asked to focus on different goals during their problem-solving practice session. Students in the product goal condition were told to minimize the number of words in their summary sentences. Girls assigned to the process goal condition where told to focus on practicing each of the writing strategy steps. In the hierarchical shifting goal condition, girls started with a process goal and then changed to outcome goals when the strategy was automatized. This study included a wide array of self-regulatory measures, including postpractice measures of task performance, self-efficacy beliefs, intrinsic interest, attribution, and self-satisfaction.

It was found that students who shifted goals hierarchically outperformed their peers in the process goal condition who, in turn, outperformed individuals who used only outcome goals in the accuracy of problem solutions. Shifting goals also produced higher self-satisfaction measures, self-efficacy beliefs, and intrinsic interest in the task than either static process or outcome goals. Girls with shifting goals or with process goals made significantly more attributions for unsuccessful practice attempts to strategies, and these strategy attributions were highly predictive of subsequent self-satisfaction reactions and self-efficacy and intrinsic interest forethought beliefs. This study revealed a cyclical relation between goal setting, writing performance, self-satisfaction reflections, and subsequent forethought phase self-efficacy and intrinsic interest beliefs.

Self-Efficacy Expectations

The self-efficacy expectations of problem solvers can greatly influence their motivation to persist in problem-solving efforts (Bandura, 1997; Zimmerman, 2000). Zimmerman and Ringle (1981) exposed young elementary school children to an adult model who unsuccessfully attempted to solve a wire-puzzle problem and who verbalized optimism or pessimism about reaching a solution. Then the children were given a similar wire puzzle to solve. The task used in this study involved separating two interlocked wires. Although it was not visually apparent, the wires were bent close enough to prevent the puzzle from being solved, and this feature made the puzzle a demanding test of the children's persistence in achieving a solution. After attempting to separate the wires for up to 15 minutes, the youngsters were posttested for efficacy for eventually solving it. The children were subsequently given an embedded word puzzle to assess their transfer. Youngsters who observed the model make optimistic comments about eventually solving the puzzle displayed higher perceptions of self-efficacy and persistence in solving a similar wire puzzle than children who observed a pessimistic model. Similar verbal optimism effects were evident in the children's perceptions of self-efficacy and persistence in solving the embedded word puzzle.

Schunk, Hansen, and Cox (1987) investigated the effects of self-efficacy and modeling on elementary school students' learning to solve fraction problems. Mastery models performed flawlessly from the outset, whereas coping models gradually improved their performance. These researchers expected the coping models to be especially beneficial to students with a low sense of self-efficacy because these students will perceive their own performances as similar to those of coping models. In this study, the peer-mastery model easily grasped the operations and verbalized positive achievement beliefs, whereas the peer-coping model initially made errors and verbalized negative coping states (e.g., "I need to pay attention to what I'm doing"). Eventually, the coping model's problem-solving behavior and verbalizations matched those of the mastery model. Observing peer-coping models led to higher self-efficacy for learning, more rapid problem solving during practice, higher posttest self-efficacy, and greater fraction skill than observing mastery models.

Intrinsic Interest

Zimmerman (1985) studied the relationship between self-efficacy beliefs and intrinsic interest of elementary school children. The influence of the form and the meaning of rewards on self-efficacy and interest was investigated experimentally. Regarding the form of the rewards, tangible rewards involved small amounts of money, and verbal rewards involved statements of praise. Regarding the self-evaluative meaning of the rewards, a normative criterion indicated the child's performance was "better than most students," whereas a performance criterion indicated approval for merely working on the task. The problem task, the block design subtest of the Wechsler Intelligence Scale for Children, requires learners to assemble various blocks to match a visually illustrated solution. Normative rewards were hypothesized to improve two measures of intrinsic interest: pupils' perceptions of self-efficacy and free choice/valuing of the block design task. It was found that normative rewards increased students' self-efficacy perceptions, free choice, and value ratings of this task more than did rewards for task completion. The form of the rewards (tangible vs. verbal) was not significant, but the self-evaluative meaning of the rewards significantly improved the children's self-efficacy beliefs and intrinsic interest. These results reveal how self-evaluative information can influence self-motivation for further problem solving.

Goal Orientation

Schunk (1996) studied the impact of goal setting and self-evaluation on the achievement, self-efficacy, and goal orientations of average achieving elementary school children. A learning or task goal orientation assessed students' desire to independently understand and master general academic work and a performance or ego goal orientation assessed students' desire to perform well on general academic work to please the teacher and avoid trouble. The children received modeled demonstrations of a strategy for solving fraction problems and then had opportunities to practice their problem-solving skills and self-evaluate the results. These students were also given either a learning goal (i.e., learning how to solve the problems) or a performance goal (i.e., solving all the problems). Schunk found that setting goals affected students' goal orientation beliefs as well as their perceptions of self-efficacy and problem-solving achievement. He found that setting learning goals significantly improved self-efficacy, achievement, and learning or task goal orientations and decreased performance or ego orientations.

Strategy Use

It is well known (Schneider & Pressley, 1989) that teaching students to use problem-solving strategies does not guarantee their continued use or generalization to similar tasks unless other self-regulation processes and a wide array of motivation beliefs are involved. Providing information about when and where to apply a learned strategy and making sure that students understand its utility are possible metacognitive factors that can facilitate transfer (Pressley & McCormick, 1995), but what about the impact of strategy utility information on students' motivation? There is evidence that strategy value information enhances perceptions of self-efficacy. In research by Schunk and Rice (1987), children were shown a strategy for discovering the main ideas when reading short passages of a comprehension test. Children in a first experiment received specific strategy value information, general strategy value information, specific plus general information, or no strategy value information before learning. The specific information focused on the value of the strategy to the task at hand; the general information conveyed the value of the strategy to all reading tasks. Students who received the combined specific and general information displayed higher self-efficacy beliefs and comprehension levels than students in the other conditions, who did not differ.

In a second experiment, children received strategy value information before problem solving, specific strategy effectiveness feedback during problem solving, or the combination of strategy value and strategy effectiveness feedback. The feedback was designed to link the children's improved performance to their use of the comprehension location strategy. Students who received combined strategy value and effectiveness feedback treatment displayed significantly greater self-efficacy and problem-solving skills than students in the other conditions, who did not differ.

The impact of explicit strategies to solve problems in enhancing students' motivation and achievement has been widely documented. We have already discussed many studies (especially by Schunk and colleagues) in which modeling was widely used to convey strategies and enhance self-efficacy. One problem-solving strategy that has been singled out for investigation is self-instruction. Schunk and Cox (1986) taught students to verbalize aloud subtraction steps during their solution of problems. Some students verbalized the steps throughout all problems (i.e., continued verbalization), whereas other students verbalized aloud during the first half of problem solving but not during the second half (i.e., discontinued verbalization). A third group did not verbalize. Continued verbalization led to higher posttest self-efficacy and subtraction skill than discontinued verbalization or no verbalization. Although verbalization strategy training improved students' motivation and achievement, it apparently was not internalized to a covert level in this study.

Self-Monitoring

Schunk (1983c) studied the influence of self-monitoring on motivation and solution of subtraction problems with deficient elementary school children. A self-monitoring group reviewed their work at the end of each practice session and recorded the number of workbook pages they had completed. A social monitoring[2] group had their work reviewed at the end of each session by an adult who recorded the number of pages completed. A no monitoring control group practiced without self- or social-monitoring. Schunk found that self- and social-monitoring groups displayed significantly higher self-efficacy, persistence, and achievement, than the no-monitoring group. The two progress monitoring groups did not differ on any measure, and thus the presence of monitoring rather than the agent of monitoring (self vs. social) was responsible for the enhanced problem-solving achievement and motivation.

In the previously mentioned study by (Zimmerman and Kitsantas (1999) of writing-revision problems by high school girls, a second treatment was included with goal setting: self-monitoring in the form of record keeping. Half of the girls in the outcome goal condition were told to record the number of words from the combined sentence in their practice examples, and half of the girls in the process goal condition were told to record the writing-strategy steps they used correctly. Half of the girls in the hierarchical shifting goal condition started recording writing-strategy steps used correctly and then changed to recording the number of words from the combined sentences after the strategy was automatized. Thus, the records for process goal groups focused on strategy steps properly executed, and the records for outcome goals focused on the total number of words of each summary sentence. It was found that self-recording improved revision problem solving, self-efficacy beliefs, self-satisfaction reactions, and intrinsic interest in the task regardless of the girls' form of goal setting. This study showed the cyclical impact of self-monitoring on problem-solving success, self-satisfaction reactions, and subsequent forethought phase self-efficacy and intrinsic interest.

Self-Evaluation Judgments

Schunk and Ertmer (1999) studied the role of self-evaluation in conjunction with goal setting with college students enrolled in a computer applications course. Four types of strategies were taught for solving various Hypercard problems. These strategies focused on four key dimensions of self-regulation (Zimmerman, 1994): motives (e.g., find ways to motivate

---

[2] Schunk referred to the adult monitoring condition as external monitoring, but we have chosen the label *social monitoring* to convey the social nature of this support.

myself to finish a lab project even when it holds little interest), methods (e.g., locate and use appropriate manuals when I need to accomplish an unfamiliar computer task), performance outcomes (e.g., set specific goals for myself in this course), and social/environmental resources (e.g., find peers who will give critical feedback on early versions of my projects). At the start of each of three laboratory sessions, some students were given a goal of learning various Hypercard tasks, which coincided with the unit objectives, whereas other students were given the performance goal of doing their work and trying their best. At the end of the second session, students assigned to the self-evaluation condition evaluated their progress in acquiring Hypercard skills, and at the end of the project, all students were posttested. Adopting learning goals led to higher self-efficacy, strategy competence, and strategy use than adopting performance goals (without self-evaluating). Goal setting interacted with self-evaluation: Students with learning goals without self-evaluating judged their self-efficacy higher than did students with performance goals who self-evaluated. Clearly, students who were focused on their performance success were adversely affected when they self-evaluated.

Attribution Judgments

The role of attribution judgments in motivating and guiding mathematical problem solving has been studied extensively by Schunk and his colleagues (Schunk, 1983a, 1984b; Schunk & Cox, 1986; Schunk & Rice, 1987). For example, Schunk (1983a) gave students one of four types of feedback for positive problem-solving outcomes: ability, effort, ability plus effort, and none. Ability feedback took the form, "You're good at this," whereas effort feedback took the form, "You have been working hard." During problem-solving practice, students received one of the four types of attribution feedback and then were posttested for subtraction skill, self-efficacy beliefs, and self-perceived effort. Schunk found that ability feedback promoted self-efficacy and skill more than did the other three conditions. Students in the effort and ability-plus-effort conditions outperformed those in the control condition in subtraction skill. Students given effort feedback (i.e., effort alone and ability plus effort) judged their expenditure of effort to be higher than students in the ability group who, in turn, significantly surpassed the effort of students in the control group.

An important point to consider when interpreting Schunk's investigations is the fact that attribution feedback was given for *positive* outcomes rather than *negative* ones. By contrast, the study by Zimmerman and Kitsantas (1999) focused on attributions for negative outcomes for an important reason. Attributing successful outcomes to one's ability enhances students' learning and self-efficacy beliefs better than attributing to mere effort because students prefer to believe their success is a permanent personal characteristic rather than a fleeting quality of their efforts. However, the critical issue to self-regulation of problem solving is sustaining effort in the face of repeated negative feedback, and in these cases, strategy attributions have been found to improve self-efficacy and problem solutions more than effort or ability attributions because strategy attributions sustain hope until all possible strategies have been tested and found wanting.

EDUCATIONAL IMPLICATIONS

Because problem solving requires high levels of self-motivation and self-regulatory skill, dysfunctions in either area will diminish people's solution efforts. With regard to motivation, when learners are unwilling to undertake or to persist in problem solving, it is important for teachers to determine whether such learners are deficient in self-efficacy, outcome expectations, intrinsic interest, learning goal orientation, or some combination of these beliefs. Distinctive pedagogical interventions are required to remedy deficiencies in each type of motivational belief. For example, students who are inefficacious need to have their self-efficacy reassured, whereas students who are unaware of the benefits of potential outcomes need to know them (Schunk, 1983b, 1983c). Students who do not value a task for its intrinsic qualities can benefit from social models who express preference for or interest in a task (Zimmerman & Koussa, 1979). However, these boosts in motivation will be short-lived without enhancing students' self-regulatory control of the solution processes as well (Bandura, 1997; Zimmerman, 1995).

There is evidence that problem solvers with little self-regulation have difficulty focusing on key elements of problems, envisioning solution goals, and self-monitoring their progress (DeCorte, Verschaffel, & Op 'T Eyne, 2000). These shortcomings lead cyclically to faulty self-evaluative judgments and adverse attributions. This deficient self-regulatory sequence undermines all forms of self-motivation. To develop committed and successful problem solvers, educators need to capitalize on the cyclical relationship between motivational beliefs and self-regulatory processes. For example, when analyzing problems in either formal or informal contexts, learners need to identify the major problem elements and use that information to estimate possible solutions. Without a clear sense of the end point in the problematic task, learners are unable to self-monitor and self-evaluate attempted solutions accurately. Although the process of estimating solutions has often been emphasized by national groups of math instructors (e.g., National Council of Teachers of Mathematics, 1989), teachers seldom incorporate estimation training into their instruction, and few students spontaneously acquire this skill on their own. An additional self-regulatory capability involves the use of specific strategies rather than amorphous discovery to solve problems. Although discovery learning can lead to effective solutions for problems, it is usually unsystematic, and when it fails, learners tend to ascribe causation to their ability rather than to their technique. By contrast, students who envision problem solving in strategic terms make more systematic changes in solution efforts and attribute causation to their strategy choice (Zimmerman & Kitsantas, 1997). In this way, students' use of effective self-regulatory techniques has been shown to have a major impact on self-motivational processes that underlie their commitment to attain a solution to a problem.

How can teachers foster greater self-regulation of problem solving? We recommend initially the use of instructional models, such as peers or teachers, to demonstrate application of self-regulatory techniques and provide supportive feedback. These social models can show students how to set goals, focus on the relevant information, estimate solutions, select or construct strategies, interpret the results, and modify their future efforts. According to a social cognitive perspective (Zimmerman, 2000), these problem-solving skills can be acquired most effectively by training conducted according to a four-level hierarchy. First, a *observation level* of problem-solving skill is attained when observers induce the underlying strategy from a model's performance and can predict further moves verbally before the model actually displays them. Second, a *emulation level* of problem-solving skill is attained when observers can emulate the strategy with verbal guidance and feedback from the instructor. Third, a *self-control level* of problem-solving skill is attained when observers can apply the model's strategy on similarly structured problems on their own. Fourth, a *self-regulation level* of problem-solving skill is attained when observers can adapt the model's solution strategy to unstructured (informal) problems on their own. Thus, problem-solving skill is most easily acquired from social sources – namely, a model who can provide feedback – and then is shifted to self-directive sources in similarly structured contexts before it is adapted to unstructured contexts. There is evidence that the motivation and problem-solving skill of learners who follow this four-step process are superior to those of learners who skipped steps (Zimmerman & Kitsantas, 1997, 1999; Kitsantas, Zimmerman, & Cleary, 2000).

CONCLUSION

Historically, researchers have given relatively little attention to the role of motivation and personal resourcefulness in explaining problem-solving efforts. We believe that this limitation is in part due to researchers' preoccupation with studying problem solving in formal contexts where problems are structured to be clear, interesting, and soluble. Problem solving in informal contexts involves unique challenges, and it requires additional cognitive and/or behavioral skills and sources of motivation to succeed.

These skills include anticipating and defining implicit or subtle problems and transcending initial boundaries of problem contexts. In addition, problem solvers in informal contexts need high levels of motivation to sustain recursive behavioral efforts. When researchers have examined the processes that expert problem solvers use in informal contexts as well as formal ones, there is evidence of high motivation and widespread use of self-regulatory processes.

Current research on self-regulation of learning has sought to identify key sources of motivation during problem-solving in a variety of contexts, and a cyclical problem-solving model was presented involving three sequential phases: forethought, performance, and self-reflection. The interdependency of self-regulatory processes and associated motivation beliefs within these three phases was described, and research documenting these cyclical relations was summarized. Performance phase processes, such as strategy use and self-monitoring, and self-reflection phase processes, such as self-evaluating, attributing causation, and self-satisfaction reactions, have significant impact on self-motivational beliefs, such as self-efficacy judgments, outcome expectations, intrinsic task interest, and goal orientations. Research on self-regulation of problem solving in informal contexts, such as problem-based learning in medical schools and practice, has demonstrated the importance of self-regulatory processes and associated sources of motivation. Finally, the pedagogical value of a cyclical phase model in developing self-sustaining motivation during solution efforts was discussed along with research showing the effectiveness of a hierarchical sequence of social and self-directed training levels. This body of research has clearly demonstrated that effective problem solvers need more than mere knowledge about a problem task to succeed; they need high levels of motivation, metacognition, and motoric competence. When these components of problem solving are self-regulated cyclically, learners will experience the heightened sense of personal agency that can sustain long-term solution efforts.

REFERENCES

Ames, C. (1992). Classrooms: Goals, structures and student motivation. *Journal of Educational Psychology, 84*(3), 261–271.
Bandura, A. (1991). Self-regulation of motivation through anticipatory and self-reactive mechanisms. In R. A. Dienstbier (Ed.), *Perspectives on motivation: Nebraska symposium on motivation* (Vol. 38, pp. 69–164). Lincoln: University of Nebraska Press.
Bandura, A. (1997). *Self-efficacy: The exercise of control.* New York: W. H. Freeman.
Bandura, A., & Cervone, D. (1986). Differential engagement of self-reactive influences in cognitive motivation. *Organizational Behavior and Human Decision Processes, 38,* 92–113.

Bandura, A., & Schunk, D. H. (1981). Cultivating competence, self-efficacy, and intrinsic interest through proximal self-motivation. *Journal of Personality and Social
Psychology, 41*, 586–598.

Bloom, B. S. (1985). *Developing talent in young people*. New York: Ballantine Books.

Brown, J. S., Collins, A., & Duguid, P. (1989). Situated cognition and the culture of
learning. *Educational Researcher, 18*, 32–42.

Bruning, R. H., Schraw, G. J., & Ronning, R. R. (1995). *Cognitive psychology and
instruction* (2nd ed.). Upper Saddle River, NJ: Merrill.

Carver, C. S., & Scheier, M. F. (2000). On the structure of behavioral self-regulation.
In M. Boekaerts, P. Pintrich, & M. Zeidner (Eds.), *Self-regulation: Theory, research,
and applications* (pp. 42–84). Orlando, FL: Academic Press.

Chase, W. G., & Simon, H. A. (1973). Perception in chess. *Cognitive Psychology, 4*,
55–81.

Chi, M. T. H., Glaser, R., & Rees, E. (1982). Expertise in problem solving. In R. J.
Sternberg (Ed.), *Advances in psychology of human intelligence* (Vol. 1, pp. 7–75).
Hillsdale, NJ: Lawrence Erlbaum Associates.

Cleary, T. J., & Zimmerman, B. J. (2001). Self-regulation differences during athletic
practice by experts, non-experts, and novices. *Journal of Applied Sport Psychology,
13*, 185–206.

Deci, E. L. (1975). *Intrinsic motivation*. New York: Plenum.

De Corte, E., Verschaffel, L., & Op 'T Eyne, P. (2000). Self-regulation: A characteristic
and goal of mathematics education. In M. Boekaerts, P. Pintrich, & M. Zeidner
(Eds.), *Self-regulation: Theory, research, and applications* (pp. 687–726). Orlando, FL:
Academic Press.

Dweck, C. S. (1988). Motivational processes affecting learning. *American Psychologist, 41*, 1040–1048.

Elstein, A. S., Shulman, L. S., & Sprafka, S. A. (1978). *Medical problem solving*.
Cambridge, MA: Harvard University Press.

Ericsson, K. A., & Charnes, N. (1994). Expert performance: Its structure and acquisition. *American Psychologist, 49*, 725–747.

Ericsson, A. K., Lehman, A. C. (1996). Expert and exceptional performance: Evidence of maximal adaptation to task constraints. *Annual Review of Psychology, 47*,
273–305.

Evensen, D. H., & Hmelo, C. E. (Eds.). (2000). *Problem-based learning: A research perspective on learning interactions*. Mahwah, NJ: Lawrence Erlbaum and Associates.

Garcia, T., & Pintrich, P. R. (1994). Regulating motivation and cognition in the classroom: The role of self-schemas and self-regulatory strategies. In D. H. Schunk
& B. J. Zimmerman (Eds.), *Self-regulation of learning and performance: Issues and
educational applications* (pp. 127–53). Hillsdale, NJ: Erlbaum.

Garfield, C. A., & Bennett, Z. H. (1985). *Peak performance: Mental training techniques
of the world's greatest athletes*. New York: Warner Books.

Gick, M. L., & Holyoak, K. J. (1980). Analogical problem solving. *Cognitive Psychology, 12*, 306–355.

Gick, M. L., & Holyoak, K. J. (1983). Schema induction and analogical transfer.
Cognitive Psychology, 15, 1–38.

Kitsantas, A., Zimmerman, B. J., & Cleary, T. (2000). The role of observation and
emulation in the development of athletic self-regulation. *Journal of Educational
Psychology, 91*, 241–250.

Kuhl, J. (1985). Volitional mediators of cognitive behavior consistency: Self-regulatory processes and action versus state orientation. In J. Kuhl & J. Beckman (Eds.), *Action control* (pp. 101–128). New York: Springer.

Langer, E. (1989). *Mindfulness*. Reading, MA: Perseus Books.

Lepper, M. R., & Hodell, M. (1989). Intrinsic motivation in the classroom. In C. Ames & R. Ames (Eds.), *Research on motivation in education* (Vol. 3, pp. 255–296). Hillsdale, NJ: Erlbaum.

Locke, E. A., & Latham, G. P. (1990). *A theory of goal setting and task performance*. Englewood Cliffs, NJ: Prentice-Hall.

Loehr, J. E. (1991). *The mental game*. New York: Penguin Books.

Lundeberg, M. A. (1987). Metacognitive aspects of reading comprehension: Studying understanding in legal case analysis. *Reading Research Quarterly, 22,* 407–432.

Mach, E. (1988). *Great contemporary pianists speak for themselves*. Dover Books: Toronto, Canada.

Mayer, R. E. (1992). *Thinking, problem solving, cognition* (2nd ed.). New York: W. H. Freeman.

Mayer, R. E. (1998). Cognitive, metacognitive, and motivational aspects of problem solving. *Instructional Science, 26,* 49–63.

McClelland, D., Atkinson, J. W., Clarke, R. A., & Lowell, E. L. (1953). *The achievement motive*. New York: Appleton-Century-Crofts.

Moore, M. T. (1990). Problem finding and teacher experience. *Journal of Creative Behavior, 24,* 39–58.

National Council of Teachers of Mathematics. (1989). *Curriculum and evaluation standards for school mathematics*. Reston, VA: National Council of Teachers of Mathematics.

Newell, A., & Simon, H. A. (1972). *Human problem solving*. Englewood Cliffs, NJ: Prentice Hall.

Nicholls, J. (1984). Conceptions of ability and achievement motivation. In R. Ames & C. Ames (Eds.), *Research on motivation in education* (pp. 39–73). Academic Press.

Pintrich, P. R., & Schunk, D. H. (1996). *Motivation in education*. Englewood Cliffs, NJ: Prentice Hall.

Powers, W. T. (1998). *Making sense of behavior: The meaning of control*. New Canaan, CT: Benchmark Press.

Pressley, M. (1977). Imagery and children's learning: Putting the picture in developmental perspective. *Review of Educational Research, 47,* 586–622.

Pressley, M., & Levin, J. R. (1977). Task parameters affecting the efficacy of a visual imagery learning strategy in younger and older children. *Journal of Experimental Child Psychology, 24,* 53–59.

Pressley, M., & McCormick, C. (1995). *Advanced educational psychology: For educators, researchers, and policymakers*. New York: HarperCollins College Publishers.

Pressley, M., & Woloshyn, V., et al. (1995). *Cognitive strategy instruction that really improves children's academic performance* (2nd ed.). Cambridge, MA: Brookline Books.

Resnick, L. B. (1985). Cognition and instruction: Recent theories of human competence. In B. L. Hammonds (Ed.), *Psychology and learning: The master lecture series* (Vol. 4, pp. 127–186).

Schneider, W., & Pressley, M. (1989). *Memory development between 2 and 20*. New York: Springer-Verlag.

Schunk, D. H. (1983a). Ability versus effort attributional feedback on children's achievement: A self-efficacy analysis. *Journal of Educational Psychology, 75,* 848–856.

Schunk, D. H. (1983b). Goal difficulty and attainment information: Effects on children's achievement behaviors. *Human Learning, 2,* 107–117.

Schunk, D. H. (1983c). Progress self-monitoring: Effects on children's self-efficacy and achievement. *Journal of Experimental Education, 51,* 89–93.

Schunk, D. H. (1984a). The self-efficacy perspective on achievement behavior. *Educational Psychologist, 19,* 48–58.

Schunk, D. H. (1984b). Sequential attributional feedback and children's achievement behaviors. *Journal of Educational Psychology, 76,* 1159–1169.

Schunk, D. H. (1990). Goal setting and self-efficacy during self-regulated learning. *Educational Psychologist, 25,* 71–86.

Schunk, D. H. (1996). Goal and self-evaluative influences during children's cognitive skill learning. *American Educational Research Journal, 33,* 359–382.

Schunk, D. H. (2000). *Learning theories: An educational perspective* (3rd ed.). Prentice-Hall: Upper Saddle River, NJ.

Schunk, D. H., & Cox, P. D. (1986). Strategy training and attributional feedback with learning disabled students. *Journal of Educational Psychology, 78,* 201–209.

Schunk, D. H., & Ertmer, P. A. (1999) Self-regulatory processes during computer skill acquisition: Goal and self-evaluative influences. *Journal of Educational Psychology.*

Schunk, D. H., Hansen, A. R., & Cox, P. D. (1987). Peer model attributes and children's achievement behaviors. *Journal of Educational Psychology, 79,* 54–61.

Schunk, D. H. & Rice, J. M. (1985). Verbalization of comprehension strategies: Effects on children's achievement outcomes. *Human Learning, 4,* 1–10.

Schunk, D. H., & Rice, J. M. (1987). Enhancing comprehension skill and self-efficacy with strategy value information. *Journal of Reading Behavior, 19,* 285–302.

Schunk, D. H., & Swartz, C. W. (1993). Goals and progress feedback: Effects on self-efficacy and writing achievement. *Contemporary Educational Psychologist, 18,* 337–354.

Schunk, B. J., & Zimmerman, B. J. (1994). Self-regulation in education: Retrospect and prospect. In D. H. Schunk & B. J. Zimmerman (Eds.), *Self-regulation of learning and performance: Issues and educational applications* (pp. 305–314.) Hillsdale, NJ: Erlbaum.

Simon, H. A. (1979). Information processing models of cognition. *Annual Review of Psychology, 30,* 363–396.

Voss, J. F., Greene, T. R., Post, T. A., & Penner, B. C. (1983). Problem solving skill in the social sciences. In G. H. Bower (Ed.), *The psychology of learning and motivation: Advances in research and theory* (Vol. 17, pp. 165–213). New York: Academic Press.

Weiner, B. (1979). A theory of motivation for some classroom experiences. *Journal of Educational Psychology, 71,* 3–25.

Weiner, B. (1985). An attributional theory of motivation and emotion. *Psychological Review, 92,* 548–573.

Weiner, B. (1986). *An attributional theory of motivation and emotion.* New York: Springer-Verlag.

Weinstein, C. E., & Mayer, R. F. (1986). The teaching of learning strategies. In M. C. Wittrock (Ed.), *Handbook of research on teaching* (3rd ed., pp. 315–327). New York: Macmillan.

Zimmerman, B. J. (1985). The development of "intrinsic" motivation: A social learning analysis. In G. J. Whitehurst (Ed.), *Annals of child development* (pp. 117–160). Greenwich, CT: JAI Press.

Zimmerman, B. J. (1989). A social cognitive view of self-regulated academic learning. *Journal of Educational Psychology, 81,* 329–339.

Zimmerman, B. J. (1994). Dimensions of academic self-regulation: A conceptual framework for education. In D. H. Schunk & B. J. Zimmerman (Eds.), *Self-regulation of learning and performance: Issues and educational applications* (pp. 3–21). Hillsdale, NJ: Erlbaum.

Zimmerman, B. J. (1995). Self-efficacy and educational development. In A. Bandura (Ed.), *Self-efficacy in changing societies* (pp. 202–231). New York: Cambridge University Press.

Zimmerman, B. J. (1996). Self-regulation involves more than metacognition: A social cognitive perspective. *Educational Psychologist, 30,* 217–221.

Zimmerman, B. J. (1998). Academic studying and the development of personal skill: A self-regulatory perspective. *Educational Psychologist, 33,* 73–86.

Zimmerman, B. J. (2000). Attainment of self-regulation: A social cognitive perspective. In M. Boekaerts, P. Pintrich, & M. Zeidner (Eds.), *Self-regulation: Theory, research, and applications* (pp. 13–39). Orlando, FL: Academic Press.

Zimmerman, B. J., Bonner, S., Evans, D. & Mellins, R. (1999). Self-regulating childhood asthma: A developmental model of family change. *Health Education & Behavior, 26,* 53–69.

Zimmerman, B. J., & Kitsantas, A. (1996). Self-regulated learning of a motoric skill: The role of goal setting and self-monitoring. *Journal of Applied Sport Psychology, 8,* 60–75.

Zimmerman, B. J., & Kitsantas, A. (1997). Developmental phases in self-regulation: Shifting from process goals to outcome goals. *Journal of Educational Psychology, 89,* 1–8.

Zimmerman, B. J., & Kitsantas, A. (1999). Acquiring writing revision skill: Shifting from process to outcome self-regulatory goals. *Journal of Educational Psychology, 91,* 1–10.

Zimmerman, B. J., & Koussa, R. (1979). Social influences on children's toy preferences: Effects of model rewardingness and affect. *Contemporary Educational Psychology, 4,* 55–66.

Zimmerman, B. J., & Lebeau, R. B. (2000). A commentary on self-directed learning. In D. H. Evensen & C. E. Hmelo (Eds.), *Problem-based learning: A research perspective on learning interactions* (pp. 299–313). Mahwah, NJ: Erlbaum.

Zimmerman, B. J., & Martinez-Pons, M. (1992). Perceptions of efficacy and strategy use in the self-regulation of learning. In D. H. Schunk & J. Meece (Eds.), *Student perceptions in the classroom: Causes and consequences* (pp. 185–207). Hillsdale, NJ: Erlbaum.

Zimmerman, B. J., & Paulsen, A. S. (1995). Self-monitoring during collegiate studying: An invaluable tool for academic self-regulation. In P. Pintrich (Ed.), *New directions in college teaching and learning: Understanding self-regulated learning* (No. 63, Fall, pp. 13–27). San Francisco, CA: Jossey-Bass, Inc.

Zimmerman, B. J., & Ringle, J. (1981). Effects of model persistence and statements of confidence on children's self-efficacy and problem solving. *Journal of Educational Psychology, 73,* 485–493.

9

Feeling and Thinking: Implications for Problem Solving

Norbert Schwarz and Ian Skurnik

INTRODUCTION

Consistent with the classic juxtaposition of reason and emotion, moods and emotions have long been assumed to interfere with problem solving. Recent advances in psychology's understanding of the interplay of feeling and thinking suggest a more complex story: Positive as well as negative moods and emotions can facilitate as well as inhibit problem solving, depending on the nature of the task. Moreover, the same feeling may have differential effects at different stages of the problem-solving process. In addition, nonaffective feelings, such as bodily sensations and cognitive experiences (e.g., fluency of recall or perception), may also influence problem solving, often paralleling the effects observed for affective feelings. This chapter summarizes key lessons learned about the interplay of feeling and thinking and addresses their implications for problem solving. To set the stage, we begin with a summary of key elements of the problem-solving process.

ELEMENTS OF PROBLEM SOLVING

In the most general sense, "a *problem* arises when we have a goal – a state of affairs that we want to achieve – and it is not immediately apparent how the goal can be attained" (Holyoak, 1995, p. 269). Consistent with the spatial metaphors of ordinary language use, where we "search for a way to reach the goal," "get lost" in a problem, meet "roadblocks" or have to "backtrack," problem solving is typically conceptualized as search through a metaphorical space (Duncker, 1945). The *problem space* (Newell & Simon, 1972) consists of an *initial state*, a *goal state*, and a number of *intermediate states*. Sets of *operators* serve to move from one state to another, and additional *path constraints* may impose limits on the paths to solution. "The relative ease of solving a problem will depend on how successful the solver has been in representing crucial elements of the task environment in his problem space" (Simon, 1978, p. 276).

Attempts to search the problem space by examining all possible operator sequences quickly exceed individuals' computational abilities due to combinatorial explosion. Hence, people typically rely on *heuristic search* strategies, attending only to a small number of alternatives that they deem promising. The choice of proper heuristics on the basis of knowledge about the problem domain is at the heart of intelligent problem solving, and *expertise* in a domain can be conceptualized as "the acquisition of knowledge that restricts the need for extensive search" (Holyoak, 1995, p. 271). This knowledge allows experts to organize elements of the problem situation into meaningful chunks (e.g., Chase & Simon, 1973) and to draw on patterns of relations between problem elements that facilitate the transfer of knowledge acquired in one situation to a related one (e.g., Holyoak & Koh, 1987). As we see below, moods and emotions have been found to influence whether people spontaneously adopt a top-down, knowledge-driven or a bottom-up, data-driven strategy of information processing (e.g., Bless & Schwarz, 1999) and may hence influence how we represent a problem and search the problem space. Moreover, the affective connotations of a problem, as well as the problem solver's affective state, may influence which knowledge becomes accessible in memory to serve as input into analogical problem-solving strategies (e.g., Hesse, Kauer, & Spies, 1997).

As Holyoak (1995, p. 285) noted, "the search perspective seems most appropriate when the problem solver has a clear goal, understands the initial state and constraints, and knows exactly what operators might be useful." Most of the problems we face in daily life, however, are of a different quality. They are *ill-defined* (Reitman, 1964) and lack a clear definition of one or more of the crucial components of the problem space. In this case, people face decisions that have received little attention in the cognitive literature: Is the current state bad enough to warrant some action? Is the goal attainable and do I have the resources to do so? Is the solution I have in mind "good enough"? These assessments are likely to be profoundly influenced by people's affective states, as we see below.

The remainder of this chapter addresses these possibilities in some detail. Before we turn to the influence of moods and emotions on human reasoning, however, it is useful to introduce some terminological distinctions.

AFFECT, MOODS, AND EMOTIONS

Affect is often used as a synonym for emotions but can also simply refer to valence. While all moods and emotions are affective, not all affective things are moods or emotions. Thus, a formal reasoning problem may be embedded in material that has a positive or negative *affective tone*, yet this manipulation would not necessarily induce a corresponding emotional experience in the problem solver. In contrast, *mood* and *emotion* refer to subjective states that have an experiential, cognitive, and physiological component. Emotions are thought to reflect the ongoing, implicit appraisal of situations with respect to positive or negative implications for the individual's goals and concerns (e.g., Arnold, 1960). They have a specific referent (what we feel emotional about), and are usually characterized by a short rise time, high intensity, and limited duration. The concept of mood, on the other hand, refers to the feeling state itself when the object or cause is not in the focus of attention. In fact, people are often unaware of the causes of their moods, which may include minor events (such as finding a dime; e.g., Isen, 1987) as well as background variables such as a lack of daylight or exercise (see Thayer, 1996). Hence, moods lack a specific referent and usually come about gradually, are of low intensity, and may endure for some time. These differences are apparent in ordinary language use when we say that we are afraid "of" or angry "about" something, but "in" a good mood. As a result, emotions draw our attention to the eliciting event and are likely to interrupt other ongoing activity. Moods, on the other hand, remain in the background, and it is this diffuse and unfocused quality that accounts for their pervasive influence, as we see below (for more detailed discussions of these conceptual distinctions, see Clore, Schwarz, & Conway, 1994; Morris, 1989; Schwarz & Clore, 1996).

In addition to these affective feelings, *bodily sensations* such as arousal or proprioceptive feedback can serve as a source of information that influences human information processing (for a review, see Schwarz & Clore, 1996). Finally, cognitive activity is accompanied by *cognitive experiences*, such as the experience of ease or difficulty of recall (e.g., Schwarz, 1998) or perceptual fluency (e.g., Jacoby, Kelley, & Dywan, 1989), which exert an influence on information processing in their own right. Unfortunately, these cognitive experiences are beyond the scope of the present chapter.

In numerous studies, affective feelings have been found to influence evaluative judgment, the spontaneous adoption of different strategies of information processing, and the material that is likely to be retrieved from memory. We address each of these aspects in turn.

FEELINGS AND EVALUATIONS

Unless we are explicitly asked to solve a problem presented to us, the first step in the problem-solving sequence is to identify whether there is a problem at all. If there is, we need to evaluate the feasibility of different paths to a solution in light of our resources and need to evaluate the outcome of different steps along the way. If the problem is ill-defined, it may not be obvious whether we reached a solution, and we need to determine whether a given candidate is "good enough" to terminate the process. Our feelings at the time may profoundly influence our conclusions at each of these steps.

Moods

Numerous studies have demonstrated that individuals evaluate nearly anything more positively when they are in a happy rather than sad mood, ranging from consumer goods and the state of the economy to the quality of their lives (see Clore et al., 1994; Forgas, 1995; Schwarz & Clore, 1996 for reviews). In most studies, moods have been experimentally induced by minor events (e.g., finding a dime or receiving a cookie), by exposure to valenced material (e.g., watching a sad video or recalling a happy event from one's past), or by natural circumstances (e.g., sunny or rainy weather), with similar results across different manipulations.

The impact of moods on judgment has been traced to two different processes. One approach (to be addressed in more detail in a later section) assumes that being in a happy (or sad) mood increases the accessibility of positively (or negatively) valenced material in memory, resulting in a mood-congruent database on which the judgment is based (e.g., Bower, 1981; Forgas, 1995; Isen, Shalker, Clark, & Karp, 1978). An alternative approach (Schwarz & Clore, 1983, 1988) assumes that individuals may simplify the judgment task by asking themselves, "How do I feel about this?" In doing so, they may misread their preexisting mood state as their affective response to the target of judgment, resulting in more positive evaluations under happy rather than sad moods. If so, mood effects on evaluative judgment should not be obtained when the informational value of the mood for the judgment at hand is called into question.

Several studies support this prediction (for a review, see Schwarz & Clore, 1996). For example, Schwarz and Clore (1983) called people on sunny or rainy days and asked them to report their life satisfaction. Not surprisingly, they reported higher general life satisfaction when they were in a good (sunny days) rather than bad (rainy days) mood. More important, this difference in life satisfaction was eliminated when the interviewer asked as a private aside, "Before we begin, how's the weather down there where you live?," thus drawing respondents' attention to a transient cause of their current mood. Note that such discounting effects (Kelley, 1972) are incompatible with the assumption that mood effects on judgment are mediated by mood-congruent recall. The interviewer's remark only discredits the implications of one's current feelings, but not the implications of any happy or sad life events that may have come to mind. Accordingly, findings of this type demonstrate that feelings can serve as a source of information in their own right, unless their informational value is called into question. For this reason, the influence of moods is more pervasive than the influence of emotions. Given that emotions have a specific referent, they inform us about our response to this particular referent, whereas the diffuse nature of moods facilitates their misinterpretation as an apparent response to a wide range of different targets of judgment (e.g., Keltner, Locke, & Audrain, 1993).

In sum, moods can influence evaluative judgments either by serving as a source of information in their own right or by influencing what comes to mind. In either case, individuals arrive at mood-congruent evaluations.

Implications for Problem Solving

The reliable emergence of mood effects in evaluative judgment suggests a number of hypotheses that have received little attention in the problem-solving literature.

Is There a Problem?

A problem arises when we perceive a discrepancy between the current state and a goal state and it is not immediately apparent how the discrepancy can be eliminated. Whether happy or sad moods are likely to increase the perceived discrepancy depends on whether the mood is brought to bear on the evaluation of the current state or of the goal state.

First, assume that people draw on their mood to evaluate the current state. In this case, being in a bad mood should result in a more negative evaluation of the current situation, and hence a larger perceived discrepancy to the goal state. In fact, the respondents in Schwarz and Clore's (1983) weather experiment reported a higher desire to change their lives when they were called on a rainy rather than sunny day – a desire that presumably reflects that they identified a discrepancy that presents a classic ill-defined problem, namely, "improving one's life." As Runco (1994) noted, dissatisfaction with the current state is an important instigator of creative problem solving, and judgments of (dis)satisfaction are reliably influenced by people's mood (e.g., Keltner et al., 1993; Schwarz & Clore, 1983; Schwarz, Strack, Kommer, & Wagner, 1987).

Conversely, assume that individuals bring their mood to bear on the goal state. In this case, being in a good mood would increase the perceived attractiveness of the goal, again increasing the perceived discrepancy. Thus, negative as well as positive moods may increase the perceived discrepancy, depending on whether the mood is brought to bear on the evaluation of the current state or of the goal state. Influences of this type are difficult to observe in the laboratory, where the sheer fact that a task is presented conveys that something needs to be done (see Schwarz, 1996), thus eliminating the need to identify whether there is a problem in the first place.

Am I Likely to Attain the Goal?

Having detected a problem, individuals are unlikely to tackle it when they think that the goal is unattainable in light of their resources. A considerable body of research indicates that individuals in a happy mood are more optimistic about their resources, and less likely to expect major obstacles, than individuals in a sad mood (e.g., Brown & Mankowski, 1993; Johnson & Tversky, 1983). Hence, individuals in a positive mood may be more likely to initiate problem-solving strategies. This tendency is further compounded by sad individuals' tendency to set higher performance standards for themselves. At first glance, this tendency is surprising in light of sad individuals' pessimistic assessment of the necessary resources. Yet when they ask themselves, "How satisfied will I be when I reach this goal?," the answer is negative, resulting in upward adjustments of the goal (e.g., Cervone, Kopp, Schauman, & Scott, 1994). As a result, sad individuals set higher goals and are less optimistic that they can achieve them, resulting in a decreased likelihood of action initiation.

How Am I Doing?

While working on the problem, individuals have to assess the quality of their performance: Are they getting closer to the goal or not? Unless the criteria for intermediate states are well defined, people may again draw on their apparent affective response in making this assessment. Consistent with the negative impact of moods on satisfaction judgments, several studies indicate that individuals in a bad mood are likely to evaluate their performance more negatively than individuals in a good mood (e.g., Hirt, McDonald, & Melton, 1996; Martin, Ward, Achée, & Wyer, 1993). In response to this negative assessment, they keep searching for a better solution, whereas happy individuals are satisfied and terminate the search process. As a result, we may expect that happy individuals are more likely to settle for a suboptimal solution, but are more satisfied with it, than sad individuals, who strive for a better solution but remain dissatisfied with it nevertheless.

As Martin et al. (1993; see also Martin & Stoner, 1996) demonstrated, however, this prediction holds only when a *performance criterion* is used as the termination criterion, as is likely to be the case for everyday problems of real world importance. In other cases, people may not ask themselves how well they are doing, but how much they enjoy working on the task. Many of the intellectual problems presented in laboratory settings may lend themselves to this criterion in the absence of instructions that ensure perceived relevance to a personal goal. When an *enjoyment criterion* is used, being in a good mood indicates that the task is fun, whereas being in a bad mod indicates that it is not. Accordingly, happy individuals keep going, whereas sad individuals terminate the task under this criterion, as Martin et al. (1993) observed.

We surmise that contingencies of this type account for many of the apparently inconsistent findings in the literature on mood and problem solving. The answer to the apparently simple question, "Does being in a good mood increase or decrease effort expenditure?" is a resounding "It depends" (Martin et al., 1993): When the task is framed in a way that evokes a performance criterion, being in a good mood decreases effort; yet when it evokes an enjoyment criterion, being in a good mood increases effort. Unfortunately, which criterion is evoked may depend as much on the general introduction or contextual cues as on the task itself, rendering it difficult to determine from sketchy methods sections what might have been going on in a given study.

Accepting a Solution

One implication of the preceding discussion is that happy individuals should be more likely to follow a satisficing strategy (Simon, 1967), accepting the first satisfactory solution they generate. In contrast, individuals in a sad mood should be more likely to follow an optimizing strategy, reflecting that they are less likely to be satisfied with any given solution (cf. Kaufmann & Vosburg, 1997).

Summary

As this selective discussion indicates, problem solving entails a large number of evaluative judgments, of which we addressed only a few. In light of the pervasive influence of moods on evaluative judgment across a large range of content domains, it is safe to assume that moods can affect problem solvers' decisions at each step along the way from the (usually neglected) detection of a problem to the acceptance of a solution. The specific effect, however, depends on which decision the mood is brought to bear. Given that moods lack a clear referent, they can be misread as responses to large number of different targets of judgment, with often opposite outcomes, as our discussion illustrated. Although the empirical evidence bearing on the above conjectures is limited, the exploration of these possibilities provides a promising avenue for future research.

FEELINGS AND PROCESSING STYLES: COGNITIVE TUNING

People are more likely to rely on their preexisting knowledge structures and routines, which have served them well in the past, when things go smoothly and they do not face any hurdles. Once complications arise, they shift from a top-down processing style to a bottom-up processing style, paying increased attention to the details at hand (cf. Wegner & Vallacher, 1986). A diverse body of studies indicates that our feelings can provide information that elicits such shifts in processing style. This is best documented for happy and sad moods as well as proprioceptive feedback that provides approach or avoidance information.

Moods

In general, individuals in a sad mood are likely to use a systematic, data-driven, bottom-up strategy of information processing, with considerable attention to detail. In contrast, individuals in a happy mood are likely to rely on preexisting general knowledge structures, using a top-down, heuristic strategy of information processing, with less attention to detail (for reviews, see Bless & Schwarz, 1999; Schwarz & Clore, 1996). These differences can again be traced to the informative functions of feelings (Schwarz, 1990). We usually feel bad when we encounter a threat of negative or a lack of positive outcomes, and feel good when we obtain positive outcomes and are not threatened by negative ones. Hence, our moods reflect the state of our environment, and being in a bad mood signals a problematic situation, whereas being in a good mood signals a benign situation. These signals have cognitive and motivational consequences, which are highly adaptive under most circumstances.

When facing a problematic situation, we are usually motivated to do something about it. Any attempt to change the situation, however, initially requires a careful assessment of its features, an analysis of their causal links, detailed explorations of possible mechanisms of change, as well as an anticipation of the potential outcomes of any action that might be initiated. Consistent with these conjectures, being in a negative affective state is associated with a narrowed focus of attention (e.g., Broadbent, 1971; Bruner, Matter, & Papanek, 1955; Easterbrook, 1959) and a higher level of spontaneous causal reasoning (e.g., Bohner, Bless, Schwarz, & Strack, 1988). Similarly, failure to obtain a desired outcome shifts attention to a lower level of abstraction, resulting in more detailed representations (e.g., Wegner & Vallacher, 1986). These influences foster bottom-up, data-driven processing. Moreover, it may seem unwise to rely on one's usual routines and preexisting general knowledge structures without further consideration of the specifics under these conditions, thus discouraging top-down strategies. Finally, we may be unlikely to take risks in a situation that is already marked problematic, and may therefore avoid simple heuristics and uncertain solutions.

Conversely, when we face a benign situation that poses no particular problem, we may see little need to engage in detailed analyses and may rely on our usual routines and preexisting knowledge structures, which served us well in the past. This encourages less effortful, top-down processing as a default, *unless* current goals require otherwise. In pursuing such goals, we may be willing to take some risk, given that the general situation is considered safe. As a result, simple heuristics may be preferred over more effortful, detail-oriented judgmental strategies; new procedures and possibilities may be explored; and unusual, creative associations may be explored.

In combination, these conjectures suggest that our cognitive processes are tuned to meet the situational requirements signaled by our feelings (Schwarz, 1990; Schwarz & Clore, 1996; see also Fiedler, 1988). Note that this *cognitive tuning* hypothesis does not entail that happy individuals are somehow unable, or generally unwilling, to engage in systematic processing. Rather, it entails only that the mood *itself* does not signal a situation that poses particular processing requirements. Hence, the spontaneously adopted heuristic processing style and reliance on preexisting knowledge structures should be easy to override, rendering processing under happy moods more flexible than processing under sad moods. In contrast, the systematic processing style fostered by negative moods should be difficult to override, reflecting that it would be maladaptive to ignore a potential "problem" signal (see Schwarz, 2001, for a more detailed discussion).

As expected based on theory, mood effects on processing style are eliminated when the informational value of the mood is undermined. When we are aware, for example, that we may feel bad only because of the lousy weather, our bad mood carries little information about the task at hand, and its influence on task performance is attenuated or eliminated (e.g., Sinclair, Mark, & Clore 1994). This finding parallels the observation that mood effects on evaluative judgment are eliminated under similar conditions (e.g., Schwarz & Clore, 1983), consistent with the informative functions logic. Note that this finding is incompatible with competing approaches that trace mood effects on processing style to mood-congruent recall. These approaches (Isen, 1987; Mackie & Worth, 1989) draw on variants of Bower's (1981) model of mood-congruent memory and assume that being in a good mood facilitates the recall of positive material from memory. Positive material stored in memory is believed to be more tightly organized and interconnected than negative material, resulting in the recall of a large amount of information. This extensive recall, in turn, is assumed by some authors to tax individuals' cognitive capacity, thus interfering with detail-oriented processing under happy moods, forcing individuals to rely on simplifying heuristics (e.g., Mackie & Worth, 1989). In contrast, others (e.g., Isen, 1987) assume that this extensive recall of interconnected material results in a more "complex cognitive context" (Isen, 1987, p. 237) that facilitates novel associations between disparate ideas in working memory, which are actively explored when individuals are in a good mood. The available data do not provide consistent support for either of these assumptions. In general, negative events have been found to elicit more causal analysis and rumination than positive events, presumably resulting in more interconnected representations of negative material (see Clore et al., 1994, for a more detailed discussion). Moreover, other researchers suggested that being in a sad (rather than happy) mood is more likely to tax individuals' cognitive capacity (e.g., Ellis & Ashbrook, 1988). Neither of these assumptions, however, can account for the observation that mood effects on processing style are eliminated when the informational value of the mood is undermined. In addition, memory-based accounts of processing-style effects are incompatible with recent research that documents parallel effects for the information provided by bodily feedback and situational cues. Before we address these parallels, however, it is useful to illustrate the differences in processing style elicited by being in a happy and sad mood with a prototypical example.

An Illustration: Moods and the Use of Scripts

As an illustration, consider a study on the use of scripts, that is, general knowledge structures pertaining to what transpires in social settings such as a restaurant (Schank & Abelson, 1977). Employing a dual-task paradigm, Bless, Clore, et al. (1996) had happy and sad participants listen to a tape-recorded story about having dinner at a restaurant that contained script-consistent as well as script-inconsistent information. While listening to the story, participants worked on a concentration test that required them to mark certain letters on a work sheet. Note that good performance on the concentration test requires detail-oriented processing, whereas the restaurant story can be understood by engaging either in script-driven top-down processing or in data-driven bottom-up processing. As predicted, happy participants were likely to recognize previously heard script-inconsistent information and showed high rates of erroneous recognition of previously not presented script-consistent information. This pattern indicates that they relied on their general knowledge about restaurant visits in encoding the information, rendering unusual acts highly salient and memorable. As usual, however, this reliance on general knowledge structures came at the expense of increased intrusion errors. Neither of these effects was obtained for sad participants, indicating that they were less likely to draw on the script.

Given that top-down processing is less taxing than bottom-up processing, we may further expect that happy participants do better on a secondary task. Confirming this prediction, happy participants outperformed sad participants on the concentration test.

In combination, these findings indicate that moods influence the spontaneously adopted processing style under conditions where different processing styles are compatible with the individual's goals and task demands, as was the case for comprehending the restaurant story. Under these conditions, sad individuals are likely to spontaneously adopt a systematic, detail-oriented, bottom-up strategy that is usually adaptive in problematic situations, whereas happy individuals rely on a less effortful top-down strategy. Yet when task demands (as in the case of the concentration test;

Bless, Clore et al., 1996) or explicit instructions (e.g., Bless, Bohner, Schwarz, & Strack, 1990) require detail-oriented processing, happy individuals are able and willing to engage in the effort.

Bodily Feedback

The cognitive tuning logic has recently been extended to *bodily sensations*, which may also signal benign or problematic situations (Friedman & Förster, 2000). In general, people try to approach situations that are characterized by a promise of positive, or a lack of negative, outcomes. Conversely, they try to avoid situations that entail a threat of negative outcomes or lack positive ones. If so, bodily responses that are typically associated with approach situations may elicit the heuristic, top-down processing style spontaneously preferred in benign situations, whereas bodily responses that are typically associated with avoidance situation may elicit the systematic, bottom-up processing style spontaneously preferred in problematic situations. One bodily response that is closely associated with approach is the contraction of the arm flexor, which is involved in pulling an object closer to the self. Conversely, contraction of the arm extensor is involved in pushing an object away from the self and is closely associated with avoidance. Hence, arm flexion provides bodily feedback that is usually associated with approaching positive stimuli, whereas arm extension provides bodily feedback that is usually associated with avoiding negative stimuli (see Cacioppo, Priester, & Berntson, 1993; Priester, Cacioppo, & Petty, 1996). In fact, affectively neutral stimuli encoded during arm flexion are later preferred over neutral stimuli encoded during arm extension, presumably reflecting the approach/avoidance information provided by the bodily feedback (Cacioppo et al., 1993; see also Chen & Bargh, 1999).

Taking advantage of this association, Friedman and Förster (2000) asked seated participants to press the right palm upward against the bottom of the table (arm flexion), or downward against the top of the table (arm extension). Although these movements engage the same muscles, they have no surface similarity to pulling an object closer, or pushing it away, thus avoiding the introduction of demand characteristics. As theoretically predicted, arm flexion fostered a heuristic processing style, whereas arm extension fostered a systematic processing style. We return to the results of these studies in some detail below.

Situational Cues

Consistent with the above reasoning, Soldat, Sinclair, and Mark (1997; Sinclair, Soldat, & Mark, 1998) and Ottati, Terkildsen, and Hubbard (1997) observed that affectively valenced situational cues may serve similar functions. Specifically, Ottati and colleagues showed that communicators who deliver a message with a happy, smiling face are likely to evoke a heuristic processing style in their audience, whereas communicators who deliver the same message with a somber face are likely to evoke a systematic processing style. In a similar vein, Soldat and colleagues presented reasoning tasks from the Graduate Record Examination on colored paper and observed that upbeat colors fostered heuristic processing, whereas more depressing colors fostered systematic processing. Again, we return to these findings below.

In combination, the available findings suggest that our strategies of information processing are tuned to meet the requirements of the specific situation. Information that characterizes the situation as problematic fosters the spontaneous adoption of a systematic, detail-oriented, bottom-up processing style. In contrast, information that characterizes the situation as benign fosters the spontaneous adoption of a top-down processing style that relies on preexisting knowledge structures and routines, unless currently active goals require otherwise. The "benign" or "problematic" signal can be external (e.g., situational cues or encountered hurdles) or internal (e.g., moods or bodily feedback), with similar effects observed in either case.

Implications for Problem Solving

The above differences in processing style have potentially far-reaching implications for problem solving, but the derivation of specific predictions for a given task situation requires close attention to theoretically specified contingencies, as the example of moods may illustrate. First, performance on problems that benefit from adopting a bottom-up processing style and considerable attention to detail should be facilitated when the problem solver is in a sad mood, but impeded when the problem solver is in a happy mood. Second, performance on problems that benefit from adopting a top-down processing style, or from the playful exploration of novel options, should be facilitated when the problem solver is in a happy mood, but impeded when the problem solver is in a sad mood. Third, as seen in the script example (Bless, Clore, et al., 1996), an individual's spontaneous preference for different processing styles can be overridden by clear task demands or instructions. Hence, the predicted effects should be most reliably observed when the task allows for different processing styles and their choice is not constrained by instructions. Finally, no mood effects are expected when problem solvers are aware that their current mood is due to some irrelevant source, thus undermining the mood's informational value (e.g., Sinclair et al., 1994).

Next, we provide a selective review of the available evidence. As noted earlier, the interplay of feeling and thinking has been most extensively studied in areas outside the traditional problem-solving literature, and we include a broad sample of reasoning tasks. We begin with tasks on which performance is likely to benefit from being in a sad mood and continue to tasks that benefit from being in a good mood, paying particular attention to creative problem solving.

Person Perception

A common but ill-defined problem of everyday life is forming an accurate impression of others. To do so, we can rely on detailed individuating information about the specific target person or can simplify the task by drawing on preexisting knowledge structures, such as stereotypes pertaining to the target's social category (Brewer, 1988; Bodenhausen, 1990; Fiske & Neuberg, 1990; Macrae, Milne, & Bodenhausen, 1994). Consistent with the above perspective, being in a good mood reliably increases stereotyping (e.g., Bodenhausen, Kramer, & Süsser, 1994; Bodenhausen, Sheppard, & Kramer, 1994), unless the target person is clearly inconsistent with the stereotype, thus undermining the applicability of the general knowledge structure (e.g. Bless, Schwarz, & Wieland, 1996). In contrast, being in a sad mood reliably decreases stereotyping and increases the use of individuating information (for a review, see Bless, Schwarz, & Kemmelmeier, 1996). Across many person-perception tasks, individuals in a chronic or temporary sad mood have been found to make more use of detailed individuating information, to show less halo effects, to be less influenced by the order of information presentation, and to be more accurate in performance appraisals than individuals in a happy mood, with individuals in a neutral mood falling in between (e.g., Edwards & Weary, 1993; Hildebrand-Saints & Weary, 1989; Sinclair, 1988; Sinclair & Mark, 1992). Throughout, these findings indicate a preponderance of top-down processing under happy moods, and bottom-up processing under sad moods.

Persuasion

Another common and equally ill-defined problem of daily life is the assessment of persuasive appeals. In general, a message that presents strong arguments is more persuasive than a message that presents weak arguments, provided that recipients are motivated and able to process the content of the message and to elaborate on the arguments. If recipients do not engage in message elaboration, the advantage of strong over weak arguments is eliminated (see Eagly & Chaiken 1993; Petty & Cacioppo, 1986, for reviews). Numerous studies demonstrated that sad individuals are more likely to engage in spontaneous message elaboration than happy individuals, with individuals in a neutral mood falling in between (for a review, see Schwarz, Bless, & Bohner, 1991). As a result, sad individuals are strongly influenced by compelling arguments and not influenced by weak arguments, whereas happy individuals are moderately, but equally, influenced by both. Conversely, happy individuals are more likely than sad individuals to rely on heuristic strategies in assessing the validity of the message, paying attention to cues such as the communicator's status or expertise in forming a judgment (e.g., Worth & Mackie, 1987). Hence, a strong message fares better with a sad than with a happy audience, but if communicators have nothing compelling to say, they are well advised to put recipients into a good mood, providing some cues that indicate high expertise and trustworthiness.

Paralleling these effects of recipients' mood, Ottati et al. (1997) observed that the same message is less likely to be scrutinized when presented by a communicator with a smiling, happy face than when presented by a communicator with a neutral, somber face. They suggested that communicator's conveyed affect can serve informative functions that parallel recipients' own moods. Finally, as noted earlier, the spontaneously adopted processing style can be overridden by other goals (e.g., Wegener, Petty, & Smith, 1995) or explicit task instructions (e.g., Bless et al., 1990). What characterizes the information processing of happy individuals is not a general cognitive or motivational impairment, but a tendency to spontaneously rely on simplifying heuristics and general knowledge structures in the absence of goals that require otherwise.

Covariation Detection
Another task that benefits from bottom-up processing and attention to detail is the assessment of covariation. Across a wide range of tasks, from estimating correlations from a scatterplot (Sinclair & Mark, 1995) to determining the extent to which an outcome depends on one's actions (Alloy, 1988), participants in a sad mood have been found to outperform participants in a good mood. Where control conditions were included, participants in a neutral mood typically fell in between these extremes (see Sinclair & Mark, 1992, for a review).

Analytic Reasoning Tasks and Logic Problems
We may further assume that the higher attention to detail that characterizes processing under sad moods will also facilitate performance on analytic reasoning tasks. The bulk of the available data is consistent with this prediction, yet parallel effects have not been observed for mathematics problems and some logic problems.

For example, Fiedler (1988) reported that sad participants produced fewer inconsistencies in multiattribute decision tasks than happy participants. Specifically, the latter were twice as likely as the former to violate transitivity by producing inconsistent triads of the form A > B and B > C, but A < C. Similarly, Melton (1995) observed that happy participants performed worse on syllogisms than participants in a neutral mood. Specifically, happy participants were more likely to select an unqualified conclusion and to give answers consistent with the atmosphere heuristic.

Extending the cognitive tuning logic to bodily feedback, Friedman and Förster (2000, Experiment 7) predicted that bodily feedback that provides a problem signal would improve performance on analytical reasoning tasks taken from the Graduate Record Exam, relative to bodily feedback that provides a benign signal. The bodily feedback used was the arm flexion or extension task discussed above, which provides feedback that is usually associated with approach (flexion) or avoidance (extension) reactions. The data confirmed this prediction, and participants in the arm extension condition solved nearly twice as many problems correctly as participants in the arm flexion condition. Finally, Soldat et al. (1997) presented analytic reasoning tasks, also taken from the Graduate Record Exam, on paper that had an upbeat red, or a somewhat depressing blue, color. They observed that participants performed better when the tasks were printed on blue rather than red paper. It is important that neither the bodily feedback nor the color cues resulted in changes in participants' self-reported mood. In combination, these findings suggest that subtle cues, such as bodily feedback or the affective connotation of the paper on which the task is presented, can serve as "problem" signals that elicit the more systematic reasoning style usually associated with negative moods.

On the other hand, other studies revealed performance deficits under depressed affect across a variety of mathematics and complex logic tasks (for a review, see Clore et al., 1994). In our reading, such mixed findings are to be expected for such tasks because none of the hypothesized processes will necessarily result in improved performance. On the one hand, greater attention to detail per se will not improve performance if the application of an algorithm is needed to which the individual does not have access. Moreover, greater attention to detail may increase the risk that the individual gets side-tracked by irrelevant features. Heuristic processing strategies, on the other hand, may similarly facilitate or impede performance, depending on whether the available heuristic is applicable to the current task. Finally, the judgment processes discussed in the preceding section may influence individuals' effort-expenditure and termination decisions, further complicating the picture.

Decision Making

Extending the above observations to decision making, Luce, Bettman, and Payne (1997) observed that information processing under negative affect "becomes more extensive and proceeds more by focusing on one attribute at a time" (p. 384), consistent with the assumption that negative feelings foster a more detail-oriented processing style. Moreover, Hertel, Neuhof, Theuer, and Kerr (2000) observed pronounced mood effects on individuals' decision behavior in a chicken game. Consistent with the present theorizing, their findings suggest that individuals in a happy mood are likely to heuristically imitate the behavior of other players, whereas individuals in a sad mood base their moves on a rational analysis of the structure of the game.

Categorization

Theoretically, the detail-oriented, bottom-up processing style associated with negative moods should foster the formation of fine-grained, narrow categories, whereas the top-down, heuristic processing style associated with positive moods should foster the formation of more inclusive categories. Numerous studies are consistent with this prediction (see Isen, 1987; Schwarz & Clore, 1996). For example, Isen and Daubman (1984) observed that happy participants were more likely to include unusual exemplars in a category than were participants in a neutral mood, assigning, for example "feet" and "camel" to the category "vehicles" and "cane" to the category "clothing." Moreover, happy individuals sorted colored chips into a smaller number of piles, again indicating more inclusive categorization. Reversing the categorization task, Hirt, Levine, McDonald, Melton, and Martin (1997) provided participants with a category and asked them to list exemplars. As expected, happy participants listed more unusual exemplars than sad participants, again indicating more inclusive categorization.

To account for these findings, it is typically assumed that being in a good mood results in the recall of mood-congruent positive material, which is believed to be more diverse and interconnected than positive material, as discussed above (Isen, 1987). These findings are, however, also consistent with the cognitive tuning logic (Schwarz, 1990). A diagnostic test would require experiments that undermine the informational value of participants' mood through attribution manipulations (Schwarz & Clore, 1983; Sinclair et al., 1994), but such experiments are not available for categorization tasks.

Findings reported by Friedman and Förster (2000, Experiment 6), however, support the cognitive tuning approach. Using the arm flexion/extension task, which provides an approach (flexion) or avoidance (extension) signal, these authors observed that participants who were induced to flex their arms provided more inclusive categorizations on Isen and Daubman's (1984) task, relative to a control. Conversely, participants who were induced to extend their arms provided less inclusive categorizations relative to a control. These differences were observed in the absence of any differences on mood measures, suggesting that the observed results are indeed due to the information provided by the bodily feedback rather than any changes in participants' mood that may have elicited mood-congruent recall.

Finally, the available findings are again consistent with the assumption that the spontaneously adopted processing style can be overridden by task instructions, rendering processing under positive moods highly flexible.

For example, Murray, Sujan, Hirt, and Sujan (1990) observed that happy participants sorted self-characteristics into finer groupings than did neutral mood participants.

Remote Associates

As may be expected on the basis of the categorization findings, happy individuals typically outperform sad or neutral-mood individuals on Mednick's (1962) remote associates test (e.g., Isen, Daubman, & Nowicki, 1987). Similarly, happy participants list more unusual first associates in response to neutral words than do sad or neutral-mood participants (e.g., Isen, Johnson, Mertz, & Robinson, 1985). In combination with the categorization findings, these observations suggest that being in a happy mood should facilitate creative problem solving (see Isen, 1987). This proposal has received considerable support.

Creativity and Insight

In a highly influential experiment, Isen and Daubman (1984) observed that being in a happy mood facilitated performance on a classic insight problem, namely, Duncker's (1945) candle task, relative to being in a neutral or sad mood (see Greene & Noice, 1988, for a replication). Isen (1987) suggested that this finding reflects that happy moods facilitate the recall of diverse material from memory, resulting in a more "complex cognitive context" that facilitates novel connections and insights. Alternatively, the cognitive tuning assumption (Schwarz, 1990) suggests that being in a good mood signals a benign situation that is conducive to playful exploration, which is discouraged by the problem signal provided by negative moods. Again, the most diagnostic test of these competing accounts would be experiments that vary the perceived informational value of participants' mood, yet such studies are not available.

Friedman and Förster's (2000) ingenious studies on bodily feedback, however, provide strong support for the cognitive tuning hypothesis. As theoretically predicted, the approach feedback provided by arm flexion facilitated creative problem solving across several tasks, whereas the avoidance feedback provided by arm extension impeded it. Specifically, participants who flexed their arms were more likely to break the set than participants who extended their arms, resulting in better performance on Witkin, Oltman, Raskin, and Karp's (1971) Embedded Figure Test (Experiment 1) as well as Ekstrom, French, Harman, and Dermen's (1976) Snowy Picture Test (Experiment 2). The Embedded Figure Test requires the identification of figures hidden in complex visual patterns, whereas the Snowy Picture Test requires the identification of familiar objects hidden in patterns of visual noise ("snow"). Performance on both tasks is facilitated by the application of familiar concepts to the hidden figures, while disregarding irrelevant detail and breaking the set imposed by the distractor. Finally, arm flexion improved the perceptual restructuring of fragmented visual images on Ekstrom et al.'s (1976) Gestalt Completion Test (Experiments 3 and 4). Both breaking the set and restructuring have traditionally been assumed to play a central role in creative insight (e.g., Wertheimer, 1959; see Schooler & Melcher, 1995, for a review).

Analogies

In addition, Friedman and Förster (2000, Experiment 5) observed that the approach feedback provided by arm flexion improved performance on a verbal analogy task (Amthauer, 1970) of the type *forest : trees = meadow : ?*, relative to arm extension. Their findings suggest that the processing style associated with being in a good mood may facilitate analogical transfer on insight problems in the absence of the helpful cues usually needed for successful transfer (see Gick & Holyoak, 1980, 1983).

Summary

As this selective review indicates, our feelings can profoundly influence our performance across a diverse range of reasoning tasks. Moods and bodily sensations that are usually associated with problematic situations foster the spontaneous adoption of a detail-oriented, bottom-up processing style. Conversely, moods and bodily sensations that are usually associated with a benign situation foster the spontaneous adoption of a more heuristic, top-down processing style and seem to encourage more playful exploration of novel options. One way to make sense of these influences is suggested by the informative functions approach to the interplay of feeling and thinking (Bless & Schwarz, 1999; Schwarz, 1990). This approach proposes that our feelings inform us about the benign or problematic nature of the current situation and that our cognitive processes are tuned to meet the respective situational requirements. Consistent with this proposal, the otherwise obtained mood effects on processing style and evaluative judgment are eliminated when the informational value of our current feelings is called into question through (mis)attribution manipulations (e.g., Schwarz & Clore, 1983; Sinclair et al., 1994).

FEELINGS AND THOUGHT CONTENT: AFFECTIVE TONE

In addition to serving as information in their own right, moods can also influence which information we recall from memory. In general, we are more likely to recall material that is congruent rather than incongruent with our mood at the time of recall. Following initial demonstrations by Isen et al. (1978), Bower (1981, 1991) conceptualized these effects in an associative network model of memory. Moods are thought to function as central nodes in an associative network, which are linked to related ideas, events of corresponding valence, autonomic activity, and muscular and expressive patterns. When new material is learned, it is associated with the nodes that are active at learning. Accordingly, material acquired while in a particular mood is linked to the respective mood node. When the person is in the same mood later on, activation spreads from the mood node along the pathways, increasing the activation of other nodes, which represent the related material. When the activation exceeds a certain threshold, the represented material comes into consciousness. This model makes two key predictions: First, memory is enhanced when the affective state at the time of encoding matches the affective state at the time of retrieval (*state-dependent learning*). Thus, we are more likely to recall material acquired in a particular mood when we are in the same, rather than a different, mood at the time of recall. Second, any given material is more likely to be retrieved when its affective tone matches the individual's mood at the time of recall (*mood-congruent memory*). Thus, information of a positive valence is more likely to come to mind when we are in a happy rather than sad mood.

Although both predictions received considerable empirical support in experimental and clinical research, this research also revealed a number of complications that are beyond the scope of this chapter (see Blaney, 1986; Clore et al., 1994; Morris, 1989; Singer & Salovey, 1988). In general, mood-congruent recall is most likely to be obtained for self-referenced material, such as autobiographical events, that meets the conditions of both of the above hypotheses: When something good (or bad) happens to us, it puts us in a positive (or negative) affective state, and its subsequent recall is facilitated when we are again in a similar affective state. Note that this situation simultaneously provides for matching mood states at learning and recall, thus satisfying the conditions of state-dependent learning, as well as for matches between the valence of the material and the mood at recall, thus satisfying the conditions of mood-congruent memory.

As noted in the preceding sections, mood-congruent recall has been used to account for mood-congruent judgment as well as mood-induced differences in processing style (see Forgas & Bower, 1998; Isen, 1987). We think that the feelings-as-information perspective provides a more parsimonious account for the available data and do not return to these issues. Instead, we focus on another aspect of problem solving, namely, the affective tone of the material.

Implications for Problem Solving

Performance on many problems is facilitated when we can recruit a useful analogy (see Holyoak, 1995). The mood and memory perspective offers three different predictions in this regard. First, the state-dependent learning hypothesis predicts that an analogy should be more likely to be recalled when the mood at the time of problem solving matches the mood at the time the analogy was encoded, irrespective of the affective tone of the analogy itself. Second, the mood-congruent recall hypothesis predicts that a positively or negatively toned analogy will be more likely to be recalled when the mood at problem solving matches rather than mismatches the affective tone of the analogy. Third, the assumption that all valenced material is linked to a few emotion nodes in memory suggests that an analogy is more likely to be recalled when the affective tone of the analogy matches the affective tone of the problem, independent of the person's mood at the time. Finally, problem solvers may prefer analogies with a matching affective tone not only because they are more accessible, but also because the affective surface similarity suggests higher relevance. We are not aware of studies that systematically tested these different predictions, with one exception.

Specifically, Hesse, Kauer, and Spies (1997) reported findings pertaining to a physical reasoning problem (the so-called Magnus effect) that support the prediction that affective surface similarities increase the likelihood that a specific analogy is recruited. To manipulate the affective tone of the target problem, Hesse et al. (1997) embedded the problem in irrelevant details that conveyed a pleasant or unpleasant experience. For example, the pleasant version opened with, "When I think back to 1924–25, I am filled with pride. My baby daughter Felice had just been born, and I had finally found employment again." In contrast, the opening line of the unpleasant version was, "I have almost nothing but bad memories of 1924–25. My daughter Hertha had recently died of pneumonia, and as an unemployed man it was difficult to make ends meet for my family." Distractor problems and source problems with a known solution were constructed in a similar way. Think-aloud protocols showed that participants predominantly referred to source problems that matched the target problem in affective tone. Moreover, participants evaluated source problems with a matching affective tone as more promising than source problems with a mismatching affective tone. These effects were observed in the absence of any influence of affective tone on participants' self-reported mood.

These findings and the extant literature on the impact of gain and loss framing, stimulated by Kahneman and Tversky's (1979) prospect theory, suggest that explorations of affective tone provide a promising avenue for further research.

A NOTE ON SPECIFIC EMOTIONS

Over the last two decades, researchers have made more progress in understanding the influence of mood on cognition than in understanding the influence of specific emotions. This is in part due to the simple fact that mild moods are easier to induce within the constraints imposed by human subject committees than specific emotions. Theoretically, the conceptual principles discussed for moods apply to emotions as well, although with some important constraints.

Emotions as a Source of Information

Recall that emotions have a specific referent (what we feel emotional about), a short rise time, and high intensity (see Clore et al., 1994). As a result, it is usually clear what we feel emotional about, and we are less likely to misread our emotions as a response to some unrelated stimulus than is the case for diffuse moods (see Keltner, Locke, & Audrain, 1993, for experimental support). As a result, emotions are most likely to influence assessments of unrelated targets after some delay, for example, after our specific anger dissipated, leaving us in a diffuse irritated mood (Bollnow, 1956).

Given that emotions primarily inform us about the eliciting event, it is not surprising that they focus our attention on this event and interrupt other ongoing activity, thus restructuring our processing priorities (Frijda, 1988; Simon, 1967). Moreover, the information that emotions provide about the eliciting event is more specific than the information provided by global moods. Emotions reflect implicit appraisals, and the experience of a given emotion indicates that the underlying appraisal pattern has been met (for a review of appraisal theories, see Clore et al., 1994; for a detailed model, see Ortony, Clore, & Collins, 1988). Accordingly, feelings of fear have been found to affect judgments of risk but not judgments of blame, whereas feelings of anger affect judgments of blame, but not judgments of risk (e.g., Gallagher & Clore, 1985). Similarly, Keltner, Ellsworth, and Edwards (1993) observed in several experiments that angry participants assigned more responsibility to human agents than to impersonal circumstances, whereas the reverse held for sad participants, consistent with the different appraisal patterns underlying anger and sadness.

In sum, specific emotions convey more specific information than diffuse moods and have more specific and localized effects. As in the case of moods, however, the influence of emotions on judgment is eliminated when the informational value of the emotion for the judgment at hand is called into question (Keltner, Locke, & Audrain, 1993; Schwarz, Servay, & Kumpf, 1985).

Emotions and Processing Style

From a feelings-as-information perspective, the specific appraisal pattern underlying a given emotion should allow us to understand which processing requirements are conveyed by the emotion. Several authors have recently pursued such an extension of the cognitive tuning assumptions (Schwarz, 1990) to specific emotions (Lerner & Keltner, 2000; Raghunathan

& Pham, 1999; Tiedens & Linton, 2001), although the few available findings are limited to negative emotions. They converge on the conclusion that different negative emotions have different effects, which can be predicted on the basis of the underlying appraisal pattern. For example, Tiedens and Linton (2001) observed in a persuasion paradigm that sad individuals engaged in systematic message processing, whereas angry individuals did not. They suggested that this difference reflects that the appraisal pattern underlying sadness entails uncertainty, which triggers more extensive reasoning, whereas the appraisal pattern underlying anger does not.

CONCLUDING REMARKS

As this selective review illustrates, psychologists have made considerable progress in understanding the interplay of feeling and thinking. As one may have expected, the emerging story is more complex than the early literature suggested, and positive as well as negative feelings can facilitate as well as impede problem solving. Unfortunately, our current understanding is mostly limited to the role of moods – and even in this domain, several crucial issues await empirical investigation, as noted earlier. We are optimistic, however, that future research will successfully specify which processing requirements are signaled by the appraisal pattern underlying specific emotions and hence likely to be elicited by the respective emotional experience. Together with a better understanding of task characteristics, this would go a long way toward understanding the impact of specific emotions on specific types of tasks.

REFERENCES

Alloy, L. B. (1988). *Cognitive processes in depression.* New York: Guilford Press.

Amthauer, R. (1970). *I-S-T 70: Intelligenz-Struktur-Test* [I-S-T 70: Intelligence Structure Test] (3rd ed.). Göttingen, Germany: Hogrefe.

Arnold, M. B. (1960). *Emotion and personality.* New York: Columbia University Press.

Blaney, P. H. (1986). Affect and memory: A review. *Psychological Bulletin, 99,* 229–246.

Bless, H., Bohner, G., Schwarz, N., & Strack, F. (1990). Mood and persuasion: A cognitive response analysis. *Personality and Social Psychology Bulletin, 16,* 331–345.

Bless, H., Clore, G. L., Schwarz, N., Golisano, V., Rabe, C., & Wölk, M. (1996). Mood and the use of scripts: Does being in a happy mood really lead to mindlessness? *Journal of Personality and Social Psychology, 71,* 665–679.

Bless, H., Schwarz, N., & Kemmelmeier, M. (1996). Mood and stereotyping: The impact of moods on the use of general knowledge structures. *European Review of Social Psychology, 7,* 63–93.

Bless, H., & Schwarz, N. (1999). Sufficient and necessary conditions in dual process models: The case of mood and information processing. In S. Chaiken and Y. Trope (Eds.), *Dual process theories in social psychology* (pp. 423–440). New York: Guilford.

Bless, H., Schwarz, N., & Wieland, R. (1996). Mood and stereotyping: The impact of category membership and individuating information. *European Journal of Social Psychology, 26*, 935–959.

Bodenhausen, G. V. (1990). Stereotypes as judgmental heuristics: Evidence of circadian variations in discrimination. *Psychological Science, 1*, 319–322.

Bodenhausen, G. V., Kramer, G. P., & Süsser, K. (1994). Happiness and stereotypic thinking in social judgment. *Journal of Personality and Social Psychology, 66*, 621–632.

Bodenhausen, G. V., Sheppard, L. A., & Kramer, G. P. (1994). Negative affect and social judgment: The differential impact of anger and sadness. *European Journal of Social Psychology, 24*, 45–62.

Bohner, G., Bless, H., Schwarz, N., & Strack, F. (1988). What triggers causal attributions? The impact of valence and subjective probability. *European Journal of Social Psychology, 18*, 335–345.

Bollnow, O. F. (1956). *Das Wesen der Stimmungen* [The nature of moods]. Frankfurt: Klostermann.

Bower, G. H. (1981). Mood and memory. *American Psychologist, 36*, 129–148.

Bower, G. H. (1991). Mood congruity of social judgments. In J. P. Forgas (Ed.), *Emotion and social judgments* (pp. 31–53). Oxford, UK: Pergamon.

Brewer, M. B. (1988). A dual process model of impression formation. In T. K. Srull & R. S. Wyer (Eds.), *Advances in social cognition* (Vol. 1, pp. 1–36). Hillsdale, NJ: Lawrence Erlbaum Associates.

Broadbent, D. E. (1971). *Decision and stress*. London: Academic Press.

Brown, J. D., & Mankowski, T. A. (1993). Self-esteem, mood, and self-evaluation: Changes in mood and the way you see you. *Journal of Personality and Social Psychology, 64*, 421–430.

Bruner, J. S., Matter, J., & Papanek, M. L. (1955). Breadth of learning as a function of drive-level and maintenance. *Psychological Review, 62*, 1–10.

Cacioppo, J. T., Priester, J. R., & Berntson, G. G. (1993). Rudimentary determinants of attitudes II: Arm flexion and extension have differential effects on attitudes. *Journal of Personality and Social Psychology, 65*, 5–17.

Cervone, D., Kopp, D. A., Schaumann, L., & Scott, W. D. (1994). Mood, self-efficacy, and performance standards: Lower moods induce higher standards for performance. *Journal of Personality and Social Psychology, 67*.

Chase, W. G., & Simon, H. A. (1973). The mind's eye in chess. In W. G. Chase (Ed.), *Visual information processing*. New York: Academic Press.

Chen, M., & Bargh, J. A. (1999). Consequences of automatic evaluations: Immediate behavioral predispositions to approach or avoid the stimulus. *Personality and Social Psychology Bulletin, 25*, 215–224.

Clore, G. L., Schwarz, N., & Conway, M. (1994). Affective causes and consequences of social information processing. In R. S. Wyer, & T. K. Srull (Eds.), *Handbook of social cognition* (2nd ed., Vol. 1, pp. 323–418). Hillsdale, NJ: Erlbaum.

Damasio, A. R. (1994). *Descarte's Error: Emotion, Reason and the Human Brain*. New York: Grosset/Putnam.

Duncker, K. (1945). On problem solving. *Psychological Monographs, 58*.

Eagly, A. H., & Chaiken, S. (1993). *The psychology of attitudes*. Fort Worth, TX: Harcourt Brace Jovanovich.

Easterbrook, J. A. (1959). The effect of emotion on cue utilization and the organization of behavior. *Psychological Review, 66,* 183–201.

Edwards, J. A., & Weary, G. (1993). Depression and the impression-formation continuum: Piecemeal processing despite the availability of category information. *Journal of Personality and Social Psychology, 64,* 636–645.

Ekstrom, R. B., French, J. W., Harman, H. H., & Dermen, D. (1976). *Manual for kit of factor-referenced cognitive tests.* Princeton, NJ: ETS.

Ellis, H. C., & Ashbrook, P. W. (1988). Resource allocation model of the effects of depressed mood states on memory. In K. Fiedler & J. Forgas (Eds.), *Affect, cognition, and social behavior.* Toronto: C. J. Hogrefe.

Fiedler, K. (1988). Emotional mood, cognitive style, and behavior regulation. In K. Fiedler & J. Forgas (Eds.), *Affect, cognition, and social behavior* (pp. 100–119). Toronto: Hogrefe International.

Fiske, S. T., & Neuberg, S. L. (1990). A continuum of impression formation, from category-based to individuating processes: Influences of information and motivation on attention and interpretation. In M. P. Zanna (Ed.), *Advances in experimental social psychology* (Vol. 23, pp. 1–74). San Diego, CA: Academic Press.

Forgas, J. P. (1995). Emotion in social judgments: Review and a new affect infusion model (AIM). *Psychological Bulletin, 117,* 39–66.

Forgas, J. P., & Bower, G. H. (1988). Affect in social and personal judgments. In K. Fiedler & J. Forgas (Eds.), *Affect, cognition, and social behavior* (pp. 183–207). Toronto: Hogrefe International.

Friedman, R. S., & Förster, J. (2000). The effects of approach and avoidance motor actions on the elements of creative insight. *Journal of Personality and Social Psychology, 79,* 477–492.

Frijda, N. H. (1986). *The emotions.* New York: Cambridge University Press.

Frijda, N. H. (1988). The laws of emotion. *American Psychologist, 43,* 349–358.

Gallagher, D., & Clore, G. L. (1985). *Effects of fear and anger on judgments of risk and blame.* Paper presented at the meetings of the Midwestern Psychological Association, Chicago.

Gick, M. L., & Holyoak, K. J. (1980). Analogical problem solving. *Cognitive Psychology, 12,* 306–355.

Gick, M. L., & Holyoak, K. J. (1983). Schema induction and analogical transfer. *Cognitive Psychology, 15,* 1–38.

Greene, T. R., & Noice, H. (1988). Influence of positive affect upon creative thinking and problem solving in children. *Psychological Reports, 63,* 895–898.

Hertel, G., Neuhof, J., Theuer, T., & Kerr, N. L. (2000). Mood effects on cooperation in small groups: Does positive mood simply lead to more cooperation? *Cognition and Emotion, 14,* 441–472.

Hesse, F. W., Kauer, G., & Spies, K. (1997). Effects of emotion-related surface similarity in analogical problem solving. *American Journal of Psychology, 110,* 357–383.

Hildebrand-Saints, L., & Weary, G. (1989). Depression and social information gathering. *Personality and Social Psychology Bulletin, 15,* 150–160.

Hirt, E. R., Levine, G. M., McDonald, H. E., Melton, R. J., & Martin, L. L. (1997). The role of mood in quantitative and qualitative aspects of performance: Single or multiple mechanisms? *Journal of Experimental Social Psychology, 33,* 602–629.

Hirt, E. R., McDonald, H. E., & Melton, R. J. (1996). Processing goals and the affect-performance link. In L. L. Martin & A. Tesser (Eds.), *Striving and feeling: Interactions among goals, affect, and self-regulation* (pp. 303–328). Hillsdale, NJ: Erlbaum.

Holyoak, K. J. (1995). Problem solving. In E. E. Smith & D. Osherson (Eds.), *An invitation to cognitive science: Thinking* (2nd ed., Vol. 3, pp. 267–296). Cambridge, MA: MIT Press.

Holyoak, K. J., & Koh, K. (1987). Surface and structural similarity in analogical transfer. *Memory & Cognition, 15,* 332–340.

Isen, A. M. (1984). Toward understanding the role of affect in cognition. In R. S. Wyer, Jr., & T. K. Srull (Eds.), *Handbook of social cognition* (Vol. 3, pp. 179–236). Hillsdale, NJ: Erlbaum.

Isen, A. M. (1987). Positive affect, cognitive processes, and social behavior. In L. Berkowitz (Ed.), *Advances in experimental social psychology* (Vol. 20, pp. 203–253). New York: Academic Press.

Isen, A. M., & Daubman, K. A. (1984). The influence of affect on categorization. *Journal of Personality and Social Psychology, 47,* 1206–1217.

Isen, A. M., Daubman, K. A., & Nowicki, G. P. (1987). Positive affect facilitates creative problem solving. *Journal of Personality and Social Psychology, 52,* 1122–1131.

Isen, A. M., Johnson, M. M. S., Mertz, E., & Robertson, G. F. (1985). The influence of positive affect on the unusualness of word associations. *Journal of Personality and Social Psychology, 48,* 1413–1426.

Isen, A. M., Shalker, T. E., Clark, M. S., & Karp, L. (1978). Affect, accessibility of material in memory, and behavior: A cognitive loop? *Journal of Personality and Social Psychology, 36,* 1–12.

Jacoby, L. L., Kelley, C. M., & Dywan, J. (1989). Memory attributions. In H. L. Roediger & F. I. M. Craik (Eds.), *Varieties of memory and consciousness: Essays in honour of Endel Tulving* (pp. 391–422). Hillsdale, NJ: Erlbaum.

Johnson, E., & Tversky, A. (1983). Affect, generalization, and the perception of risk. *Journal of Personality and Social Psychology, 45,* 20–31.

Kahneman, D., & Tversky, A. (1979). Prospect theory: An analysis of decision under risk. *Econometrica, 47,* 363–391.

Kaufmann, G., & Vosburg, S. K. (1997). "Paradoxical" mood effects on creative problem-solving. *Cognition & Emotion, 11,* 151–170.

Kelley, H. H. (1972). *Causal schemata and the attribution process.* Morristown, NJ: General Learning Press.

Keltner, D., Ellsworth, P., & Edwards, K. (1993). Beyond simple pessimism: Effects of sadness and anger on social perception. *Journal of Personality and Social Psychology, 64,* 740–752.

Keltner, D., Locke, K. D., & Audrain, P. C. (1993). The influence of attributions on the relevance of negative feelings to satisfaction. *Personality and Social Psychology Bulletin, 19,* 21–30.

Lerner, J. S., & Keltner, D. (2000). Beyond valence: Toward a model of emotion-specific influences on judgment and choice. *Cognition & Emotion, 14,* 473–492.

Luce, M., Bettman, J., & Payne, J. W. (1997). Choice processing in emotionally difficult decisions. *Journal of Experimental Psychology: Learning, Memory, and Cognition, 23,* 384–405.

Mackie, D. M., & Worth, L. T. (1989). Cognitive deficits and the mediation of positive affect in persuasion. *Journal of Personality and Social Psychology, 57,* 27–40.

Macrae, C. N., Milne, A. B., & Bodenhausen, G. V. (1994). Stereotypes as energy-saving devices: A peek inside the cognitive toolbox. *Journal of Personality and Social Psychology, 66,* 37–47.

Martin, L. L., & Stoner, P. (1996). Mood as input: What we think about how we feel determines how we think. In L. L. Martin & A. Tesser (Eds.), *Striving and feeling: Interactions among goals, affect, and self-regulation* (pp. 279–301). Hillsdale, NJ: Erlbaum.

Martin, L. L., Ward, D. W., Achée, J. W., & Wyer, R. S. (1993). Mood as input: People have to interpret the motivational implications of their moods. *Journal of Personality and Social Psychology, 64,* 317–326.

Mednick, S. T. (1962). The associative basis of the creative process. *Psychological Review, 69,* 220–232.

Melton, R. J. (1995). The role of positive affect in syllogism performance. *Personality and Social Psychology Bulletin, 21,* 788–794.

Morris, W. N. (1989). *Mood: The frame of mind.* New York: Springer-Verlag.

Murray, N., Sujan, H., Hirt, E. R., & Sujan, M. (1990). The influence of mood on categorization: A cognitive flexibility interpretation. *Journal of Personality and Social Psychology, 43,* 1244–1255.

Newell, A., & Simon, H. A. (1972). *Human problem solving.* Englewood Cliffs, NJ: Prentice-Hall.

Ortony, A., Clore, G. L., & Collins, A. (1988). *The cognitive structure of emotions.* London: Cambridge University Press.

Ottati, V., Terkildsen, N., & Hubbard, C. (1997). Happy faces elicit heuristic processing in a televised impression formation task: A cognitive tuning account. *Personality and Social Psychology Bulletin, 23,* 1144–1156.

Petty, R., & Cacioppo, J. (1986). *Communication and persuasion: Central and peripheral routes to attitude change.* New York: Springer-Verlag.

Priester, J. R., Cacioppo, J. T. & Petty, R. E. (1996). The influence of motor processes on attitudes toward novel versus familiar semantic stimuli. *Personality and Social Psychology Bulletin, 22,* 442–447.

Raghunathan, R., & Pham, M. T. (1999). All negative moods are not created equal: Motivational influences of anxiety and sadness on decision making. *Organizational Behavior and Human Decision Performance, 79,* 56–77.

Reitman, W. (1964). Heuristic decision procedures, open constraints, and the structure of ill-defined problems. In W. Shelley & G. L. Bryan (Eds.), *Human judgments and optimality.* New York: Wiley.

Runco, M. A. (1994). *Problem finding, problem solving, and creativity.* Norwood, NJ: Ablex.

Schank, R., & Abelson, R. (1977) *Scripts, plans, goals and understanding: An inquiry into human knowledge structures.* Hillsdale, NJ: Erlbaum.

Schooler, J. W., & Melcher, J. (1995). The ineffability of insight. In S. M. Smith, T. B. Ward, & R. A. Finke (Eds.), *The creative cognition approach* (pp. 97–134). New York: Guilford.

Schwarz, N. (1990). Feelings as information: Informational and motivational functions of affective states. In E. T. Higgins & R. Sorrentino (Eds.), *Handbook* of motivation and cognition: Foundations of social behavior (Vol. 2, pp. 527–561). New York: Guilford Press.

Schwarz, N. (1996). *Cognition and communication: Judgmental biases, research methods and the logic of conversation*. Hillsdale, NJ: Erlbaum.

Schwarz, N. (1998). Accessible content and accessibility experiences: The interplay of declarative and experiential information in judgment. *Personality and Social Psychology Review, 2,* 87–99.

Schwarz, N. (2001). Feelings as information: Implications for affective influences on information processing. In L. L. Martin & G. L. Clore (Eds.), *Theories of mood and cognition: A user's handbook* (pp. 159–176). Mahwah, NJ: Erlbaum.

Schwarz, N., Bless, H., & Bohner, G. (1991). Mood and persuasion: Affective states influence the processing of persuasive communications. In M. Zanna (Ed.), *Advances in experimental social psychology* (Vol. 24, pp. 161–199). San Diego, CA: Academic Press.

Schwarz, N., & Clore, G. L. (1983). Mood, misattribution, and judgments of well-being: Informative and directive functions of affective states. *Journal of Personality and Social Psychology, 45,* 513–523.

Schwarz, N., & Clore, G. L. (1988). How do I feel about it? Informative functions of affective states. In K. Fiedler & J. Forgas (Eds.), *Affect, cognition, and social behavior* (pp. 44–62). Toronto: Hogrefe International.

Schwarz, N., & Clore, G. L. (1996). Feelings and phenomenal experiences. In E. T. Higgins & A. Kruglanski (Eds.), *Social psychology: Handbook of basic principles* (pp. 433–465). New York: Guilford.

Schwarz, N., Servay, W., & Kumpf, M. (1985). Attribution of arousal as a mediator of the effectiveness of fear-arousing communications. *Journal of Applied Social Psychology, 15,* 74–78.

Schwarz, N., Strack, F., Kommer, D., & Wagner, D. (1987). Soccer, rooms and the quality of your life: Mood effects on judgments of satisfaction with life in general and with specific life-domains. *European Journal of Social Psychology, 17,* 69–79.

Simon, H. (1967). Motivational and emotional controls of cognition. *Psychological Review, 74,* 29–39.

Simon, H. A. (1978). Information processing theory of human problem solving. In W. K. Estes (Ed.), *Handbook of learning and cognitive processes* (Vol. 5). Hillsdale, NJ: Erlbaum.

Sinclair, R. C. (1988). Mood, categorization breadth, and performance appraisal: The effects of order of information acquisition and affective state on halo, accuracy, information retrieval, and evaluations. *Organizational Behavior and Human Decision Processes, 42,* 22–46.

Sinclair, R. C., & Mark, M. M. (1992). The influence of mood state on judgment and action: Effects on persuasion, categorization, social justice, person perception, and judgmental accuracy. In L. L. Martin & A. Tesser (Eds.), *The construction of social judgment* (pp. 165–193). Hillsdale, NJ: Erlbaum.

Sinclair, R. C., & Mark, M. M. (1995). The effects of mood state on judgmental accuracy: Processing strategy as a mechanism. *Cognition and Emotion, 9,* 417–438.

Sinclair, R. C., Mark, M. M., & Clore, G. L. (1994). Mood-related persuasion depends on misattributions. *Social Cognition, 12,* 309–326.

Sinclair, R. C., Soldat, A. S., & Mark, M. M. (1998). Affective cues and processing strategy: Color coded forms influence performance. *Teaching of Psychology, 25,* 130–132.

Singer, J. A., & Salovey, P. (1988). Mood and memory: Evaluating the network theory of affect. *Clinical Psychology Review, 8,* 211–251.

Soldat, A. S., Sinclair, R. C., & Mark, M. M. (1997). Color as an environmental processing cue: External affective cues can directly affect processing strategy without affecting mood. *Social Cognition, 15,* 55–71.

Thayer, R. E. (1996). *The origin of everyday moods.* New York: Oxford University Press.

Tiedens, L. Z., & Linton, S. (2001). Judgment under emotional certainty and uncertainty: The effects of specific emotions on information processing. *Journal of Personality and Social Psychology, 81,* 973–988.

Wegener, D. T., Petty, R. E., & Smith, S. M. (1995). Positive mood can increase or decrease message scrutiny. *Journal of Personality and Social Psychology, 69,* 5–15.

Wegner, D. M., & Vallacher, R. R. (1986). Action identification. In R. M. Sorrentino & E. T. Higgins (Eds.), *Handbook of motivation and cognition: Foundations of social behavior* (pp. 550–582). New York: Guilford.

Wertheimer, M. (1959). *Productive thinking.* New York: Harper & Row.

Witkin, H. A., Oltman, P. K., Raskin, E., & Karp, S. A. (1971). *A manual for the embedded figures test.* Palo Alto, CA: Consulting Psychologist Press.

Worth, L. T., & Mackie, D. M. (1987). Cognitive mediation of positive mood in persuasion. *Social Cognition, 5,* 76–94.

Zajonc, R. B. (1980). Feeling and thinking: Preferences need no inferences. *American Psychologist, 35,* 151–175.

ACKNOWLEDGMENT

Preparation of this chapter was supported by a fellowship from the Center for Advanced Study in the Behavioral Sciences, Stanford, CA, to the first author.

10

The Fundamental Computational Biases of Human Cognition

Heuristics That (Sometimes) Impair Decision Making and Problem Solving

Keith E. Stanovich

Consider the following syllogism. Ask yourself whether it is valid – whether the conclusion follows logically from the two premises:

Premise 1: All living things need water.
Premise 2: Roses need water.
Therefore, Roses are living things.

What do you think? Judge the conclusion either logically valid or invalid before reading on.

If you are like about 70% of the university students who have been given this problem, you will think that the conclusion is valid. And if you did think that it was valid, like 70% of university students who have been given this problem, you would be wrong (Markovits & Nantel, 1989; Sá, West, & Stanovich, 1999; Stanovich & West, 1998c). Premise 1 says that all living things need water, not that all things that need water are living things. So just because roses need water, it doesn't follow from Premise 1 that they are living things. If that is still not clear, it probably will be after you consider the following syllogism with exactly the same structure:

Premise 1: All insects need oxygen.
Premise 2: Mice need oxygen.
Therefore, Mice are insects.

Now it seems pretty clear that the conclusion does not follow from the premises. If the logically equivalent "mice" syllogism is solved so easily, why is the "rose" problem so hard? Well for one thing, the conclusion (roses are living things) seems so reasonable and you know it to be true in the real world. And that is the rub. Logical validity is not about the believability of the conclusion; it is about whether the conclusion necessarily follows from the premises. The same thing that made the rose problem so hard made the mice problem easy. The fact that "mice are insects" is not definitionally true in the world we live in might have made it easier to see that the conclusion did not follow logically from the two premises.

In both of these problems, prior knowledge about the nature of the world (that roses are living things and that mice are not insects) was becoming implicated in a type of judgment (judgments of logical validity) that is supposed to be independent of content. In the rose problem prior knowledge was interfering, and in the mice problem prior knowledge was facilitative. In fact, if we really wanted to test a person's ability to process the relationships in this syllogism, we might have used totally unfamiliar material. For example, we might have told you to imagine you were visiting another planet and that you found out the following two facts:

All animals of the hudon class are ferocious.
Wampets are ferocious.

We might then ask you to evaluate whether it logically follows that: Wampets are animals of the hudon class. We can see here that the conclusion does not follow. Research has shown that it is easier to see that the conclusion lacks validity in this unfamiliar version than it is in the rose version, but it is harder to see that the conclusion does not follow in the unfamiliar version than it is in the mice version (Markovits & Nantel, 1989; Sá et al., 1999). These differences prove that factual knowledge is becoming implicated in both the rose and mice problems, even though the content of syllogisms should have no impact on their logical validity. The effect on the rose problem is large. Only about 32% of university students solve it (Sá et al., 1999), whereas the same participants respond correctly 78% of the time on logically equivalent versions with unfamiliar material (versions where prior knowledge does not get in the way).

The rose problem illustrates one of the fundamental computational biases of human cognition: the tendency to automatically bring prior knowledge to bear when solving problems. The fact that prior knowledge is implicated in performance on this problem, even when the person is explicitly told to ignore the real-world believability of the conclusion, illustrates that this tendency toward contextualizing problems with prior knowledge is so ubiquitous that it cannot easily be turned off – hence its characterization here as a fundamental computational bias[1] (one that pervades virtually all

[1] It cannot be emphasized enough that the term "bias" is used throughout this chapter to denote "a preponderating disposition or propensity" (*The Compact Edition of the Oxford Short English Dictionary*, p. 211) and not a processing *error*. That a processing bias does not necessarily imply a cognitive error is a point repeatedly emphasized by the critics of the heuristics and biases literature (Funder, 1987; Gigerenzer, 1996a; Hastie & Rasinski, 1988; Kruglanski & Ajzen, 1983), but in fact it was always the position of the original heuristics and biases researchers themselves (Kahneman, 2000; Kahneman & Tversky, 1973, 1996; Tversky & Kahneman, 1974). Thus, the use of the term *bias* here is meant to connote "default value" rather than "error." Under the assumption that computational biases result

thinking, whether we like it or not). Of course, the tendency to use prior knowledge to supplement problem solving is more often a help than a hindrance. Nevertheless, it is argued below that there are certain improbable but important situations in modern life in which the fundamental computational biases must be overridden, and that failure to do so can have negative real-life consequences. As research summarized in Baron (1998), Belsky and Gilovich (1999), Dawes (1988), Sutherland (1992), and Thaler (1992) has shown, because of the failure to override fundamental computational biases, physicians choose less effective medical treatments; people fail to accurately assess risks in their environment; information is misused in legal proceedings; millions of dollars are spent on unneeded projects by government and private industry; parents fail to vaccinate their children; unnecessary surgery is performed; animals are hunted to extinction; billions of dollars are wasted on quack medical remedies; and costly financial misjudgments are made.

In the remainder of this chapter, I describe a collection of related processing styles that I have termed *the fundamental computational biases of human cognition* (Stanovich, 1999). It is argued, consistent with arguments in evolutionary psychology (e.g., Badcock, 2000; Barkow, Cosmides, & Tooby, 1992; Buss, 1999, 2000; Cartwright, 2000; Cosmides & Tooby, 1994; Pinker, 1997; Plotkin, 1998; Tooby & Cosmides, 1992), that these fundamental computational biases are resident in the brain because they were adaptive in the so-called environment of evolutionary adaptedness (EEA) that existed throughout the Pleistocene (Buss, 1999). In short, it is argued that these computational biases make evolutionary sense. Nevertheless, it is also argued that despite their usefulness in the EEA, and despite the fact that even in the present environment they are more useful than not, the modern world presents situations in which the type of contextualization rendered by the fundamental computational biases proves extremely problematic. Such situations are numerically minority situations, but they tend to be ones where a misjudgment tends to have disproportionately large consequences for a person's future utility maximization – for the future fulfillment of the person's life's goals, whatever those goals may be (see Baron, 1993, 1994). In these situations, in order for people to maximize personal utility, they will need to override the fundamental computational biases. We will see that humans have available other cognitive structures (with somewhat different processing architectures) to use in such situations, structures that have the capability of overriding the fundamental computational biases.

In short, in situations where the present human environment is similar to the EEA, the human brain is characterized by fundamental computational

from evolutionary adaptations of the brain (Cosmides & Tooby, 1994), it is likely that they are efficacious in many situations.

biases that bring massive amounts of stored contextual information to bear on the problem. However, when technological societies present new problems that confound these evolutionarily adapted mechanisms, humans must use cognitive mechanisms that are in part cultural inventions (see Dennett, 1991) to override the fundamental computational biases that, in these situations, will prime the wrong response. These culturally induced processing modes more closely resemble the abstract, rule-based, serial processes in many more traditional models of problem solving (Rips, 1994; Sloman, 1996).

THE FUNDAMENTAL COMPUTATIONAL BIASES

The fundamental computational biases of human cognition work separately and sometimes in combination to ensure that problems with which we are faced are heavily contextualized. They are part of the automatic inferential machinery of the brain that supplements problem solving with stored declarative knowledge, linguistic information, and social knowledge. These processes provide rich supplemental knowledge to augment the sometimes fragmentary and incomplete information we receive when faced with a real-world problem. The four interrelated biases that I introduce here are: (1) the tendency to contextualize a problem with as much prior knowledge as is easily accessible, even when the problem is formal and the only solution is a content-free rule; (2) the tendency to "socialize" problems, even in situations where interpersonal cues are few; (3) the tendency to see deliberative design and pattern in situations that lack intentional design and pattern; (4) the tendency toward a narrative mode of thought.

Automatic Contextualization: The Use of Prior Knowledge and Context

The property of cognition illustrated in the rose syllogism problem is sometimes termed *knowledge projection* (Stanovich, 1999). In the rose example, we can see why the tendency to supplement problems with prior knowledge is deemed an automatic tendency. It cannot be "shut off," even in situations (such as that of judging logical validity) where knowledge gets in the way and the problem solver is actively trying to suppress it. The automatic activation of prior knowledge is not limited to syllogistic reasoning problems. Experiments have shown it to operate in several different problem-solving domains and in several different paradigms (Banaji & Greenwald, 1995; Evans, Over, & Manktelow, 1993; Greenwald, McGhee, & Schwartz, 1998; Kunda, 1999; Nickerson, 1999; Nickerson, Baddeley, & Freeman, 1987; Sá & Stanovich, 2001; Sá et al., 1999; Stanovich, 1999; Stanovich & West, 1997).

Before looking at some of these additional domains, it should be noted that sometimes the knowledge that is brought to bear on a problem is not accurate. This does not change the nature or logic of the phenomenon. In fact, what often is projected onto a problem is not knowledge at all but, instead, inadequately substantiated opinion. Thus, since philosophers often define knowledge as justified true belief, in some paradigms in cognitive psychology, strictly speaking, what we are looking at is not knowledge projection, because the belief may not be justified or true. In some cases, we should be talking about belief projection rather than knowledge projection. Nevertheless, we do not distinguish the two here, because the line between them can be very fuzzy and because they appear to reflect an underlying phenomenon that is very similar (Sá & Stanovich, 2001).

One belief projection paradigm that has been extensively studied in the reasoning literature is the evaluation of information in 2 × 2 contingency tables (Levin, Wasserman, & Kao, 1993; Schustack & Sternberg, 1981; Stanovich & West, 1998d). For example, in one such paradigm, participants are asked to evaluate the efficacy of a drug based on a hypothetical well-designed scientific experiment. They are told that:

150 people received the drug and were not cured
150 people received the drug and were cured
75 people did not receive the drug and were not cured
300 people did not receive the drug and were cured

They are asked to evaluate the effectiveness of the drug based on this information. In this case, they have to detect that the drug is ineffective. In fact, not only is it ineffective, it is positively harmful. Only 50% of the people who received the drug were cured (150 out of 300), but 80% of those who did *not* receive the drug were cured (300 out of 375).

The drug context of this problem is fairly neutral to most participants. But it is easy to trigger prior knowledge and belief by using problems that have more content. For example, in one study, Richard West and I (Stanovich & West, 1998d) asked participants to evaluate the outcome of an experiment to test whether having siblings is associated with sociability. The association presented was the same as in the drug experiment:

150 children had siblings and were not sociable
150 children had siblings and were sociable
75 children did not have siblings and were not sociable
300 children did not have siblings and were sociable

Now, however, it was more difficult for our participants (who, as a group, *did* think that sociability was positively associated with having siblings) to see that, in these data, having siblings was *negatively* associated with sociability. As in the rose syllogism problem, prior knowledge/belief automatically colored the evaluation of the data. The fact that the numerical paradigm here was quite different from the verbal reasoning domain of syllogistic reasoning indicates the generality of the phenomenon.

Controlled studies (e.g., Broniarczyk & Alba, 1994; King & Koehler, 2000; Levin et al., 1993; Nisbett & Ross, 1980) have demonstrated that when people have a prior belief that two variables are connected, they tend to see that connection even in data in which the two variables are totally unconnected. Unfortunately, this finding generalizes to some real-world situations that adversely affect people's lives. For example, many psychological practitioners continue to believe in the efficacy of the Rorschach Test. This is the famous inkblot test in which the client responds to blotches on a white paper. Because the inkblots lack structure, the theory is that people will respond to them in the same style that they typically respond to ambiguity and thus reveal "hidden" psychological traits. The test is called *projective* because the clients presumably "project" unconscious psychological thoughts and feelings in their responses to the inkblots. The problem with all of this is that there is no evidence that the Rorschach Test provides any additional diagnostic utility when used as a "projective" test (Dawes, 1994; Garb, Florio, & Grove, 1998; Lilienfeld, 1999; Lilienfeld, Wood, & Garb, 2000; Shontz & Green, 1992; Widiger & Schilling, 1980; Wood, Nezworski, & Stejskal, 1996). Belief in the Rorschach Test arises from the phenomenon of illusory correlation. Clinicians see relationships in response patterns because they believe they are there, not because they are actually present in the pattern of responses being observed (Broniarczyk & Alba, 1994; Chapman & Chapman, 1967, 1969; King & Koehler, 2000).

One final paradigm illustrates the range of tasks in which knowledge/belief projection has been studied. The paradigm derives from the informal reasoning and problem-solving research tradition (Baron, 1995; Klaczynski, Gordon, & Fauth, 1997; Kuhn, 1991, 1993, 1996; Perkins, Farady, & Bushey, 1991; Sternberg & Wagner, 1986; Voss, Perkins, & Segal, 1991). Unlike deductive reasoning paradigms where there is a single right answer to a problem, research on informal reasoning tries to mimic the type of argumentation and reasoning that goes on in everyday life. This type of argumentation relies on inductive arguments more than deductive arguments. Good arguments in these more realistic contexts tend to be probabilistic and tend to be what philosophers call defeasible: Unlike deductive arguments, they can be defeated by additional information that can be brought to bear (see Hilton, 1995; Johnson-Laird, 1999; Oaksford & Chater, 1995; Pollock, 1995; Stevenson & Over, 1995).

Richard West and I (see Stanovich & West, 1997) developed an argument evaluation test of informal reasoning ability and we can use it to illustrate how belief projection operates in this domain by considering one problem from it. In this particular problem, the respondents are presented with a protagonist, Dale, who believes a particular proposition. In this case, the proposition is that "Students, not the general public, should have the ultimate voice in setting university policies." Dale is said to justify the belief with the following argument: "Because students are the ones who must pay the costs of running the university through tuition, they should have the ultimate voice in setting university policies." A critic then attacks Dale's justification with the following counterargument: "Tuition covers less than one half the cost of an education at most universities" (the respondent is told to assume that this is factually correct). Finally, Dale rebuts the critic with the following argument: "Because it is the students who are directly influenced by university policies, they are the ones who should make the ultimate decisions." Respondents are asked to rate the quality of Dale's rebuttal argument, and they are specifically focused on Dale's argument as a rebuttal of the counterargument made by the critic. Furthermore, the respondents are very specifically reminded to evaluate the quality of the rebuttal *independently* of their feelings about Dale's original belief.

This problem was given to eight university professors of philosophy and psychology, and all but one of them agreed that the rebuttal argument was weak because it lacked relevance as a refutation of the critic's counterargument. However, a group of university students (who had a mean prior belief about the matter that corresponded to "agree" on the response scale) gave the rebuttal argument a mean rating of "strong" on the scale. The influence of prior belief was confirmed more directly by the finding that the students who agreed with the original proposition rated Dale's rebuttal significantly more highly than those who disagreed with the original proposition put forward by Dale. In our subsequent work with the argument evaluation test, we have found that belief projection operates in a variety of informal reasoning situations and across a host of topics including taxes, the legal drinking age, car safety, the validity of interviews, fairness of Social Security, child care, welfare payments, prison sentencing, the speed limit, the death penalty, the voting age, labor unions, and the effects of secondhand smoke.

The three tasks discussed here – syllogistic reasoning, reasoning about numerical covariation data, and informal reasoning – are just a small sampling from a large number of paradigms that have demonstrated the tendency to contextualize a problem-solving situation with prior knowledge and prior belief, even when the problem requires content-free inference and evaluation procedures. These findings confirm the observation of Evans, Barston, and Pollard (1983) that "specific features of problem content, and their semantic associations, constitute the dominant influence on thought" (p. 295).

The tendency to supplement formal, decontextualized problems with prior knowledge is often commented on in both the problem-solving and decision-making literatures. It seems that even in problems that are viewed purely formally by the experimenter, the slightest bit of real-world information seems to provoke contextual inferences. For example, Doherty and Mynatt (1990) used a relatively sparse toy problem to study Bayesian reasoning:

> Imagine you are a doctor. A patient comes to you with a red rash on his fingers. What information would you want in order to diagnose whether the patient has the disease Digirosa? Below are four pieces of information that may or may not be relevant to the diagnosis. Please indicate *all* of the pieces of information that are necessary to make the diagnosis, but *only* those pieces of information that are necessary to do so.

Participants then chose from the alternatives listed in the order: % of people without Digirosa who have a red rash, % of people with Digirosa, % of people without Digirosa, and % of people with Digirosa who have a red rash. These alternatives represented the choices of $P(D/\sim H)$, $P(H)$, $P(\sim H)$, and $P(D/H)$, respectively, from Bayes's rule for conditioning hypotheses based on data. Our concern here is not with Bayes's rule per se, but the fact that even in a problem as stripped down as this one, participants tended to import contextual information based on their prior knowledge (contextual information that in this case could only be disruptive because all necessary information is already in the problem). Doherty and Mynatt (1990) observed that many participants "brought real-world knowledge to the task, knowledge about the relations between symptoms and diseases in general and knowledge about rashes in particular" (p. 8). These participant responses exemplify the tendency toward automatic contextualization that Evans et al. (1993) stress is often a generally adaptive characteristic of thought: "The purpose of reasoning is best served by drawing inferences from all our beliefs, not just from an artificially restricted set of premises" (p. 175).

Philosopher Nicholas Rescher (1988) emphasizes how contextualization with prior knowledge beyond the explicitly stated is a pervasive aspect of cognitive life. For example, Rescher (1988) draws attention to the enthymematic character of much human reasoning and problem solving. In logic, a syllogism with an unstated premise is called an enthymeme. In his logic text, Kelley (1990) provides the example "John will support the gun control law because he's a liberal" and notes that the implicit argument is: (a) All liberals support gun control; (b) John is a liberal; (c) John will support a gun control law. But (a) is unstated, so the argument is enthymematic. Rescher argues that "we frequently make substantive assumptions about how things stand in the world on the basis of experience or inculcation, and the incorrect conclusions people draw can stem from these *assumptions* rather than from any error of inferential reasoning" (pp. 195–196). In reviewing the earlier literature on content effects in reasoning and problem solving, Evans (1982) refers to how it is a ubiquitous finding that "in effect, the subject reasons with an augmented problem space, enriched by relevant personal experience" (p. 225). The enthymematic reasoning styles that form one aspect of the fundamental computational bias are thus natural and nearly universal reasoning styles of human beings, perhaps because of their evolutionary adaptiveness (Cosmides & Tooby, 1992; Pinker, 1997). They will thus facilitate reasoning when context reinforces the conclusion of any explicitly stated information (see Stevenson, 1993). But, equally obviously, they will be maladaptive when the situation demands a *non*enthymematic reasoning style (one where context must be ignored or decoupled).

The enthymematic aspect of the fundamental computational bias thus guarantees that when the environment calls on a person to fix beliefs via a content-free construal – without supplementing with additional inferred information – then they will reason poorly. An example is provided by the most investigated task in the entire reasoning and problem-solving literature: Wason's (1966) selection task. The participant is shown four cards lying on a table showing two letters and two numbers (A, D, 3, 8). They are told that each card has a number on one side and a letter on the other and that the experimenter has the following rule (of the "if P, then Q" type) in mind with respect to the four cards: "If there is a vowel on one side of the card, then there is an even number on the other side." The participant is then told that he/she must turn over whichever cards are necessary to determine whether the experimenter's rule is true or false. Performance on such abstract versions of the selection task is extremely low (Evans, Newstead, & Byrne, 1993; Manktelow, 1999; Newstead & Evans, 1995). Typically, less than 10% of participants make the correct selections of the A card (P) and 3 card (not-Q) – the only two cards that could falsify the rule. The most common incorrect choices made by participants are the A card and the 8 card (P and Q) or the selection of the A card only (P).

Numerous alternative explanations for the preponderance of incorrect PQ and P responses have been given (see Evans, Newstead, & Byrne, 1993; Hardman, 1998; Johnson-Laird, 1999; Liberman & Klar, 1996; Margolis, 1987; Newstead & Evans, 1995; Oaksford & Chater, 1994; Sperber, Cara, & Girotto, 1995; Stanovich & West, 1998a). Notably, several of these alternative explanations involve the assumption that the participant is reading more into the instructions than is actually there. For example, Oaksford and Chater's (1994) analysis of the selection task assumes that participants approach the task as an inductive problem in data selection with assumptions about the relative rarity of the various *classes* (vowels, odd numbers) of cards. That is, despite the fact the instructions refer to *four cards only*, it is proposed that the participant is thinking that they are sampling from four *classes* (a bunch of vowels, a bunch of consonants, etc.). Now imagine that you are verifying the statement "if you eat tripe you will get sick" in the real world. Of course you would sample from the class "people who eat tripe" to verify or falsify it. However, would you sample from the class of "people who are not sick"? Probably not, because this class is too big. But you might well sample from the class "people who are sick" to see if any of them have eaten tripe.

Such an approach to the problem is entirely enthymematic. The participant is assumed to be adding details and context to the problem, none of which is present in the actual instructions. Nothing at all has been said in the instructions about *classes*; the instructions refer to four cards only. But the alternative explanation of Oaksford and Chater (1994) assumes that the participants are thinking in terms of sampling from classes of cards. Participants even have implicit hypotheses about the relative rarity of these classes according to the particular model of performance championed by Oaksford and Chater (1994). Also, despite the fact that the instructions speak in terms of determining truth and falsity, most participants are thought to ignore this and instead to think in terms of inductive probabilities. In short, the deductive requirements of the instructions violate the fundamental computational bias of most participants, who proceed instead to solve a contextualized, familiar, inductive version of the problem.

Margolis (1987) has proposed another highly enthymematic interpretation on the part of participants to explain the incorrect choice, one that again involves the participant thinking about categories even when nothing about categories has been mentioned in the instructions. He argues that some individuals develop an open reading of the task (in terms of choosing entire categories) rather than a closed reading (in terms of choosing individual cards). Margolis (1987) demonstrates the distinction by suggesting a selection task in which participants are given the rule: "If it says swan on one side of a card, it must say white on the other." Given the four categories of cards – swan, raven, black, white – the participants are asked which categories they would need to examine exhaustively to test whether there has been a violation of the rule. Many people familiar with selection tasks do not recognize that this is not a selection task in the traditional sense. The correct answer is not that categories P and not-Q should be picked. In this open scenario, only P *or* not-Q need be chosen, but not both. Examining all swans will reveal any violations of the rule, as will examining all black things. But examining both provides only a redundant opportunity to see a violation. This open scenario (where one chooses categories) is different from the closed selection task scenario where one must check designated exemplars of the stated rule. If the participant views the task from an open scenario, then P-only is a reasonable choice. If the participant adopts a biconditional interpretation, then they should choose categories P and Q – the modal response in the selection task.

There are continuing disputes about whether either the Oaksford and Chater (1994) or the Margolis (1987) interpretation of the selection task is the correct one (see Gebauer & Laming, 1997; Griggs, 1989; Hardman,

1998; Oaksford & Chater, 1995, 1996; Sperber et al., 1995; Stanovich & West, 1998a). It looks instead as if there a variety of different interpretations that could lead to the PQ response and that the task is probably characterized by multiple interpretations (see Gebauer & Laming, 1997). The key point is that both of these interpretations posit the recruitment of knowledge and scenarios *extrinsic* to the instructions – an enthymematic style of reasoning that adds unstated information to further contextualize the problem.

The Tendency to "Socialize" Abstract Problems

Hilton (1995) describes the following conversational exchange:

Q: How is your family?
A: Fairly well, thank you.

Then he asks us to consider the same man who answered the above question engaging in the next exchange with a different person, perhaps even on the same day:

Q: How is your wife?
A. Not too good I'm afraid.
Q: And how is your family?
A: Extremely well, thank you.

The man has answered the exact same question ("How is your family?") in two different ways on the same day. Should we consider the man's responses irrational? Hilton (1995) argues that of course we would not. Context is everything here. What if the man's wife had recently lost a close friend but the man's two children were doing just great? That might have provoked the "fairly" well in the first exchange because the man took "family" to mean wife and kids. But in the second instance the man had already provided information about his wife, so he feels bound to interpret "family" as "the kids only" so that he does not burden the questioner with knowledge that the questioner already has.

Hilton (1995) analyzes this case in terms of Grice's (1975) norms of rational communication (see Hilton & Slugoski, 2000; Sperber & Wilson, 1986; Sperber et al., 1995), which require that the speaker be cooperative with the listener, and one of the primary ways that speakers attempt to be cooperative is by not being redundant. The key to understanding the so-called Gricean maxims of communication is to see that to understand a speaker's meaning, the listener must comprehend not only the meaning of what is spoken, but also what is implicated in a given context, assuming that the speaker intends to be cooperative. So, for example, Hilton (1995) notes that the statement "I went to the cinema last night" is taken to imply that you saw a film even though that was not explicitly stated. Hilton (1995) points out that the "default assumption of conversational rationality enjoins . . . [a person] to go beyond the information given in making inferences about what is required of them" (p. 257). These additional pieces of information are termed conversational implicatures. Hilton (1995) illustrates that these implicatures share properties with inductive inference. For example, they are ampliative: They are conclusions that contain more information than the premises (see also Levinson, 1995).

Grice (1975; see also Hilton, 1995; Hilton & Slugoski, 2000; Levinson, 1983, 1995; Schwarz, 1996; Sperber & Wilson, 1986) embeds under his superordinate principle of communicative cooperativeness four maxims: quality (try to make sure that your contribution is true), quantity (make your contribution informative but do not make it more informative than is required), relation (make your contribution relevant), and manner (do not be unnecessarily ambiguous or obscure). Hilton (1995) stresses that the Gricean maxims apply not just to the production of speech but to our comprehension and interpretation as well. Indeed, he develops the idea that humans automatically apply them, even in situations that are not characterized by interactive exchange. Hilton (1995) argues that people treat even decontextualized and depersonalized situations as conversational exchanges with an active interlocutor: "that no utterance is depersonalized, all messages have a source, and that reasoning and inference processes typically operate on socially communicated information" (p. 267). In short, people tend to treat even depersonalized communications as quasipersonal linguistic encounters in a social context. As in our previous discussion of the automatic recruitment of prior knowledge, this too is a type of automatic use of stored information. But in the present case, the additional information that is recruited is information about pragmatic expectancies in conversational exchanges. As with the use of prior knowledge, the linguistic socialization of situations is most often a useful cognitive skill (indeed, a necessary and quite astounding one; see Levinson, 1995). However, as is argued in a section below, it can create difficulties for problem solving in a modern technological society with its high degree of decontextualization.

It has not proven difficult to find experimental situations where Gricean implicatures were operating to make the solution of a decontextualized problem difficult. Consider the demonstration by Tversky and Kahneman (1983) that people show a conjunction fallacy in probabilistic reasoning. An example is provided by the much-investigated Linda Problem (Tversky & Kahneman, 1983):

Linda is 31 years old, single, outspoken, and very bright. She majored in philosophy. As a student, she was deeply concerned with issues of discrimination and social justice, and also participated in anti-nuclear demonstrations. Please rank the following statements by their probability, using 1 for the most probable and 8 for th̲ probable.

a. Linda is a teacher in an elementary school
b. Linda works in a bookstore and takes Yoga classes
c. Linda is active in the feminist movement
d. Linda is a psychiatric social worker
e. Linda is a member of the League of Women Voters
f. Linda is a bank teller
g. Linda is an insurance salesperson
h. Linda is a bank teller and is active in the feminist movement

Because alternative h (Linda is a bank teller and is active in the feminist movement) is the conjunction of alternatives c and f, the probability of h cannot be higher than that of either c (Linda is active in the feminist movement) or f (Linda is a bank teller), yet 85% of the participants in Tversky and Kahneman's (1983) study rated alternative h as more probable than f, thus displaying the conjunction fallacy. Those investigators argued that logical reasoning on the problem (all feminist bank tellers are also bank tellers, so h cannot be more probable than f) was trumped by a heuristic based on so-called representativeness that primes answers to problems based on an assessment of similarity (a feminist bank teller seems to overlap more with the description of Linda than does the alternative "bank teller"). Of course, logic dictates that the subset (feminist bank teller)–superset (bank teller) relationship should trump assessments of representativeness when judgments of probability are at issue.

A large literature on the conjunction effect has established that representativeness is not the only reason that the conjunction effect occurs (Hertwig & Gigerenzer, 1999). However, our interest here is in several explanations that posit that participants are imposing on the problem social assumptions of conversational relevance (Adler, 1984, 1991; Dulany & Hilton, 1991; Hertwig & Gigerenzer, 1999; Hilton, 1995; Hilton & Slugoski, 2000; Macdonald & Gilhooly, 1990; Slugoski & Wilson, 1998). Hilton (1995), for example, provides a Gricean explanation of participants' behavior on the Linda Problem. Under the assumption that the detailed information given about the target means that the experimenter knows a considerable amount about Linda, then it is reasonable to think that the phrase "Linda is a bank teller" in the list of alternatives does not contain the phrase "and is not active in the feminist movement" because the experimenter already knows this to be the case. If "Linda is a bank teller" is interpreted in this way, then rating h as more probable than f no longer represents a conjunction fallacy. Indeed, there is some evidence that participants are reading this into the problem (Dulany & Hilton, 1991; Hertwig & Gigerenzer, 1999; Messer & Griggs, 1993; Politzer & Noveck, 1991; Tversky & Kahneman, 1983).

Schwarz (1996) discusses a host of demonstrations such as this, situations in the reasoning and problem-solving literature where participants interpret depersonalized and decontextualized communications as if they were personalized communications from someone engaged in an ongoing interaction with them. The phenomenon is real. But this leaves the question of why *would* someone interpret the words on a sheet of paper from an experimenter or survey researcher (who is often not even physically present) as an exchange in an ongoing personalized discussion? Recent speculative, interdisciplinary theories about the origins of human intelligence may provide the answer. These theories, although varied in their details, all posit that much of human intelligence has foundations in social interaction (Baldwin, 2000; Barton & Dunbar, 1997; Blackmore, 1999; Brothers, 1990; Bugental, 2000; Byrne & Whiten, 1988; Caporael, 1997; Cosmides, 1989; Cosmides & Tooby, 1992; Cummins, 1996; Dunbar, 1998; Gibbard, 1990; Gigerenzer, 1996b; Goody, 1995; Humphrey, 1976, 1986; Jolly, 1966; Kummer, Daston, Gigerenzer, & Silk, 1997; Levinson, 1995; Mithen, 1996; Tomasello, 1998, 1999; Whiten & Byrne, 1997).

In a seminal essay that set the stage for this hypothesis, Nicholas Humphrey (1976) argued that the impetus for the development of primate intelligence was the need to master the social world more so than the physical world. Based on his observation of nonhuman primates, Humphrey concluded that the knowledge and information processing necessary to engage efficiently with the physical world seemed modest compared with the rapidly changing demands of the social world. Humphrey posited that these social demands are associated with higher intelligence. Humphrey's hypotheses (and other related speculations; see Jolly, 1966) in part helped to spawn a host of research on so-called Machiavellian intelligence (Byrne & Whiten, 1988; Whiten & Byrne, 1997): the ability to engage in multiple and rapidly changing cooperative and competitive interchanges with a host of conspecifics and maintain these relationships over a long period of time.

The key aspects of Humphrey's (1976) speculations that are critical for the present discussion are that all further advances in cognitive capabilities were built upon a social substrate and that these social mechanisms are still present in our brains and pervasively color all of our cognition. They were not *replaced* by the more analytic intelligence developed in humans. Thus, a social orientation toward problems is always available as a default processing mode when computational demands become onerous. The cognitive architecture is one where analytic cognition was laid down on top of the modules for social cognition that were already in place. In this feature, the architecture proposed is like Dennett's (1996) notion of four different "kinds of minds" that all overlap with each other in the brain and that all are simultaneously active in controlling behavior (see Stanovich & West, 2000).

Because the social exchanges that provided the environment of evolutionary adaptation for social intelligence involved fluid transactional exchanges with partners engaged in their own dynamic problem solving, Humphrey (1976) argues that the thinking styles involved became the dominant or default ways of approaching problems. Humphrey felt that this processing bias – the "predisposition among people to try to fit nonsocial material into a social mould" (p. 312) – would always compete with subsequent types of intelligence ("kinds of minds") that might develop. The cognitive illusions demonstrated by three decades of work in problem solving, reasoning, and decision making (Evans, 1989; Kahneman, Slovic, & Tversky, 1982; Kahneman & Tversky, 1996, 2000; Stanovich, 1999) seem to bear this out. As in the Linda Problem and four-card selection task discussed above, the literature is full of problems where an abstract, decontextualized – but computationally expensive – approach is required for the normatively appropriate answer. However, often alongside such a solution resides a tempting social approach ("oh, yeah, the author of this knows a lot about Linda") that with little computational effort will prime a response.

In short, the social intelligence hypothesis posits that evolutionary pressures were focused more on negotiating cooperative mutual intersubjectivity than on understanding the natural world. Having as its goals the ability to model other minds in order to read intention and to make rapid interactional moves based on those modeled intentions, interactional intelligence (to use Levinson's [1995] term) is composed of the mechanisms that support a Gricean theory of communication that relies on intention attribution. This social, or interactional, intelligence forms that substrate on which all future evolutionary and cultural developments in modes of thought are overlaid.

Thus, as Humphrey (1976) puts it, "for better or worse, styles of thinking which are primarily suited to social problem-solving colour the behaviour of man and other primates even toward the inanimate world" (p. 316). This social orientation toward the inanimate world leads to one of the other fundamental computational biases that is both a strength of cognition and also sometimes a source of error when dealing with the abstract aspects of the modern technological world: the tendency to see deliberate design and pattern in situations that lack intentional design.

Seeing Intentional Design in Random Events

The tendency of a socially based human intelligence to respond as if in a social dynamic even when faced with the impersonal or random has other consequences as well, particularly when faced with unpatterned events in the world. As Humphrey (1976) noted, "thus the gambler at the roulette table, who continues to bet on the red square precisely because he has already lost on red repeatedly, is behaving as though he expects the behaviour of the roulette wheel to respond eventually to his persistent overtures" (p. 313). Levinson (1995) proposes that the interactional intelligence behind conversational understanding operates with an important default: that the conversational puzzles it is trying to solve were intentionally "*designed* to be solved and the clues have been designed to be sufficient to yield a determinate solution" (p. 238). This makes it hard to fathom the concept of a "design without a designer" that is at the heart of the concept of evolution (Dawkins, 1986; Dennett, 1995). As Denzau and North (1994) have argued, "it may be an evolutionarily superior survival trait to have explanations for inexplicable phenomena; or this may just be a by-product of the curiosity which helps make humans model builders" (pp. 12–13).

Levinson argues that there are important "spill-over" problems when interactional intelligence, rather than analytic intelligence, is used to decode the structure of the natural world. As a result

> we see design in randomness, think we can detect signals from outer space in stellar X-rays, suspect some doodles on archaeological artifacts to constitute an undiscovered code, detect hidden structures in Amazonian myths. If we are attuned to think that way, then that is perhaps further evidence for the biases of interactional intelligence: in the interactional arena, we must take all behaviour to be specifically designed to reveal its intentional source. (p. 245)

There is plenty of evidence for the "spill-over" effects that Levinson posits – instances where we carry over assumptions about human design into situations where it is absent. What in particular confounds our quest for structure are situations infused with chance and randomness. The social intelligence hypothesis posits that our voracious search for the purposive meaning behind communicative events – our relentless search for an intentional explanation (see Levinson, 1995) – was an adaptive characteristic that allowed us to predict important events in the social world. But we impose this relentless search for patterns on *everything* in the world, and sometimes this extremely adaptive aspect of human cognition backfires on us.

The quest for conceptual understanding is maladaptive when it takes place in an environment in which there is nothing to conceptualize. Humphrey (1976), in a passage cited above, mentioned the gambler's fallacy – the tendency for people to see links between events in the past and events in the future when the two are really independent. For example, the number that comes up on a roulette wheel is independent of the outcome that preceded it. Yet after five or six consecutive reds, many bettors switch to black, thinking that it is now more likely to come up. However, the roulette wheel has no memory of what has happened previously. The probability of red and black is still equal.

This pattern – the so-called gambler's fallacy – is not restricted to the inexperienced or novice gambler. Research has shown that even habitual gamblers, who play games of chance over 20 hours a week, still display belief in the gambler's fallacy (Wagenaar, 1988). Also, it is important to realize that the gambler's fallacy is not restricted to games of chance. The gambler's fallacy operates in any domain that has a chance component, such as sporting events and stock markets (see Andreassen, 1987). It operates in any domain in which chance plays a substantial role (that is, in almost *everything*). The genetic makeup of babies is an example. Psychologists, physicians, and marriage counselors often see couples who, after having two female children, are planning a third child because "We want a boy, and it's *bound* to be a boy this time." This, of course, is the gambler's fallacy. The probability of having a boy (approximately 50 percent) is exactly the same after having two girls as it was in the beginning.

The tendency to see pattern and design in randomness is especially characteristic of people who interact with the financial markets that play such a large role in modern technological societies. Financial analysts routinely concoct elaborate explanations for every little fluctuation in stock market prices. In fact, much of this variability is simply random fluctuation (Malkiel, 1999; Shefrin & Statman, 1986; Shiller, 1987). Nevertheless, stock market "analysts" continue to imply to their customers (and perhaps believe themselves) that they can "beat the market" when there is voluminous evidence that the vast majority of them can do no such thing. If you had bought all of the 500 stocks in the Standard and Poor's Index and simply held them throughout the 1970s (what we might call a no-brain strategy), you would have had higher returns than 80 percent of the money managers on Wall Street (Malkiel, 1999). If you had done the same thing in the 1980s and 1990s, you would have beaten two-thirds of the money managers on Wall Street (Malkiel, 1999; Updegrave, 1995). You would also have beaten 80 percent of the financial newsletters that subscribers buy at rates of up to $500 per year (Kim, 1994).

The tendency to see design in every random happenstance – especially when the happenstance is a salient event that happens to *us* – is illustrated in a humorous anecdote related by Dawes (1991). He wrote about meeting an inmate from a prison education program run by the university for which Dawes was working. The inmate had been a bartender in a tavern and had also had a side job collecting gambling debts (at gunpoint if necessary). One day, he was sent to another state, Oregon, to collect a sum of money. When he got to Oregon, he cornered the man owing the money and drew out his gun. Just then, the police jumped from hiding and arrested him on the spot. After telling Dawes the story, the inmate declared confidently that he would never go to jail again. When Dawes asked how he knew that he would never go to jail again, the inmate replied, "Because I'll never go to Oregon again!"

Now what was wrong with the inmate's thinking? If we ignore its context and accept it on its own terms, the inmate's deduction isn't bad. Dawes (1991) wrote:

> People laugh when I tell that story, but viewed in non-probabilistic terms, the enforcer's inference isn't that bad. He had collected debts at gunpoint many times without being arrested, and he had been in Oregon only once. To believe that there was something special about Oregon that "caused" his arrest is compatible with the canons of inductive inference. (p. 245)

The problem here is not the inference per se, but the focus on trying to explain a *particular* instance. The inmate was trying to explain why he was arrested in *Oregon* – why he was arrested that particular time. And it was this focus on the instance – *this particular case* – that was leading the inmate to an absurd conclusion. Instead, the inmate should have been thinking probabilistically. There was some probability of his being arrested each time he collected debts at gunpoint (perhaps three times in 100). The inmate had done it many times. This time he got arrested. It was simply one of those three times. A general trend (such-and-such a probability of being arrested each time he collected a debt at gunpoint) explains why he was arrested. There was probably nothing unique about the fact that it happened to be in Oregon. But instead, the prisoner saw some special "design" specific to Oregon.

Computer scientist Marvin Minsky (1985) has said that "whatever happens, where or when, we're prone to wonder who or what's responsible. This leads us to discover explanations that we might not otherwise imagine, and that help us predict and control not only what happens in the world, but also what happens in our minds. But what if those same tendencies should lead us to imagine things and causes that do not exist? Then we'll invent false gods and superstitions and see their hand in every chance coincidence" (p. 232). Philosopher Daniel Dennett (1995) alludes to this characteristic of thought when discussing the trouble people have in understanding how the process of evolution produces adaptive design through random variation, differential survival, and heredity. A perplexing question that evolution presents us with is, "Could something exist for a reason without its being *somebody's* reason?" (p. 25).

Writer Annie Dillard (1999) alludes to how the tendency to see design often proves embarrassing to the "keenest thinkers" in every religion who are faced with explaining to skeptical rationalists the "presenting face of religion" in the form of its mass superstitions: "In New Mexico in 1978 the face of Jesus arose in a tortilla. 'I was just rolling out my husband's burrito . . . ,' the witness began her account. An auto parts store in Progresso, Texas, attracted crowds when an oil stain on its floor resembled the Virgin Mary. Another virgin appeared in 1998 in Colma, California, in hardened sap on a pine trunk. At a Nashville coffee shop named Bongo Java, a cinnamon bun came out of the oven looking like Mother Teresa – the nun bun, papers called it. In 1996 in Leicester, England, the name of Allah appeared in a halved eggplant" (pp. 76–77). In short, it is not difficult to enumerate many examples of our social intelligence defaulting to the assumption that all fluctuations that we see are due to intentional design. The world that determined a critical substrate of our intelligence was a world populated with other organisms who were transforming the environment with their own plans (see Humphrey, 1976, p. 45). Humphrey (1976) and others (e.g., Levinson, 1995) argue that we evolved to decipher such plans, and the social decipherer, the intentional interpreter in our brains (Wolford, Miller, & Gazzaniga, 2000), does not automatically decouple itself from problems when it is not needed. Chance fluctuations will thus routinely confound such a mechanism if it is not decoupled. And of course, chance and randomness infuse many events in our global, interactive modern world.

The Narrative Mode of Thought

The fourth fundamental computational bias is once again a bias that leads to the contextualization of problem solving. It is mentioned here only briefly because it has been extensively discussed in the literature. This fourth bias is the tendency toward a narrative mode of thought. Perhaps Bruner's (1986, 1990, 1996) treatments of this mode of thought are the most well known in psychology, but a number of authors from numerous cross-disciplinary perspectives have reiterated related themes (e.g., Carrithers, 1995; Dennett, 1991; Goody, 1977; Margolis, 1987; Oatley, 1992, 1996, 1999; Schank, 1991). Many characteristics of the narrative mode of thought are closely related to the contextualizing features of the fundamental computational biases discussed previously. For example, people thinking in the narrative mode are biased toward interpreting problems in terms of stories involving agents acting instrumentally to fulfill their goals (Dennett, 1987).

Dennett (1991) has emphasized the role of the narrative in forming our sense of self. In his Multiple Drafts theory of consciousness and its evolution, the self is viewed as a narrative center of gravity, the result of distributed brain centers constantly churning narrative-like language representations in order to aid in behavioral control. Narratives are the main medium by which we present ourselves to ourselves, thus constructing, from our constant storytelling with ourselves as the main protagonist, a sense of self that then becomes the main story we tell to others. Dennett emphasizes the naturalness and automaticity of the narratives about the self:

> Our fundamental tactic of self-protection, self-control, and self-definition is not spinning webs or building dams, but telling stories, and more particularly concocting and controlling the story we tell others – and ourselves – about who we are. And just as spiders don't have to think, consciously and deliberately, about how to spin their webs, and just as beavers, unlike professional human engineers, do not consciously and deliberately plan the structures they build, we (unlike *professional* human storytellers) do not consciously and deliberately figure out what narratives to tell and how to tell them. Our tales are spun, but for the most part we don't spin them; they spin us. Our human consciousness, and our narrative selfhood, is their product, not their source. (p. 418)

Flanagan (1996) emphasizes the naturalness – and the automatic properties – of our narrative tendencies in his discussion of dreams as epiphenomena of the evolutionarily useful tendency to make sense of stimuli by putting them into narrative structures. He argues that "it did us a lot of good to develop a cortex that makes sense out of experience while awake, and the design is such that there are no costs to this sense-maker always being ready to do its job" (p. 36). The result is the bizarre weaving together of the random cascades of neuronal firing that occur during sleep. The narrative maker is working as ever, but during sleep is working with degraded and chaotic stimuli. It grinds away nonetheless. The fragmented semi-narrative of dreams thus becomes further evidence of the modes of thought that are our defaults in our waking hours as well.

Perhaps Carrithers's (1995) discussion of the narrative mode has the closest affinity with the social intelligence hypothesis of Humphrey (1976) and others. He notes that stories "have the capacity to frame a markedly intricate and elaborate flow of social events, indeed just the sort of flow that seems even more characteristic of human than of other social primate societies" (p. 261). Carrithers emphasizes the binding function of narratives, that they tie together many-sided interactions over a considerable period of time. He shares Bruner's (1986) emphasis on the narrative as sequencing the consequences of intentional action, as well as structuring and exploring the consequences of emotional reactions (see Oatley, 1992, 1996, 1999), but emphasizes the role of narrative in solving the evolutionary problem of social coordination (see Levinson, 1995).

Margolis (1987) argues that people have a tendency to fill in contextual information when a problem is not "narrativized" or does not contain a schema that is familiar to the participant: "In the impoverished environment of the set-piece puzzle, therefore, we may impute a wider context to the problem that is not only not there at all but perhaps is flatly inappropriate" (pp. 143–144). The tendency to supplement purely formal problems with prior knowledge often takes the form of a constructed narrative that is largely free of the constraints of information actually presented in the problem.[2] Margolis has pointed out that it is not uncommon for a participant to concoct a task construal that is so discrepant from anything in the problem as set (even if narratively coherent in itself) that it represents a serious cognitive error: "An anomalous response will almost always in fact be a reasonably logical response to another question (as Henle has claimed), and in particular to a question that means something in the life experience of the individual giving the response. But the other question will often turn out to be a logically irrelevant or absurd interpretation of the context that actually prompted the response" (p. 6).

Many authors emphasizes the "naturalness" of the narrative mode for most real-world situations, and the corresponding unnaturalness of the analytic (scientific and abstract) mode of thinking. For example, Oatley (1996) notes that "one of the properties of the narrative mode is that objects expressed in this mode, that is to say, stories about agents, slip easily into the mind.... [in contrast] the mind is more resistant to objects based on the paradigmatic [analytic] mode. At least such objects need elaborate cultural assistance to allow them to enter the mind, for example, knowledge about how to reason mathematically, how to understand statistical data presented in tables and diagrams, or how to draw inferences validly from scientific experiments" (p. 123). Likewise, Carrithers (1995) emphasizes that the narrative mode is not well suited to generalization but works more on the basis of particular to particular. If the former is the focus, then abstract, essayist-styled (Olson, 1977, 1994), scientific thought is the most efficient mode. This contrast between the analytic scientific styles of thought and those reflected in the fundamental computation biases is the focus of other sections of this chapter below.

THE EVOLUTIONARY ADAPTIVENESS OF THE FUNDAMENTAL COMPUTATIONAL BIASES

Each of the fundamental computational biases discussed previously is a functional aspect of human cognition. Indeed, they are fundamental precisely because they are basic information-processing adaptations that arose in our evolutionary history probably long before the more abstract features of analytic intelligence (Mithen, 1996). Many investigators have painted compelling theoretically and empirically based explanations of why these computational biases developed in the course of human evolution

---

[2] Epstein, Donovan, and Denes-Raj (1999) note that many investigators have commented on the tendency of participants to spontaneously produce narrative responses to the Linda problem.

(Cosmides & Tooby, 1992; Humphrey, 1976, 1986; Mithen, 1996; Pinker, 1997). The socialization of problems and the tendency to see deliberate design in undesigned parts of the environment follow from the evolutionary assumptions behind the social intelligence hypothesis: that attributing intentionality in order to predict the behavior of conspecifics and to coordinate behavior with them (see Gibbard, 1990) was a major evolutionary hurdle facing the social primates, in many cases more computationally complex than mastering the physical environment (Humphrey, 1976). The tendency to see design may have other evolutionary sources. For example, Dennett (1991) discusses the "innate tendency to treat every changing thing at first as if it had a soul" (p. 32). He speculates that this tendency is innate because it is an evolutionary design trick that is "a shortcut for helping our time-pressured brains organize and think about the things that need thinking about if we are to survive" (p. 32).

The ubiquitous tendency to adopt what Dennett (1978, 1987) calls the intentional stance underlies many of the fundamental computational biases (particularly, the tendency to see human design in the world and to socialize problems). There appear to be biologically based brain structures devoted to supporting the intentional stance toward other animate beings (Baron-Cohen, 1995). However, these mechanisms do not appear to be modular in Fodor's (1983) strict sense, because they are not informationally encapsulated – they do draw on information from domain-general parts of the brain (Baron-Cohen, 1998; Thomas & Karmiloff-Smith, 1998; Tsimpli & Smith, 1998). Instead, they reflect a processing style that infuses much of cognition because they were early developing aspects of intelligence. Evolutionarily later aspects of analytic cognition (see Dennett, 1991, 1996; Mithen, 1996) did not replace these older socially based mechanisms but were built on top of them. Thus, aspects of social intelligence infuse even abstract problems that are best solved with later developing (see Mithen, 1996; Reber, 1992a, 1992b) analytic intelligence.

Finally, there exist many theoretical arguments for why the automatic contextualization of problems with prior knowledge might be adaptive (see Stanovich, 1999). For example, Evans and Over (1996) provide arguments in favor of the adaptiveness of contextualization and the nonoptimality of always decoupling prior beliefs from problem situations ("beliefs that have served us well are not lightly to be abandoned," p. 114). Their argument parallels the reasons that philosophy of science has moved beyond naive falsificationism (see Howson & Urbach, 1993). Scientists do not abandon a richly confirmed and well-integrated theory at the first little bit of falsifying evidence, because abandoning the theory might actually decrease explanatory coherence (Thagard, 1992). Similarly, Evans and Over (1996) argue that beliefs that have served us well in the past should be hard to dislodge, and projecting them on to new information – because of their past efficacy – might help in assimilating the new information.

This argument for the adaptiveness of contextualization was termed the *knowledge projection argument* by Stanovich (1999) because it reappears in a remarkably diverse set of disciplines and specialties within cognitive science. For example, philosopher Hilary Kornblith (1993) stresses that "mistaken beliefs will, as a result of belief perseverance, taint our perception of new data. By the same token, however, belief perseverance will serve to color our perception of new data when our preexisting beliefs are accurate.... If, overall, our belief-generating mechanisms give us a fairly accurate picture of the world, then the phenomenon of belief perseverance may do more to inform our understanding than it does to distort it" (p. 105).

This argument – that in a natural ecology where most of our prior beliefs are true, projecting our beliefs on to new data will lead to faster accumulation of knowledge – has been used to explain the false consensus effect in social psychology (Dawes, 1989, 1990; Hoch, 1987; Krueger & Zeiger, 1993), findings on expectancy effects in learning (Alloy & Tabachnik, 1984), biases in evaluating scientific evidence (Koehler, 1993), realism effects in attributing intentionality (Mitchell, Robinson, Isaacs, & Nye, 1996), syllogistic reasoning (Evans, Over, & Manktelow, 1993), and informal reasoning (Edwards & Smith, 1996). Alloy and Tabachnik (1984) summarize the generic case for knowledge projection, arguing for the general adaptiveness of such contextualization: Because "covariation information provided in an experiment may represent only one piece of conflicting evidence against the background of the large body of data about event covariations summarized by an expectation, it would be normatively appropriate for organisms to weight their expectations more heavily than situational information in the covariation judgment process" (p. 140). Of course, Alloy and Tabachnik emphasize that we must project from a largely *accurate* set of beliefs in order to obtain the benefit of knowledge projection. In a sea of inaccurate beliefs, the situation is quite different (see Stanovich, 1999, Chapter 8, for a discussion).

FACILITATING REASONING BY FITTING PROBLEMS TO THE FUNDAMENTAL COMPUTATIONAL BIASES

Evolutionary psychologists have shown that many of the problems that are difficult for people in their abstract forms can be made easier to solve if they are contextualized, particularly if they are contextualized in ways that are compatible with the representations used by specific evolutionarily adapted modules (see Cosmides & Tooby, 1992, 1996; Gigerenzer & Hoffrage, 1995). The most famous demonstration involves Wason's (1966) four-card selection task described above. The abstract rule (if there is a vowel on one side of the card, then there is an even number on the other side) is notoriously difficult, and this has been known for some time (Evans,

Newstead, & Byrne, 1993). At first it was thought that the abstract content of the vowel/number rule made the problem hard for people and that more real-life or "thematic," nonabstract problems would raise performance markedly. Investigators tried examples like the following "Destination Rule": "If 'Baltimore' is on one side of the ticket, then 'plane' is on the other side of the ticket." The fours cards facing the participant said:

| Destination: **Baltimore** | Destination: **Washington** | Mode of Travel: **Plane** | Mode of Travel: **Train** |

Surprisingly, this type of content did not improve performance at all (Cummins, 1996; Manktelow & Evans, 1979; Newstead & Evans, 1995; Stanovich & West, 1998a). Most participants still picked either P and Q or the P card only. The correct P, not-Q solution escaped the vast majority.

However, Griggs and Cox (1982) were the first to use a thematic version of the task that did markedly improve performance in their experiment and in many subsequent experiments by other investigators (Cummins, 1996; Dominowski, 1995; Newstead & Evans, 1995; Pollard & Evans, 1987). Here is a particularly easy version of the Griggs and Cox rule used by my research group (Stanovich & West, 1998a). Do the problem and experience for yourself how easy it is:

Imagine that you are a police officer on duty, walking through a local bar. It is your job to ensure that the drinking laws are in effect in this bar. When you see a person engaging in certain activities, the laws specify that certain conditions must first be met. One such law is "If a person is drinking beer then the person must be over 21 years of age." Each of the boxes below represents a card lying on a table. There are two pieces of information about a person on each card. Whether or not the person is drinking beer is on one side of the card and the person's age is on the other side. For two of the people, you can see their age, but you cannot see what they are drinking. For the other two people, you can see what they are drinking, but you cannot see their age. Your task is to decide whether or not this law is being broken in the bar. Circle the card or cards you would definitely need to turn over to decide whether or not the law is being broken. You may select any or all of the cards.

| Age: **22** | Age: **18** | Drink: **Beer** | Drink: **Coke** |

Many people answer the Drinking Age problem correctly, including many people who answer the abstract version incorrectly. This is true even though the underlying logical structure of the two problems are seemingly the same. The answer to both is to pick P and not-Q – in this problem, Beer and Age 18.

With the invention of the Drinking Age problem, researchers had finally found a way to get participants to give the right answer to the Wason four-card selection task after 15 years of research (at the time of the Griggs & Cox, 1982, report). Joy was short-lived however, because researchers immediately began to doubt whether the reasoning process leading to correct responses on the abstract version was anything like the reasoning process leading to correct responses on the Drinking Age version. That is, despite the surface similarity of the two rules, investigators began to think that they were actually tapping fundamentally different reasoning mechanisms. The Destination rule, for example, is what is called an indicative rule: a rule concerning the truth status of a statement about the world. In contrast, the Drinking Age rule is a so-called deontic rule. Deontic reasoning problem solving concerns thinking about the rules used to guide human behavior, about what "ought to" or "must" be done. Cummins (1996) terms a deontic rule a rule about "what one may, ought, or must not do in a given set of circumstances" (p. 161; see also Manktelow, 1999; Manktelow & Over, 1991). A number of theorists have argued that deontic rules and indicative rules engage different types of mental mechanisms.

The most famous of these proposals was in a highly influential paper by Cosmides (1989), one of the leading figures in the move to ground psychology in evolutionary theory that swept through psychology in the 1990s (for summaries, see Buss, 1999; Cosmides & Tooby, 1992, 1994, 1996; Geary & Bjorklund, 2000; Pinker, 1997; Plotkin, 1998). She proposed that evolution has built processing systems (what she termed *Darwinian algorithms*) exclusively concerned with social exchange in human interactions. These algorithms embody the basic rule "if you take a benefit, then you must pay a cost" and are extremely sensitive "cheater detectors": They react strongly to instances where an individual takes a benefit without paying the cost. In the Drinking Age problem, an individual underage and drinking beer is just that: a cheater. Thus, with this rule, the possibility of an 18-year-old drinking beer (the P and not-Q case) becomes very salient because the rule automatically triggers an evolutionary algorithm specifically concerned with detecting card selections that happen to be correct. The indicative rule of course does not trigger such a Darwinian algorithm. Evolution has provided no special module in the brain for solving indicative problems. The tools for solving such problems are largely cultural inventions (Dennett, 1991; Jepson, Krantz, & Nisbett, 1983; Krantz, 1981; McCain, 1991; Stanovich, 1999; Thagard & Nisbett, 1983), and the brain processes supporting them are fragile because they demand much computational capacity (Dennett, 1991; Evans & Over, 1996, 1999; Stanovich & West, 2000).

Cosmides's (1989) hypothesis is not the only explanation for the superior performance in the Drinking Age problem (see Cheng & Holyoak, 1985; Evans & Over, 1996; Kirby, 1994; Manktelow, 1999; Manktelow & Over, 1991; Manktelow, Sutherland, & Over, 1995; Oaksford & Chater, 1994, 1996). Other theorists have taken issue with her emphasis on a domain-specific and informationally encapsulated modules for regulating social exchange. However, the alternative explanations do share some family resemblances with Cosmides's (1989) account. They tend to view the Drinking Age task as a problem of pragmatic rationality rather than epistemic rationality. Indicative selection tasks tap epistemic rationality: They probe how people test hypotheses about the nature of the world. In contrast, deontic tasks tap pragmatic rationality: They concern how actions should be regulated and what people should *do* in certain situations. Given the arguments of the social intelligence theorists, we again might expect the mechanisms for the former to be evolutionarily younger (see Mithen, 1996; Reber, 1992a, 1992b) and more computationally cumbersome (Dennett, 1991; Evans & Over, 1996, 1999; Stanovich & West, 2000). If participants do not use the computationally expensive processes of analytic intelligence (Dennett, 1991; Stanovich, 1999) to solve the indicative task, then they must rely on automatic heuristics such as Evans's (1996) relevance heuristic. This heuristic generates a primitive, so-called matching response of P and Q: The participant is primed to choose just the two cards mentioned in the rule. The problem is that, in the indicative task, these heuristics do not lead to the correct response.

Consistent with this interpretation are some individual difference data from my own lab (Stanovich & West, 1998a). Richard West and I have found that there were large intelligence differences in abstract selection task problems. The minority of individuals who answered correctly had significantly higher SAT scores than those that did not, and the difference was quite large in magnitude (effect sizes of roughly .500 to .800). In contrast, cognitive ability differences between those who answered deontic problems such as the Drinking Age problem correctly and incorrectly are considerably smaller (effect sizes of roughly .050 to .400).

A similar pattern is apparent on other tasks where the fundamental computational biases lead to overall poor performance on noncontextualized task versions. Take the conjunction fallacy illustrated above (the Linda Problem). Evolutionary psychologists have argued that the human cognitive apparatus is more adapted to dealing with frequencies than with probabilities (Brase, Cosmides, & Tooby, 1998; Cosmides & Tooby, 1996; Gigerenzer & Hoffrage, 1995). It has been found that when tasks such as the Linda Problem are revised in terms of estimating the frequency of categories rather than judging probabilities, that performance is improved (see Fiedler, 1988; Gigerenzer, 1991, 1993). My research group has replicated this finding, but we again found that cognitive ability differences are much smaller in the frequentist versions of these problems (Stanovich & West, 1998b).

My research group (1999; Stanovich & West, 2000) has reported other instances of this trend. Specifically, the abstract, noncontextualized versions of many problem-solving and reasoning problems usually produces large cognitive ability differences. Versions of many of these problems designed with considerations of evolutionary psychology in mind have indeed produced vastly superior performance overall. However, these same versions often attenuate individual differences in analytic intelligence. I have argued (1999) that these findings are reconciled by clearly distinguishing evolutionary adaptation from normative (or individual) rationality. In this distinction lies a possible rapprochement between the researchers who have emphasized the flaws in human cognition (Kahneman & Tversky, 1973, 1996, 2000) and the evolutionary psychologists who have emphasized the optimality of human cognition (Cosmides & Tooby, 1994, 1996; Gigerenzer & Todd, 1999). What is useful here is to use Dawkins's (1976) replicator/vehicle terminology to distinguish between evolutionary adaptation at the level of the gene and instrumental rationality (utility maximization given goals and beliefs) at the level of the individual person.

Distinguishing optimization at the level of the replicator from optimization at the level of the vehicle can reconcile both the impressive record of descriptive accuracy enjoyed by a variety of adaptationist models (Anderson, 1990, 1991; Oaksford & Chater, 1994, 1996, 1998) with the fact that cognitive ability sometimes dissociates from the response deemed optimal on an adaptationist analysis (Stanovich & West, 2000). For example, Oaksford and Chater (1994) have had considerable success in modeling the abstract selection task as an inductive problem in which optimal data selection is assumed (see also Oaksford, Chater, Grainger, & Larkin, 1997). Their model predicts the modal response of P and Q and the corresponding dearth of P and not-Q choosers. Similarly, Anderson (1990, pp. 157–160) models the 2 × 2 contingency assessment experiment using a model of optimally adapted information processing and shows how it can predict the much-replicated finding that the D cell (cause absent and effect absent) is vastly underweighted (see also Friedrich, 1993; Klayman & Ha, 1987). Finally, a host of investigators (Adler, 1984, 1991; Dulany & Hilton, 1991; Hilton, 1995; Hilton & Slugoski, 2000; Levinson, 1995) have stressed how a model of rational conversational implicature predicts that violating the conjunction rule in the Linda Problem reflects the adaptive properties of interactional intelligence.

Yet in all three of these cases – despite the fact that the adaptationist models predict the modal response quite well – individual differences analyses demonstrate associations that *also* must be accounted for. Correct responders on the abstract selection task (P and not-Q choosers, not those choosing P and Q) are higher in cognitive ability. In the 2 × 2 covariation detection experiment, it is those participants weighting cell D more *equally* (not those underweighting the cell in the way that the adaptationist model dictates) who are higher in cognitive ability (Stanovich & West, 1998d). Finally, despite conversational implicatures indicating the opposite, individuals of higher cognitive ability disproportionately tend to adhere to the conjunction rule. These patterns make sense if it is assumed (1) that there are two systems of processing, sometimes labeled heuristic and analytic (see Evans & Over, 1996; Sloman, 1996; Stanovich, 1999), (2) that the two systems of processing are optimized for different situations and different goals, and (3) that in individuals of higher cognitive ability there is a greater probability that the analytic system will override the heuristic system.

This differential proclivity for override could become important in situations where the two systems compute different responses. Richard West and I (Stanovich, 1999; Stanovich & West, 2000) have argued that this is more likely to happen in situations where the human cognitive system has instantiated conflicting goals. Differing goals might characterize different levels of computational complexity in a "tower of intellect" model of the type popularized by Dennett (1991, 1995, 1996) and illustrated by the title of his book *Kinds of Minds*. In such a conception, more computationally complex cognitive structures do not *replace* simpler ones, but are posited to operate in *parallel*. Specifically, what we must be concerned about are situations where the evolutionary adapted goals (instantiated in the evolutionarily older heuristic mechanisms) do not coincide with personal goals in the current environment, which are more likely to be tracked by systems displaying a more flexible, analytic intelligence (Sternberg, 1997).

In short, the critical situations are those where the interests of the replicators and the vehicle do not coincide (again, to use Dawkins's [1976] terms). Evolutionary psychologists are prone to emphasize situations where genetic goals and personal goals coincide. They are not wrong to do so because this is often the case. Accurately navigating around objects in the natural world was adaptive during the EEA, and it similarly serves our personal goals as we carry out our lives in the modern world. Likewise with other evolutionary adaptations: It is a marvel that humans are exquisite frequency detectors (Hasher & Zacks, 1979), that they infer intentionality with almost supernatural ease (Levinson, 1995), and that they acquire a complex language code from impoverished input (Pinker, 1994) – and all of these mechanisms serve personal goal fulfillment in the modern world. But none of this means that the overlap is necessarily 100%.

First, evolutionary biology is full of examples where the genes instantiate strategies that necessitate sacrificing the vehicle. Dawkins's book *The Extended Phenotype* (1982) contains many such examples. For instance, the genes have little interest in the vehicle they build once it is beyond its reproductive years, which is why many creatures (such as salmon) die immediately after reproducing. But as humans, we *are* interested in our postreproductive longevity, thus we have a clear example of genetic goals and individual goals coming apart. Skyrms (1996) devotes an entire book on evolutionary game theory to showing that instrumental goal optimization for an individual organism might not coincide with adaptive fitness. He concludes that "if evolutionary game theory is generalized to allow for correlation of encounters between players and like-minded players, then strongly dominated strategies – at variance with both rational decision and game theory – can take over the population. . . . When I contrast the results of the evolutionary account with those of rational decision theory, I am not criticizing the normative force of the latter. I am just emphasizing the fact that the different questions asked by the two traditions may have different answers" (pp. x–xi). Skyrms's book articulates the environmental and population parameters under which "rational choice theory completely parts ways with evolutionary theory" (p. 106; see also Cooper, 1989). The point is that local maximization in the sense of genetic fitness is not the same as the maximization of expected utility for the individual.

Unfortunately, the modern world tends to create situations where some of the default values of evolutionarily adapted cognitive systems are not optimal. Many of these situations implicate the fundamental computational biases discussed previously. These biases serve to radically contextualize problem-solving situations. In contrast, modern technological societies continually spawn situations where humans must decontextualize information, where they must deal abstractly (Adler, 1984) and in a depersonalized manner with information. Such situations require the active suppression of the personalizing and contextualizing styles that characterize the fundamental computational biases. These situations may not be numerous, but they tend to be in particularly important domains of modern life – indeed, they in part *define* modern life in postindustrial knowledge-based societies.

THE FUNDAMENTAL COMPUTATIONAL BIASES AND THE PROBLEMS OF MODERN SOCIETY

Mechanisms designed for survival in preindustrial times are clearly sometimes maladaptive in a technological culture. Our mechanisms for storing and utilizing energy evolved in times when fat preservation was efficacious. These mechanisms no longer serve the goals of people in a technological society where a Burger King is on every corner. Likewise, the cognitive mechanisms that lead us to stray from normative models that would maximize utility are probably mechanisms that once were fitness enhancing but now serve to thwart our goals (see Baron, 1993, 1994, 1998; Stanovich, 1999).

It is argued here that many of the fundamental computational biases are now playing this role. Such biases directly conflict with the demands for decontextualization that a highly bureaucratized society puts on its citizens. Indeed, this is often why schools have to explicitly teach such skills of cognitive decontextualization. Donaldson (1978, 1993) views this as one of the primary tasks of schooling (see Anderson, Reder, & Simon, 1996). She argues that "what is involved in the mind's movement from 'seven fishes' to 'seven' is abstraction indeed, but it is more: it is a dramatic decontextualization. In the contexts of our ordinary life we have to deal with quantities of fishes but we never encounter seven" (p. 90). She emphasizes how, in order to master a variety of abstract rule systems (mathematics, logic, etc.), decontextualization must become a comfortable thinking style for a learner: "If the intellectual powers are to develop, the child must gain a measure of control over his own thinking and he cannot control it while he remains unaware of it. The attaining of this control means prising thought out of its primitive unconscious embeddedness in the immediacies of living in the world and interacting with other human beings. It means learning to move beyond the bounds of human sense. It is on this movement that all the higher intellectual skills depend" (Donaldson, 1978, p. 123).

This point is a recurring theme in the literature of cognitive development (e.g., Neimark, 1987; Piaget 1972; Sigel, 1993). Indeed, many developmental theorists, as have influential cognitive psychologists (e.g., Kahneman & Tversky, 1982), emphasize how schooling teaches children to decouple reasoning from the pragmatic inferences of language comprehension. For example, in a paper discussing developmental trends in reasoning, Chapman (1993) draws the specific link between the ability to decouple pragmatic knowledge in the interests of reasoning logically: "[C]hildren who have mastered the pragmatic rules of language may have to unlearn some of these rules when it comes to formal reasoning. More precisely, they may have to learn that particular contexts exist in which those rules do not apply" (p. 104).

Of course, all of this emphasis on decoupling pragmatic processes of natural language understanding is quite unnatural – unnatural in the sense that it is evolutionarily unprecedented and that it requires overriding many cognitive heuristics that are probably highly automatized (Pollock, 1995; Stanovich, 1999). But it is not just for success in school that we inculcate the decontextualization skills emphasized by Donaldson (1978, 1993). Increasingly, modern society is demanding such skills (Frank & Cook, 1995; Gottfredson, 1997; Hunt, 1995, 1999) – and in some cases it is rendering economically superfluous anyone who does not have them (Bronfenbrenner, McClelland, Wethington, Moen, & Ceci, 1996; Frank & Cook, 1995).

Modern society creates many situations that require radical decontextualization, that require one or more of the fundamental computational biases to be overridden by analytic intelligence. For example, many aspects of the contemporary legal system put a premium on detaching prior belief and world knowledge from the process of evidence evaluation. There has been understandable vexation at odd jury verdicts rendered because of jury theories and narratives concocted during deliberations that had nothing to do with the evidence but instead that were based on background knowledge and personal experience. For example, members of a Baltimore jury acquitted a murder defendant who had been identified by four witnesses and had confessed to two people because "they had invented their own highly speculative theory of the crime" (Gordon, 1997, p. 258). In this case, the perpetrator had wanted to plea bargain for a 40-year sentence, but this was turned down at the request of the victim's family. Similarly, in Lefkowitz's (1997) account of the trial of several teenagers in an affluent New Jersey suburb who brutally exploited and raped a young girl who was intellectually disabled, one juror concocted the extenuating circumstance that one defendant thought he was attending an "initiation rite" even though no evidence for such a "rite" had been presented in months of testimony.

The point is that in a particular cultural situation where detachment and decoupling is required, the people who must carry out these demands for decontextualization are often unable to do so even under legal compulsion. Posttrial reports of juries in a "creative," "narrative," or highly enthymematic mode have incited great debate. If the polls are to be believed, a large proportion of Americans were incensed at the jury's acquittal of O. J. Simpson. Similar numbers were appalled at the jury verdict in the first trial of the officers involved in the Rodney King beating. What both juries failed to do was to decontextualize the evidence in their respective cases, and each earned the wrath of their fellow citizens because it is a cultural (and legal) expectation of citizenship that people should be able to carry out this cognitive operation in certain settings.

The need to decontextualize also characterizes many work settings in contemporary society. Consider the common admonition in the retail service sector of "the customer is always right." This admonition is often interpreted to include even instances where customers unleash unwarranted verbal assaults that are astonishingly vitriolic. The service worker is supposed to remain polite and helpful under this onslaught, despite the fact that such emotional social stimuli are no doubt triggering evolutionarily instantiated modules of self-defense and emotional reaction. All of this emotion, all of these personalized attributions – all fundamental computational biases – must be set aside by the service worker, and instead an abstract rule that "the customer is always right" must be invoked in this special, socially constructed domain of the market-based transaction. The worker must realize that he or she is not in an *actual* social interaction with this person (which if true, might call for socking them in the nose!), but in a special, indeed, "unnatural" realm where different rules apply.

Numerous theorists have warned about a possible mismatch between the fundamental computational biases and the processing requirements of many tasks in a technological society containing many abstract and decontextualized symbolic artifacts. Hilton (1995) warns that the default assumption of interactional intelligence may be wrong for many technical settings because "many reasoning heuristics may have evolved because they are adaptive in contexts of social interaction. For example, the expectation that errors of interpretation will be quickly repaired may be correct when we are interacting with a human being but incorrect when managing a complex system such as an aircraft, a nuclear power plant, or an economy. The evolutionary adaptiveness of such an expectation to a conversational setting may explain why people are so bad at dealing with lagged feedback in other settings" (p. 267).

Concerns about the real-world implications of the failure to engage in necessary cognitive abstraction (see Adler, 1984) were what led Luria (1976) to warn against minimizing the importance of decontextualizing thinking styles. In discussing the syllogism, he notes that "a considerable proportion of our intellectual operations involve such verbal and logical systems; they comprise the basic network of codes along which the connections in discursive human thought are channeled" (p. 101). Likewise, regarding the subtle distinctions on many decontextualized language tasks, Olson (1986) has argued that "the distinctions on which such questions are based are extremely important to many forms of intellectual activity in a literate society. It is easy to show that sensitivity to the subtleties of language are crucial to some undertakings. A person who does not clearly see the difference between an expression of intention and a promise or between a mistake and an accident, or between a falsehood and a lie, should avoid a legal career or, for that matter, a theological one" (p. 341).

Olson's statement reflects a stark fact about modern technological societies: They are providing lucrative employment only for those who can master complexity, make subtle quantitative and verbal distinctions, and reason in decontextualized ways (Bronfenbrenner et al., 1996; Frank & Cook, 1995; Gottfredson, 1997; Hunt, 1995, 1999). Objective measures of the requirements for cognitive abstraction have been increasing across most job categories in technological societies throughout the past several decades (Gottfredson, 1997). This is why measures of the ability to deal with abstraction remains the best employment predictor and the best earnings predictor in postindustrial societies (Brody, 1997; Gottfredson, 1997; Hunt, 1995).

Adler (1991) emphasizes the point that not to make important linguistic, probabilistic, and logical distinctions in a complex social environment has real costs and represents more than just the failure to play an artificial game:

> The conversationally induced problem of a lack of shared understanding is a subtle one, not due to any blatant verbal trick. It is reasonable to conjecture that the subtlety results in part from participants'

limited skill with the rule the experimenter wants to study. To be specific: Our greater pragmatic sophistication alone does not explain the differences in the dominant adult responses to the conjunction effect compared to the Piaget class-inclusion studies. The difference between the number of members of a class and the number of a proper sub-class is so obvious to us that we readily permit the conversationally untoward question – "Are there more dimes or coins?" – at face value. Our greater resistance to the violation of the maxims in the conjunction-effect experiment is partly due, I believe, to a certain lack of either accessibility to or confidence in – though not competence with – the conjunction rule for probabilities. If this is so, then the fact that subjects do not understand the experimenter as he intends his words is itself some evidence of a weakness in subjects' understanding of the scope of the conjunction rule in everyday reasoning. (p. 265)

Einhorn and Hogarth (1981) highlight the importance of decontextualized environments in their discussion of the optimistic and pessimistic views of the cognitive biases revealed in laboratory experimentation. They note that "the most optimistic asserts that biases are limited to laboratory situations which are unrepresentative of the natural ecology" (p. 82), but they go on to caution that "in a rapidly changing world it is unclear what the relevant natural ecology will be. Thus, although the laboratory may be an unfamiliar environment, lack of ability to perform well in unfamiliar situations takes on added importance" (p. 82).

Critics of the abstract content of most laboratory tasks and standardized tests have been misguided on this very point. The issue is that, ironically, the argument that the laboratory tasks and tests are not like "real life" is becoming less and less true. "Life," in fact, is becoming more like the tests! Try using an international ATM machine with which you are unfamiliar, or try arguing with your HMO about a disallowed medical procedure. In such circumstances, we invariably find out that our personal experience, our emotional responses, our stimulus-triggered intuitions about social justice are all worthless. All are for naught when talking over the phone to the representative looking at a computer screen displaying a spreadsheet with a hierarchy of branching choices and conditions to be fulfilled. The social context, the idiosyncrasies of individual experience, the personal narrative – all are abstracted away as the representatives of modernist technological-based services attempt to "apply the rules." Consider Toronto writer Todd Mercer (2000) trying to fly across the continent on short notice to be with his 83-year-old father undergoing emergency surgery. Calling Canadian Airlines and finding out that the last-minute scheduled airline fare was $3,120, Mercer asked whether there was any discount that applied to his situation and was informed that he might be eligible for an "imminent death discount" by, as Mercer puts it, "no less a medical/spiritual authority" than the telephone ticket agent. Prodded for the definition of "imminent death," the ticket agent quotes from a document outlining the details of the "bereavement travel program" that clarifies the program's requirements when illness rather than death is the reason for the travel. The ticket agent relates that the person in question must be a patient in intensive care, a patient in the final stages of cancer, or a patient involved in a serious accident. Merton's father had an aortic aneurysm, which made him a "walking time bomb" according to his doctor, but he had not yet gone into surgery and had not yet been put into intensive care. The ruling was that such a situation was in "a gray area" and, as a result, the ticket agent stonewalled by saying that "not all operations are life threatening. The imminent death discount is not meant just for operations. It is meant for imminent death" – the latter defined as above, and another round of technical and nuanced argument between Mercer and the ticket agent ensued. This is life in the First World in the early part of the twenty-first century.

The abstract, semantic games encountered by Mercer are nothing compared with what a person faces when deciding on whether to apply for a tax deduction for an infirm relative who lived outside Canada for the year 1994. Canada Customs and Revenue Agency will advise the person: "Your dependent must be: – your or your spouse's child or grandchild, if that child was born in 1976 or earlier and is physically or mentally infirm; or – a person living in Canada at any time in the year who meets all of the following conditions. The person must have been: – your or your spouse's parent, grandparent, brother, sister, aunt, uncle, niece, or nephew; – born in 1976 or earlier; and – physically or mentally infirm." Given the ubiquitousness of such abstract directives in our informational and technology-saturated society, it just seems perverse to argue the "unnaturalness" of decontextualized reasoning skills when such skills are absolutely necessary in order to succeed in our society. If one has the postindustrial goal of, say, "going to Princeton," then the only way to fulfill that goal in our current society *is* to develop such cognitive skills. Situations that require abstract thought and/or the ability to deal with complexity will increase in number as more niches in postindustrial societies require these intellectual styles and skills (Gottfredson, 1997; Hunt, 1995). For intellectuals to use their abstract reasoning skills to argue that the "person in the street" is in no need of such skills of abstraction is like a rich person telling someone in poverty that money is not really all that important.

To the extent that modern society increasingly requires the fundamental computational biases to be overridden, then dissociations between evolutionary and individual rationality will become more common. Cosmides and Tooby (1996) argue that "in the modern world, we are awash in numerically expressed statistical information. But our hominid ancestors did not have access to the modern accumulation which has produced, for the first time in human history, reliable, numerically expressed statistical information about the world beyond individual experience. Reliable numerical statements about single event probabilities were rare or nonexistent in the Pleistocene" (p. 15). "It is easy to forget that our hominid ancestors did not have access to the modern system of socially organized data collection, error checking, and information accumulation. . . . In ancestral environments, the only external database available from which to reason inductively was one's own observations" (Brase et al., 1998, p. 5).

Precisely. I am living in a technological society where I must: decide which HMO to join based on just such statistics; figure out whether to invest in a Roth IRA; decide what type of mortgage to purchase; figure out what type of deductible to get on my auto insurance; decide whether to trade in a car or sell it myself; decide whether to lease or to buy; think about how to apportion my retirement funds; and decide whether I would save money by joining a book club. And I must make all of these decisions based on information represented in a manner for which my brain is not adapted (in none of these cases have I coded individual frequency information from my own personal experience). To reason normatively in all of these domains (in order to maximize my own personal utility), I am going to have to deal with probabilistic information represented in nonfrequentistic terms – in representations that the evolutionary psychologists have shown are different from my well-adapted algorithms for dealing with frequency information (Cosmides & Tooby, 1996; Gigerenzer & Hoffrage, 1995).

Consider the work of Brase et al. (1998), who improved performance on a difficult probability problem (Bar-Hillel & Falk, 1982; Falk, 1992; Granberg, 1995) by presenting the information as frequencies and in terms of whole objects, both alterations designed to better fit the frequency-computation systems of the brain. In response to a query about why the adequate performance observed was not even higher given that our brains contain such well-designed frequency-computation systems, Brase et al. (1998) replied that "in our view it is remarkable that they work on paper-and pencil problems at all. A natural sampling system is designed to operate on actual events" (p. 13). The problem is that in a symbol-oriented postindustrial society, we are presented with paper-and pencil problems all the time, and much of what we know about the world comes not from the perception of actual events but from abstract information preprocessed, prepackaged, and condensed into symbolic codes such as probabilities, percentages, tables, and graphs (the voluminous statistical information routinely presented in *USA Today* comes to mind).

What we are attempting to combat here is a connotation implicit in some discussions of findings in evolutionary psychology (e.g., Gigerenzer & Todd, 1999) and indeed in the situated cognition literature as well (see Anderson et al., 1996) that there is nothing to be gained from being able to understand a formal rule at an abstract level (the conjunction rule of probability, etc.) and no advantage in flexibly overriding the fundamental computational biases. To the contrary, modern technological society often puts a premium on the use of such abstract tools. Adler (1984) emphasizes that the efficiency of the cognitive modules underlying intention attribution and social cooperation just as surely extract certain costs. He argues that such costs occur "in situations where the naturalness of our expectations under the cooperative principle leads us to miss subtle, but significant deviations from those expectations" (p. 174). He cites a now-famous experiment by Langer, Blank, and Chanowitz (1978) where a confederate attempts to cut into a line at a copy machine. In one condition a good reason is given ("May I use the Xerox machine, because I'm in a rush?"), and in the other a redundant explanation is given ("May I use the Xerox machine, because I have to make copies?"). Despite the fact that the second explanation is much less informative than the first, the compliance rates in the two conditions did not differ. Langer (1989; Langer et al., 1978) terms the compliance in the second case "mindless" and Adler (1984) analyzes it in terms of overly generalizing the Gricean Cooperative Principle. The default assumption that a contribution will be selectively relevant – in this case, that a real reason will follow the request – is false in this condition, yet it triggers exactly the same compliance behavior because it is not overridden ("Yes but *all* of us are in line to make copies. Why should you go first?").

Langer-type examples of mindlessness abound in many important domains. *Consumer Reports* (April 1998) chronicles how some dealers put an item costing $500 and labeled ADM on many automobile price stickers. The dealers are hoping that some people will not ask what ADM means. The dealers are also hoping that even after asking and being told that it means "additional dealer markup" that some consumers will not fully process what that means and will not inquire further about what this additional dealer markup feature is that they are paying for. In short, the dealers are hoping that analytic intelligence will not override Langer-type "mindlessness" and allow the customer to ascertain that ADM is not a feature on the car at all, that it simply represents a request from the dealer to contribute $500 more to the dealership, as if it were a charity. As one dealer put it, "every once in a while somebody pays it, no questions asked" (p. 17). A mindless response here, a failure to override automatic heuristics, and the consumer could simply throw away a good chunk of hard-earned income. The modern consumer world is simply littered with such traps, and, often, the more costly the product, the more such traps there are (e.g., automobiles, mutual funds, mortgage closing costs).

Modern mass communication technicians have become quite skilled at implying certain conclusions without actually stating those conclusions (for fear of lawsuits, bad publicity, etc.). Advertisements rely on the fundamental computational biases (particularly its enthymematic processing feature) to fill in the missing information. Of course, such techniques are not limited to election and product advertising. The glossy brochures that our universities send out, full of fresh-faced young people in a wholesome learning environment, have the same logic. Margolis (1987; see Margolis, 1996) warns of the ubiquitousness of this situation in modern society: "We can encounter cases where the issue is both out-of-scale with everyday life experience and contains important novelties, so that habitual responses can be highly inappropriate responses. The opportunity for unrecognized contextual effects akin to the scenario effects . . . [demonstrated in the laboratory] can be something much more than an odd quirk that shows up in some contrived situation" (p. 168).

As discussed previously, evolutionary psychologists have shown that some problems can be efficiently solved if represented one way (to coincide with how the brain modules represent information) but not if represented in another way (e.g., as single-event probabilities rather than frequencies; see Gigerenzer, Hoffrage, & Kleinbolting, 1991). Nevertheless, they often seem to ignore the fact that the world will not always *let* us deal with representations that are optimally suited to our evolutionarily designed cognitive mechanisms. For example, in a series of elegant experiments, Gigerenzer et al. (1991) have shown how at least part of the overconfidence effect in knowledge calibration studies is due to the unrepresentative stimuli used in such experiments, stimuli that do not match the participants' stored cue validities that are optimally tuned to the environment. But there are many instances in real life when we are suddenly placed in environments where the cue validities have changed. Metacognitive awareness of such situations and strategies for suppressing incorrect confidence judgments generated by automatic responses to cues will be crucial here. Every high school musician who aspires to a career in music has to recalibrate when they arrive at university and see large numbers of talented musicians for the first time. If they persist in their old confidence judgments, they may not change majors when they should. Many real-life situations where accomplishment yields a new environment with even more stringent performance requirements share this logic. Each time we "ratchet up" in the competitive environment of a capitalist economy (Frank & Cook, 1995) we are in a situation just like the overconfidence knowledge calibration experiments with their unrepresentative materials. It is important to have learned strategies that will temper one's overconfidence in such situations (Koriat, Lichtenstein, & Fischhoff, 1980).

ABSTRACTION AND THE FUNDAMENTAL COMPUTATIONAL BIASES IN EDUCATION

In an article titled "Abstraction Is Uncooperative," Adler (1984) points out that what is called for in many problem-solving and reasoning tasks (and certainly in many tasks in the heuristics and biases literature) is abstraction: extracting from a given problem representation only the features that fit a general pattern. In the process of abstraction "we are rendering information inessential to the formal structure irrelevant" (p. 165). But Adler points out that the Gricean Cooperative Principle is directly in conflict with the demands of abstraction. The cooperativeness principle that everything about the experimenter's contribution is relevant (the instructions, the context, every bit of content that is presented) is diametrically opposed to the requirements of abstraction: that we treat as inessential everything that does not fit a certain formal structure.

As Donaldson (1978, 1993) argues, education serves, both explicitly and implicitly, to suppress Gricean tendencies in order to make adopting an abstract stance a more natural processing style. This is why education – at all levels – is often, deliberately and correctly, "not like real life." Much educational effort is expended demonstrating that so-called recipe knowledge must be supplemented by abstract knowledge in order to enable true understanding. The term *recipe knowledge*, coined by psychologist Leigh Shaffer (1981), is the knowledge of the way to use an artifact without knowledge of the fundamental principles that govern its functioning. For example, most people know many things about how to use a telephone. But many are completely ignorant of the physical principles on which the operation of the telephone is based. They do not know why it does what it does; they know only that they can make it work. Our knowledge of many technological products in our society is also recipe knowledge. Of course, this is not an entirely negative thing. Indeed, most technological products have been designed precisely *to* be used without knowledge of all the principles on which they are based (the well-known "user-friendly" concept). But it is important to understand the limitations of recipe knowledge. It does not contain the generalizable, universal principles that allow a full understanding of the physical and social world.

A problem arises when people mistakenly view recipe knowledge as the ultimate goal of university education. Such knowledge is inevitably contextually embedded and nongeneralizable. By its very nature it is perspective-dependent and even discourages perspective switching, because much recipe knowledge is designed for use only within a particular perspective or context. Thus, everything about it works against the principles of decontextualized thinking, the importance of which I have outlined earlier. In fact, in an article on the importance of decentering cognitive styles in education, Floden, Buchmann, and Schwille (1987) stress that "unless students can break with their everyday experience in thought, they cannot see the extraordinary range of options for living and thinking; and unless students give up many commonsense beliefs, they may find it impossible to learn disciplinary concepts that describe the world in reliable, often surprising ways" (p. 485). The deepest concepts across the whole range of human knowledge – from the arts to science to moral philosophy to language – require the ability to cognize across various perspectives and situations. They require a person to see a local situation as part of a more global whole, to go beyond situation- or perspective-specific thinking. Students can begin to gain access to this knowledge only if they are first decentered from the egocentric assumption that their environment, milieu, or perspective is the only one there is, and that the immediately surrounding context is uniformly relevant to solving the problem.

Theorists such as Bereiter (1997) and Dennett (1991, 1996) have emphasized how such decontextualizing cognitive styles are computationally expensive, "unnatural," and therefore rare. As Bereiter (1997) notes, "symbolic processes are themselves exceptional and by no means representative of the great bulk of cognitive activity. . . . They are acquired processes, culturally mediated, that enable the brain to act as if it were a different kind of device from what it had evolved to be. The device we simulate in our conscious thinking is a logic machine" (pp. 292–293). These "unrepresentative" types of cognitive styles have to be taught because they are instantiated in an evolutionary recent virtual machine (see Dennett, 1991) simulated by the massively parallel brain. This virtual machine is a serial processor (a von Neumann machine), and it is a powerful mechanism for logical, symbolic thought. However, not only is this serial process computationally expensive to simulate, but it is a cultural product. It is part of what Dennett (1991) calls the Gregorian brain: the part of the brain that is capable of exploiting the mental tools discovered by others (see also Clark, 1997).

Why has schooling increasingly focused on the thinking styles of the capacity-demanding serial processes of the brain? It is conjectured here that the reason is that, increasingly, modernism requires an override of the fundamental computational biases of human cognition by the serial processes of the virtual machine (what I [Stanovich, 1999], extrapolating from various dual-process theorists, call System 2). In short, the processes fostered by education are what they are because modern society is what it is. Modernism has meant decontextualization. School-like processes of cognitive decontextualization gradually replace personalized interactions that are highly contextualized as modernist forces (e.g., market mechanisms) spread further into every corner of the world and every aspect of modern life. Philosopher Robert Nozick (1993) describes the theme of Max Weber's writings as explicating how "economic and monetary calculation, bureaucratic rationalization, general rules and procedures came to replace action based on personal ties, and market relations were extended to new arenas" (p. 180).

This shift from premodern to modernist societies was discussed recently by social theorist Francis Fukuyama (1999), who uses the distinction in sociology between gemeinschaft ("community") and gesellschaft ("society"). The former – characteristic of premodern European peasant society – consists of "a dense network of personal relationships based heavily on kinship and on the direct, face-to-face contact that occurs in a small, closed village. Norms were largely unwritten, and individuals were bound to one another in a web of mutual interdependence that touched all aspects of life. . . . Gesellschaft, on the other hand, was the framework of laws and other formal regulations that characterized large, urban, industrial societies. Social relationships were more formalized and impersonal; individuals did not depend on one another for mutual support to nearly the same extent" (pp. 8–9). These two different societal structures no doubt call for different cognitive mechanisms in order to optimally fulfill their cognitive demands.

Gemeinschaft is clearly most compatible with the fundamental computational biases of human cognition; it is closer to the EEA in which those computational biases were selected for. Gesellschaft, in contrast, would seem to call for cognitive processes to override those biases on many occasions. School-like cognition – with its contextual overrides – is shaping minds to the requirements of gesellschaft. The requirements of gemeinschaft are probably handled quite efficiently by evolutionary adaptations that are a universal endowment of human cognition.

Consider the tensions between the modern and premodern that still exist in society and how often we resolve them in favor of the former. You are a university faculty member and two students come to you requesting exemptions from a course requirement that neither has taken. They both want to graduate at the end of this term. Student A relates to you a heartfelt and quite probably true tale of personal woe. Money is low; her single mother is ill; loan possibilities are exhausted; failure to graduate will make job possibilities (and hence the probability of *repaying* the loans) slim; getting a new lease on an apartment in a tight rental market will be impossible – and the list goes on. All of the details you ascertain to be true, but they are conjoined with one troublesome fact: The student has provided no "reason" why she did not take the required course. This all contrasts with student B, a comfortable student who is a sorority member and who drives a late-model convertible to your class. This student has found a "loophole" in the requirements: a complicated interaction between the changing course requirements of your department over the years and how the university registrar gives credit for courses taken at community colleges in a neighboring state. Which student do you think will be more likely to receive your dispensation? The premodern wars with the modern here. In my experience with universities, the behavior dictated by modernism usually prevails. Student B is likely to be more successful in her request. She has a "reason": She has shown how the "rules" support her position; she appeals to the regulations that govern academic life as they are officially registered in university documents. Student A provides none of these things. She fulfills none of the requirements or regulations with her heartfelt contextualization of her situation. The department's academic adviser may well sympathize with her plight, but he will argue that "his hands are tied" because she cannot produce a decontextualized reason – an applicable rule in the published regulations – that would support her request. This example reflects the tension of the premodern and the modern and how the latter often triumphs in such conflicts. In a fascinatingly recursive way, demands for radical decontextualization form a large part of the context of modern society! This is in fact part of the stress of modern life, its constant requirement that we override fundamental computational biases that are a natural default mode of the human cognitive apparatus.

REFERENCES

Adler, J. E. (1984). Abstraction is uncooperative. *Journal for the Theory of Social Behaviour, 14,* 165–181.
Adler, J. E. (1991). An optimist's pessimism: Conversation and conjunctions. In E. Eells & T. Maruszewski (Eds.), *Probability and rationality: Studies on L. Jonathan Cohen's philosophy of science* (pp. 251–282). Amsterdam: Editions Rodopi.
Alloy, L. B., & Tabachnik, N. (1984). Assessment of covariation by humans and animals: The joint influence of prior expectations and current situational information. *Psychological Review, 91,* 112–149.
Anderson, J. R. (1990). *The adaptive character of thought.* Hillsdale, NJ: Erlbaum.
Anderson, J. R. (1991). Is human cognition adaptive? *Behavioral and Brain Sciences, 14,* 471–517.
Anderson, J. R., Reder, L. M., & Simon, H. A. (1996). Situated learning and education. *Educational Researcher, 25*(4), 5–11.
Andreassen, P. (1987). On the social psychology of the stock market: Aggregate attributional effects and the regressiveness of prediction. *Journal of Personality and Social Psychology, 53,* 490–496.
Badcock, C. (2000). *Evolutionary psychology: A critical introduction.* Cambridge, UK: Polity Press.
Baldwin, D. A. (2000). Interpersonal understanding fuels knowledge acquisition. *Current Directions in Psychological Science, 9,* 40–45.
Banaji, M., & Greenwald, A. G. (1995). Implicit gender stereotyping in judgments of fame. *Journal of Personality and Social Psychology, 68,* 181–198.
Bar-Hillel, M., & Falk, R. (1982). Some teasers concerning conditional probabilities. *Cognition, 11,* 109–122.
Barkow, J., Cosmides, L., & Tooby, J. (Eds.). (1992). *The adapted mind.* New York: Oxford University Press.
Baron, J. (1993). *Morality and rational choice.* Dordrecht: Kluwer.
Baron, J. (1994). Nonconsequentialist decisions. *Behavioral and Brain Sciences, 17,* 1–42.
Baron, J. (1995). Myside bias in thinking about abortion. *Thinking and Reasoning, 1,* 221–235.
Baron, J. (1998). *Judgment misguided: Intuition and error in public decision making.* New York: Oxford University Press.

Baron-Cohen, S. (1995). *Mindblindness: An essay on autism and theory of mind.* Cambridge, MA: MIT Press.

Baron-Cohen, S. (1998). Does the study of autism justify minimalist innate modularity? *Learning and Individual Differences, 10,* 179–192.

Barton, R. A., & Dunbar, R. (1997). Evolution of the social brain. In A. Whiten & R. W. Byrne (Eds.), *Machiavellian intelligence II: Extensions and evaluations* (pp. 240–263). Cambridge: Cambridge University Press.

Belsky, G., & Gilovich, T. (1999). *Why smart people make big money mistakes – And how to correct them: Lessons from the new science of behavioral economics.* New York: Simon & Schuster.

The benevolence of self-interest. (1998, December 12). *The Economist,* 80.

Bereiter, C. (1997). Situated cognition and how to overcome it. In D. Kirshner & J. A. Whitson (Eds.), *Situated cognition: Social, semiotic, and psychological perspectives* (pp. 3–12). Mahwah, NJ: Erlbaum.

Blackmore, S. (1999). *The meme machine.* New York: Oxford University Press.

Brase, G. L., Cosmides, L., & Tooby, J. (1998). Individuation, counting, and statistical inference: The role of frequency and whole-object representations in judgment under uncertainty. *Journal of Experimental Psychology: General, 127,* 3–21.

Brody, N. (1997). Intelligence, schooling, and society. *American Psychologist, 52,* 1046–1050.

Bronfenbrenner, U., McClelland, P., Wethington, E., Moen, P., & Ceci, S. J. (1996). *The state of Americans.* New York: Free Press.

Broniarczyk, S., & Alba, J. W. (1994). Theory versus data in prediction and correlation tasks. *Organizational Behavior and Human Decision Processes, 57,* 117–139.

Brothers, L. (1990). The social brain: A project for integrating primate behaviour and neuropsychology in a new domain. *Concepts in Neuroscience, 1,* 27–51.

Bruner, J. (1986). *Actual minds, possible worlds.* Cambridge, MA: Harvard University Press.

Bruner, J. (1990). *Acts of meaning.* Cambridge, MA: Harvard University Press.

Bruner, J. (1996). Frames for thinking: Ways of making meaning. In D. R. Olson & N. Torrance (Eds.), *Modes of thought: Explorations in culture and cognition* (pp. 93–105). New York: Cambridge University Press.

Bugental, D. B. (2000). Acquisitions of the algorithms of social life: A domain-based approach. *Psychological Bulletin, 126,* 187–219.

Buss, D. M. (1999). *Evolutionary psychology: The new science of the mind.* Boston: Allyn and Bacon.

Buss, D. M. (2000). The evolution of happiness. *American Psychologist, 55,* 15–23.

Byrne, R. W., & Whiten, A. (Eds.). (1988). *Machiavellian intelligence: Social expertise and the evolution of intellect in monkeys, apes, and humans.* Oxford: Oxford University Press.

Caporael, L. R. (1997). The evolution of truly social cognition: The core configurations model. *Personality and Social Psychology Review, 1,* 276–298.

Carrithers, M. (1995). Stories in the social and mental life of people. In E. N. Goody (Ed.), *Social intelligence and interaction: Expressions and implications of the social bias in human intelligence* (pp. 261–277). Cambridge: Cambridge University Press.

Cartwright, J. (2000). *Evolution and human behavior.* Cambridge, MA: MIT Press.

Chapman, L., & Chapman, J. (1967). Genesis of popular but erroneous psychodiagnostic observations. *Journal of Abnormal Psychology, 72,* 193–204.

Chapman, L., & Chapman, J. (1969). Illusory correlation as an obstacle to the use of valid psychodiagnostic signs. *Journal of Abnormal Psychology, 74,* 271–280.

Chapman, M. (1993). Everyday reasoning and the revision of belief. In J. M. Puckett & H. W. Reese (Eds.), *Mechanisms of everyday cognition* (pp. 95–113). Hillsdale, NJ: Erlbaum.

Cheng, P. W., & Holyoak, K. J. (1985). Pragmatic reasoning schemas. *Cognitive Psychology, 17,* 391–416.

Clark, A. (1997). *Being there: Putting brain, body, and world together again.* Cambridge, MA: MIT Press.

Cooper, W. S. (1989). How evolutionary biology challenges the classical theory of rational choice. *Biology and Philosophy, 4,* 457–481.

Cosmides, L. (1989). The logic of social exchange: Has natural selection shaped how humans reason? Studies with the Wason selection task. *Cognition, 31,* 187–276.

Cosmides, L., & Tooby, J. (1992). Cognitive adaptations for social exchange. In J. Barkow, L. Cosmides, & J. Tooby (Eds.), *The adapted mind* (pp. 163–205). New York: Oxford University Press.

Cosmides, L., & Tooby, J. (1994). Beyond intuition and instinct blindness: Toward an evolutionarily rigorous cognitive science. *Cognition, 50,* 41–77.

Cosmides, L., & Tooby, J. (1996). Are humans good intuitive statisticians after all? Rethinking some conclusions from the literature on judgment under uncertainty. *Cognition, 58,* 1–73.

Cummins, D. D. (1996). Evidence for the innateness of deontic reasoning. *Mind & Language, 11,* 160–190.

Dawes, R. M. (1988). *Rational choice in an uncertain world.* San Diego, CA: Harcourt, Brace Jovanovich.

Dawes, R. M. (1989). Statistical criteria for establishing a truly false consensus effect. *Journal of Experimental Social Psychology, 25,* 1–17.

Dawes, R. M. (1990). The potential nonfalsity of the false consensus effect. In R. M. Hogarth (Ed.), *Insights into decision making* (pp. 179–199). Chicago: University of Chicago Press.

Dawes, R. M. (1991). Probabilistic versus causal thinking. In D. Cicchetti & W. Grove (Eds.), *Thinking clearly about psychology: Essays in honor of Paul E. Meehl* (Vol. 1, pp. 235–264). Minneapolis: University of Minnesota Press.

Dawes, R. M. (1994). *House of cards: Psychology and psychotherapy built on myth.* New York: Free Press.

Dawkins, R. (1976). *The selfish gene* (new edition, 1989). New York: Oxford University Press.

Dawkins, R. (1982). *The extended phenotype.* New York: Oxford University Press.

Dawkins, R. (1986). *The blind watchmaker.* New York: Norton.

Dennett, D. C. (1978). *Brainstorms: Philosophical essays on mind and psychology.* Cambridge, MA: MIT Press.

Dennett, D. (1987). *The intentional stance.* Cambridge, MA: MIT Press.

Dennett, D. C. (1991). *Consciousness explained.* Boston: Little, Brown.

Dennett, D. C. (1995). *Darwin's dangerous idea: Evolution and the meanings of life.* New York: Simon & Schuster.

Dennett, D. C. (1996). *Kinds of minds: Toward an understanding of consciousness.* New York: Basic Books.

Denzau, A. T., & North, D. C. (1994). Shared mental models: Ideologies and institutions. *Kyklos, 47*, 3–31.

Dillard, A. (1999). *For the time being*. Toronto: Penguin Books Canada.

Doherty, M. E., & Mynatt, C. (1990). Inattention to P(H) and to P(D/~H): A converging operation. *Acta Psychologica, 75*, 1–11.

Dominowski, R. L. (1995). Content effects in Wason's selection task. In S. E. Newstead & J. S. B. T. Evans (Eds.), *Perspectives on thinking and reasoning* (pp. 41–65). Hove, UK: Erlbaum.

Donaldson, M. (1978). *Children's minds*. London: Fontana Paperbacks.

Donaldson, M. (1993). *Human minds: An exploration*. New York: Viking Penguin.

Dulany, D. E., & Hilton, D. J. (1991). Conversational implicature, conscious representation, and the conjunction fallacy. *Social Cognition, 9*, 85–110.

Dunbar, R. (1998). Theory of mind and the evolution of language. In J. R. Hurford, M. Studdert-Kennedy, & C. Knight (Eds.), *Approaches to the evolution of language* (pp. 92–110). Cambridge: Cambridge University Press.

Edwards, K., & Smith, E. E. (1996). A disconfirmation bias in the evaluation of arguments. *Journal of Personality and Social Psychology, 71*, 5–24.

Einhorn, H. J., & Hogarth, R. M. (1981). Behavioral decision theory: Processes of judgment and choice. *Annual Review of Psychology, 32*, 53–88.

Epstein, S., Donovan, S., & Denes-Raj, V. (1999). The missing link in the paradox of the Linda conjunction problem: Beyond knowing and thinking of the conjunction rule, the intrinsic appeal of heuristic processing. *Personality and Social Psychology Bulletin, 25*, 204–214.

Evans, J. St. B. T. (1982). *The psychology of deductive reasoning*. London: Routledge.

Evans, J. St. B. T. (1989). *Bias in human reasoning: Causes and consequences*. London: Erlbaum Associates.

Evans, J. St. B. T. (1996). Deciding before you think: Relevance and reasoning in the selection task. *British Journal of Psychology, 87*, 223–240.

Evans, J. St. B. T., Barston, J., & Pollard, P. (1983). On the conflict between logic and belief in syllogistic reasoning. *Memory & Cognition, 11*, 295–306.

Evans, J. St. B. T., Newstead, S. E., & Byrne, R. M. J. (1993). *Human reasoning: The psychology of deduction*. Hove, UK: Erlbaum.

Evans, J. St. B. T., & Over, D. E. (1996). *Rationality and reasoning*. Hove, UK: Psychology Press.

Evans, J. St. B. T., & Over, D. E. (1999). Explicit representations in hypothetical thinking. *Behavioral and Brain Sciences, 22*, 763–764.

Evans, J. St. B. T., Over, D. E., & Manktelow, K. (1993). Reasoning, decision making and rationality. *Cognition, 49*, 165–187.

Falk, R. (1992). A closer look at the probabilities of the notorious three prisoners. *Cognition, 43*, 197–223.

Fiedler, K. (1988). The dependence of the conjunction fallacy on subtle linguistic factors. *Psychological Research, 50*, 123–129.

Flanagan, O. (1996). *Self expressions: Mind, morals, and the meaning of life*. New York: Oxford University Press.

Floden, R. E., Buchmann, M., & Schwille, J. R. (1987). Breaking with everyday experience. *Teacher's College Record, 88*, 485–506.

Fodor, J. (1983). *Modularity of mind*. Cambridge: MIT Press.

Frank, R. H., & Cook, P. J. (1995). *The winner-take-all society*. New York: Free Press.

Friedrich, J. (1993). Primary error detection and minimization (PEDMIN) strategies in social cognition: A reinterpretation of confirmation bias phenomena. *Psychological Review, 100,* 298–319.

Fukuyama, F. (1999). *The great disruption: Human nature and the reconstitution of social order.* New York: Free Press.

Funder, D. C. (1987). Errors and mistakes: Evaluating the accuracy of social judgment. *Psychological Bulletin, 101,* 75–90.

Garb, H. N., Florio, C. M., & Grove, W. M. (1998). The validity of the Rorschach and the Minnesota Multiphasic Personality Inventory. *Psychological Science, 9,* 402–404.

Geary, D. C., & Bjorklund, D. F. (2000). Evolutionary developmental psychology. *Child Development, 71,* 57–65.

Gebauer, G., & Laming, D. (1997). Rational choices in Wason's selection task. *Psychological Research, 60,* 284–293.

Gibbard, A. (1990). *Wise choices, apt feelings: A theory of normative judgment.* Cambridge, MA: Harvard University Press.

Gigerenzer, G. (1991). How to make cognitive illusions disappear: Beyond "heuristics and biases." *European Review of Social Psychology, 2,* 83–115.

Gigerenzer, G. (1993). The bounded rationality of probabilistic mental models. In K. Manktelow & D. Over (Eds.), *Rationality: Psychological and philosophical perspectives* (pp. 284–313). London: Routledge.

Gigerenzer, G. (1996a). On narrow norms and vague heuristics: A reply to Kahneman and Tversky (1996). *Psychological Review, 103,* 592–596.

Gigerenzer, G. (1996b). Rationality: Why social context matters. In P. B. Baltes & U. Staudinger (Eds.), *Interactive minds: Life-span perspectives on the social foundation of cognition* (pp. 319–346). Cambridge: Cambridge University Press.

Gigerenzer, G., & Hoffrage, U. (1995). How to improve Bayesian reasoning without instruction: Frequency formats. *Psychological Review, 102,* 684–704.

Gigerenzer, G., Hoffrage, U., & Kleinbolting, H. (1991). Probabilistic mental models: A Brunswikian theory of confidence. *Psychological Review, 98,* 506–528.

Gigerenzer, G., & Todd, P. M. (1999). *Simple heuristics that make us smart.* New York: Oxford University Press.

Goody, E. N. (Ed.). (1995). *Social intelligence and interaction: Expressions and implications of the social bias in human intelligence.* Cambridge: Cambridge University Press.

Goody, J. (1977). *The domestication of the savage mind.* New York: Cambridge University Press.

Gordon, R. A. (1997). Everyday life as an intelligence test: Effects of intelligence and intelligence context. *Intelligence, 24,* 203–320.

Gottfredson, L. S. (1997). Why g matters: The complexity of everyday life. *Intelligence, 24,* 79–132.

Granberg, D. (1995). The Monte Hall dilemma. *Personality and Social Psychology Bulletin, 31,* 711–723.

Greenwald, A. G., McGhee, D. E., & Schwartz, J. L. K. (1998). Measuring individual differences in implicit cognition: The implicit association test. *Journal of Personality and Social Psychology, 74,* 1464–1480.

Grice, H. P. (1975). Logic and conversation. In P. Cole & J. Morgan (Eds.), *Syntax and semantics: Vol. 3., Speech acts* (pp. 41–58). New York: Academic Press.

Griggs, R. A. (1989). To "see" or not to "see": That is the selection task. *Quarterly Journal of Experimental Psychology, 41A,* 517–529.

Griggs, R. A., & Cox, J. R. (1982). The elusive thematic-materials effect in Wason's selection task. *British Journal of Psychology, 73,* 407–420.

Hardman, D. (1998). Does reasoning occur on the selection task? A comparison of relevance-based theories. *Thinking and Reasoning, 4,* 353–376.

Hasher, L., & Zacks, R. T. (1979). Automatic processing of fundamental information: The case of frequency of occurrence. *Journal of Experimental Psychology: General, 39,* 1372–1388.

Hastie, R., & Rasinski, K. A. (1988). The concept of accuracy in social judgment. In D. Bar-Tal & A. Kruglanski (Eds.), *The social psychology of knowledge* (pp. 193–208). Cambridge: Cambridge University Press.

Hertwig, R., & Gigerenzer, G. (1999). The conjunction fallacy revisited: How intelligent inferences look like reasoning errors. *Journal of Behavioral Decision Making, 12,* 275–305.

Hilton, D. J. (1995). The social context of reasoning: Conversational inference and rational judgment. *Psychological Bulletin, 118,* 248–271.

Hilton, D. J., & Slugoski, B. R. (2000). Judgment and decision making in social context: Discourse processes and rational inference. In T. Connolly, H. R. Arkes, & K. R. Hammond (Eds.), *Judgment and decision making: An interdisciplinary reader* (2nd ed., pp. 651–676). Cambridge, MA: Cambridge University Press.

Hoch, S. J. (1987). Perceived consensus and predictive accuracy: The pros and cons of projection. *Journal of Personality and Social Psychology, 53,* 221–234.

Howson, C., & Urbach, P. (1993). *Scientific reasoning: The Bayesian approach* (2nd ed). Chicago: Open Court.

Humphrey, N. (1976). The social function of intellect. In P. P. G. Bateson & R. A. Hinde (Eds.), *Growing points in ethology* (pp. 303–317). London: Faber & Faber.

Humphrey, N. (1986). *The inner eye.* London: Faber & Faber.

Hunt, E. (1995). *Will we be smart enough? A cognitive analysis of the coming workforce.* New York: Russell Sage Foundation.

Hunt, E. (1999). Intelligence and human resources: Past, present, and future. In P. Ackerman, P. Kyllonen, & R. Richards (Eds.), *Learning and individual differences: Process, trait, and content determinants* (pp. 3–28). Washington, DC: American Psychological Association.

Jepson, C., Krantz, D., & Nisbett, R. (1983). Inductive reasoning: Competence or skill? *Behavioral and Brain Sciences, 6,* 494–501.

Johnson-Laird, P. N. (1999). Deductive reasoning. *Annual Review of Psychology, 50,* 109–135.

Jolly, A. (1966). Lemur social behaviour and primate intelligence. *Science, 153,* 501–506.

Kahneman, D. (2000). A psychological point of view: Violations of rational rules as a diagnostic of mental processes. *Behavioral and Brain Sciences, 23,* 681–683.

Kahneman, D., Slovic, P., & Tversky, A. (Eds.). (1982). *Judgment under uncertainty: Heuristics and biases.* Cambridge: Cambridge University Press.

Kahneman, D., & Tversky, A. (1973). On the psychology of prediction. *Psychological Review, 80,* 237–251.

Kahneman, D., & Tversky, A. (1982). On the study of statistical intuitions. *Cognition, 11,* 123–141.

Kahneman, D., & Tversky, A. (1996). On the reality of cognitive illusions. *Psychological Review, 103*, 582–591.

Kahneman, D., & Tversky, A. (Eds.). (2000). *Choices, values, and frames*. New York: Cambridge University Press.

Kelley, D. (1990). *The art of reasoning*. New York: Norton.

Kim, J. (1994, September). Watch out for investing newsletters luring you with outdated returns. *Money Magazine*, 12–13.

King, R. N., & Koehler, D. J. (2000). Illusory correlations in graphological inference. *Journal of Experimental Psychology: Applied, 6*, 336–348.

Kirby, K. N. (1994). Probabilities and utilities of fictional outcomes in Wason's four-card selection task. *Cognition, 51*, 1–28.

Klaczynski, P. A., Gordon, D. H., & Fauth, J. (1997). Goal-oriented critical reasoning and individual differences in critical reasoning biases. *Journal of Educational Psychology, 89*, 470–485.

Klayman, J., & Ha, Y. (1987). Confirmation, disconfirmation, and information in hypothesis testing. *Psychological Review, 94*, 211–228.

Koehler, J. J. (1993). The influence of prior beliefs on scientific judgments of evidence quality. *Organizational Behavior and Human Decision Processes, 56*, 28–55.

Koriat, A., Lichtenstein, S., & Fischhoff, B. (1980). Reasons for confidence. *Journal of Experimental Psychology: Human Learning and Memory, 6*, 107–118.

Kornblith, H. (1993). *Inductive inference and its natural ground*. Cambridge, MA: MIT Press.

Krantz, D. H. (1981). Improvements in human reasoning and an error in L. J. Cohen's. *Behavioral and Brain Sciences, 4*, 340–341.

Krueger, J., & Zeiger, J. (1993). Social categorization and the truly false consensus effect. *Journal of Personality and Social Psychology, 65*, 670–680.

Kruglanski, A. W., & Ajzen, I. (1983). Bias and error in human judgment. *European Journal of Social Psychology, 13*, 1–44.

Kuhn, D. (1991). *The skills of argument*. Cambridge: Cambridge University Press.

Kuhn, D. (1993). Connecting scientific and informal reasoning. *Merrill-Palmer Quarterly, 38*, 74–103.

Kuhn, D. (1996). Is good thinking scientific thinking? In D. R. Olson & N. Torrance (Eds.), *Modes of thought: Explorations in culture and cognition* (pp. 261–281). New York: Cambridge University Press.

Kummer, H., Daston, L., Gigerenzer, G., & Silk, J. B. (1997). The social intelligence hypothesis. In P. Weingart, S. D. Mitchell, P. J. Richerson, & S. Maasen (Eds.), *Human by nature: Between biology and the social sciences* (pp. 157–179). Mahwah, NJ: Lawrence Erlbaum Associates.

Kunda, Z. (1999). *Social cognition: Making sense of people*. Cambridge, MA: MIT Press.

Langer, E. J. (1989). *Mindfulness*. Reading, MA: Addison-Wesley.

Langer, E. J., Blank, A., & Chanowitz, B. (1978). The mindlessness of ostensibly thoughtful action: The role of "placebic" information in interpersonal interaction. *Journal of Personality and Social Psychology, 36*, 635–642.

Lefkowitz, B. (1997). *Our guys: The Glen Ridge rape and the secret life of the perfect suburb*. Berkeley: University of California Press.

Levin, I. P., Wasserman, E. A., & Kao, S. F. (1993). Multiple methods of examining biased information use in contingency judgments. *Organizational Behavior and Human Decision Processes, 55*, 228–250.

Levinson, S. C. (1983). *Pragmatics*. Cambridge: Cambridge University Press.

Levinson, S. C. (1995). Interactional biases in human thinking. In E. Goody (Ed.), *Social intelligence and interaction* (pp. 221–260). Cambridge: Cambridge University Press.

Liberman, N., & Klar, Y. (1996). Hypothesis testing in Wason's selection task: Social exchange cheating detection or task understanding. *Cognition, 58*, 127–156.

Lilienfeld, S. O. (1999). Projective measures of personality and psychopathology: How well do they work? *Skeptical Inquirer, 23*(5), 32–39.

Lilienfeld, S. O., Wood, J. M., & Garb, H. N. (2000). The scientific status of projective techniques. *Psychological Science in the Public Interest, 1*, 27–66.

Luria, A. R. (1976). *Cognitive development: Its cultural and social foundations*. Cambridge, MA: Harvard University Press.

Macdonald, R. R., & Gilhooly, K. J. (1990). More about Linda *or* conjunctions in context. *European Journal of Cognitive Psychology, 2*, 57–70.

Malkiel, B. G. (1999). *A random walk down Wall Street*. New York: W. W. Norton.

Manktelow, K. I. (1999). *Reasoning & thinking*. Hove, UK: Psychology Press.

Manktelow, K. I., & Evans, J. S. B. T. (1979). Facilitation of reasoning by realism: Effect or non-effect? *British Journal of Psychology, 70*, 477–488.

Manktelow, K. I., & Over, D. E. (1991). Social roles and utilities in reasoning with deontic conditionals. *Cognition, 39*, 85–105.

Manktelow, K. I., Sutherland, E., & Over, D. E. (1995). Probabilistic factors in deontic reasoning. *Thinking and Reasoning, 1*, 201–219.

Margolis, H. (1987). *Patterns, thinking, and cognition*. Chicago: University of Chicago Press.

Margolis, H. (1996). *Dealing with risk*. Chicago: University of Chicago Press.

Markovits, H., & Nantel, G. (1989). The belief-bias effect in the production and evaluation of logical conclusions. *Memory & Cognition, 17*, 11–17.

McCain, R. A. (1991). A linguistic conception of rationality. *Social Science Information, 30*(2), 233–255.

Mercer, T. (2000, September 16). Navigating the shark-eat-shark world of "compassionate" airfares. *The Globe and Mail* (Toronto), T5.

Messer, W. S., & Griggs, R. A. (1993). Another look at Linda. *Bulletin of the Psychonomic Society, 31*, 193–196.

Minsky, M. (1985). *The society of mind*. New York: Simon & Schuster.

Mitchell, P., Robinson, E. J., Isaacs, J. E., & Nye, R. M. (1996). Contamination in reasoning about false belief: An instance of realist bias in adults but not children. *Cognition, 59*, 1–21.

Mithen, S. (1996). *The prehistory of mind: The cognitive origins of art and science*. London: Thames and Hudson.

Neimark, E. (1987). *Adventures in thinking*. San Diego, CA: Harcourt Brace Jovanovich.

Newstead, S. E., & Evans, J. St. B. T. (Eds.). (1995). *Perspectives on thinking and reasoning*. Hove, UK: Erlbaum.

Nickerson, R. S. (1999). How we know – and sometimes misjudge – what others know: Imputing one's own knowledge to others. *Psychological Bulletin, 125*, 737–759.

Nickerson, R. S., Baddeley, A., & Freeman, B. (1987). Are people's estimates of what other people know influenced by what they themselves know? *Acta Psychologica, 64,* 245–259.

Nisbett, R. E., & Ross, L. (1980). *Human inference: Strategies and shortcomings of social judgment.* Englewood Cliffs, NJ: Prentice-Hall.

Nozick, R. (1993). *The nature of rationality.* Princeton, NJ: Princeton University Press.

Oaksford, M., & Chater, N. (1994). A rational analysis of the selection task as optimal data selection. *Psychological Review, 101,* 608–631.

Oaksford, M., & Chater, N. (1995). Theories of reasoning and the computational explanation of everyday inference. *Thinking and Reasoning, 1,* 121–152.

Oaksford, M., & Chater, N. (1996). Rational explanation of the selection task. *Psychological Review, 103,* 381–391.

Oaksford, M., & Chater, N. (1998). *Rationality in an uncertain world.* Hove, UK: Psychology Press.

Oaksford, M., Chater, N., Grainger, B., & Larkin, J. (1997). Optimal data selection in the reduced array selection task (RAST). *Journal of Experimental Psychology: Learning, Memory, and Cognition, 23,* 441–458.

Oatley, K. (1992). *Best laid schemes: The psychology of emotions.* Cambridge: Cambridge University Press.

Oatley, K. (1996). Emotions, rationality, and informal reasoning. In J. V. Oakhill & A. Garnham (Eds.), *Mental models in cognitive science: Essays in honor of Phil Johnson-Laird* (pp. 1–22). Hove, UK: Psychology Press.

Oatley, K. (1999). Why fiction may be twice as true as fact: Fiction as cognitive and emotional simulation. *Review of General Psychology, 3,* 101–117.

Olson, D. R. (1977). From utterance to text: The bias of language in speech and writing. *Harvard Educational Review, 47,* 257–281.

Olson, D. R. (1986). Intelligence and literacy: The relationships between intelligence and the technologies of representation and communication. In R. J. Sternberg & R. K. Wagner (Eds.), *Practical intelligence* (pp. 338–360). Cambridge: Cambridge University Press.

Olson, D. R. (1994). *The world on paper.* Cambridge, UK: Cambridge University Press.

Perkins, D. N., Farady, M., & Bushey, B. (1991). Everyday reasoning and the roots of intelligence. In J. Voss, D. Perkins, & J. Segal (Eds.), *Informal reasoning and education* (pp. 83–105). Hillsdale, NJ: Erlbaum.

Piaget, J. (1972). Intellectual evolution from adolescence to adulthood. *Human Development, 15,* 1–12.

Pinker, S. (1994). *The language instinct.* New York: William Morrow.

Pinker, S. (1997). *How the mind works.* New York: Norton.

Plotkin, H. (1998). *Evolution in mind: An introduction to evolutionary psychology.* Cambridge, MA: Harvard University Press.

Politzer, G., & Noveck, I. A. (1991). Are conjunction rule violations the result of conversational rule violations? *Journal of Psycholinguistic Research, 20,* 83–103.

Pollard, P., & Evans, J. St. B. T. (1987). Content and context effects in reasoning. *American Journal of Psychology, 100,* 41–60.

Pollock, J. L. (1995). *Cognitive carpentry: A blueprint for how to build a person.* Cambridge, MA: MIT Press.

Reber, A. S. (1992a). The cognitive unconscious: An evolutionary perspective. *Consciousness and Cognition, 1,* 93–133.

Reber, A. S. (1992b). An evolutionary context for the cognitive unconscious. *Philosophical Psychology, 5,* 33–51.

Rescher, N. (1988). *Rationality: A philosophical inquiry into the nature and rationale of reason.* Oxford: Oxford University Press.

Rips, L. J. (1994). *The psychology of proof.* Cambridge, MA: MIT Press.

Sá, W., & Stanovich, K. E. (2001). The domain specificity and generality of mental contamination: Accuracy and projection in mental content judgments. *British Journal of Psychology, 92,* 281–302.

Sá, W., West, R. F., & Stanovich, K. E. (1999). The domain specificity and generality of belief bias: Searching for a generalizable critical thinking skill. *Journal of Educational Psychology, 91,* 497–510.

Schank, R. (1991). *Tell me a story.* New York: Scribner's.

Schustack, M. W., & Sternberg, R. J. (1981). Evaluation of evidence in causal inference. *Journal of Experimental Psychology: General, 110,* 101–120.

Schwarz, N. (1996). *Cognition and communication: Judgmental biases, research methods, and the logic of conversation.* Mahwah, NJ: Lawrence Erlbaum Associates.

Shaffer, L. (1981). The growth and limits of recipe knowledge. *Journal of Mind and Behavior, 2,* 71–83.

Shefrin, H., & Statman, M. (1986). How not to make money in the stock market. *Psychology Today, 20,* 53–57.

Shiller, R. (1987). The volatility of stock market prices. *Science, 235,* 33–37.

Shontz, F., & Green, P. (1992). Trends in research on the Rorschach: Review and recommendations. *Applied and Preventive Psychology, 1,* 149–156.

Sigel, I. E. (1993). The centrality of a distancing model for the development of representational competence. In R. Cocking & K. Renninger (Eds.), *The development and meaning of psychological distance* (pp. 141–158). Hillsdale, NJ: Erlbaum.

Skyrms, B. (1996). *The evolution of the social contract.* Cambridge: Cambridge University Press.

Sloman, S. A. (1996). The empirical case for two systems of reasoning. *Psychological Bulletin, 119,* 3–22.

Slugoski, B. R., & Wilson, A. E. (1998). Contribution of conversation skills to the production of judgmental errors. *European Journal of Social Psychology, 28,* 575–601.

Sperber, D., Cara, F., & Girotto, V. (1995). Relevance theory explains the selection task. *Cognition, 57,* 31–95.

Sperber, D., & Wilson, D. (1986). *Relevance: Communication and cognition.* Cambridge, MA: Harvard University Press.

Stanovich, K. E. (1999). *Who is rational? Studies of individual differences in reasoning.* Mahweh, NJ: Erlbaum.

Stanovich, K. E., & West, R. F. (1997). Reasoning independently of prior belief and individual differences in actively open-minded thinking. *Journal of Educational Psychology, 89,* 342–357.

Stanovich, K. E., & West, R. F. (1998a). Cognitive ability and variation in selection task performance. *Thinking and Reasoning, 4,* 193–230.

Stanovich, K. E., & West, R. F. (1998b). Individual differences in framing and conjunction effects. *Thinking and Reasoning, 4,* 289–317.

Stanovich, K. E., & West, R. F. (1998c). Individual differences in rational thought. *Journal of Experimental Psychology: General, 127,* 161–188.

Stanovich, K. E., & West, R. F. (1998d). Who uses base rates and P(D/~H)? An analysis of individual differences. *Memory & Cognition, 28,* 161–179.

Stanovich, K. E., & West, R. F. (2000). Individual differences in reasoning: Implications for the rationality debate? *Behavioral and Brain Sciences, 23,* 645–726.

Sternberg, R. J. (1997). The concept of intelligence and its role in lifelong learning and success. *American Psychologist, 52,* 1030–1037.

Sternberg, R. J., & Wagner, R. K. (Eds.). (1986). *Practical intelligence.* Cambridge: Cambridge University Press.

Stevenson, R. J. (1993). Rationality and reality. In K. Manktelow & D. Over (Eds.), *Rationality: Psychological and philosophical perspectives* (pp. 61–82). London: Routledge.

Stevenson, R. J., & Over, D. E. (1995). Deduction from uncertain premises. *Quarterly Journal of Experimental Psychology, 48A,* 613–643.

Sutherland, S. (1992). *Irrationality: The enemy within.* London: Constable.

Thagard, P. (1992). *Conceptual revolutions.* Princeton, NJ: Princeton University Press.

Thagard, P., & Nisbett, R. E. (1983). Rationality and charity. *Philosophy of Science, 50,* 250–267.

Thaler, R. H. (1992). *The winner's curse: Paradoxes and anomalies of economic life.* New York: Free Press.

Thomas, M., & Karmiloff-Smith, A. (1998). Quo vadis modularity in the 1990s? *Learning and Individual Differences, 10,* 245–250.

Tomasello, M. (1998). Social cognition and the evolution of culture. In J. Langer & M. Killen (Eds.), *Piaget, evolution, and development* (pp. 221–245). Mahwah, NJ: Lawrence Erlbaum Associates.

Tomasello, M. (1999). *The cultural origins of human cognition.* Cambridge, MA: Harvard University Press.

Tooby, J., & Cosmides, L. (1992). The psychological foundations of culture. In J. Barkow, L. Cosmides, & J. Tooby (Eds.), *The adapted mind* (pp. 19–136). New York: Oxford University Press.

Tsimpli, I., & Smith, N. (1998). Modules and quasi-modules: Language and theory of mind in a polyglot savant. *Learning and Individual Differences, 10,* 193–216.

Tversky, A., & Kahneman, D. (1974). Judgment under uncertainty: Heuristics and biases. *Science, 185,* 1124–1131.

Tversky, A., & Kahneman, D. (1983). Extensional versus intuitive reasoning: The conjunction fallacy in probability judgment. *Psychological Review, 90,* 293–315.

Updegrave, W. L. (1995, August). Why funds don't do better. *Money Magazine,* 58–65.

Voss, J., Perkins, D. & Segal J. (Eds.). (1991). *Informal reasoning and education.* Hillsdale, NJ: Erlbaum.

Wagenaar, W. A. (1988). *Paradoxes of gambling behavior.* Hove, UK: Erlbaum.

Wason, P. C. (1966). Reasoning. In B. Foss (Ed.), *New horizons in psychology* (pp. 135–151). Harmonsworth, UK: Penguin.

Whiten, A., & Byrne, R. W. (Eds.). (1997). *Machiavellian intelligence II: Extensions and evaluations.* Cambridge: Cambridge University Press.

Widiger, T., & Schilling, M. (1980). Towards a construct validation of the Rorschach. *Journal of Personality Assessment, 44,* 450–459.

Wolford, G., Miller, M. B., & Gazzaniga, M. S. (2000). The left hemisphere's role in hypothesis formation. *Journal of Neuroscience, 20,* 1–4.

Wood, J. M., Nezworski, T., & Stejskal, W. J. (1996). The comprehensive system for the Rorschach: A critical examination. *Psychological Science, 7,* 3–10.

ACKNOWLEDGMENT

Preparation of this chapter was supported by a grant from the Social Sciences and Humanities Research Council of Canada to Keith E. Stanovich.

11

Analogical Transfer in Problem Solving

Miriam Bassok

When people encounter a novel problem, they might be reminded of a problem they solved previously, retrieve its solution, and use it, possibly with some adaptation, to solve the novel problem. This sequence of events, or "problem-solving transfer," has important cognitive benefits: It saves the effort needed for derivation of new solutions and may allow people to solve problems they wouldn't know to solve otherwise. Of course, the cognitive benefits of problem-solving transfer are limited to the case in which people retrieve and apply a solution to an analogous problem that, indeed, can help them solve the novel problem (*positive transfer*). But people might be also reminded of and attempt to transfer a solution to a nonanalogous problem (*negative transfer*) and thereby waste their cognitive resources or arrive at an erroneous solution. The challenge facing researchers and educators is to identify the conditions that promote positive and deter negative problem-solving transfer. In this chapter, I describe how researchers who study analogical transfer address this challenge. Specifically, I describe work that examined how problem similarity affects transfer performance and how people determine whether the learned and the novel problems are similar. Throughout the chapter I highlight the relevance of research on analogical transfer to instructional contexts and illustrate the main concepts and findings with examples of mathematical word problems.

SIMILARITY IN SURFACE AND STRUCTURE

As in every other case of learning generalization, the main variable that mediates problem-solving transfer is the degree of similarity between the learned (*base*) and novel (*target*) problems. Transfer is quite common between highly similar problems, especially when people encounter the problems in the same or similar context. For example, students are very likely to solve end-of-the-chapter textbook problems using worked-out solutions of similar problems in that chapter (e.g., Chi & Bassok, 1989; LeFevre &

Dixon, 1986). Unfortunately, when the similarity between the base and the target problems is less obvious, people often fail to notice the relevance of a previously learned base solution to the target problem. For example, there appears to be little transfer from textbook math and physics problems to analogous real-life problems (e.g., Lave, 1988; McClosky, 1983; Nunes, Schliemann, & Carraher, 1993).

Although highly similar problems are more likely to be solved in a similar way than dissimilar problems, reliance on overall similarity may lead to negative transfer and block positive transfer. This is because problems that appear to be highly similar might actually entail different solutions, and problems that appear to be quite different might actually entail similar solutions. To understand the conditions that promote flexible transfer, it is necessary to understand the mechanism by which similarity affects transfer performance. To this end, researchers who study analogical transfer make a principled distinction between similarity in the problems' *structure* and *surface* (Gentner, 1983), which often coincides with the distinction between aspects of similarity that are and are not relevant to the problem solutions (e.g., Holyoak, 1985).

Structural similarity refers to similarity in the way the respective variables in the base and the target problems are interrelated (e.g., LIVES IN (bird, nest) in the base problem and LIVES IN (person, house) in the target). It is solution relevant because when the variables of distinct problems are organized into identical (isomorphic) or similar (homomorphic) relational structures, the problems can be usually solved in the same or similar way. Surface similarity refers to similarity of the particular entities that serve as arguments of the problem structures (e.g., similarity between a bird and a person in the LIVES IN relation), the problems' phrasing, story line, and the context in which people encounter the problems (e.g., in school or out). These aspects of problems are often solution irrelevant in the sense that they have no direct bearing on the problems' solutions.

To illustrate the surface-structure distinction in problem solving, consider the following two arithmetic word problems:

> *Problem 1*: Jane, Sue, and Mary want to start a ribbon collection. Jane has three ribbons, Sue has seven, and Mary has six. How many ribbons do these girls have altogether?
>
> *Problem 2*: Jane and Sue are wrapping three gift boxes for Mary's birthday. They want to decorate the boxes with six ribbons and use the same number of ribbons on each box. How many ribbons should they use for each box?

On the surface, Problems 1 and 2 are quite similar: They describe the same characters (Jane, Sue, and Mary) and share some objects (ribbons) and numbers (3 and 6). However, these problems differ in their underlying structures and therefore require different mathematical solutions: Problem 1 involves three sets of objects that have to be combined (an addition solution), whereas Problem 2 involves one set of objects that has to be partitioned into three equal subsets (a division solution).

The complementary case involves problems that differ on the surface but share the same underlying structure and therefore can be solved in the same way. To illustrate, consider a third arithmetic word problem:

Problem 3: John and Rick enjoy seeing movies together. They saw four movies in June, five in July, and two in August. How many movies did they see altogether?

On the surface, Problems 1 and 3 appear to be quite different: They involve different characters (three girls vs. two boys), different sets of objects (ribbons vs. movies), and different numbers of objects in the respective object sets (3, 7, and 6 vs. 4, 5, and 2). Yet these differences are irrelevant to the problems' solutions. The solution-relevant similarity between these two problems is that they share the same underlying structure (i.e., three sets of objects that have to be combined) and therefore entail the same mathematical solution (i.e., addition).

As the above examples illustrate, the solution-irrelevant surface similarities between problems are usually much more salient than the solution-relevant structural similarities. Because people are more likely to notice surface than structural similarities, they might fail to notice that problems that differ in surface have a similar structure. That is, salient surface differences between structurally similar base and target problems (e.g., Problems 1 and 3) may hinder positive transfer. By the same logic, salient surface similarities between problems that differ in structure (e.g., Problems 1 and 2) increase the likelihood of negative transfer. Of course, people may erroneously retrieve a highly similar but nonanalogous problem, and then realize their mistake when they subsequently attempt to apply the retrieved solution to the novel problem. That is, problem-solving transfer involves several component processes that may be differentially affected by similarities in surface and structure. Indeed, using problem variants similar in design to the above arithmetic word problems, researchers who study analogical transfer show that surface and structural similarities have different effects on (1) *access* to the base analog in memory, and (2) *application* of the retrieved base solution to the target problem.[1] In the next section, I describe the methodology and the main findings from this line of research.

The above examples of arithmetic word problems also suggest that the impact of surface similarity on transfer performance will crucially depend on a person's ability to determine which aspects of the given problem

---

[1] This dichotomy is not exhaustive and glosses over some important distinctions. For example, access involves reminding and retrieval (Ross, 1984), and application involves mapping, inferences, and adaptation (Holyoak, Novick, & Melz, 1994).

are solution relevant and which are not. A preschooler might perceive Problems 1 and 2 as similar, relying solely on the problems' surface similarity. By contrast, a middle-school student, who also understands the problem structures, is likely to perceive these same problems as different. I describe findings from two lines of research that examined the relation between problem understanding and transfer performance. First, I discuss instructional interventions that managed to facilitate positive problem-solving transfer by helping people understand the structure of the base problem. Then, I discuss findings from studies in which individual differences in people's background knowledge and learning ability led to corresponding individual differences in people's sensitivity to surface and structural similarities between problems.

After describing the differential impact of similarities in surface and structure on transfer performance, I address the fact that these two components of problem similarity are often correlated in a nonarbitrary way, and that people tend to exploit such helpful regularities. For example, Problems 1 and 3 both contain the word "altogether" in their question statement, which is very common in texts of addition but not division word problems. Noticing this surface similarity in phrasing, students may assume (here, correctly) that the two problems have a similar structure that differs from the structure of Problem 2. That is, people use surface similarity as a cue for likely similarity in structure. Another way in which people exploit the correlation between surface and structure is using each problem's surface to understand its structure. For example, students might infer (here correctly) that a problem involving similar entities (e.g., ribbons in Problem 1 or movies in Problems 3) has an addition structure, whereas a problem involving functionally related entities (e.g., ribbons and gift boxes in Problem 2) has a division structure. I describe some work, mainly from my laboratory, showing that transfer performance depends on similarity between such interpreted problem structures.

EFFECTS OF SURFACE AND STRUCTURAL SIMILARITY ON ACCESS AND APPLICATION

A typical paradigm in research on analogical transfer involves two consecutive sessions. In the first session (training), subjects in the experimental condition solve or read the solutions to one or more base problems. In the second session (transfer), which is usually administered after a period of time ranging from a few minutes to about a week, the subjects are asked to solve one or more target problems. The base and the target problems are designed to provide researchers with separate estimates of the relative impact of surface and structural similarity on transfer performance. In most studies, the base and the target problems are analogous: They share a similar structure but differ in their surface characteristics. Some studies also use base and target problems that are similar both in their surface and in their structure (i.e., literal similarity) or only in their surface (i.e., mere appearance).

To determine transfer performance, the target solutions of subjects in the experimental condition are compared with those of control subjects who did not receive training on analogous or similar base problems or who received training on unrelated problems that differ from the targets in both surface and structure. Transfer in the analogy and literal-similarity training conditions, if any, should be positive (i.e., higher rate of success and/or shorter solution time in the experimental than in the control condition). Transfer in the mere-appearance training condition, if any, should be negative (i.e., lower rate of success and/or longer solution time in the experimental than in the control condition). Some studies also examine whether the experimental subjects explicitly mention the relevance of the base problems and whether their solution methods and the errors they commit show traces of the learned base solutions.

As I have mentioned earlier, positive transfer between analogous problems may fail because people fail to access the relevant base analog in memory and/or because they fail to apply the base solution to the target. To separate these two component processes, researchers compare transfer performance of subjects who were and who were not explicitly informed that the base solution is relevant to the target (i.e., hint and no-hint conditions, respectively). In the no-hint, or *spontaneous transfer*, condition, positive transfer requires both successful access to and successful application of the base solution. In the hint, or *informed transfer*, condition, positive transfer requires only successful application. The logic of this design allows researchers to infer that (1) lower transfer performance in the no-hint than in the hint condition indicates difficulties in access and (2) failure of transfer in the hint condition indicates difficulties in application.

Using variants of this basic methodology, researchers found that both surface and structural similarity can affect both access and application. However, access is much more sensitive to the salient surface than to the deeper structural similarity between problems, whereas application is much more sensitive to structural than to surface similarities. Below, I describe some representative studies that illustrate this pattern of results, first for spontaneous and then for informed transfer.

Spontaneous Transfer

Gick and Holyoak's (1980) study is probably the best known illustration of access failure caused by solution-irrelevant differences between base and target analogs. In this study, college students first read a solution to a military problem (the base) in which small army troops managed to destroy a heavily guarded fortress by simultaneously attacking it from different directions. The essence of the base solution was that simultaneous convergence of weak and relatively harmless forces on a focal point creates a powerful focal force. After learning this solution, the subjects were asked to solve an analogous medical problem (the target). The target problem, adapted from Duncker (1945), described a medical doctor who wanted to destroy a malignant stomach tumor using X-ray radiation. The tumor could be destroyed only with high-intensity X-rays. However, such high-intensity rays would also destroy the healthy tissue surrounding the tumor. The subjects' task was to find a method by which the doctor could use X-rays to destroy the tumor without harming the healthy tissue.

The correct solution to the target problem, which is analogous to the base solution, requires a simultaneous convergence of low-intensity X-rays on the focal tumor. This solution is quite rare among control subjects (about 10%). Surprisingly, the frequency of the simultaneous-convergence solution was only slightly higher among subjects in the no-hint transfer condition (about 30%). That is, only about 20% of the subjects may have spontaneously transferred the analogous solution from the base to the target problem. In sharp contrast to this low level of spontaneous transfer, about 75% of the subjects in the informed transfer condition came up with the convergence solution – 45% more than in the no-hint condition. This pattern of results indicates that surface differences between the military and the medical problems severely impaired subjects' ability to notice the relevance of the analogous base solution. At the same time, these surface differences did not impair subjects' ability to exploit the structural correspondence between the military base and the medical target when they were informed that the base solution could help them solve the target. That is, surface differences between analogous problems affected access without affecting application.

Spencer and Weisberg (1986) used similar problem analogs (adapted from Gick and Holyoak's [1983] follow-up study), but administered the training and transfer sessions in different locations: in a laboratory and in a classroom. This additional surface difference between the contexts in which the subjects encountered the base and the target problems completely eliminated spontaneous transfer. Holyoak and Koh (1987) found the complementary results: They increased the overall level of spontaneous transfer (access) by increasing the level of surface similarity between the base and the target problems. Specifically, they used base analogs that described simultaneous convergence of laser beams or ultrasound waves, which were more similar to converging X-rays than were the converging army troops in the original Gick and Holyoak (1980) study. Moreover, because people consider X-rays as more similar to laser beams than to ultrasound waves, spontaneous transfer to the X-rays target was higher from the laser-beam than from the ultrasound-waves version of the base analog. In general, decreasing or increasing the degree of surface similarity between the base and the target problems (i.e., objects, story line, phrasing, context) leads to a corresponding decrease or increase in the likelihood of spontaneous transfer.

In addition to varying the degree of surface similarity between the base and the target problems, Holyoak and Koh (1987) also examined whether different levels of structural similarity affect spontaneous access.[2] Specifically, they compared transfer to the radiation target problem from base analogs that either matched or did not match the target in their causal structure. In all the base analogs, a research assistant fixed a broken filament of an expensive light bulb by focusing several low-intensity laser beams (or ultrasound waves) on the bulb's filament. In the causally matching base, the justification for using low-intensity forces was protecting the fragile glass surrounding the filament, analogous to protecting the healthy tissue in the radiation target. In the causally mismatching base, the justification for using this same solution was that none of the available machines could emit the high-intensity laser beams (waves) that were necessary for fixing the filament. Holyoak and Koh found that, for a given level of surface similarity, spontaneous transfer from the structurally matching base was significantly higher than from the structurally mismatching base. Although structural similarity helped people access an analogous base, surface similarity was clearly the main contributor to spontaneous transfer.

Informed Transfer

Structural differences between base and target problems can significantly impede even informed transfer. The main reason for such effects is that structural differences often require nontrivial adaptation of the learned solution to the target problem (e.g., Novick & Holyoak, 1991; Reed, 1987; Reed, Dempster & Ettinger, 1985; Reed, Ernst, & Banerji, 1974). For example, Reed et al. (1974) examined transfer between two homomorphic river-crossing problems. One problem (MC) required moving three missionaries and three cannibals across a river, under the constraint that cannibals cannot outnumber missionaries in the boat or on either side of the river. The second problem (JH) required moving three husbands and three wives across a river, under the constraint that a wife cannot be left in the presence of another man unless her husband is present.

The MC and the JH problems have similar structures, with the husbands corresponding to the missionaries and the wives to the cannibals. However, the JH problem has a structural pairing constraint (husbands paired with wives) that does not exist in the MC problem. This additional structural constraint requires a significant change to the solution of the MC problem,

---

[2] Gentner and Landers (1985) used a similar design and report similar findings for stories rather than problems.

because one has to keep track of which wife is paired with which husband. Indeed, this adaptation completely blocked informed transfer from the MC to the JH problem. At the same time, informed transfer in the opposite direction did occur. Subjects transferred the more constrained JH solution to the less constrained MC problem without any adaptation by preserving the pairing constraint, even though it was not necessary to the solution of the MC problem.

Bassok and Olseth (1995) found a similar asymmetry in transfer between mathematical word problems that described situations of either discrete or continuous change. Transfer in the discrete to continuous direction was high and straightforward because the subjects believed that they could treat continuous change as a series of discrete changes and therefore applied the learned (discrete) solution to continuous problems without any adaptations. At the same time, transfer in the continuous to discrete direction was virtually blocked. The subjects could not transform discrete change into continuous change and therefore made various (unsuccessful) attempts to adapt the learned continuous solution to the discrete problems. In general, structural differences between analogous problems lead to asymmetries in informed transfer whenever they entail, or are believed to entail, difficult solution adaptation in one direction but not in the other.

Structural differences between problem analogs can impair informed transfer even when they do not entail any variable transformations or solution adaptations. For example, Holyoak and Koh (1987) found that informed transfer from the light-bulb to the tumor problem was impaired by differences between the justification for administering the convergence solution (e.g., high-intensity forces were unavailable in the base but were dangerous in the target). One reason for such effects is that, before people can transfer the learned solution (with or without adaptation), they have to align the representations of the base and the target problems (Gentner, 1983). That is, they have to establish one-to-one mappings between the entities and the relations in the corresponding structures (e.g., the filament corresponds to the tumor; attacking the fortress corresponds to destroying the tumor). Differences between the causal structures of the base and the target problems introduce significant difficulties to the alignment process.

The alignment (or mapping) process can be also affected by surface similarities between the specific entities that serve as arguments of the corresponding problem structures (Bassok, Wu, & Olseth, 1995; Gentner & Toupin, 1986; Ross, 1987, 1989). The work of Brian Ross (1987, 1989) that examined informed transfer of solutions to probability word problems nicely illustrates such effects. In one experimental condition, college students received a training example of a permutation problem in which cars were randomly assigned to mechanics (base). Then they were asked to apply the learned solution to an isomorphic permutation problem in which scientists were randomly assigned to computers (target). Subjects received the relevant equation, $1/n[n-1][n-2]\dots[n-r+1]$, and were asked to instantiate it with the appropriate values (i.e., n = the number of scientists).

In the target problem, scientists had to be placed in the structural role of the cars (because both were the randomly assigned sets) and computers in the structural role of the mechanics (because both were the sets of assignees). However, the subjects erroneously solved the target problem by placing scientists in the role of the mechanics and computers in the role of the cars. That is, they solved the target problem as if computers were assigned to scientists rather than scientists to computers. Ross explained such erroneous solutions by the fact that, during mapping, subjects tend to place similar objects in similar structural roles (i.e., object mapping). Specifically, subjects placed scientists in the structural role of the mechanics because both were animate objects, and placed computers in the role of the cars because both were inanimate objects.

Unlike structural differences that impair application because they require (or are believed to require) mindful adaptation of the base solution, or because they introduce structural mismatches that hinder the alignment process, the effects of object similarity on mapping performance appear to be quite mindless. Below I describe evidence showing that, in addition to such mindless effects, people use objects to interpret the problem's structure. This interpretive process might introduce inferred structural differences between mathematically isomorphic base and target problems that, in turn, lead to erroneous alignment and adaptation.

To summarize, people often fail to spontaneously access potentially relevant base analogs that differ from the target in their story line, phrasing, or context (for a review, see Reeves & Weisberg, 1994). Such salient surface differences between analogous problems do not impair informed transfer, although surface similarities between the specific objects in the base and the target problems can lead to misapplications of the learned solutions. In a complementary fashion, the less salient similarities and differences between the structures of analogous problems have a lesser effect on access, but can significantly affect informed transfer.

The differential impact of surface and structural similarity on access and application is captured in several computational models of these two processes (e.g., Falkenhainer, Forbus, & Gentner, 1989; Forbus, Gentner, & Law, 1995; Holyoak & Thagard, 1989; Hummel & Holyoak, 1997; Thagard, Holyoak, Nelson, & Gochfeld, 1990). The proposed models differ in many processing assumptions. Nonetheless, all models posit that people include in their problem representations aspects of both surface and structure. For example, they might represent the military problem used by Gick and Holyoak (1980) as DESTROY (army troops, fortress) and the analogous medical problem as DESTROY (X-rays, tumor). When people attempt to retrieve or apply previously learned solutions, mismatches in aspects of surface (e.g., army troops differ from X-rays; a fortress differs from a tumor) compete with matches in the solution-relevant aspects of structure (e.g., the DESTROY relation). Of course, matches in surface (e.g., two medical problems involving X-rays) would support matches in structure. Furthermore, consistent with the empirical findings, surface and structural matches are weighted differently, and their relative weights differ for access and mapping.

UNDERSTANDING AND STRUCTURAL ABSTRACTION

Why would people include aspects of surface in their problem representations if such inclusion leads to failures of analogical transfer? People might be uncertain about which aspects of the learned problems are, in fact, relevant to the solution. If so, inclusion of content, context, and phrasing in problem representations could protect them from potentially misleading generalizations to problems that differ in any one of these aspects (Medin & Ross, 1989). Support for this account comes from studies that significantly increased transfer performance by helping people understand which aspects of the base problem are solution relevant (e.g., Bassok & Holyoak, 1989; Brown, 1989; Catrambone, 1994; Catrambone & Holyoak, 1989; Dunbar, 2001; Gick & Holyoak, 1983; Gick & McGarry, 1992; Needham & Begg, 1991; Reed, 1993; Ross & Kennedy, 1990; Wertheimer, 1959).

One instructional intervention that helps people distinguish between the solution-relevant and -irrelevant aspects of problems is presenting people with two or more base analogs during training and asking them to compare the problems. The logic behind this intervention is that, by comparing problems that differ in surface but entail the same solution, people are likely to notice the solution-relevant structure that is common to the problems. It is important that a joint representation of the problems, or their intersection, would be a relatively surface-free abstract structure that eliminates the possibility of mismatches with surface aspects of target analogs. The abstraction-by-intersection training method is very common in educational settings. For example, students in formal domains usually receive several word problems that differ in their cover stories but share the same mathematical structure (Bassok & Holyoak, 1993). Of course, when all the training problems happen to describe a particular situation, people are likely to preserve this commonality and abstract a situation-specific problem schema or problem category (e.g., a schema for distance problems).

Gick and Holyoak (1983) have shown that the abstraction-by-intersection method can significantly increase analogical transfer of the converging-forces solution. In this study, subjects received either one or two convergence problems during training and, in the two-problem condition, the subjects were asked to summarize the similarity between the base problems. As predicted, the abstraction manipulation significantly increased both spontaneous and informed transfer to the target tumor problem. It is important that the relative benefit of the two-problem training interacted with the quality of subjects' summaries. Subjects whose summaries correctly captured the solution-relevant structural similarities between the two base analogs were much more likely to spontaneously transfer the convergence solution than were subjects whose summaries did not reveal correct structural abstraction. Gick and Holyoak also found that providing subjects with a summary of the key principle in each analog or with a diagram that depicted the convergence principle increased the frequency of correct structural summaries and led to a corresponding increase in the frequency of transfer solutions.

The individual differences in Gick and Holyoak (1983) indicate that multiple analogs do not guarantee abstraction. Rather, they provide an opportunity for a successful problem comparison that could lead to structural abstraction. In general, many instructional interventions can promote understanding of the base solution or lead to structural abstraction, but the likelihood of successful abstraction is modulated by peoples' background knowledge and learning abilities. Several studies have shown that differences in people's ability to understand the solution of training problems lead to corresponding differences in transfer performance. For example, researchers compared transfer performance of older and younger children (Gentner & Toupin, 1986), students with good and poor learning skills (Chi, Bassok, Lewis, Reimann, & Glaser, 1989), and relative experts and novices in a given domain (Novick, 1988). The general findings of these studies was that older children, good learners, and domain experts were more sensitive to structural similarities and less sensitive to surface differences between analogous problems than were younger children, poor learners, and domain novices.

It is interesting that good structural understanding of a training problem does not, in itself, secure spontaneous transfer. This is because even people who have good understanding of a given base tend to include aspects of surface in their problem representations. Given that aspects of surface affect access more than they affect application, the relative advantage of good structural understanding is more apparent in postaccess processes. Novick's (1988) study nicely illustrates the differential impact of domain understanding on access and application. Novick examined transfer of mathematical solutions by college students with high and low mathematical SATs (i.e., relative experts and novices in mathematics, respectively). She found that, in both groups, surface similarities between nonanalogous problems led to negative transfer. However, only the "expert" subjects realized that they had retrieved a nonanalogous base and, subsequently, recovered from their initial access errors.

One might wonder why it is that even people who have good understanding of the base solution, such as the math "experts" in Novick (1988), tend to preserve aspects of surface in their problem representations. A reasonable explanation of this tendency is that knowledge is most likely to be applied in the context in which it was learned (e.g., a military strategy is more likely to be applied in a military than in a medical context). Hence, inclusion of highly predictive aspects of surface has the potential benefit of speeding up retrieval and application of the learned solutions to the most relevant contexts. Hinsley, Hayes, and Simon (1977) have documented such speed-up effects in adults who were highly familiar with categories of mathematical word problems. These researchers found that, after reading no more than a few words of an algebra word problem, mathematically sophisticated subjects could correctly identify the problem's category (e.g., a work problem, a distance problem), and thereby access schematic information relevant to the problem's solution.

The speed-up effects in Hinsley et al. (1977) occurred because the cover stories of mathematical word problems are highly positively correlated with the correct mathematical solutions (Mayer, 1981). People who have extensive experience in solving such problems learn these predictive regularities. Hence, when they abstract a schema for word problems that share a common structure and lead to a similar solution, they include in their schematic representations the typical story line and the entities that tend to appear in the problem cover stories (e.g., moving objects, time and speed of travel). For the same reason, people tend to retain in their schematic representations various aspects of phrasing, such as keywords or word order, which provide highly reliable syntactic (surface) cues to the correct problem solutions. For example, students learn that the word "altogether" indicates that they should use addition, whereas the word "less" indicates that they should use subtraction (Nesher & Teubal, 1975), or that the word "times" indicates multiplication rather than division (English, 1997).

Because the phrasing of word problems is highly positively correlated with particular mathematical operations, reliance on syntactic cues leads to a high proportion of correct solutions. In fact, only problems that are purposely designed to undo or reverse the typical correlation (e.g., the keyword "less" appears in a problem that requires addition) reveal students' extensive reliance on similarity in the syntactic aspects of problems. It is important, and consistent with the findings of Novick (1988), that even students who have good understanding of the mathematical word problems use the syntactic surface cues as a convenient short-cut strategy to identify potentially relevant problem solutions. The difference between students with good and poor mathematical understanding is that the former, but not the later, can (and typically do) check the appropriateness of the retrieved solutions (Paige & Simon, 1966).

To summarize, people often retain aspects of surface in their problem representations because they do not know which aspects of the learned problem are and are not solution relevant. Instructional interventions that promote understanding of the learned solution lead to structural abstraction, which decreases the amount of surface in the representation of the base and thereby increases the likelihood of positive transfer. The effectiveness of such interventions is modulated by differences in people's background knowledge and learning ability. Good learners are more likely than poor learners to understand the derivation of a single worked-out solution, and are more likely to look for and successfully induce structural abstractions from multiple problem analogs. Yet even people who have good understanding of the base solution tend to retain aspects of surface in their problem representations. This is because aspects of surface are often good predictors for the most relevant contexts of application.

EFFECTS OF SURFACE ON STRUCTURAL ABSTRACTION

The work I described in the previous section, which relates individual differences in problem understanding to transfer performance, underscores the fact that problem similarity is a highly subjective psychological variable. One reason for the subjective nature of similarity is that it is actively constructed in a process that involves comparison between the internal representations of the problems (Markman & Gentner, 1993; Medin, Goldstone, & Gentner, 1993). It is important that the internal problem representations that enter into the comparison process are also actively constructed. In this section, I address the constructive process by which people understand problems. In particular, I describe work showing that people use a problem's surface to infer, or interpret, the problem's structure. This interpretive process may lead people to construct different *interpreted structures* for structurally isomorphic problems that differ in layout, phrasing, or cover story. The inferred structural differences, in turn, are likely to affect problem-solving transfer.

Several studies have shown that variants of structurally isomorphic problems differ in their difficulty and are solved in qualitatively different ways (e.g., Bassok et al., 1995; Cheng & Holyoak, 1985; Duncker, 1945; Hayes & Simon, 1974; Kintsch & Greeno, 1985; Kotovsky, Hayes, & Simon, 1985; Maier & Burke, 1967; Tversky & Kahnemann, 1981). To illustrate, Kotovsky et al. (1985) presented college students with two isomorphs of the Tower of Hanoi problem. In both problems, the subjects had to place disks of different sizes on top of each other according to a prespecified set of rules, but in one of the problems the disks supposedly represented acrobats. The subjects had little difficulty placing a large disk on top of a small one, but they refrained from this same move when the discs represented acrobats. The authors explained the greater difficulty of the jumping-acrobats problem by the structural constraint, inferred from subjects' world knowledge, that a large acrobat cannot jump on the shoulders of a small one without hurting him.

In other words, the results of Kotovsky et al. (1985) show that the entities in structurally isomorphic problems led people to construct different interpreted structures for these problems. The jumping-acrobats problem described entities that implied an inherently asymmetric semantic relation (i.e., small acrobats can jump on the shoulders of big acrobats, but not vice versa). By contrast, the literal disk problem described entities whose relational roles were not constrained by people's prior knowledge (i.e., a small disk can be placed on a large disk, or vice versa). People incorporated the inferred relational symmetry and asymmetry into their representations of the problem structures.

Object-based relational inferences, similar to those in Kotovsky et al. (1985), also mediate people's interpretation and solution of mathematical word problems. Bassok and her colleagues have shown that middle school, high school, and college students use the semantic symmetry implied by pairs of object sets that appear in the texts of mathematical word problems to infer the mathematical symmetry of the problems. When the paired object sets (e.g., tulips and vases) imply an asymmetric semantic relation (tulips are contained in vases, but not vice versa), people infer that the problem has an asymmetric mathematical structure (e.g., division, where $a/b \neq b/a$). But when the paired object sets (e.g., tulips and daisies) imply a symmetric semantic relation (e.g., both tulips and daisies are flowers), people infer that the problem has a symmetric mathematical structure (e.g., addition, where $a + b = b + a$). Such semantic interpretations, or *semantic alignments*, affect the way college students and textbook writers construct arithmetic word problems (Bassok, Chase, & Martin, 1998). They also determine the relative difficulty of mathematically isomorphic division problems (Bassok & Martin, 1997) and, as I elaborate later, affect how students solve mathematically isomorphic probability problems (Bassok et al., 1995).

The interpretive effects described above have important implications for problem-solving transfer. To this point, I have described work showing that people retain the content, context, and phrasing of problems in their problem representations, and that the retained surface aspects of base problems may create mismatches with the surface aspects of analogous targets. However, to the extent that people use aspects of surface to understand the problem's structure, similarities and differences in problem surface can also affect transfer in a different way. In particular, differences in the surface of analogous base and target problems might lead people to infer different interpreted structures for these problems. When this happens, transfer could fail because of the inferred structural mismatches between the base and the target problems rather than, or in addition to, direct mismatches in aspects of surface. Below I describe two studies in which the objects that served as arguments of mathematical word problems led to semantic alignments that, in turn, affected problem-solving transfer.

Inferred Symmetry and Asymmetry

Ling Ling Wu, Karen Olseth, and I constructed mathematically isomorphic probability word problems that we expected to induce, via semantic alignments, either symmetric or asymmetric interpreted mathematical structures (Bassok et al., 1995).[3] All the word problems in our studies had the same mathematical structure (random permutations) and required the same mathematical solution. They described a person who randomly assigned three elements from one set (n) to three elements from a different set (m) and asked for the probabilities of such random assignments. The objects in the assigned set and in the set of assignees (denoted by n and m, respectively) were either symmetric or asymmetric. We expected that these two types of object sets would lead subjects to infer that the problems have, respectively, either symmetric or asymmetric mathematical structures.

Table 11.1 presents two representative problems from Experiment 1 in Bassok et al. (1995). In the first problem (asymmetric sets), computers are randomly assigned to secretaries; in the second problem (symmetric sets), doctors from one hospital are randomly assigned to doctors from another hospital. Note that, irrespective of whether a manager assigns computers to secretaries or secretaries to computers (asymmetric sets), the outcome is that secretaries get computers rather than vice versa (i.e., an asymmetric semantic relation). By contrast, when a chairperson assigns doctors from one hospital to doctors from another hospital (symmetric sets) the doctors end up working with each other (i.e., a symmetric semantic relation). That is, the semantic outcome of the assignment process depends on the semantic symmetry of the two sets and is not affected by the direction of assignment specified in the problem's text.

To validate the effectiveness of our semantic manipulation, we first examined whether the symmetry of the paired sets affects how people represent the mathematical structures of these novel and rather complex word problems. We asked undergraduate students from the University of Chicago and Northwestern University to solve either the symmetric or the asymmetric permutation word problems as best they could. To

---

[3] In Bassok et al. (1995), we modified the problems and the procedure used by Ross (1989), such that we could examine the relative contribution of semantic alignments and direct object mapping. I do not discuss this issue here, and only describe evidence that demonstrates the impact of semantic alignments on analogical transfer.

TABLE 11.1. *Examples of semantically asymmetric and symmetric permutation problems in Bassok, Wu, and Olseth (1995)*

Asymmetric (Computers and Secretaries): In a big publishing company, some
secretaries will get to work on new personal computers. The company received
a shipment of 21 computers, with serial numbers in a running order from 10075
through 10095. There are 25 secretaries in this company who would like to work
on a new computer. The names of the secretaries are listed in order of their work
experience, from the most experienced secretary to the least experienced one.
The manager of the company randomly assigns computers to secretaries according to
the work experience of the secretaries. What is the probability that the three most
experienced secretaries will get to work on the first three computers (10075,
10076, and 10077), respectively?

Symmetric (Doctors and Doctors): In a medical meeting, doctors from a Minnesota
Hospital will get to work in pairs with doctors from a Chicago Hospital. There
is a list of 20 doctors from Chicago, arranged in alphabetical order. There are
16 doctors from Minnesota who would like to work with the doctors from
Chicago. The names of the Minnesota doctors are listed in the order of their
Social Security numbers, from highest to lowest. *The chairman of the meeting
randomly assigns doctors from Minnesota to doctors from Chicago* according to the
alphabetical order of the Chicago doctors. What is the probability that the first
three doctors on the Minnesota Hospital's Social Security number list will get
to work with the first three doctors on the Chicago Hospital's alphabetical list,
respectively?

---

minimize the effects of familiarity with such problems, we analyzed only
the incorrect solutions. We transformed each (incorrect) numerical solution into an algebraic equation, and examined whether the paired object
sets (m and n) played symmetric or asymmetric structural roles in these
equations.

We found that, indeed, the erroneous solutions to these unfamiliar
word problems reflected semantic alignments. In the asymmetric condition (secretaries-computers), most subjects (87%) placed the numbers representing the paired object sets in mathematically asymmetric roles (e.g.,
$m^3/n!$, $1/n^3$). By contrast, in the symmetric condition (doctors-doctors),
most subjects (78%) placed the numbers representing the paired object
sets in mathematically symmetric roles (e.g., $3/(m + n)!$, $(m + n)/(mn)^3$).
That is, subjects inferred that the asymmetric and symmetric semantic relations (e.g., "get," "work with") correspond, respectively, to asymmetric and
symmetric mathematical relations. They inferred such subjectively distinct
mathematical structures for mathematically isomorphic word problems.

After their initial attempt at solving these novel permutation problems,
the subjects received a short chapter that introduced them to the relevant
probability concepts and provided them with the equation for solving such

problems. For three random drawings, which was the case in all the word problems we used, the equation is $1/n[n-1][n-2]$. Note that the only variable in this equation is the number of elements in the assigned set (n). In this sense, the mathematical equation is asymmetric (i.e., only one of the two sets mentioned in the problem's text is relevant to the problem's solution). The training session ended with a worked-out solution to the permutation word problem (the base) the subjects had initially failed to solve on their own. Following the training session, subjects received a novel permutation problem (the target) together with the learned equation ($1/n[n-1][n-2]$) and were asked to instantiate the equation for the target problem. That is, they had to choose which of the two object sets in the target problem was the randomly assigned set (n).

The pattern of transfer results revealed large and significant effects of semantic alignments. For example, after learning a solution to an asymmetric base problem in which computers were assigned to secretaries, most subjects (89%) solved correctly an asymmetric target problem in which prizes were assigned to students. However, only 60% of the subjects solved correctly a symmetric target problem in which children from one school were assigned to children from another school. That is, the correctness of the solution to the target problem depended on the similarity between the interpreted mathematical structures subjects inferred, via semantic alignments, for the formally isomorphic base and target problems.

It is interesting that some subjects were so confident that the semantically asymmetric base problem differed in its mathematical structure from the semantically symmetric target problem that they crossed out the correct asymmetric equation we presented with the target problem and, instead, constructed an incorrect symmetric equation. In other words, they crossed out the one-set equation (n) and, instead, constructed an equation in which both sets, m and n, played symmetric mathematical roles. For example, one participant combined the two sets of children ($m + n$), and sampled pairs of children from the combined set. The following is an excerpt from this participant's verbal protocol:

> What's that have to do with 16 kids from 20 kids? . . . So you have to take all the kids from one and all the kids from the other. . . . Sum of elements is 36, . . . so 36, 34, 32. . . . Every time you do this you take out 2.

Just as the subjects who constructed incorrect symmetric equations for the semantically symmetric base problems before the training session, subjects who were trained on semantically asymmetric base problems constructed incorrect symmetric equations for the semantically symmetric target problems.

In addition to the inferred structural discrepancy between the semantically symmetric and asymmetric permutation problems, semantic knowledge affected subjects' decisions about which of the two asymmetric sets should be the assigned set and which should be the set of assignees. For example, in one experimental condition subjects received a worked-out solution to a permutation problem in which caddies were randomly assigned to golfers. Following this training, 94% of the subjects solved correctly a mathematically isomorphic problem in which prizes were randomly assigned to students, but only 17% solved correctly a mathematically isomorphic problem in which students were randomly assigned to prizes. That is, subjects were operating under the assumption that the direction of assignment in the base and target problems is compatible with the outcome of assignment. Because golfers get caddies and not vice versa (base), and because students get prizes and not vice versa (target), they understood that the direction of assignment in the target must be from prizes to students.

The same assumption guided subjects' solutions when one of the paired sets appeared in both the base and the target problems. For example, after receiving a worked-out solution to a problem in which caddies were randomly assigned to golfers, some subjects received a target problem in which caddies were randomly assigned to carts and others received a target problem in which carts were randomly assigned to caddies. As mentioned earlier in the chapter, previous studies on analogical mapping have shown that people prefer to place similar objects in similar structural roles (Gentner & Toupin, 1986; Ross, 1989). Because in the base problem caddies were the assigned set, reliance on object similarity would dictate better performance on the "caddies assigned to carts" than on the "carts assigned to caddies" target problem. However, because subjects engaged in semantic alignments, they understood that the direction of assignment is compatible with the outcome of assignment. In the base problem, golfers got caddies, and in the target problem, caddies got carts. Hence, subjects understood that carts were assigned to caddies. That is, contrary to what would be predicted by direct object similarity, 94% of the subjects solved correctly the "carts assigned to caddies" problem, but only 24% solved correctly the "caddies assigned to carts" problem.

To summarize, we found that semantically symmetric and asymmetric object sets lead people to construct symmetric and asymmetric interpreted structures for mathematically isomorphic probability problems. Similarities and differences between such interpreted structures affected analogical transfer. The effects of semantic alignments were powerful enough to override the impact of direct object similarities on analogical mapping.

Inferred Continuity and Discreteness

Karen Olseth and I examined the effects of semantic alignments on transfer between analogous algebra, economics, and physics word problems

(Bassok & Olseth, 1995).[4] All the problems in our study described constant change and could be solved in the same way. However, the constantly changing entities (e.g., the rate at which ice is melting off a glacier vs. the rate at which ice is delivered to a restaurant) were selected to induce inferences about manner of change (continuous vs. discrete, respectively). We conjectured that people would treat the inferred manner of change as a structural constraint that should be reflected in the corresponding mathematical solution (e.g., a linear function vs. an arithmetic progression, respectively). We therefore hypothesized that matches and mismatches in the inferred manner of change would affect transfer performance. For example, we predicted that transfer from a continuous base (e.g., speed of a car in miles/hr) will be higher to a continuous target (e.g., melting ice in lb/month) than to a discrete target (e.g., ice deliveries in lb/month).

We first established that college students spontaneously infer the manner in which various entities change with time. We established the existence of such inferences using a categorization task (Bassok & Olseth, 1995) and by analyzing the gestures that accompanied verbal descriptions of constant change problems (Alibali, Bassok, Olseth, Syc, & Goldin-Meadow, 1999). For example, we found that subjects made discrete gestures when describing constant change in salary ($/year), but made continuous gestures when describing constant change in the value of a coin ($/year). We then proceeded to examine whether and how matches and mismatches in the implied manner of change affect spontaneous and informed transfer.

We used an experimental design that varied orthogonally the manner of change in the base and the target problems. College students first learned to solve either discrete or continuous base problems in the context of one domain and then solved either a discrete or a continuous target problem as a pretest to learning another domain. To control for possible effects of other types of matches and mismatches between the base and the target problems, we compared transfer from continuous and discrete base problems with pairs of continuous and discrete target problems that were equated in units and phrasing. Table 11.2 presents one continuous (speed) and one discrete (investment) base problem, each with its matching pair of continuous and discrete targets. Note that the same problems served different roles in different experiments. For example, in one experiment (Experiment 4), students who studied physics (speed base) received the investment problem

---

[4] The experiments on manner of change follow up on previous work in which Keith Holyoak and I compared transfer of the same solution procedure learned in the context of either algebra or physics (Bassok, 1990; Bassok & Holyoak, 1989). In that earlier work, we predicted that because algebra training is more conducive to structural abstraction than is physics training, people will be more likely to transfer the learned solution from algebra to physics than vice versa. Our findings supported this prediction.

TABLE 11.2. *Continuous (speed) and discrete (investment) base problems, each with its matching pair of continuous and discrete targets in Bassok and Olseth (1995)*

Continuous Base (Speed): The speed of an airplane increases at a constant rate during a period of 12 minutes from 10 miles/min to 34 miles/min. What distance, in miles, will the plane travel during the 12-minute period?

    Continuous Target (Population): The rate of population growth in a certain country increased steadily during the last 12 years from 3,000 people/year to 15,000 people/year. How many people in total were added to the population during the 12-year period?

    Discrete Target (Attendance): An annual arts & crafts fair is held on November 1st every year. The attendance rate at the annual fair increased steadily during the last 12 years from 3,000 people/year to 15,000 people/year. How many people total attended the fair during the 12-year period?

Discrete Base (Investment): During the last 16 months the monthly deposits into a certain savings account constantly increased from \$200/month to \$440/month. How much money in total was deposited into the account during the 16-month period?

    Continuous Target (Melting Ice): The rate at which ice melts off a glacier steadily increases over an 8-week period from 50 lb/week to 106 lb/week. What is the total weight of the ice that will melt off the glacier over the 8-week period?

    Discrete Target (Ice Delivery): Ice is delivered to a restaurant once a week over an 8-week period. The weight of the deliveries steadily increases from 50 lb the first week to 106 lb the 8th week. What is the total weight of the ice that will be delivered over the 8-week period?

---

as a target, whereas students who studied economics (investment base) received the speed problem as a target.

As predicted, when the base problem was understood to describe continuous change (speed), transfer to continuous targets (matching manner) was frequent, but transfer to discrete targets (mismatching manner) was rare. For example, significantly more subjects used the distance equation learned for physics problems dealing with changing speed (continuous) to find the number of people in the continuous-population than in the discrete-attendance target (71% vs. 27%, respectively). Because the continuous and discrete target problems were matched in all other aspects of content and phrasing (e.g., both referred to people/year), these results indicate that matches and mismatches in the inferred manner of change were responsible for this overwhelming difference in the frequency of spontaneous transfer. To our surprise, mismatches in manner of change did not impair spontaneous transfer from base problems that described discrete change. Following an economics training session in which subjects learned to solve investment problems (discrete), spontaneous transfer was similarly high

TABLE 11.3. *Examples of verbal protocols that accompanied informed transfer in the discrete-to-continuous and continuous-to-discrete conditions in Bassok and Olseth (1995)*

Discrete (investments) to continuous (speed)

The sum would equal to what you start with plus what you end with divided by 2. So, start with 10 + 34 is 44, divided by 2 equals 22, times 12 is 264 . . . miles.

Continuous (speed) to discrete (investments)

Alignment 1, mapping:

> I guess I'm supposed to apply those equations to this somehow, or they're analogs. Uhh, all right then: Initial payment would correspond to initial speed and final payment to final speed, and so, average payment would be their sum divided by . . .

Alignment 2, repeat 12 times:

> But wait, I was thinking whether I should use each month as an initial payment, in other words, apply this 12 times. But I don't want to do that. It's too much work.

Back to Alignment 1, solution:

> I'm going to see if I can come out with the right answer by just treating it with the first and last month's payments. So, I add 232 and 100 and get 332, then divide by 2 gives 166 . . .

Hesitation between Alignment 1 and 2:

> I guess . . . umm, that's my *average payment*. How much money total over a year . . . uhh, *12 average payments?* 166 times 12 is 1,992.

---

to the discrete ice-delivery target (100%) and to the continuous melting-ice target (88%).

The asymmetric impact of mismatches in manner of change on the frequency of spontaneous transfer (i.e., high transfer in the discrete-to-continuous direction and low transfer in the continuous-to-discrete direction) was accompanied by an asymmetry in the relative difficulty of mapping (i.e., informed transfer). An analysis of the informed-transfer solutions revealed that subjects had no difficulty aligning the representations of discrete base and continuous target problems, but found it quite difficult to align continuous base and discrete target problems. Table 11.3 presents a representative excerpt of a verbal protocol from each of the two mismatching-transfer conditions. The top panel of Table 11.3 shows a straightforward instantiation of the sum-of-investments equation (discrete base) with values of the speed problem (continuous target). The bottom panel shows repeated attempts to apply the distance equation (continuous base) to the investment problem (discrete target), which involve shifts in alignment and explicit variable mappings.

As mentioned earlier in this chapter, the asymmetry in transfer between problems with mismatching manner of change reflects a difference in the possibility of reinterpreting the target such that it fits the representation of the base. Transfer in the discrete-to-continuous condition was possible because continuous change in the target problems could be transformed (parsed) into an arithmetic series of discrete values and therefore fit the discrete structure of the base. For example, when the rate at which ice is melting off a glacier constantly increases over a period of eight weeks from 50 lb/week to 106 lb/week, the melting rate increases every week by a constant (8 lb/week). Moreover, the consecutive discrete values (58 lb/week, 64 lb/week, . . .) actually exist. This type of transfer was impossible in the continuous-to-discrete condition because, in order to transform discrete targets to fit a continuous base structure, people would have to hypothesize values that are unlikely to exist (e.g., hypothesize continuous deliveries of ice to a restaurant).

To summarize, we found evidence for semantic alignments in word problems that described constant change. Subjects used their world knowledge to infer whether the entities described in the cover stories changed discretely or continuously, and treated the inferred manner of change as a structural constraint that should be reflected in the mathematical solution of the problem. Such semantic alignments affected both spontaneous and informed transfer. Mismatches in the interpreted mathematical structures blocked transfer in the continuous to discrete direction but did not block transfer in the discrete to continuous direction.

SUMMARY AND CONCLUDING REMARKS

I began this chapter with the general notion that problem-solving transfer depends on the degree of similarity between a learned and a novel problem. Then I pointed out the need to distinguish between aspects of similarity that are and are not relevant to problem solutions. I described research on analogical transfer that makes a principled distinction between similarity in problems' surface and structure. These two types of problem similarity have different effects on retrieval and application of analogous problems. People rely heavily on salient surface similarities in content, context, and phrasing to retrieve potentially relevant prior problems. As a result, they may fail to retrieve useful problem analogs from other knowledge domains, or even problems from the same domain but learned in a different context. Moreover, people might erroneously retrieve similar but nonanalogous problems. Fortunately, when they attempt to apply the retrieved solutions, people are mainly guided by the solution-relevant similarities in structure. At least those people who understand the problem well can notice their mistakes and recover from their retrieval errors.

Although transfer performance can be explained in terms of problem similarity, the same pair of analogous problems can be perceived as similar by people who understand the problem structures and as different by people who do not. Given that structural similarity can assist in access of relevant analogs and enables recovery from negative transfer, the most efficient way to secure analogical transfer in problem solving is helping people understand the solution-relevant structural aspects of the learned problems. For example, one might present people with several analogous problems that differ in surface and ask them to figure our why these problems are similar. In designing such interventions, it is important to realize that people use surface to understand the problem's structure. In particular, they draw structural inferences based on their semantic knowledge about the entities that appear in the problem. For example, people can readily understand the inherent mathematical asymmetry of the division operation if the entities in the example problem (e.g., tulips and vases) evoke an asymmetric semantic relation, but might fail to understand it when the entities evoke a symmetric semantic relation (e.g., tulips and daisies).

In describing the findings from research on analogical problem solving, I used examples of mathematical word problems and some unique riddle problems, such as problems describing a general attacking a fortress or missionaries and cannibals crossing a river. Strictly speaking, mathematical word problems differ from riddles in at least three (not independent) respects. First, word problems exemplify mathematical solutions and therefore are likely to be encoded as members of a general problem category. By contrast, riddle problems are likely to be perceived and encoded as unique cases. Second, the texts of mathematical word problems have standardized phrases that can serve as highly reliable cues to problem structures. Such standardized cues do not exist in unique riddles. Third, analogical transfer between mathematical word problems can be mediated either by structural similarity of the problem situations or by the mathematical structure that is common to these problems. By contrast, unique riddles can share only structural similarity of their problem situations.

One would expect that the above differences between unique riddles and mathematical word problems should lead to significant differences in transfer performance. Although such predictions are worth testing, the overall pattern of research findings pertaining to both types of problems appears to be virtually the same. In both cases, access is most sensitive to surface similarities, whereas application is most sensitive to structural similarities; better structural understanding fosters spontaneous and informed transfer; and the entities in the problems people encounter affect which structures people abstract. These similarities attest to the robustness of the extant research findings and the relevance of basic research on analogical transfer to instructional contexts. The current challenge facing researchers and educators is to design instructional interventions that implement these findings.

REFERENCES

Alibali, M. W., Bassok, M., Olseth, K. L., Syc, S., & Goldin-Meadow, S. (1999). Illuminating mental representations through speech and gesture. *Psychological Science, 10*, 327–333.

Bassok, M. (1990). Transfer of domain-specific problem solving procedures. *Journal of Experimental Psychology: Learning, Memory, and Cognition, 16*, 522–533.

Bassok, M., Chase, V. M, & Martin, S. A. (1998). Adding apples and oranges: Alignment of semantic and formal knowledge. *Cognitive Psychology, 35*, 99–134.

Bassok, M., & Holyoak, K. J. (1989). Interdomain transfer between isomorphic topics in algebra and physics. *Journal of Experimental Psychology: Learning, Memory, and Cognition, 15*, 153–166.

Bassok, M., & Holyoak, K. J. (1993). Pragmatic knowledge and conceptual structure: Determinants of transfer between quantitative domains. In D. K. Detterman & R. J. Sternberg (Eds.), *Transfer on trial: Intelligence, cognition, and instruction* (pp. 68–98). Norwood, NJ: Ablex Publishing Corp.

Bassok, M., & Martin, S. A. (1997, November). *Object-based interpretation of arithmetic word problems*. Paper presented at the 38th annual meeting of the Psychonomic Society, Philadelphia, PA.

Bassok, M., & Olseth, K. L. (1995). Object-based representations: Transfer between cases of continuous and discrete models of change. *Journal of Experimental Psychology: Learning, Memory, and Cognition, 21*, 1522–1538.

Bassok, M., Wu, L., & Olseth, K. L. (1995). Judging a book by its cover: Interpretative effects of content on problem solving transfer. *Memory & Cognition, 23*, 354–367.

Brown, A. L. (1989). Analogical learning and transfer: What develops? In S. Vosniadou & A. Ortony (Eds.), *Similarity and analogical reasoning* (pp. 369–412). Cambridge: Cambridge University Press.

Catrambone, R. (1994). Improving examples to improve transfer to novel problems. *Memory & Cognition, 22*, 606–615.

Catrambone, R., & Holyoak, K. J. (1989). Overcoming contextual limitations on problem-solving transfer. *Journal of Experimental Psychology: Learning, Memory, and Cognition, 15*, 1147–1156.

Cheng, P. W., & Holyoak, K. J. (1985). Pragmatic reasoning schemas. *Cognitive Psychology, 17*, 391–416.

Chi, M. T. H., & Bassok, M. (1989). Learning from examples via self-explanations. In L. B. Resnick (Ed.), *Knowing, learning, and instruction: Essays in honor of Robert Glaser* (pp. 251–282). Hillsdale, NJ: Erlbaum.

Chi, M. T. H., Bassok, M., Lewis, M. W., Reimann, P., & Glaser, R. (1989). Self-explanations: How students study and use examples in learning to solve problems. *Cognitive Science, 13*, 145–182.

Dunbar, K. (2001). The analogical paradox: Why analogy is so easy in naturalistic settings, yet so difficult in the psychological laboratory. In D. Gentner, K. J. Holyoak, & B. N. Kokinov (Eds.), *The analogical mind: Perspectives from cognitive science* (Chapter 12, pp. 401–433). Cambridge, MA: MIT Press.

Duncker, K. (1945). On problem solving. *Psychological Monographs, 58* (No. 270).

English, L. (1997). Children's reasoning processes in classifying and solving computational word problems. In L. English (Ed.), *Mathematical reasoning: Analogies, metaphors, and images* (Chapter 6, pp. 191–220). Hillsdale, NJ: Erlbaum.

Falkenhainer, B., Forbus, K. D., & Gentner, D. (1989). The structure mapping engine: Algorithm and examples. *Artificial Intelligence, 41,* 1–63.

Forbus, K. D., Gentner, D., & Law, K. (1995). MAC/FAC: A model of similarity-based retrieval. *Cognitive Science, 19,* 141–205.

Gentner, D. (1983). Structure-mapping: A theoretical framework for analogy. *Cognitive Science, 7,* 155–170.

Gentner, D., & Landers, R. (1985). Analogical reminding: A good match is hard to find. *Proceedings of the International Conference on Systems, Man and Cybernetics* (pp. 306–355). Tucson, AZ: International Conference on Systems, Man and Cybernetics.

Gentner, D., & Toupin, C. (1986). Systematicity and surface similarity in the development of analogy. *Cognitive Science, 10,* 277–300.

Gick, M. L., & Holyoak, K. J. (1980). Analogical problem solving. *Cognitive Psychology, 12,* 306–355.

Gick, M. L., & Holyoak, K. J. (1983). Schema induction and analogical transfer. *Cognitive Psychology, 15,* 1–38.

Gick, M. L., & McGarry, S. J. (1992). Learning from mistakes: Inducing analogous solution failures to a source problem produces later successes in analogical transfer. *Journal of Experimental Psychology: Learning, Memory, and Cognition, 18,* 623–639.

Hayes, J. R., & Simon, H. A. (1974). Understanding written problem instructions. In L. W. Gregg (Ed.), *Knowledge and cognition.* Hillsdale, NJ: Lawrence Erlbaum Associates.

Hinsley, D. A., Hayes, J. R., & Simon, H. A. (1977). From words to equations: Meaning and representation in algebra word problems. In M. A. Just & P. A. Carpenter (Eds.), *Cognitive processes in comprehension* (pp. 89–106). Hillsdale, NJ: Erlbaum.

Holyoak, K. J. (1985). The pragmatics of analogical transfer. In G. H. Bower (Ed.), *The psychology of learning and motivation* (Vol. 19, pp. 59–87). New York: Academic Press.

Holyoak, K. J., & Koh, K. (1987). Surface and structural similarity in analogical transfer. *Memory & Cognition, 15,* 332–340.

Holyoak, K. J., Novick, L. R., & Melz, E. R. (1994). Component processes in analogical transfer: Mapping, pattern completion, and adaptation. In K. J. Holyoak & J. A. Barnden (Eds.), *Analogical connections* (Vol. 2, pp. 113–180). Norwood, NJ: Ablex.

Holyoak, K. J., & Thagard, P. (1989). Analogical mapping by constraint satisfaction. *Cognitive Science, 13,* 295–355.

Hummel, J. E., & Holyoak, K. J. (1997). Distributed representations of structure: A theory of analogical access and mapping. *Psychological Review, 104,* 427–466.

Kintsch, W., & Greeno, J. G. (1985). Understanding and solving word arithmetic problems. *Psychological Review, 92,* 109–129.

Kotovsky, K., Hayes, J. R., & Simon, H. A. (1985). Why are some problems hard?: Evidence from Tower of Hanoi. *Cognitive Psychology, 17,* 248–294.

Lave, J. (1988). *Cognition in practice: Mind, mathematics and culture in everyday life.* Cambridge, MA: Cambridge University Press.

LeFevre, J., & Dixon, P. (1986). Do written instructions need examples? *Cognition and Instruction, 3,* 1–30.

Maier, N. R. F., & Burke, R. J. (1967). Response availability as a factor in the problem-solving performance of males and females. *Journal of Personality and Social Psychology, 5*, 304–310.

Markman, A. B., & Gentner, D. (1993). Structural alignment during similarity comparisons. *Cognitive Psychology, 25*, 431–467.

Mayer, R. E. (1981). Frequency norms and structural analysis of algebra story problems into families, categories, and templates. *Instructional Science, 10*, 135–175.

McClosky, M. (1983). Naive theories of motion. In D. Gentner & A. L. Stevens (Eds.), *Mental models* (Chapter 13, pp. 299–324). Hillsdale, NJ: Lawrence Erlbaum.

Medin, D. L., Goldstone, R. L., & Gentner, D. (1993). Respects for similarity. *Psychological Review, 100*, 254–278.

Medin, D. L., & Ross, B. H. (1989). The specific character of abstract thought: Categorization, problem solving, and induction. In R. J. Sternberg (Ed.), *Advances in the psychology of human intelligence* (Vol. 5, pp. 189–223). Hillsdale, NJ: Erlbaum.

Needham, D., & Begg, I. (1991). Problem-oriented training promotes spontaneous analogical transfer, memory-oriented training promotes memory for training. *Memory & Cognition, 19*, 543–557.

Nesher, P. & Teubal, E. (1975). Verbal cues as an interfering factor in verbal problem solving. *Educational Studies in Mathematics, 6*, 41–51.

Novick, L. R. (1988). Analogical transfer, problem similarity, and expertise. *Journal of Experimental Psychology: Learning, Memory, and Cognition, 14*, 510–520.

Novick, L. R., & Holyoak, K. J. (1991). Mathematical problem solving by analogy. *Journal of Experimental Psychology: Learning, Memory, and Cognition, 17*, 398–415.

Nunes, T., Schliemann, A. D., & Carraher, D. W. (1993). *Street mathematics and school mathematics*. Cambridge, UK: Cambridge University Press.

Paige, J. M., & Simon, H. A. (1966). Cognitive processes in solving algebra word problems. In B. Kleinmuntz (Ed.), *Problem solving: Research, method, and theory* (pp. 51–119). New York: John Wiley & Sons.

Reed, S. K. (1987). A structure-mapping model for word problems. *Journal of Experimental Psychology: Learning, Memory, and Cognition, 13*, 124–139.

Reed, S. K. (1993). A schema-based theory of transfer. In D. K. Detterman & R. J. Sternberg (Eds.), *Transfer on trial: Intelligence, cognition, and instruction* (pp. 39–67). Norwood, NJ: Ablex Publishing.

Reed, S. K., Dempster, A., & Ettinger, M. (1985). Usefulness of analogous solutions for solving algebra word problems. *Journal of Experimental Psychology: Learning, Memory, and Cognition, 11*, 106–125.

Reed, S. K., Ernst, G., & Banerji, R. (1974). The role of analogy in transfer between similar problems. *Cognitive Psychology, 6*, 436–450.

Reeves, L. M., & Weisberg, R. W. (1994). The role of content and abstract information in analogical transfer. *Psychological Bulletin, 115*, 381–400.

Ross, B. H. (1984). Remindings and their effects in learning a cognitive skill. *Cognitive Psychology, 16*, 371–416.

Ross, B. H. (1987). This is like that: The use of earlier problems and the separation of similarity effects. *Journal of Experimental Psychology: Learning, Memory, and Cognition, 13*, 629–639.

Ross, B. H. (1989). Distinguishing types of superficial similarities: Different effects on the access and use of earlier problems. *Journal of Experimental Psychology: Learning, Memory, and Cognition, 15*, 456–468.

Ross, B. H., & Kennedy, P. T. (1990). Generalizing from the use of earlier examples in problem solving. *Journal of Experimental Psychology: Learning, Memory, and Cognition, 16,* 42–55.

Spencer, R., & Weisberg, R. (1986). Is analogy sufficient to facilitate transfer during problem solving? *Memory & Cognition, 14,* 442–449.

Thagard, P. H., Holyoak, K. J., Nelson, G., & Gochfeld, D. (1990). Analog retrieval by constraint satisfaction. *Artificial Intelligence, 46,* 259–310.

Tversky, A., & Kahnemann, D. (1981). The framing of decisions and the psychology of choice. *Science, 211,* 453–458.

Wertheimer, M. (1959). *Productive thinking.* New York: Harper & Row.

PART IV

CONCLUSIONS AND INTEGRATION

Problem Solving – Large/Small, Hard/Easy, Conscious/Nonconscious, Problem-Space/ Problem-Solver

The Issue of Dichotomization

Kenneth Kotovsky

The chapters in this volume, together and separately, make a convincing case that problem solving is an extraordinarily broad, perhaps all-encompassing, and somewhat daunting domain. In dealing with the challenges presented by the breadth of the domain, they virtually all follow a broadly similar strategy that is hinted at in the title of this chapter. Each chapter implements this strategy differently, but when taken together, the chapters provide an illuminating approach to this difficult subject.

The breadth of issues that affect problem solving is revealed by the range of chapter topics, which includes motivation, creativity, emotion, transfer of knowledge, language parsing, intellectual ability, expertise, and many more topics or issues involved in the study of problem solving. The range is daunting, but the collection of chapters nonetheless forms a book that coheres and brings together a vast collection of findings and theories that illuminate this central aspect of our thinking. The breadth arises from the fact that problem solving is essentially synonymous with thinking, and thinking is in one manner or another affected by virtually all of the equipment a person brings to bear on a problem, as well as the full range of environmental influences that define the problem, its problem space, and its solution. Despite this incredible breadth and the resultant different foci of the chapters, the authors present a number of common themes or perspectives that help bring coherence to the volume.

A feeling for the breadth of the domain, as well as the common focus on major issues within it, can perhaps best be appreciated via a consideration of what those issues are together with the chapters that devote serious attention to them. A sampling of the major foci, along with the chapters that particularly address them, is included in Table 12.1. The table demonstrates the wide range of topics that are intrinsic to problem solving, but also how quite diverse chapters nonetheless have similar focal issues. This combination of an incredibly broad domain with a focus on common issues from a variety of perspectives defines a central tension in problem solving

TABLE 12.1. *Examples of shared foci on problem-solving issues*

Problem-solving issue	Chapters with a significant focus on the issue
Mental representation	Pretz, Naples, & Sternberg; Hambrick & Engle (Chapters 1 and 6)
Role of knowledge	Pretz, Naples, & Sternberg; Wenke & Frensch; Lubart & Mouchiroud; Hambrick & Engle; Whitten & Graesser; Schwarz & Skurnik (Chapters 1, 3, 4, 6, 7, and 9)
Focus on insights	Pretz, Naples, & Sternberg; Davidson (Chapters 1 and 5)
Cognitive processes	Pretz, Naples, & Sternberg; Wenke & Frensch; Schwarz & Skurnik (Chapters 1, 3, and 9)
Explicit/implicit distinction and dual task method	Wenke & Frensch; Stanovich (Chapters 3 and 10)
Role of hints	Davidson; Bassok (Chapters 5 and 11)
Focus on creativity	Lubart & Mouchiroud; Whitten & Graesser (Chapters 4 and 7)
Role of intelligence	Wenke & Frensch; Schwarz & Skurnik (Chapters 3 and 9)
Influence of motivation and/or emotion	Lubart & Mouchiroud; Whitten & Graesser; Zimmerman & Campillo (Chapters 4, 7, and 8)
Role of learning and development of expertise	Ericsson; Wenke & Frensch; Hambrick & Engle; Zimmerman & Campillo (Chapters 2, 3, 6, and 8)
Problem size and scope or type (well/ill defined)	Pretz, Naples, & Sternberg; Davidson; Hambrick & Engle; Stanovich (Chapters 1, 5, 6, and 10)
Multistage models of problem solving	Pretz, Naples, & Sternberg; Lubart & Mouchiroud; Davidson; Zimmerman & Campillo (Chapters 1, 4, 5, and 8)

research. To the extent that problem-solving is synonymous with thinking, its study excludes very little psychology; to understand problem-solving in its full richness entails understanding how we think and behave in the environments we inhabit and move through. This is the essence and definition of psychology. There is thus not much that is excluded if problem solving is defined broadly. The domain includes not only the traditional – the problem of proving a theorem, of solving an equation, of calculating an orbit, of designing a sports car, or even of negotiating the end to a war – but also the less obvious – the problem of forming a relationship, of attaining expertise, of parsing a sentence, of delineating figure from ground in a visual image, and so on. One way in which this breadth is handled in this volume is as noted above, via a shared focus on central issues. Another way in which the challenging breadth of problem solving is dealt with within the chapters is described next.

TABLE 12.2. *Typologies (dichotomizations) of the space of problem solving*

Chapter	Typologies (dichotomies) introduced
Pretz, Naples, & Sternberg; Wenke & Frensch; Schwartz & Skurnik	Well-defined vs. ill-defined problems, three-part division of the problem-solving process (recognition, definition, and representation)
Wenke & Frensch	Complex vs. noncomplex problems, explicit vs. implicit processes
Lubart & Mouchiroud	Creative vs. noncreative problem solving, four-stage model of creativity
Davidson	Insightful vs. noninsightful problem solving, problem finding vs. problem solving, insight vs. search, four-stage model of problem solving (preparation, incubation, illumination, and verification), three-part model of insight generation (selective encoding, selective combination, and selective comparison)
Stanovich	Computational biases and heuristics vs. abstract reasoning
Bassock	Surface vs. structural similarity in transfer, hard vs. easy problems, continuous vs. discrete problems
Zimmerman & Campillo	Expert (self-motivated) vs. novice problem solvers
Whitten & Graesser	Surface vs. deep linguistic structure in problem descriptions
Schwarz & Skurnik	Feeling vs. thinking, top-down vs. bottom-up search, positive vs. negative moods
Hambrick & Engle	Working memory vs. short-term memory, storage limitations vs. processing limitations, American approach (individual differences) vs. European approach (universal findings)
Ericsson	Expert vs. novice, deliberate vs. nondeliberate practice, laboratory vs. real-world problem solving

The tactic that the authors use in responding to this challenge is actually two-fold. Each chapter takes on a particular aspect or dimension of problem solving, while usually acknowledging the remaining breadth of influences. More interesting, each chapter attempts to delineate its area of study and render it understandable via the strategy of generating something of a typology of that area, usually in the form of a simple dichotomy. Some of these dichotomies are illustrated in Table 12.2.

The set of typologies in Table 12.2 is not exhaustive but nonetheless shows the basic approach that the authors have taken in attempting to grapple with the size and complexity of the domain. One question that can be asked is whether this approach to generating dichotomies or other typologies is the "right" one for understanding problem solving, or more particularly, whether these dichotomies are the right ones to use. The first answer to this question is an unambiguous "yes" in that all of them have led to good experiments and promising theories that are amply represented and described in this set of chapters, and to hypotheses that will no doubt lead to further experimentation and understanding. In addition, many of the authors, even as they take on different topics, have converged on the same set of dichotomies. For example, the issue of well-defined versus ill-defined problems is a dichotomy that is used in the chapters by Pretz et al. as a central organizing principle in describing problem types, by Wenke and Frensch in defining their focus on complex problems where they find little correlation with general intellectual ability, by Schwartz and Skurnik in examining the relative roles of knowledge and mood on problem solving (where they find larger effects of affect in ill-defined problems), and in a number of other chapters as well. This convergence suggests the viability and usefulness of that problem typology for the study of problem solving.

On another level, however, the answer to the question about "correct" typologies might be somewhat less certain. There might be too much dichotomization and, at the same time, too little. (One is tempted to say "there are two kinds of issues, one of them being too much dichotomization and the other. . . .") One issue is that categorization (and, in particular, dichotomization) often distorts what are really continuous distributions of some attribute. Are problems really either well defined or ill defined, or do they vary along a continuum of definiteness? Consider by way of illustration a well-defined problem, the extrapolation of a letter sequence as in a Thurstone letter series task. A simple example: Extend the sequence AAABBBCCCDDD_ _ _. The "correct" answer is, of course, EEE, the rule being running through the alphabet sequentially in groups of three. But what if someone were to answer "AAAB," with the rule being that the sequence simply repeats itself over and over? The judgment that this is a less satisfactory or wrong answer is exactly that – a "judgment" – and the need to make a judgment of the correctness of an answer is, of course, the hallmark of an ill-defined problem. While that example might seem forced in that the correctness of the first answer is obvious, it might be less forced if the sequence was from the end of the alphabet, WWWXXXYYYZZZ _ _ _ where the choice of repeating the sequence – WWW – might seem somewhat more likely given the need to wrap the alphabet back to A in order to use the more sequential answer – AAA (Thurstone & Thurstone, 1941; Simon & Kotovsky, 1963; Kotovsky & Simon, 1973).

A similar argument can be made for ill-defined problems. A prototypical example is a design problem where the outcome is necessarily based on human judgment. For example, if the problem were to design a "good" train station, the usual criterion would be the vote of a panel of architectural judges, making this a good example of an ill-defined problem.

However, one can imagine more objective criteria (number of people per minute that can board a train, unidirectionality of people flow, escalator capability, width of platform for passenger safety) that could possibly be used to make the problem somewhat well defined as well. The point is that even as obviously dichotomizable a dimension as well- versus ill-defined problems is susceptible to being treated as more of a continuum than as a dichotomy, with important differences arising as one moves along the dimension from one end or extreme (moving a stack of disks in the Tower of Hanoi problem at the well-defined end of the continuum) through intermediate problems (as in the examples above) to the other end (painting a beautiful painting at the ill-defined end). A similar argument can be made for many if not all of the dichotomizations listed in Table 12.2, a result that would not surprise any of the authors; it is a fairly ubiquitous concomitant of dichotomization. For variables that don't involve partitioning a continuum but are natural dichotomies, one hardly ever says, "There are two kinds of . . ."; it rather goes without saying. This point does not obviate the usefulness and necessity of the typologies generated, but rather serves as a caution about the distortion that can inadvertently be introduced.

As mentioned above, there are two possible issues with dichotomization, one being that there is too much, and the other that there is too little. The second issue is that the set of dichotomies that is commonly used in the study and categorization of problem solving, even though making a significant contribution to organizing information, generating experiments, and directing theory, may itself be too delimited, and thus may miss important aspects of problem-solving behavior. That is, despite the excellence and comprehensiveness of the set of issues addressed in these chapters, there may remain some unexamined issues (and possible dichotomies) that are at a "higher" level than could be expected from chapters dealing with particular aspects of problem solving, and that are nonetheless important for an understanding of it. One such issue might be the role of the environment versus that of the problem solver in attempting to understand problem solving, an issue briefly alluded to above. This issue arises from a number of considerations, in particular the focus of many of the chapters on learning.

The suggestion that emerges from a consideration of the central and significant role that learning plays in so many aspects of problem solving and expertise acquisition is that people may be thought of as powerful generalized learning devices; with sufficient practice they can assimilate information about virtually any environment or problem space and learn to operate effectively within it. This viewpoint suggests not that the problem solver is necessarily the correct focus in our efforts to understand problem solving, but rather that much of the focus belongs on the environment and its influence on the solver as he or she moves through the problem space the environment defines. This viewpoint has been thoroughly and eloquently analyzed by Herbert A. Simon, who set much of the agenda for the study of problem solving when he presented his parable of the ant crawling through an environment that almost totally shapes his or her behavior. In his words: "An ant, viewed as a behaving system, is quite simple. The apparent complexity of its behavior over time is largely a reflection of the complexity of the environment in which it finds itself" (Simon, 1969/1981, p. 64). Simon then goes on to make the same point about humans and their thoughts, viewing man as an adaptive system whose behavior "will reflect characteristics largely of the outer environment (in the light of his goals) and will reveal only a few limiting properties of the inner environment . . ." (p. 65). This focus on the environment (or, in the spirit of dichotomization, the splitting of focus between the external environment and the inner machinery that operates in that environment) is an important perspective on problem solving that bears on many of the issues examined in this volume.

Another very general dichotomy is somewhat analogous to the above; it is the dichotomy between thought and behavior or action. This is an issue that maps onto the larger historical development of the field, as it moved from a focus on behavior to a focus on cognition. Put simply, the issue is that problem solving can be viewed as something that happens in the inner environment as a sequence of thoughts or mental events, or as something that happens in the outer environment as a sequence of actions or movements through that environment. Another of the many contributions of Herbert Simon was the search metaphor for problem solving that externalized what was essentially a hidden sequence of mental operations and, thus, made the mental operations more amenable to being studied. This perspective, along with the related methodologies of verbal reports and computer simulation, helped legitimize the study of mental processes and accomplish the transition from behaviorism to the study of cognition. The cognitive view of problem solving as an internal process of searching through a representation of the problem (a representation of some aspect of the external world) receives a great deal of attention in this volume. The dual nature of problem solving – that it can be viewed as a sequence of internal mental events or as an actual series of movements through, or actions on, an external environment (or perhaps more profitably as an interaction between these two levels or realities) – does not usually receive much overt attention or analysis. This important part of the Simon legacy has not been explored to the same extent as the separate levels have been. The focus has been on problem solving as cognition and representation to a much greater extent than on problem solving as action in the environment or on the interaction of the cognating organism with that external environment.

A final example of a limitation in the efficacy of dichotomization in understanding problem solving appropriately goes beyond the above-delineated dichotomous view of "too much/too little" to argue that another kind of distortion might also arise. Given not only the size of the domain of problem solving but also its complexity and multileveled structure, a typology at one level or across one set of issues might entail a distortion at another level or with regard to another set of issues. An example of this that we examine next concerns a common issue: implicit versus explicit processes in the attainment of insights in problem solving. The attainment of insights is often viewed as a sudden process, whereby a breakthrough occurs resulting in a sudden change in representation. Creative insights are discussed in a number of chapters, receiving the greatest attention in the informative and enlightening chapter by Davidson. The viewpoint that is presented is that consciously directed search is occurring within a representation that does not lead to the goal. During this search, and probably as a result of reaching an impasse, the problem solver suddenly changes representation and achieves the goal. The suddenness of the process is often referred to as an "Aha" experience, implying that the solver solves the problem with great suddenness, that they suddenly see the need to change representations and thus obtain a solution.

Two aspects of the above account are of primary interest here. The implicit dichotomy is between sudden solution and gradual solution, with the timing being important because it signals not only a sudden breakthrough but very different solution processes (attentionally controlled explicit processes vs. nonconscious or implicit processes). In a recent experiment, Michelle Fahey and I videotaped 32 participants solving a set of what are traditionally termed "insight problems" and found that the solutions often did not fit the description of attentionally controlled explicit processes. Many participants generated the solution, and then after some time (often 1 to 2 minutes, and as much as 3 or 4) announced that they had solved the problem. This time delay was labeled "recognition time" and was treated separately from verification time (the time from when they said they thought they had the solution until the final announcement of "Yes, I've got it" or any other equivalent of "Aha"). The average recognition times for the three insight problems they were given were 26, 63, and 23 seconds, but, given that not all participants showed a recognition time, the actual recognition times of those who did were even longer than the above average times would indicate. While it might be concluded that they "knew" they had solved it but needed to verify it before announcing the solution, that did not fit the great majority of the cases, and verification time was, to the extent possible, excluded. One piece of evidence for this is that the participants took much more time than needed for simple verification. Another piece of evidence is that the participants were instructed to give estimates of closeness to a solution, termed "feelings of warmth" or "FOW" (Metcalfe, 1986) every 30 seconds. Their FOW scores often did not change at all, but remained low right through the solution, with the immediate postsolution FOW often being equal to the presolution FOW. Only well after the solution did many of these participants increase their FOW, and that often took considerable time.

The above evidence strongly suggests that people frequently generate a solution without knowing that they have done so, and ascertain that it is the solution only after considerable examination or further consideration of it. The interesting aspect of this is not only that insights are sometimes not instantaneous, thus suggesting a needed revision of the standard view of insight generation, but that the solution is generated outside the control of consciously directed processes, and only then is consciously assimilated.

A related finding was described by Siegler (2000). He found that children learning to do arithmetic problems of the form "$a + b - b = ?$" first solve them by doing the addition and subtraction steps but then adopt a shortcut strategy of canceling the $+b$ and $-b$ steps without being aware of doing this. In other words, they actually solve the problems in a much more efficient manner than how they describe doing them. (Their descriptions continue for some time to include the plus b and minus b steps!) Again, the adoption of a new strategy seemingly occurs outside awareness.

In a similar vein, in our lab we have followed peoples' acquisition of problem-solving strategies as they learn to play strategic games (Abbaloney and Fox and Hounds) against an AI computer opponent. In this work, we collected verbal protocols and also monitored participants' performance on various strategies as they acquired them, as well as the quality of their play during the first 4 hours of their playing the games. The major finding was that there is very little relation between the time when a strategy first gets mentioned and the time when it comes to be exhibited in their play. Problem solvers exhibit a sizable increase in strategy use and in quality of play (e.g., often suddenly moving from losing 80% of their games near the beginning of play to winning close to that percentage later in their play) without their concurrent verbalizations indicating any significant strategy change occurring at the point where their play dramatically improves (Kotovsky & Garcia de Osuna, 1999). The acquisition of strategies for problem-solving tasks without concomitant awareness has also been reported by Berry and Broadbent (1984) and Reber and Kotovsky (1992, 1997), among others, and the phenomenon is discussed in the current volume in the chapter by Wenke and Frensch as well as in the chapter by Davidson.

The above findings strongly suggest that the dichotomous view of insightful problem solving may not be accurate in asserting the centrality of the suddenness of solution attainment and conscious recognition in defining a problem as an insight problem. This criticism of the temporal basis for categorizing problems as insight or noninsight problems is not all that interesting in its own right, although it does raise an issue about the usefulness of dichotomization in regard to that dimension of problem solving (suddenness of solution attainment together with awareness of approaching a solution). However, the other issue that emerges from the above work makes consideration of problem categorization on the basis of explicit or conscious and implicit or nonconscious solution domains much more interesting. The argument is a simple one. If the solution to insight problems is often or even usually generated nonconsciously, whether coming into consciousness as a sudden "Aha" or, as we have argued, emerging and then being recognized more gradually – with the conscious recognition often taking some minutes – then it suggests that insight problems are indeed solved nonconsciously. The question then becomes, What about noninsight problems? Clearly, there are problems that are solved consciously; one only has to sit and listen to high school geometry students reciting, "Let's see if side-angle-side works" to themselves just before solving a geometry proof to accept the plausibility of conscious problem solving.

However, as any problem-solver knows, whether it is an insight or not, we often sit and wait for ideas about how to proceed on problems. Where do those ideas come from? How are they generated? In even the most mundane problem-solving situations, we often sit (and sometimes stew) and wait for – what? Even the phrase "we sit and wait" implies that candidates for next moves or solutions are coming to us from somewhere, that we are more the recipient than the generator of the solution. The language itself gives away our possibly nonarticulated view that our mind is generating candidates that we (the conscious "we") wait for and then evaluate. This is in reality no different than the description that emerges from the above-cited work about insight problems. The ideas, next moves, insights, and solution candidates come into our mind, and we then become aware of them and choose to accept them and act on them or else reject them and wait for the next one to emerge. In short, the line between insight and noninsight problems is not a very firm one at all, and once again, this time with respect to different cognitive processes, the dichotomy, while a fairly obvious and frequently adopted one, seems to be limited in its contribution to our understanding of problem solving.

Given the above criticisms of what has become (and is used in this chapter as well) a standard way of attacking problem solving, we might ask in closing why dichotomization or similar styles of categorization of the phenomena of problem solving is so common. Its attractiveness is nearly overwhelming. I have only to cite work I have been involved with on contrasting hard and easy problems (Kotovsky, Hayes & Simon, 1985; Kotovsky & Simon, 1990; Simon & Kotovsky, 1963) to make the point personally obvious. The answer is in the phenomenal range of issues and behaviors that fall under the rubric of problem solving. The topic, which at first may appear innocuously manageable (as when the author of this chapter agreed to write a summary-discussion chapter) is extremely broad (almost as broad as psychology itself, as I have argued) and richly multidimensional, as perusal of the excellent chapters that make up this volume attests. The task of ordering the phenomena of problem solving and making them amenable to analysis and understanding renders the adoption of the strategy of generating often dichotomous contrasts (insight vs. noninsight, hard vs. easy, well-defined vs. ill-defined, real-life vs. laboratory, conscious vs. nonconscious, creative vs. noncreative, etc.) overwhelmingly attractive and often quite useful. It is a strategy that is well implemented in this volume and one that, despite some of the limitations that I have tried to point out, is possibly the only strategy available to us at this stage of our understanding.

While we all recognize Newton's laws of motion as only approximations to reality and delight in poking fun at Aristotelian ideas about motion as hopelessly wrong, they both provide very useful and often (especially in the case of Newton, but also for Aristotle in a friction-containing world) some wonderfully accurate predictions and a rich understanding of the phenomena. One would hate to have to invoke special relativity before deciding when to begin braking a car as we approach a stop sign. We would be equally at sea if we were required to invoke a full understanding of the domain of problem solving before solving a problem or trying to understand the processes by which it is solved. Delineating the contrasting categories to organize our findings about the cognition and behavior of problem solvers, the problems they solve, and the external environment within which they do so is the most likely avenue for scientific progress on this vast topic. To end, in the study of problem solving, as in all science, there is a right way and a wrong way to go about it and the correct way may lie somewhere between.

REFERENCES

Berry, D. C., & Broadbent, D. E. (1984). On the relationship between task performance and associated verbalizable knowledge. *Quarterly Journal of Experimental Psychology, 36A*, 209–231.

Kotovsky, K., Hayes, J. R., & Simon, H. A. (1985). Why are some problems hard? Evidence from Tower of Hanoi. *Cognitive Psychology, 17*, 248–294.

Kotovsky, K., & Simon, H. A. (1973). Empirical tests of a theory of human acquisition of concepts for sequential patterns. *Cognitive Psychology, 4*, 399–424.

Kotovsky, K., & Simon, H. A. (1990). Why are some problems really hard?: Explorations in the problem space of difficulty. *Cognitive Psychology, 22*, 143–183.

Kotovsky, K., & Garcia de Osuna, J. (1999, June 4–7). *The strategic unconscious: Some problem-solving and game-playing evidence.* Paper presented at the annual meeting of the Association for the Scientific Study of Consciousness, London, Ontario, Canada.

Metcalfe, J. A. (1986). Feeling of knowing in memory and problem solving. *Journal of Experimental Psychology: Learning, Memory & Cognition, 12*, 288–294.

Reber, P., & Kotovsky, K. (1992). Learning and problem solving under a memory load. *Proceedings of the 14th Annual Meeting of the Cognitive Science Society* (pp. 1068–1073). Bloomington, IN.

Reber, P., & Kotovsky, K. (1997). Implicit learning in problem solving: The role of working memory capacity. *Journal of Experimental Psychology, General, 126: 2,* 178–203.

Siegler, R. S. (2000). Unconscious insights. *Current Directions in Psychological Science, 9,* 79–83.

Simon, H. A. (1969/1981). *The sciences of the artificial.* Cambridge, MA: MIT Press.

Simon, H. A., & Kotovsky, K. (1963). Human acquisition of concepts for sequential patterns. *Psychological Review, 70,* 534–546.

Thurstone, L. L., & Thurstone, T. G. (1941). *Factorial studies of intelligence.* Chicago: University of Chicago Press.

Index